Your Boat's Electrical System

Your Boat's Electrical System

BY CONRAD MILLER

With an updated and enlarged

Manual of Electrical and Electronic Projects

BY ELBERT S. MALONEY

HEARST MARINE BOOKS

Library of Congress Cataloging-in-Publication Data

Miller, Conrad.
    Your boat's electrical system, 2nd revised ed. : including a manual of marine electrical work / Conrad Miller, Elbert S. Maloney.
        p.   cm.
    ISBN 0-688-08132-0
    1. Boats and boating—Electrical equipment.   I. Maloney, Elbert S. II. Title.
VM325.M54   1988
623.8'503—dc19   88-11002
                                                                     CIP

Printed in the United States of America

Second Revised Edition

1 2 3 4 5 6 7 8 9 10

BOOK DESIGN BY ARLENE GOLDBERG

Contents

PART 2: Manual of Electrical and Electronic Projects

Preface

THIS BOOK, first published in 1973, found a ready audience in the boatkeeper who enjoys doing his own maintenance. The continuing demand for the work has been gratifying, but the continuing advances in technology during the past years has made it necessary to re-issue it in this new up-dated version.

It is still a book about small-craft electricity, the circuits carrying it from its source, and those distributing it throughout the boat. Both alternating and direct current circuits are covered in a way that attempts to help a boat operator understand and care for his boat's electrical systems. To this purpose, circuits are first described, then workable approaches to maintenance or rework are suggested.

The text spills over into engine mechanics simply because the most vital parts of the engine are electrical. Consequently, ignition and starting circuits, although strictly engine components, become part of the work.

Part 2 has been substantially updated and expanded to cover the new developments in the field of marine electronics since the 1981 edition. It features such related topics as electronic equipment selection, installation and maintenance; advances in marine storage batteries and charging circuits; additional shop practices; and "hints and kinks" of boat electrical/electronic work.

The Authors

CONRAD MILLER'S interest in electrical and mechanical things was sparked by his father, who gave him transformers, electric motors, batteries, and spark coils instead of mundane toys when Miller was in first grade. By the age of eight he was on the air with a spark gap transmitter; but a few months later he was put off the air when local radio listeners found what was wrecking reception of *Amos 'n Andy*.

An avid boatman and boating writer, Miller started sailing on Barnegat Bay at the age of six, raced sneakboxes all of his boyhood, wrote his first boating magazine article at 17, and had his first book, "Small Boat Engines," published when he was 19. That was back in the early 1940s, and he has been writing about boats and engineering ever since.

His schooling included studies at Rutgers, Cornell, G.M. Technical Institute, the Command & General Staff School, and several U.S. Army technical schools.

Currently he is on the staff of Tenney Engineering Company, Union, N.J., is a regular contributor to *Motor Boating & Sailing,* consultant to NAEBM Westlawn School of Yacht Design, a member of the American Boat & Yacht Council, and member of Institute of Electrical and Electronic Engineers.

ELBERT S. MALONEY, better known as "Mack," is an active boatman who does his own installation and maintenance work. He and his wife, Mary, have lived aboard for ten years and cruised many thousands of miles. He has served for more than 20 years in the Educational Department of the U.S. Power Squadrons (Director of Education for 1971-6) and was Chief of the Department of Education, National Staff, U.S. Coast Guard Auxiliary. He holds USCG Licenses as Motorboat Operator and Ocean Operator.

Mack is an electrical engineer with B.S. and M.E.A. degrees, and was a Senior Member of the Institute of Electrical and Electronics Engineers. He has FCC Amateur and Commercial First Class Radio Licenses and is an active "ham." He is a member of the American Boat and Yacht Council and serves on the ABYC Technical Committee for Electronic Equipment.

Mack is an established boating writer—author of the current editions of *Chapman's Piloting, Seamanship, and Small Boat Handling*, and *Dutton's Navigation and Piloting*, plus a number of other books. He is a Contributing Editor of *Motor Boating & Sailing* magazine.

He now lives in Pompano Beach, cruising Florida and Bahamian waters when not writing books and magazine articles (and sometimes while doing so!).

CHAPTER 1

Fundamentals

Electricity—What Is It?

IT FLOWS through wires. It operates all manner of lights and machines aboard the boat, sparks the engine into action, bothers the compass, starts fires, causes corrosion, and can be a blessing or curse, depending upon whether it is corroding hardware or energizing a bilge pump.

But what is electricity? The dictionary says: "Electricity is one of the fundamental quantities in nature, giving rise to a magnetic field of force." But those words leave a lot untold.

Even the great Lord Kelvin had difficulty in teaching his students what electricity really is. There is a story that the famous scientist once lectured a university class on electricity and magnetism. Finishing his dissertation, he turned from the blackboard to question the students about the subject.

"Well," he asked, scanning the upturned faces, "what is electricity?"

A dozing young man at the back of the class raised his hand; then, alarmed at his own involuntary action, quickly pulled it down again. But alas, Kelvin's keen eye had sighted him.

"Ah!" said Lord Kelvin, "Mr. Smith knows what electricity is; and he is going to tell us."

The hapless young student rose, gulped, looked at his feet, and stammered, "I am sorry, sir, I have forgotten."

In the dreadful silence that followed, Kelvin drew himself up, adjusted his glasses, and glared down at the class for what seemed an eternity. Then he said: "Gentlemen, you have just witnessed one of the major tragedies of our century. Only two people know what electricity is: God and Mr. Smith. God will not tell us; and Mr. Smith has forgotten." And with that, he gathered his gown about him and swept out of the room.

We may not know all of what electricity is, but we do know that it's a force (Electromotive Force—EMF or E) which pushes a current (I) through a load (Resistance—R). Electromotive Force is measured in terms of *volts,* and it is analagous to the water pressure in a pipe. Current is measured in terms of *amperes,* and is analagous to the rate of water flow through a pipe. Resistance is measured in terms of *ohms,* and is analagous to the friction offered to the flow of water through plumbing by valves or other restrictions within the pipe.

Energy relates to total amount of work done (electricity used), while power is the rate of using energy or doing work. Power is measured in *watts,* energy in *watt-hours*—or for DC systems in *ampere-hours.* A bit later in this chapter you will learn how to deal with all these units.

Sources of Electricity

Aboard the boat, electricity flows from a variety of sources. Among these are:

1. **Storage batteries:** In the storage battery, energy is held in chemical form, being converted to electricity when an external circuit is made across its terminals. The conventional lead-acid storage battery cell puts out about two volts regardless of its physical size. To enable a storage battery to give more than two volts, cells are cascaded in *series,* each adding its voltage to the prior one. Thus, a 12-volt storage battery has six cells. As shown in Figure 1–1, the negative terminal of each cell is connected to the positive of the next.

Current capability, not voltage, depends upon the battery's physical heft. Thus, a powerful diesel engine starting battery is bigger and heavier than one used to crank an outboard motor. But their voltages may be identical. As one wag put it, looking at a motorcycle battery and comparing it to a 300-pound diesel starting battery: "That monster may offer only 12 volts, same as the tiny one; but they sure are damn big volts!"

CELLS IN SERIES

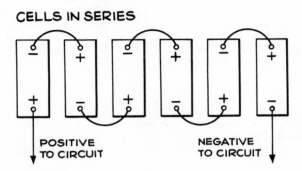

Fig. 1-1. When battery cells are strung in series, each adds its voltage to the one it follows. The six two-volt cells shown will deliver 12 volts to the external circuit.

2. **Dry Cells:** Flashlight batteries and the cells powering portable radios are called *dry cells* even though there is a wet paste inside the case. The common zinc-carbon cell generates about 1.5 volts regardless of its size, the tiny penlight cell having identical voltage to the quart-bottle-size doorbell battery. When more than 1.5 volts are required, the cells are placed in series. However, when heavier current is to be furnished, cells are wired in parallel. Now, *voltage* of the combination is the same as for one cell, but *current capability* equals that of one cell multiplied by the number of cells. This is shown in Figure 1–2.

3. **Capacitors:** Sometimes called *Condensers,* capacitors store electrical charges fed to them. They don't generate electricity in the sense that batteries do, but they take a charge from the voltage impressed on them, and store it.

The storage capability of a condenser is utilized in capacitor discharge ignition. Here, the capacitor is charged to several hundred volts, then discharged rapidly into the ignition circuit. Compared to dry or wet cells on a size or weight basis, capacitors store but little energy. However, they accept a full charge almost instantly, can store high voltage, and can release their entire reserve of energy in mere thousandths of a second.

CELLS IN PARALLEL

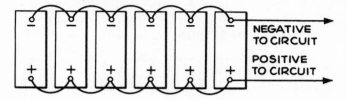

NEGATIVE
TO CIRCUIT

POSITIVE
TO CIRCUIT

Fig. 1–2. Voltage from a battery of cells connected in parallel is the same as for one cell. However, six cells, each capable of two amperes, will deliver 12 amperes to the external circuit, when wired as shown.

4. **Generator and Alternator:** Dynamic machines, these: motor-driven generators and alternators convert mechanical power to electricity, forcing it into the boat's electrical system. Voltage is a function of machine design; 6-, 12-, and 32-volt systems are typical for marine DC circuits, while alternators serving a boat's housepower needs are 120 or 240 volts (sometimes AC systems show ratings of 110 and 220 volts, or 115 and 230 volts). Current capability depends upon size, and upon how hard the rotating machine is driven.

5. **Magnetos:** Many outboards and some inboard engines derive ignition electricity from an engine-driven magneto. Sometimes a separate accessory, but often a part of the flywheel, the

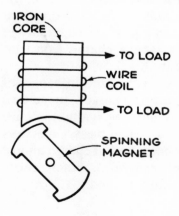

IRON
CORE

TO LOAD

WIRE
COIL

TO LOAD

SPINNING
MAGNET

Fig. 1–3 Generators, alternators, and magnetos create electricity by spinning a magnet close to a coil wound on an iron core.

14

magneto is a special purpose generator, converting engine power to electric current specifically tailored to ignition requirements.

6. **Shore Power Cord:** A common power source for boats berthed in marinas and yards, the power cord is more a link than a source of electricity. Through it flows household type alternating current; and its power handling capability depends upon its size, fittings, and the circuits feeding it.

7. **Electrochemical Reactions:** Frequently refered to by boatmen as electrolysis, electrochemical reaction between underwater hardware of different metals generates electricity. Such current is an unwelcome intruder aboard the boat. It performs no useful function, and can destroy otherwise sound hardware through electrolytic corroson, also called galvanic action.

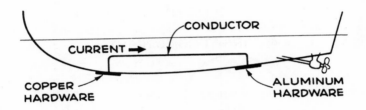

Fig. 1–4 Dissimilar metals placed under the floating hull generate electricity which flows from one to the other through any conductive path between the metals.

Kinds of Current

Direct current (DC) is the kind of electricity which flows from a battery, through its associated circuit, and back to the battery. While the circuit is energized, current flows constantly in one direction, like water flowing through a pipe.

Alternating current (AC) is the variety which comes from receptacles on the pier and from AC motor-generators aboard the boat. So far, no one has invented an AC battery. Alternating current pulsates through its wires, flowing in one direction for a fraction of a second, then reversing itself and flowing in the opposite direction. In the United States, AC pulses back and forth 60 times a second, at a frequency defined as 60 Hertz (formerly, and still commonly, called "60 cycles"). An especially useful characteristic of AC is that it can be easily transformed from one voltage to another with little energy loss, whereas DC transformation involves complicated converters or high losses, or both.

DIRECT CURRENT

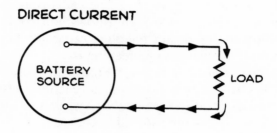

Fig. 1–5

ALTERNATING CURRENT

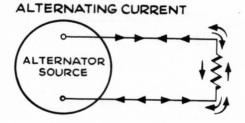

Fig. 1–6

Units of Measurement

Earlier, we introduced the terms volt, ampere, ohm, and watt. As you recall, these terms define electric parameters—for both DC and AC. Let's review the terms again:

* **Volt** expresses the pressure forcing electricity through a conductor, and is analogous to the water pressure in a pipe.

* **Ampere** describes the current, or rate of flow, through the conductor and is analogous to the rate of water flow through a pipe.

* **Ohm** defines the resistance to current flow, and is analogous to friction offered the flow of water through a pipe.

* **Watt** is a measure of electric power, just as horsepower is a measure of mechanical power. It is analogous to the water flow rate through a pipe against a given pressure head.

Ohm's Law

An electrical law originated by Georg Simon Ohm over a hundred years ago defines the relationship of voltage, current, and resistance in a circuit. Knowing any two elements, you can calculate the third. Said Georg, "Let **E** equal voltage, **I** equal current, and **R** equal resistance."

Then:

$$I = \frac{E}{R}; \quad R = \frac{E}{I}; \quad \text{and } E = IR$$

Assume that you know the voltage (**E**) is 12 volts and current (**I**) is six amperes. You can determine resistance from the second equation $R = \frac{12}{6} = 2$. Thus, the circuit has two ohms resistance.

Another example is where voltage is 120, resistance of a heater element is 24 ohms. How much current does the heater draw? $I = \frac{E}{R} = \frac{120}{24} = 5$. The heater draws five amps.

Calculating Watts

We saw that wattage is a measure of power. To find the watts being dissipated by a circuit, multiply volts times amperes (**EI** thus, if five amps flows in a 120 volt circuit, wattage is 5 × 120 = 575 watts.

Another way to compute wattage, where current and resistance are known, is to multiply current squared times resistance (**I²R** Thus, where current is 5 amps and resistance 24 ohms, I²R = 25 × 24 = 600 watts.

Measuring the units

To design electrical circuits, control their function, and trouble-shoot, we must be able to measure what's going on in the conductors. The basic measuring tools are the voltmeter, ammeter, and ohmmeter.

* The **voltmeter** is an instrument of high resistance, connected directly across the conductors or line. Because of its high resistance, it draws little current, placing a negligible load on the circuit. The meter movement senses circuit voltage, magnetically deflecting a pointer in proportion to measured voltage.

VOLTMETER

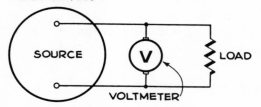

Fig. 1–7 The voltmeter is connected across the line in parallel with the load. Having high resistance, it demands little power.

* The **ammeter** is an instrument of low resistance, connected in series between the power source and load. A good ammeter has such low resistance that the power loss through it is of no consequence. Its internal movement senses circuit current, magnetically deflecting a pointer in proportion to measured current.

AMMETER

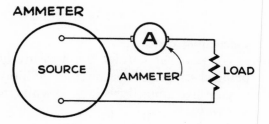

Fig. 1–8 An ammeter is wired in series with the load. Offering little resistance, it causes negligible voltage drop.

* The **ohmmeter** incorporates a penlight or flashlight battery, providing its own current for resistance measurements; and it is *always* connected to a deenergized or "dead" circuit element. The instrument comprises a cell of known voltage in series with an internal known resistance and a sensitive ammeter, called a milliammeter.

When the ohmmeter's test leads are touched together, the meter swings to zero ohms, indicating no external resistance in series with the leads. When the test leads are separated, the

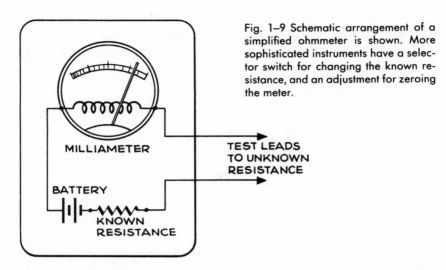

Fig. 1–9 Schematic arrangement of a simplified ohmmeter is shown. More sophisticated instruments have a selector switch for changing the known resistance, and an adjustment for zeroing the meter.

MILLIAMETER

TEST LEADS
TO UNKNOWN
RESISTANCE

BATTERY

KNOWN
RESISTANCE

meter falls to infinity, indicating substantially infinite external resistance. When the leads are placed in series with an external resistance, such as a light bulb, the meter deflects in proportion to that resistance. Normally zero will be at the right-hand end of the scale and infinity (open circuit) at the left; the scale thus reads "backwards" from scales used for voltage and current.

The Multimeter

A most useful electrician's trouble-shooting tool is the **multimeter,** a portable, sometimes pocket size, instrument incorporating all three popular meters. An inexpensive multimeter might have the following scales: Ohms center scale deflection: 6, 60, 600, 6,000, and 60,000. Volts full scale: 3, 15, 60, 300, 600, and 1,200. Current full scale, in amperes: 0.003, 0.03, 0.3, 3.0, and 10.

Most multimeters measure both AC and DC voltage. However, they only measure direct current amperes. For alternating current ampere measurements, the snap-on ammeter is used by trouble shooters.

The AC Snap-On Ammeter

The hand-held AC snap-on ammeter measures alternating

current flowing through a conductor without metal-to-metal contact with the conductor. It does so by magnetically "feeling" the current flow; and its use and operation are described later in this book.

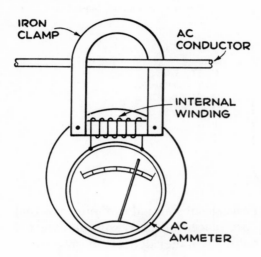

Fig. 1–10 Clipped around an insulated conductor, the alternating current ammeter measures current by detecting the pulsating magnetic field around one wire.

Wire Size vs. Gauge

As emphasized many times throughout the book, larger diameter wires offer less resistance than smaller ones, and voltage drop through them is less. Thus large diameter wires result in less power loss than skinny ones. Keep in mind that American Wire Gauge (AWG) sizes vary inversely with the diameter of the conductor; the higher the gauge number, the smaller the wire. A change of three numbers doubles or halves the resistance of the wire; a change of six numbers changes resistance by a factor of four. For example, #12 wire has a resistance of 1.62 ohms per 1000 feet; the same length of #6 has only 0.40 ohms resistance, wire #18 would have 6.51 ohms. Commonly-used wire gauges have even numbers.

Basic Circuits

Most electrical circuits fall into two categories: parallel and series. Of the two, parallel circuits are the most common in boating electricity.

* All loads are connected between the two conductors in a parallel circuit. Each load has available the same voltage as the others; and each draws current as determined by its resistance.

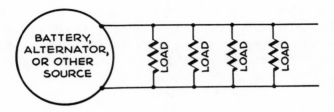

Fig. 1–11 In a parallel circuit, the loads such as lights, motors, or heaters, are wired across the power lines like ladder rungs.

* Loads are connected end-to-end, "series strung," in a series circuit. Each load sees the same current as the others. If all loads have the same resistance, each load sees voltage equal to source voltage divided by the number of loads. Thus, 10 equal light bulbs in series with a 100 volt feed will each see 10 volts.

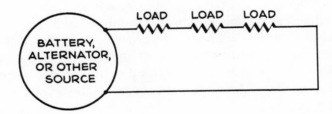

Fig. 1–12 In a series circuit, loads follow along one after the other like a string of cars on a train.

Temperature vs. Resistance

Common conductors increase in resistance as temperature increases. Keep this in mind when trouble shooting with an ohmmeter. For example, a 120-volt 100 watt light bulb offers 144 ohms resistance when burning. But its cold resistance, measured with an ohmmeter, is only 15 ohms.

Grounded Circuits

One side of a circuit, whether AC or DC, is frequently connected to ground, usually as a safety measure. In a few instances where "ground" is the frame of a metal machine, ground is used as one of the current-carrying conductors. This arrangement is used on cars and trucks, but seldom on boats. The many aspects of grounds and grounding are covered extensively in chapters that follow.

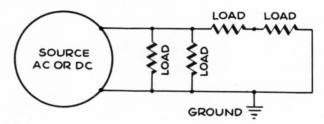

Fig. 1–13 One conductor in this series-parallel system is grounded.

DEFINING OUR TERMS

The definitions that follow take minor liberties that the scientist or electrical engineer may grouse about; but with them, the author tries to make clear the meaning of electrical and related words the way they are used in this book. Purists are invited to keelhaul the author if they deem the analogies a little salty in spots.

alternating current (AC): Electricity that flows first in one direction, then in the reverse direction through its conductors. Each wire is positive, then negative, then positive again, etc., reversing polarity typically 60 times each second. Analogous to water oscillating back and forth in a pipe.

alternator: A machine that generates alternating current. In battery-charging alternators, the generated AC is internally changed to direct current before reaching the terminals.

ampacity: Current-carrying capacity of a conductor expressed in amperes. Analogous to the diameter of a water pipe.

ampere: The amount of electricity flowing. Analogous to the

22

quantity of water flowing through a pipe. One ampere flowing through one ohm gives a voltage drop of one volt.

amphoteric: Capable of reacting chemically either as an acid or base. Aluminum is amphoteric, requiring special protection as a marine metal.

anode: The positive terminal of an electrolytic system, the one at which oxidizing reactions occur. When zinc is fastened to bronze on under-water hardware, the zinc is *anodic*.

arc: Flash of electricity across a gap, usually seen as a blue or yellow spit of flame.

armature: The spinning rotor of a DC motor or generator. Also the fixed coils (stator) in an automotive type-alternator.

autotransformer: A transformer in which there is a connection between primary and secondary windings. Some have one simple winding with a tap, one terminal being common to primary and secondary. Variac and Powerstat are trade names for variable autotransformers.

binnacle: The box, stand, or housing carrying the boat's compass.

brush: A carbon or copper spring-loaded sliding contact, bearing on a commutator or rotor, carrying current to or from the rotating member in a motor or generator.

capacitance: The size of a capacitor, its capacity, usually expressed in microfarads (μF) for boat electricity. Typical distributor capacitor (condenser) is 0.1 μF, typical motor starting capacitor: 100 μF.

capacitor: Also condenser. Component that stores electric charges. In effect, will conduct AC but block DC. Analogous to a stretchable membrane across a water pipe, allowing water to oscillate, but not flow unidirectionally.

capacity shield: In an isolation transformer, a faraday screen preventing energy transmission from shore to the boat except by desired electromagnetic means of coupling. The shield knocks out the capacitive coupling between shore and boat windings.

capacitive coupling: Transfer of energy from one component to another due to capacitance between the two.

cathode: The negative terminal of an electrolytic system, the one at which reducing reactions occur; the protected one. When zinc is fastened to bronze underwater hardware, the bronze becomes cathodic.

charger: An electrical appliance to convert alternating current to direct current of lower voltage, used to charge the boat's batteries.

circuit breaker: An automatic switch that opens its circuit upon detecting excess current. Analogous to an automatic safety valve on a pressurized water tank.

clip-on ammeter: An AC ammeter which measures current in a conductor by proximity, there being no connection other than magnetic.

commutator: Radial copper segments on the rotor of an electric motor or generator, conducting current from the brushes to the spinning windings.

conductive: State of being able to transmit an electrical current.

conductor: Material that allows electricity to flow through easily. Copper is a good conductor.

corona: A faint blue glow near the surface of an electrical conductor at high potential.

corrosion: Deterioration of hardware and other metals because of reaction with the environment.

cross fire: The undesired firing of one spark plug caused by voltage transfer from the wire serving another plug.

current sensing relay (CSR): A relay which responds to current flowing through a circuit, rather than to voltage across the circuit.

dead-front switchboard: One with no exposed live parts on the front.

deviate: To deflect the needle of a compass by local influence, as through the effect of a current-carrying conductor.

dielectric: A non-conductor. Special dielectrics are used for elements inside capacitors. Oil-impregnated paper is an example.

diode: a two-terminal component, vacuum tube or semiconductor, which passes current in one direction, blocking it in the other. Analogous to a check valve in a water pipe.

direct current (DC): Electricity that flows in one direction through a conductor. Analogous to water flowing through a pipe.

electrode: A conductor used to make electrical contact with a non-metallic surface, as with seawater or other electrolyte.

electrolysis: Passage of electricity through a liquid, such as seawater.

electrolyte: A liquid conductor of electricity, such as salt water or battery-acid solution.

electrolytic corrosion: Destruction of metals through electrolysis.

eliminator, battery: A power pack or battery charger with filtered output, suitable for operating direct current accessories from the alternating current line.

ferrite: A molded, kiln fired, magnetic transformer core material usually used for high frequency or pulse transformers.

full-wave rectifier: A circuit that changes alternating current to pulsating direct current, rectifying both halves of each cycle. Output is smoother than that of the half wave rectifier.

fuse: A thin ribbon of metal that melts or burns, opening its associated circuit on detecting excess current. Analogous to a freeze-out or blow-out plug on a pressure vessel.

galvanic anode: A "low noble" metal that protects, frequently zinc or magnesium.

galvanic corrosion: Corrosion resulting from electric current between dissimilar metals in an electrolyte.

galvanic series: A list of metals and alloys arranged according to their relative potentials in seawater. Metals close to each other on the list "fight" the least.

ganged: Switches or switch functions are ganged when the throwing of one transfers all at the same time. Circuit breakers can be ganged.

gauge: Wire diameter. Higher gauge number designates smaller wire (more resistance).

generator: A machine to generate electricity. Analogous to a water pump.

grounded: A conductor which is normally current-carrying, when at earth potential.

grounding: A conductor at earth potential which is normally non-current-carrying. Typical of safety conductors which ground equipment frames.

half-wave rectifier: A circuit that changes alternating current to pulsating direct current, rectifying only half of each cycle. Output is rougher than that of the full wave rectifier.

hot: A conductor not at ground potential. Also, one that can give a shock.

housepower: Euphemism describing 120/140 volt, single phase, 60 Hertz, alternating current used domestically, at dockside, and on board boats. The word is not in standard dictionaries.

insulator: A material that will not allow electricity to flow through. Nylon and ceramics are good insulators.

induction motor: An AC motor without brushes or commutator wherein the rotor is energized by transformer action. (Note: A *very* few induction motors, repulsion-start type, have a commutator. They are seldom seen on modern appliances.)

inductive load: An electrical load, as given by induction motor or transformer. May draw much more current from the line than is indicated by its wattage.

isolation transformer: A power transformer, located on the boat, which furnishes AC to the boat's system, coupling to shore power magnetically, but eliminating all connections by direct conductor.

loading coil: A wire-wound coil in a transmitter or a receiver circuit which makes the antenna seem electrically longer than its physical length. Often a part of the whip antenna.

locked-rotor current: The amperes which a motor draws when its shaft is locked. This is the current the motor can demand for the first split second after it is turned on, but has not yet accelerated.

microfarad (*u*F): The usual measure of a capacitor's electrical size or capacitance. A 2 *u*F unit stores twice the energy of a 1 *u*F unit at the same voltage.

Micro-Switch: A miniature switch, easily actuated, and of high current handling ability, considering its small size.

negative: The polarity of a boat's battery which is usually grounded. Polarity of the bottom of a flashlight battery. Polarity of a cathode. The electrode from which electrons flow to the anode. Symbol is −. Color code on battery charger terminals is often black.

noble: When more noble and less noble metals are electrically connected and placed in an electrolyte, such as salt water, the less noble corrodes; the more noble is protected.

ohm: Measure of resistance. Analogous to pressure drop in a water pipe when water flows; 1 ohm causes 1 volt drop when 1 ampere flows.

pinion: A small gear designed to mesh with a large gear, such as the small gear on a starter drive mechanism.

polarity: The distinction between positive and negative conductors, and also between north and south magnetic poles in a machine.

pole: Referring to a switch or relay, the number of conductors which the device can switch on and off, or transfer from one circuit to another. Single and double pole devices are most common on the boat.

polyphase: A power system with more than one phase. (See *three-phase*.)

positive: The polarity of a boat's conductors which are usually hot. Polarity of the top button on a flashlight battery. Polarity of an anode. The electrode to which electrons flow from the cathode. Symbol is +. Color code on battery chargers is usually red.

potential: Voltage.

power center: A dockside enclosure having power receptacles, fuses or circuit breakers, and sometimes a light on top.

power factor: The ratio of watts to volt-amperes in an AC circuit. At low power factor, there can be considerable current, but few watts dissipated. Analogous to a lot of water oscillating to and fro inside a pipe against a spring load, but with little water flowing from source to faucet.

Powerstat: Trade name for a variable autotransformer.

rectifier: A device or network to convert AC to DC. The word is sometimes used to describe a complete battery charger or power supply.

relay: A switch activated by a small current in its coil. Heavy duty power relays are called *contactors*.

resistance: Measured in ohms. The degree to which current is retarded from flowing. Small diameter copper wire has higher resistance than large diameter wire. Analogous to a small water pipe having greater resistance to flow than a large one.

resistive load: An electrical load of pure or almost pure resistance such as a light bulb or heating element.

rheostat: A variable resistance. Analogous to a throttling valve in a water pipe.

rotor: The spinning part of a motor, generator, or alternator.

salinity: The percentage of salts dissolved in water. Seawater has a salinity of about 3.5% in the open ocean. Brackish water has lower salinity than seawater.

short circuit: Condition where the circuit's two conductors touch together at a point between the source (such as a battery) and the termination (such as a light).

shunt: A conductor connecting two points in a circuit in parallel with another conductor. A resistor across ammeter terminals is called a shunt. Sharing the current, it will allow an ammeter of, say, 1 ampere full deflection, to measure 10 amperes.

silicon controlled rectifier (SCR): A transistor-type device which acts like a high speed relay. When a small current is passed through its trigger circuit, it "fires," allowing heavy current to flow through its main terminals.

single phase: The standard housepower electrical system where one set of waves represents the voltage.

solenoid: Wire wound as a helix. Also a term applied to plunger relays used in engine starting circuits.

stator: The fixed, stationary poles and windings in a generator or motor.

stray current corrosion: Corrosion of underwater parts caused by flow of battery current, or other current, between submerged hardware. Corrosion occurs at the electrically positive part where current flows from the metal part to the seawater.

sweat: To solder.

synchronous speed: As applied to a motor, the rpm of the rotor where the speed is locked in step with the power line frequency. A four-pole synchronous machine rotates 1,800 rpm on a 60 Hz line. Analogous to a surfboard catching a wave and riding it without ever falling behind.

tap: As applied to a motor, transformer, or coil winding: a wire connected to the winding turns somewhere between the start and finish turns.

thermal protector: A temperature-sensitive device inside a motor which shuts down the machine upon detecting that its windings are over-heated. When the motor cools, the protector resets, starting the motor again.

three-phase: A power system where three sets of waves represent the voltage; and crests of the waves are displaced 120 degrees apart. It is a three or four wire system found in factories, but is almost unknown on the pier.

throw: As applied to a switch: the number of selections it can make. A single-throw switch offers on-off. A double throw switch can connect its incoming wire or wires to two different circuits alternately, and frequently has a "center off" position. The term is applied to describe relays, also.

transformer: An AC device to magnetically couple one circuit to another. It can raise or lower the output voltage relative to the input. See also *autotransformer* and *isolation transformer*.

trip-free: A circuit breaker which will function to interrupt the current even though the reset handle is manually held against the trip.

universal motor: An electric motor with armature and brushes which will operate on AC or DC. Commonly used in hand drills and vacuum cleaners.

volt: The pressure or push behind the electricity in a circuit. Analogous to the pressure in a water pipe. One volt can push one ampere through one ohm.

vector: A line segment whose length represents magnitude and whose orientation in space represents direction. Useful for finding the resulting force when two separate forces act on a point.

watt: Measure of electrical power. In direct current, volts times amperes equals watts. In alternating current, volts times amps times power factor equals watts. Theoretically, 746 watts equals 1 horsepower.

zener diode: A semiconductor that suddenly starts to conduct at one particular voltage. Used as a stable, accurate reference voltage, somewhat like a standard cell.

CHAPTER 2

Understanding the Battery

STORAGE BATTERIES are the very heart and center of the boat's direct-current electrical system. They not only provide the enormous current (hundreds of amperes) required to start the engine, but they also contribute a moderating effect, smoothing voltage fluctuations while the charging circuits are operative.

Batteries act not only as gigantic "springs" to wind the engines into action, they also serve as electrical fly-wheels, soaking up power when the alternator pushes it into the system; returning power when the alternator cannot keep up with demands.

Battery Function

Storing hundreds of watt-hours of energy while being charged, the batteries force that work back into the electrical system during discharge. Lacking the battery's moderating effect, the boat's electrical system would show wide variations which could be damaging to lights, motors, and especially to electronic equipment. Never operate a charging system without a battery connected.

Lead-Acid Batteries

Almost without exception the batteries used on recreational and commercial small craft are of the *lead-acid* type similar to those used on cars, trucks, and busses. Most boat systems are 12-volt; a few on larger craft are 32-volt.

Understanding what makes it tick will help the intelligent boatkeeper do a good job of battery maintenance. A simple "cellar shop" experiment is interesting and demonstrates the principle behind the lead-acid battery. You may like to try it:

Hang up two strips of lead, such as two flattened lengths of solder, inside a jar on opposite sides, and keep the strips from touching. Fill the jar with dilute sulphuric acid, available from a battery shop in plastic containers. Careful! The acid will burn your hands or clothes. If you splash it, wash immediately with plenty of soap and water.

To the lead strips in the jar connect a source of direct current at about three volts, and you will then be charging your miniature cell. Bubbles will rise to the surface of the acid and one strip will turn brown, while the other strip will remain lead colored. After a period of charging, the brown strip is covered with a layer of lead peroxide and becomes the cell's positive plate. The clear lead plate becomes negative; and the two plates plus the acid now comprise a small electric cell.

After detaching the charging source, touch a pair of voltmeter probes to the dry part of the strips: You should see a potential between them of about two volts. That is the approximate *voltage* of any lead-acid cell, regardless of its size. Bigger cells

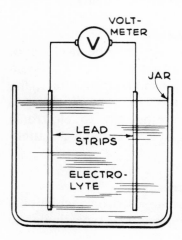

Fig. 2–1 Two strips of lead immersed in a glass of lead acid electrolyte form a basic kitchen sink experimental battery. When charged, one strip becomes positive, the other negative.

generate more *current,* but *voltage* remains the same. Remember: when higher voltage is required, cells are connected in series. Repeated charge and discharge of your small cell will increase the thickness of lead peroxide film on the positive electrode; and this will increase the cell's capacity. However, voltage will remain at about the two-volt level.

The miniature experimental cell described above works the same in principle as the big, heavy batteries on a boat. In practice, current is amplified hundreds of times because the effective area of the plates is increased in proportion. Voltage is raised to 6, 8*, or 12 as desired, through stringing of the cells in a series to form a "battery" of cells, from whence cometh the name. Surface, upon which current depends, is multiplied not only through the incorporation of many large plates, but also by corrugating, grooving, and sponging of the lead. In a high-capacity cell, sponging is important: Electrolyte can then flow through the lead's pores contacting active material many times greater in area than presented by the apparent outer surface.

The Inside Story

Engineers with Exide Power Systems Division of ESB, one of the largest battery manufacturers in the world, describe the electro-chemical action in a lead-acid battery cell in the following words:

$$\text{Discharge}$$
$$\xrightarrow{\hspace{3cm}}$$
$$PbO_2 + Pb + 2H_2SO_4 = 2\,PbSo_4 + 2H_2O$$
$$\xleftarrow{\hspace{3cm}}$$
$$\text{Charge}$$

"In a fully-charged battery all the active material of the positive plate is lead peroxide. That of the negative plate is pure sponge lead. All the acid is in the electrolyte, and the specific gravity is at maximum. As the battery discharges, some of the acid separates from the electrolyte which is in the pores of the

---

*A bank of four 8-volt batteries is used for 32-volt systems.

33

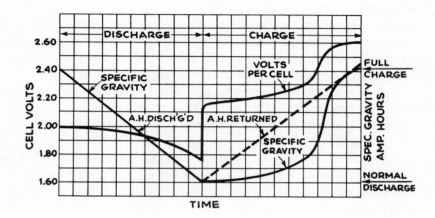

Fig. 2–2 Voltage and specific gravity characteristics during constant rate discharge and charge. Voltage rises immediately as charging starts, but specific gravity lags far behind ampere hours charged until full charge is reached.

plates. It forms a chemical combination with the active material, changing it to lead sulphate, and producing water.

"As discharge continues, additional acid is drawn from the electrolyte, while further sulphate and water is formed. As this process progresses, the specific gravity of the electrolyte gradually falls. The proportion of acid is decreasing and that of water is increasing.

"When a battery is on charge, reverse action takes place. Acid in the sulphated active material of the plates is driven out and returns to the electrolyte. Return of the acid to the electrolyte reduces sulphate in the plates and increases specific gravity of the electrolyte. Gravity continues to rise until all the acid is driven from the plates, back into the electrolyte. The plates are then free of sulphate.

"As the cells approach full charge, they cannot absorb all of the energy from the charging current. The excess current breaks up water from the electrolyte into its two components, hydrogen and oxygen, which are liberated from the cell as gases. This is the primary reason for the required addition of water to battery cells."

10.0 Charge and Discharge are Different

Rare is the boatkeeper who has not tested a battery's condition or state-of-charge with a hydrometer. Battery experts at ESB point out that decrease in specific gravity on *discharge* is proportional to the ampere-hours discharged. However, as discussed below, the rise in specific gravity indicated by a hydrometer during recharge is not uniform or proportional to the charge in ampere-hours. There is a lag.

Here's what accounts for the delay:

During the early part of the charge there is no effect to mix or stir the electrolyte. Some of the heavier acid forced from the plates fails to rise to the top of the cell and cannot be reached by the testing hydrometer. Later in the charge, when gassing is active, all of the electrolyte becomes a homogenous liquid. As gassing starts, the gravity determined at the cell's top surface, rises rapidly to full-charge level. The lag in measured specific gravity of electrolyte at the top of the cell does not mean that the battery is rejecting the charge. The effect is perfectly normal and the boatkeeper must keep the lag effect in mind when testing batteries being charged after considerable discharge.

What Voltage?

We saw that a single lead-acid cell generates nominal potential very close to two volts. However, exact voltages varies with the specific gravity of the electrolyte, and to a great extent on whether the cell is *delivering* current on discharge or *receiving* current on charge. In all batteries, 6, 8, or 12 volt, for example, open circuit no load voltage is a direct function of the electrolyte's specific gravity. Within close limits, cell voltage equals specific gravity plus 0.84. This means the open circuit voltage of a cell with electrolyte specific gravity of 1.210 will be 2.05 volts. A battery with six of these cells in series will develop a potential, unloaded, of 12.3 volts; and that theoretical value is very close to the voltage one will find on everyday batteries aboard the boat.

Effect of Load

The last paragraph describes the situation when the cells are unloaded. But assume now that a small electric motor is turned on, throwing a moderate load on the battery. Cell voltage will immediately drop due to internal resistance. As the motor runs for a while, voltage will fall still more as the motor's load discharges the battery. Finally, after continued discharge when the battery nears exhaustion, voltage drops below a value that is useful.

Effect of Charging

It was shown that when a depleted battery is placed on charge its voltage goes up, the extent of the rise increasing with charge rate. At commonly used charging rates on a six-cell 12 volt battery, voltage quickly rises to 12.6 or 12.9, then increases gradually until the charge is about 75% complete. Voltage then rises sharply, finally leveling off to maximum potential at full charge. At that point, voltage in a six-cell battery will be about 15.6 at the finish rate of charge. Because voltage varies with state-of-charge, an accurate, narrow-range voltmeter, properly interpreted, will give the battery-keeper a fair idea of the cell's charging progress.

Specific Gravity

Electrolyte nominal specific gravity varies slightly in different makes and designs of marine batteries. However, most manufacturers specify about 1.260 as the value for a fully charged cell. Specific gravity decreases as the battery discharges, increases as it charges; consequently, its value is an approximate indicator of the battery's state. Between full charge and discharge state, a typical battery will evidence a gravity drop of 125 points: Full charge gravity is 1.260, half charge 1.197, and discharged 1.135.

Temperature Effect

Standard electrolyte temperature for hydrometer readings of specific gravity is 77°F, made when electrolyte level is above the plates. In order to get accurate gravity readings, the hydrometer float indication must be corrected for temperature and electrolyte level. The corrections are applied as follows:

1. Add one gravity point for each 3°F above 77°F; alternately,

subtract one point of gravity for each 3°F below 77°F.
2. Subtract 15 points for each ½″ below normal level; alternately, add 15 points for each ½″ above normal.

From the above, it is apparent that a battery having electrolyte level ½″ above normal, and with temperature 107°F, will require plus 25 points correction. Thus, if the hydrometer reads 1.235, corrected value is 1.260, indicating the battery is fully charged.

Altered Readings

Specific gravity is never tested immediately after water is added to the cells because the fresh water on top of the cells will make the reading much too low. Time must be allowed, and the battery used, to thoroughly mix the liquids. Battery manufacturers also say that age alters the normal gravity reading, pointing out that a decrease of several points a year is normal.

How Powerful?

"The capacity of a storage battery," say Exide engineers, "is usually expressed in ampere-hours. This is simply the product of the discharge in amperes times the number of hours [the battery can sustain that discharge rate.] However, a single figure of, say, 200 ampere-hours has little significance unless qualified by the many factors influencing a battery's capacity."

Principal factors influencing total capacity are discharge rate, temperature, specific gravity, and final voltage.

Discharge Rate

The higher the amperes of the discharge rate, the less total ampere-hours a battery will deliver under otherwise like conditions. Commonly used as a standard is the eight hour rate, which, for example, would represent 12.5 amperes for eight hours, delivered by a 100 ampere-hour battery. Another common rating applied to boat batteries is the 20 hour rate. A 100 AH battery, so specified, will furnish five amperes for 20 hours before its voltage drops lower than a usable level. It is apparent that a battery of given AH capacity can do more useful work operating a small light bulb than in cranking a heavy engine.

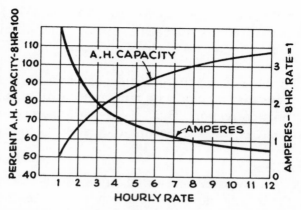

Fig. 2–3 The curves show that a battery's ampere hour capacity increases as discharge rate decreases.

Temperature Effect

Higher temperatures than 77°F increase a battery's capacity, and lower temperatures decrease it. Since engine room temperatures in powerboats frequently reach or exceed 120°F, boat battery capacity is increased as much as 15% above normal.

Gravity Influence

A new battery, originally filled with electrolyte of higher specific gravity will have greater ampere-hour capacity than one filled with fluid of lower gravity. The reader may ask the question: "Then why not fill all batteries with high gravity electrolyte?" The reason is that "high gravity" batteries enjoy a shorter useful life, and lose charge faster when standing idle.

Final Voltage

The minimum useful voltage at various rates of discharge is termed final voltage. It is accepted as lower with high rates of discharge, as when cranking a balky engine. For engine starting currents, final voltage per cell may be as low as one volt. But for low discharge rates, it may be as high as 1.85 volts. Nominal standard rating for batteries is about 1.75 volts per cell, or 10.5 volts for an ordinary 12-volt battery.

Discharge Rate

Battery engineers say that most batteries can be safely discharged at the fastest rate of current they can muster. However, the discharge must not be continued beyond the point where the cells approach exhaustion or where the voltage falls below useful value. In short, fast discharge does not hurt the unit, but overdischarge may.*

Overdischarge Hurts

Severe overdischarging can be harmful to a battery, particularly if the battery is not immediately recharged. During normal discharge a moderate amount of lead sulphate is found on the plates, and this is ok. Lead sulphate occupies more space than the sponge lead of the negative plate, so that during discharge the plate material expands slightly. However, if discharge is carried too far, the material may expand to the point where portions of it separate, losing contact with the grid, and remaining permanently as sulphate. Mechanics then refer to the battery as "sulphated."

To some extent, sulphating will occur when a battery is normally discharged and allowed to remain in that state for a long time. A typical case would be when the boat is laid up. That is one of the reasons why a battery should be kept well charged when the boat is laid away.

Normal Charging

Battery manufacturers specify a normal or finish rate of charge for each battery. This rate is the amperes of current which can safely be applied any time charging is required and which can be continued to completion of charge without causing excessive gassing or damaging temperatures.

Typical finish rates fall between four and 10 amperes per 100 ampere-hours of battery capacity at the eight hour rate. A safe rate for almost any boat battery in the 100 AH class is six amperes. Charging at that current, you will never hurt a 100

---

*See page 337 for new "deep-cycle" batteries.

ampere-hour battery: Even though the charge is continued slightly past "full," the only damage will be some lost water due to gassing.

Fast vs. Slow Charging

Accurately controlled, "fast" charging will not damage a battery. But the key to protecting the battery is *control*. An acceptable rule is that a battery may be charged at any rate in amperes that will not produce excessive gassing or raise electrolyte temperature above 125°F for short periods. Another rule, say Exide engineers, is that any rate is safe which does not force cell voltage to more than 2.4 volts per cell while the current is above the normal or finish rate of charge. Current may be continue at the finish rate whenever charging is required, regardless of cell voltage.

Completely or partially discharged conventional 12-volt batteries can safely absorb charging currents as high as 50 to 80 amperes for a short time. But as the state-of-charge rises, the rate must be promptly reduced. As charge approaches "full," current must be reduced evenly or in steps to the normal or finish rate.

Overcharging

Like excessive discharging, continued overcharging is harmful. It tends to corrode positive plate grids, weakening them physically, while increasing their electrical resistance. In addition, overcharging at high rates creates violent gassing, washing active material from the plates, and shortening cell life. If a battery's electrolyte gravity remains at full value, but the battery demands excessive make-up water, the unit is being overcharged, and the rate should be reduced. This requires lowering generator charging voltage through adjustment of the regulator. Frequently, voltage reduction as little as 5% will improve the situation greatly.

Trickle Charging

Sometimes it would seem convenient to simply plug into dockside power and leave the battery on a constant trickle charge of perhaps three quarters of an amp. Seemingly, this should maintain the battery topped up without further attention.

The method is simple; but battery manufacturers don't particularly like it. Slow, constant trickle charging is not good for conventional boat batteries. It is better to hook up the charger manually, as needed, or to rig a timer to charge the batteries once a day for a short period at the finish rate. Another good plan is to install one of the modern "marine converters" that automatically turn on or *completely* off in response to the battery's state of charge.

Dry-Charged

Some batteries are manufactured by a special process and are sold as "dry-charged." Before assembly, the plates are dried in an atmosphere free of air or oxygen. Then the cells are assembled and sealed to block out all traces of moisture. When stored in a cool, dry location, dry-charged batteries will retain most of their charge for two years, or even longer.

Before being placed in service, a dry-charged battery is filled with electrolyte having specific gravity about 10 points lower than the normal full-charge gravity. It is then given a moderate charge and placed in service. The dry-charged battery may be used immediately, although for the first few hours it may not have full capacity depending upon its length of time and condition of storage.

Distilled Water Required?

Among battery mechanics there is always a little discussion as to whether distilled or demineralized water is better for batteries than tap water. It is the opinion of Exide engineers that the vast majority of public water sources are satisfactory for marine battery use. However, the experts also say that water containing large amounts of iron and chlorine is bad for lead-acid storage batteries. Consequently, if the reader is in doubt about his local source, or about the water he may encounter while cruising, he'll find it cheap enough to buy a gallon of distilled water from a local grocery or automotive parts store; and can be carried on board for the season.

Layup

Before a battery is stored for several months, as during the boat's seasonal layup, it should first be given a good, full charge, then stored in a cool place. It must not be allowed to freeze; and, indeed, it will not freeze if it is kept charged. During layup, gravity is checked about once each six weeks, and the cells recharged when gravity dips to around 1.220. Electrolyte is never dumped from a battery during storage; the cells cannot be stored "dry"; and dumping will ruin the plates.

Safety Requirements

Both the American Boat & Yacht Council and the National Fire Protection Association have standards applying to batteries and their installation aboard boats. Important points cited in these standards apply to location, installation, and wiring methods.

Location

In a first-class installation, batteries are located so that gas given off during charging will be quickly dissipated by natural and mechanical ventilation. Naturally, they are located high enough that bilge water, even when above normal, will not reach the battery caps and terminals; and they are protected against rain and spray.

Engine starting batteries should be located as close to the starter as practicable to keep the cable lengths short and voltage drop to a minimum. Batteries must be arranged where they are easy to get at for inspection and adding of make-up water.

Installation

Batteries must be secured against shifting and pounding when the boat is in the roughest water; and those in trailered boats must be fastened tightly enough for rough road trailering. The case should be chocked on all sides and supported at the bottom by nonabsorbent insulating supports of a material not affected by acid.

To comply with the requirements of ABYC Standard E-10, all batteries must have a non-conductive and ventilated cover to prevent accidental shorting of the terminals. Also, where the hull or compartment material under the battery is aluminum, steel, or other material liable to attack by acid, a tray of lead or fiberglass must be fitted under the unit.

Wiring

Batteries are never tapped for voltages other than the total voltage of all the cells comprising the complete battery. Thus, a 12-volt battery, having 6 cells, is never center-tapped between the third and fourth to energize a separate six-volt circuit. If six volts is required aboard, it should be furnished by a separate six-volt battery.

An emergency switch capable of carrying starter current and all other currents should be wired in the "hot" battery lead as close to the battery as possible. There must be no switch in the ground strap lead.

Connections to battery posts must be husky, permanent solder-lug type clamps. Spring clips and temporary clamps are frowned upon.

Maintenance

Based upon principles laid down in this chapter, battery maintenance becomes pretty much a matter of common sense. The following are suggested maintenance procedures:

• The battery's top should be maintained as clean and dry as possible. Water and electrolyte conduct electricity from one binding post to the other, and the resulting electric leak discharges the battery. Baking soda is a good cleaning agent for battery tops; but it must be kept out of the cells at all costs. After the battery top is cleaned, it must be rinsed and then dried off bone dry.

• Voltage regulator controlling the generator or alternator is checked at least once a season. Most nominal 12-volt regulators are designed to maintain the charging circuit at about 14 volts. Higher voltage leads to over-charging on most conventionally operated boats. Lower potential, on the other hand, may allow the battery to run down. However, on sailboat auxiliary engines, ordinarily used for short intervals, the regulator may be stepped up until charging potential is about 15 volts. This will speed the charging process; and gassing should pose no problem since the engine is not run long enough to overcharge the cells substantially.

• Both cable clamps and binding posts must be brightly burnished before a connection is made. Either a stainless steel brush or coarse sandpaper will do the job.

• Battery cables, both hot and ground, must be replaced when they show signs of corrosion or fraying. Deteriorated cables cause a considerable voltage loss when high currents are drawn, as for starting engines.

• Cells are kept topped up to correct level with clean water, and are checked for state-of-charge with a hydrometer from time to time.

SYNOPSIS

Through its electrochemical process, the lead-acid battery can store a great deal of energy and can release the energy quickly. Charging takes longer than discharging. Battery potential is roughly 2 volts per cell, but is higher when the battery is charging than when discharging. Battery capacity is measured in ampere-hours. Severe overdischarge hurts lead-acid cells, but overcharging does, too. Batteries must be well secured in the boat, must be kept clean, dry, watered, and adequately charged. See also Chapter 24.

CHAPTER 3

The Modern Boat's
DC Systems

THIS CHAPTER comprises a guide on what to look for in checking over the qualities of an existing direct-current electrical system. It is also a guide on how to inspect the DC electrical installation on a new boat under consideration for purchase, and will be an aid to the owner who is expanding his existing circuits or wiring a new boat.

Material in this chapter is guided by two standards: *Safety Standards for Small Craft,* compiled by the American Boat and Yacht Council, and *Fire Protection Standards for Motor Craft, NFPA 302,* authorized by the National Fire Protection Association. What is written here applies to popular direct-current systems of six, 12, and 32 volts, or any system up to 50 volts, but not higher.

Wiring Arrangements

How often have you looked at an otherwise neat boat, perhaps one having a workmanlike shoreside AC system, and beheld a messy, haphazard looking six, 12, or 32 direct-current system? And how frequently the owner will say, "Oh well, it's only battery voltage; it can't do much harm if it does go haywire."

Such opinions are dangerous. Low-voltage DC wiring when short circuited or grounded can cause fire, corrosion, and breakdown of the boat. In fact, the National Fire Protection Association states flatly: "It is to be recognized that low voltage installations do not warrant the use of substandard materials or workmanship, particularly in motorcraft where the possible presence of flammable or explosive vapors render a spark or incandescence liable to serious consequences."

A good wiring system is simple, straightforward, easy to trace and trouble-shoot. Its switching arrangements prevent improper operation by the inexperienced, and all switches are marked to indicate their purpose. An exception to the labeling of switches is where function is obvious, as in the case of a lamp with integral switch.

Separate Systems

On a cruiser or auxiliary, in fact aboard any boat which operates in "offshore" waters, and where reliability is important, the engine starting and ignition system should be entirely separate from the boat's lighting and accessory circuits. Best practice is for each engine to have its own battery and charging circuit, while separate batteries and generators are provided for lighting, bilge pumps, DC machinery, and the like. A boat equipped in this way should also carry good jumper cables or have a cross-over switching arrangement so that one system can aid the other in emergency. But the basic wiring of the individual systems should be independent so that trouble in one is not reflected in the others.

Appropriate Voltage

Years ago the electrical systems of recreational boats were all at 6 volts, like the automobiles of those days. Now they are almost exclusively 12-volt systems, with 32 volts used on some larger craft. At the higher voltages, circuit currents, and thus voltage drops to lights and other loads, are less.

Polarity

When a new DC system is installed, or an old one reworked and modernized, it should be installed with the negative polarity grounded. Negative ground is now standard throughout the industry; and it is difficult to buy appliances and electronic gear for positive grounded boats.

Extra Circuits

A new DC electrical system, or one which is being upgraded, should be wired with fuses or circuit breakers, and terminal strips for future additional circuits. Providing for the future in this way helps assure that when new circuits are added they will be neatly, safely hooked up, and not haywired on the tail end of existing circuits, a practice which leads to overloading and possible subsequent fires.

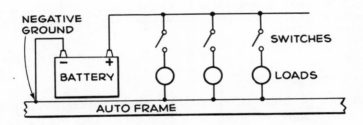

Fig. 3–1 Automobile electrical systems use a single "hot" wire and the car frame for the negative return. See Fig. 3–2 for the difference in boat electrical systems.

The Two-Wire System

Perhaps the greatest difference between automotive wiring and marine wiring is that land vehicles almost always use a one-wire system, while boats must use a two-wire arrangement. In car or truck, the positive wire is hot, feeding the lights and appliances; the chassis, frame, and body are negative, acting as ground return conductor.

The boat is different. In it the hot wire is positive, feeding the lights and appliances as in the automobile; but the negative return is not via the hull, but rather by insulated wires. Note that the boat's grounded bonding system, described in Chapter Five, is never used as a common current-carrying ground, in the manner of an automobile frame.

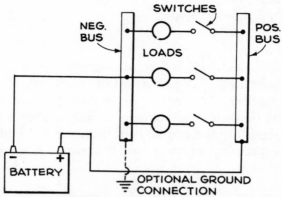

Fig. 3–2 The boat has individual bus bars and connectors. Negative is usually grounded, but a few boats use an ungrounded system where both polarities float free of ground.

Color Coding of Wires

The ABYC Standard for Wiring Identification, E-3, specifies the color coding of wires in a boat's DC system; its use will greatly facilitate the tracing of circuits and trouble-shooting. Table 3-1 lists each color code. Note that white is preferred for the negative return lead, but black is acceptable; whichever color is used for negative, the other must not be used for any purpose.

Grounded and Ungrounded Systems

Two varieties of low-voltage DC systems are used aboard modern boats, *grounded* and *ungrounded*. But the reader is asked to keep in mind that even with the grounded type, the hull or bonding is never used as a current-carrying ground. The systems are connected as follows:

The Ungrounded System

A highly recommended system, but one difficult to use in practice, especially on small boats, is the completely ungrounded system where the entire DC circuitry "floats" absolutely without ground as if it were free in space. It comprises a two-wire system in which all current-carrying conductors, including the source of

RECOMMENDED MARINE WIRING COLOR CODE
DIRECT CURRENT SYSTEMS—UNDER 50 VOLTS
(No diagram required if wiring is in compliance with Tables I and II)

Color	Item	Use
Green (G)		Bonding
White (W) or Black (B)		Return, Negative Main
Red (R)		Positive Mains, Particularly Unfused
Yellow w/Red Stripe (YR)	Starting Circuit	Starting Switch to Solenoid
Yellow (Y)	Generator or Alternator Field	Generator or Alternator Field to Regulator Field Terminal
	Bilge Blowers	Fuse or Switch to Blowers
Dark Gray (Gy)	Navigation Lights	Fuse or Switch to Lights
	Tachometer	Tachometer Sender to Gauge
Brown (Br)	Generator Armature	Generator Armature to Regulator
	Alternator Charge Light	Generator Terminal/Alternator Auxiliary Terminal to Light to Regulator
	Pumps	Fuse or Switch to Pumps
Orange (O)	Accessory Feed	Ammeter to Alternator or Generator Output and Accessory Fuses or Switches
	Accessory Common Feed	Distribution Panel to Accessory Switch
Purple (Pu)	Ignition	Ignition Switch to Coil and Electrical Instruments
	Instrument Feed	Distribution Panel to Electric Instruments
Dark Blue	Cabin and Instrument Lights	Fuse or Switch to Lights
Light Blue (Lt Bl)	Oil Pressure	Oil Pressure Sender to Gauge
Tan	Water Temperature	Water Temperature Sender to Gauge
Pink (Pk)	Fuel Gauge	Fuel Gauge to Gauge

Table 3-1 ABYC Tables show the required wiring color code for direct current systems of less than 50 volts.

power and all accessories, are completely insulated from ground or "earth" throughout the system.

The two-wire ungrounded system is recommended *provided* the entire system can be guaranteed free of grounds. That guarantee is difficult on a small boat with but one DC system. It is difficult because the use of any electrical equipment, including starters and generators, in which current-carrying conductors are connected to metallic frames, will automatically require that the system be grounded. However, all ground potential (negative) conductors must be insulated from ground right up to the point where a common ground point is provided, usually close to the propulsion engine.

The Grounded System

A two-wire system, the grounded circuitry utilizes the boat's common ground point to maintain the negative conductors at ground potential. Except for engine-mounted accessories, which may use the engine block as a common ground return, all electrical circuits must be the two-wire type, having insulated conductors to and from the power source.

Common Ground

In boats using grounded electrical systems, there should be but one common ground point. This should be located at a point well above bilge water level, and as close to the boat's batteries as possible. Only one such point should be established for each system because, among other things, more than one ground point can generate stray currents, inviting corrosion.

The following conductors may be connected directly to the common ground point, once that point is established:

- Engine starter ground return lead and ground lead of the battery.
- Main switchboard ground-return conductor.
- Bonding system conductor.
- Radio ground plate lead (if ground lead plate is installed).
- Auxiliary generator ground.

The common ground point must not be used as the common

return point for individual branch circuits. As shown in Figures 3–2 and 3–3, the return point for branch circuits is the ground bus or ground strip in the main switchboard. This bus, in turn, is then connected by heavy conductor to the common ground point.

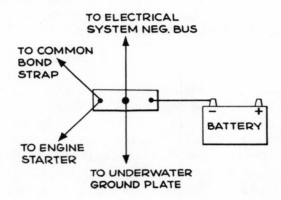

Fig. 3–3 The common ground point, located close to the battery, is the center point of a grounded system.

The majority of DC systems are of the grounded type because the engine starter ground return is the engine ground strap, and grounding is inevitable. In this arrangement, the bonding system is connected to the common ground point. However, in the ungrounded DC system, where the starter is insulated, the bonding system is not connected to the common ground point and although the point is called "ground," it actually floats at its own potential, not necessarily that of Mother Earth.

Details on the all-important bonding system are found in Chapter 5.

DC Receptacles

Common sense dictates that outlets in the direct current, low-voltage system be distinctly different from the standard 120 volt housepower variety of receptacle, assuming a boat has both systems.

Wiring near the Compass

Direct-current wiring should always be strung as far from the compass as possible because of the flow of current which deviates the instrument in proportion to the amperage. Where wires must be closer than 3 or 4 feet from the binnacle, they must be run in twisted pairs to eliminate or minimize the effect of current on the compass heading. Interesting details on electricity and its effect on the compass are found in Chapter 21.

Switchboards

In a good, safe installation, switchboards and distribution panels are accessibly located in well ventilated places, preferably outside of engine and fuel tank compartments. Where applicable, they are protected from rain, spray, or drip from the overhead. Totally enclosed switchboards and distribution panels of the deadfront type are recommended. Deadfront means that the enclosure has no live parts exposed on the front of the panel. Metal enclosures are recommended for switchboards and panels. However, wood or fiberglass may be used, providing all terminal strips, fuse blocks, and the like are mounted on nonabsorbent, noncombustible, high-quality insulating materials. The safest enclosures are lined with asbestos or other fire resistant sheeting.

Switches

Cheap landlubbery switches corrode and cause no end of trouble aboard the boat, those intended for household and automobile use often being troublemakers. A good switch for marine use should be intended for that purpose, preferably being approved by Underwriters Laboratories. If a switch is being installed in fuel tank compartment or engine space, it definitely must be approved for marine use.

Every switch should have a little plate fixed to it, or near it, indicating "on" and "off." Naturally, each switch must be rated for the amperes it is to handle. It is best to avoid switches which are not clearly marked with their current rating; and where there is doubt as to the maximum switched current, select a switch of the next higher capacity.

Terminals

Good terminals and connectors are particularly important on a boat's DC wiring system because, despite vibration and corrosive environment, they must offer continuity and low resistance to current flow. Terminal lugs recommended most highly are the swaged, or crimped, solderless, tinned copper or brass variety with ring ends. These are better than those with spade or forked ends because they will stay in place even if the stud or nut loosens. A preferred type is shown in Figure 3–4.

Fig. 3–4 Lugs with closed ends are best for marine work.

If you plan a wiring job using the approved kind of lugs, be sure to crimp the lug around the wire with the hand tool made by the manufacturer for crimping his lugs. One popular series of lugs is manufactured by Thomas & Betts, and that company also furnishes a combination crimper-cutter that does a workmanlike job of swaging. Avoid crimping with an ordinary pair of pliers; the connection so made will be mechanically and electrically weak.

A good job requires that the holes in ring type terminals be a nice fit to the stud, and that the terminal also match the size wire to which it is crimped. For extra security, it is recommended that a short length of insulating sleeving be slid over the wire at each terminal connection.

Normal Stud Size	Minimum Stud Diameter	Conductor Size*
6	.138	18 AWG
8	.164	14-16 AWG
10	.190	10, 12 AWG
¼	.250	8 AWG
⁵⁄₁₆	.3125	6 AWG
⅜	.375	4 AWG

* Based on the use of 4 conductors to each terminal stud.

Fig. 3–5 Table specifies minimum stud sizes for terminal studs, as specified by ABYC Standard E-9.

Studs

The studs to which terminals are screwed must be of the minimum size indicated in the accompanying table. In addition, good wiring practice dictates the following:

- No more than four conductors should ever be attached to one terminal stud.
- Connections must be made so there is no strain on the terminal.

Battery Terminals

Heavy noncorroding lugs must be used as storage battery connectors, and the connections to the cables should be soldered, not merely clamped. A perfect fit must mate the clamp to the binding post to assure minimum voltage drop. Very heavy current is transmitted through the connection, resulting in unacceptable voltage drop unless the connection is perfect. Hard engine starting is frequently caused by imperfect connections between battery posts and cable clamp. Details on this and other aspects of the battery are found in Chapter 2.

Wiring Installation

A prime rule in good DC wiring practice is to keep all wires routed as far above the bilge as possible. It is not hard to imagine what happens to the wiring when it gets soaked with water, oil, and the other varieties of gunk which swash around in the typical bilge.

In addition to being well above the bilge, wiring in a workmanlike installation will show many of the following qualities:

1. Conductors protected against physical damage as by being struck, walked on, or pinched by doors and hatch covers.

2. All wiring secured throughout its length each 18 inches or as otherwise required to keep it from flapping loose. Good means of security are noncorroding metal clips with antichafing material, and all-plastic clips.

3. Exposed surface wiring, subject to damage, protected by loom, conduit, neat tape wrap, or other workmanlike means.

4. Wire splices conspicuous by their scarcity. Where seen, they are neat, strong, and relieved of strain.

5. Where wiring passes through bulkheads or panels, it is protected against wear by nonchafing ferrules or soft grommets.

Wire Insulation

The purpose of insulation on DC wires is, of course, to prevent short circuits and stray current leakage to the hull or machinery. Even though voltage is low, insulation must be of high quality, enabling it to cope with the severe marine environment.

Wire for marine and general use is manufactured with various types of insulation designated *TW, THW, THWN,* etc. Applications for the various types of insulation are shown in Fig. 3–6, taken from ABYC Standard E-9.

Type	Insulation	Maximum Operating Temperature	Use
THWN	Moisture and Heat Resistant Thermoplastic	75°C 167°F	General use
XHHW	Moisture and Heat Resistant Cross Linked Synthetic Polymer	75°C 167°F	General use
MTW	Moisture, Heat, and Oil Resistant Thermoplastic	60°C	General use except machinery spaces

Fig. 3–6 Shown are conductor insulation and application specified by ABYC. Lengths of insulated wire may be purchased by type and gauge specification.

Wire Conductors

Nothing contributes more to an efficient direct-current network aboard a boat than good, adequate sized conductors. Wires which are too small for the current cause inefficiency due to voltage drop and generate heat because of excessive resistance. For a given current, wire size must increase as the distance from source to load becomes greater. Likewise, wire size must grow proportionately to current; otherwise resistance and voltage drop will be excessive. Conductors should be stranded, not solid.

The most common cause of sluggish performance in electric bilge pumps, pressure water systems, winches, refrigerators, windshield wipers and the like is undersized conductors. Remember that for a given power output, these appliances on 12 volts draw roughly ten times as much current as equivalent 120 volt items.

AWG WIRE SIZES BASED ON A 10 PER CENT VOLTAGE DROP

Total Current on Circuit in Amps.	Feet															
	20	30	40	50	60	70	80	90	100	110	120	130	140	150	160	170
12 Volts																
5	16	16	16	16	14	14	14	14	12	12	12					
10	16	14	14	12	12	12	10	10	10	10	8					
15	14	14	12	10	10	10	8	8	8	8	8					
20	12	12	10	10	8	8	8	6	6	6	6					
25	10	10	10	8	8	8	6	6	6	6	4					
32 Volts																
5	16	16	16	16	16	16	16	16	16	16	16	16	16	16	14	14
10	16	16	16	16	16	16	14	14	14	14	14	12	12	12	12	12
15	16	16	16	16	14	14	14	12	12	12	12	10	10	10	10	10
20	16	16	14	14	14	12	12	12	10	10	10	10	10	10	8	8
25	16	16	14	12	12	12	10	10	10	10	10	8	8	8	8	8
30	16	14	14	12	12	10	10	10	10	8	8	8	8	8	8	6

Fig. 3–7 Length of conductor in feet from source of current to most distant fixture and return is shown for 10% voltage drop.

Rules for Choosing Size

Conductor sizes used for cabin lighting and other circuits where voltage drop is not too critical, may be determined according to Figure 3–7, which is based on a 10% voltage drop.

Conductors used in more critical circuits, where voltage drop must be kept to a minimum (navigation lights, electronic gear, etc.) must not have more than 3% voltage drop. Here, wire size may be determined from Figure 3–8.

If the reader has a special problem and wants to calculate his own conductor size, he may use a formula to give circular mil area of wire. Once knowing the circular mil dimensions, he may refer to Figure 3–9 to find equivalent wire size. The National Fire Protection Association states that when the calculated circular mil area is less than a given value of wire gauge, the next gauge of conductor is to be used.

Formula for Conductor Size

Assuming that circular mils (CM) are desired, the formula is:

$$CM = \frac{K \times I \times L}{E}$$

where: CM = circular mils of conductor
K = 10.8 a constant representing resistance of copper
I = load current in amperes
L = conductor length from source to fixture and return
E = voltage drop at lead, in volts

Example Calculation

Suppose an electric winch is installed 40 feet from a 12-volt battery. Conductor length is 80 feet. The installer will accept a voltage drop of 1 volt to the winch, which draws 40 amperes at full load. What wire size shall he select?

$$CM = \frac{10.8 \times 40 \times 80}{1} = 34,560$$

Figure 3-9 shows that the wire size next larger than 34,560 circular mils is #4 AWG. That is the size conductor which should be selected for the winch, a pair of number fours running from the source to winch and return.

AWG WIRE SIZES BASED ON A 3 PER CENT VOLTAGE DROP

Total Current on Circuit in Amps.	20	30	40	50	60	70	80	90	100	110	120	130	140	150	160	170
									Feet							
							12 Volts									
5	14	12	12	10	10	8	8	8	8	8	6					
10	12	10	8	8	6	6	6	5	5	5	4					
15	10	8	6	6	5	5	4	4	3	3	2					
20	8	6	6	5	4	3	2	2	2	2	1					
25	8	6	5	4	3	3	2	1	1	1	0					
							32 Volts									
5	16	16	16	14	14	14	12	12	12	12	10	10	10	10	10	10
10	16	14	12	12	10	10	10	10	8	8	8	8	8	6	6	6
15	14	12	10	10	10	8	8	8	6	6	6	6	6	6	5	5
20	12	10	10	8	8	8	6	6	6	6	5	5	5	4	4	4
25	12	10	8	8	6	6	6	6	5	5	4	4	4	3	3	3

Fig. 3-8 Length of conductor in feet from source of current to most distant fixture and return is shown for 3% voltage drop.

Conductor Size, AWG	Nominal CM Area	Number of Strands	Resistance OHMS Per 1000 Ft. at 25°C
16	2,583	19	4.09
14	4,107	19	2.58
12	6,530	19	1.62
10	10,380	19	1.02
8	16,510	19	0.641
6	26,250	37	0.410
4	41,740	61	0.253
2	66,370	127	0.162
1	83,690	127	0.129
1/0	105,500	127	0.102
2/0	133,100	127	0.0811
3/0	167,800	259	0.0642
4/0	211,600	418	0.0509

Fig. 3–9 Relationship is shown between size in wire gauge and circular mil area.

Advantage of Higher Voltage

The calculation points up the advantage of higher DC voltage in the boat's system, highlighting the reason that the six-volt system was abandoned some years ago. In the winch example, if a 32-volt system were used, current would be reduced to 15 amperes, and a 3-volt drop would be reasonable. Now, the calculation becomes:

$$CM = \frac{10.8 \times 15 \times 80}{3} = 4,320$$

This indicates that a pair of #12 AWG wires would handle the winch if it operated on a nominal 32-volt system. But, consider the ridiculous situation on the old six-volt system, where current would be 80 amperes, voltage drop should not exceed 0.6 volts, and calculations show that a pair of heavy #2/0 AWG cables would be required to do an adequate job.

Fuses and Breakers

Trip-free circuit breakers and fuses are both approved for protecting the boat's circuits against overload. However, from a practical standpoint, circuit breakers are better because they need no replacement after being overloaded. There's little more frustrating than being out on the water with a blown fuse, and no replacement on board.

Two kinds of circuit breakers are available: trip-free and nontrip-free. Only the trip-free should be used. These are magnetically or thermally actuated by overload; and they cannot be bypassed manually during overload by holding the control button or handle.

Each circuit breaker or fuse should be marked, showing what circuit it serves; and each should be marked with its current rating. Where a circuit is wired with two sizes of conductor, such as #12 and #14, the protective device must be rated to protect the smaller conductor: in this case, the #14 wire.

Some devices, particularly motors, have an internal thermal circuit breaker without manual reset. This protects the device, but not the circuit wiring, and the circuit energizing such a device must still incorporate a fuse or trip-free circuit breaker.

Points to Protect

A well designed electrical system finds a correctly sized fuse or trip-free circuit breaker in the following circuit locations:

1. At the main switchboard, the heavy ungrounded conductor from the master battery switch is overload-protected. The fuse or breaker is rated not more than 125% of total switchboard load. Thus, if all the circuits attached to the switchboard can draw 40 amperes total, the main fuse or breaker can be of 50 amperes rating.

2. On larger installations having distribution panels in addition to the main switchboard, there is protection at the main board in ungrounded power feeds to the panels.

3. Each ungrounded conductor comprising a branch circuit is fused or protected by breaker.

4. Circuits which energize DC motors have a breaker or fuse in the "hot" lead; and the protection is rated not more than 125% of the motor's full load current.

Master Battery Switch

A high quality master-battery disconnect switch provides important protection to the boat, electrical system, and battery. Proper location for the master switch is very close to the batteries, wired in each ungrounded lead.

Most battery switches serving more than one battery double as selector switches, connecting one battery bank or the other to the system. Where this kind of device is used, it must be the make-before break type, connecting the second battery before disconnecting the first. This type of switch assures that at least one battery is always in the circuit. When its handle is turned, the circuit does not open; and the generator or alternator never looks into an open circuit, a situation which might cause damage.

The best battery disconnect switches incorporate an auxiliary contact which opens the field circuit of the alternator or generator when the disconnect is open. This protects the generator. Battery switches not incorporating an auxiliary field contact must be marked with a caution saying: "Do not open this switch when generator is running."

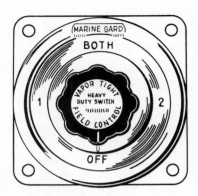

Fig. 3–10 This heavy duty battery disconnect switch incorporates an auxiliary contact to open the generator or alternator control circuit.

SYNOPSIS

For highest reliability, engine and lighting circuits should be independent. Modern DC circuits have negative ground, and the two-wire system is always used for marine work. A common ground point ties all circuits together, avoiding stray currents. Switches, terminals and other components should be designed for marine use, and battery hardware must be especially rugged. Wires should be kept well above the bilges, and should always be of more than adequate gauge. Circuit breakers must be the trip free type; and battery switches should be make-before-break. See also Chapter 23.

CHAPTER 4

Living With "Housepower" Aboard

NOT TOO MANY years ago, when there were yacht clubs but few marinas, the majority of cruisers lay at moorings off shore rather than being tied to a pier. They had no umbilical electric cord, and their electrical systems were simple battery-energized affairs of limited capacity.

Then the marina proliferated, cruisers joined runabouts at dockside, the power cord was plugged into a shoreside receptacle, and the age of "housepower" afloat blossomed. On board went a stream of appliances, as families took to spending weekends aboard at the marina: toasters, heaters, irons, refrigerators, washers, driers, deep freezers and, naturally, the TV set. As the appliances multiplied, voltage dropped, the power cord to the pier got hotter, and so did the wiring inside the boat. These are common problems today; and we shall see what to do about them shortly.

The Basic "Housepower" System

Four wires comprise the standard combination 120/240-volt AC system that you plug into at the marina. It is the same system used in towns throughout the United States and many other countries. Coded black, red, white, and green or bare, the wires function as follows:

Black wire is hot, carrying AC voltage 120 volts above ground. If you touch this wire you may get a shock.

Red wire is also hot, carrying AC voltage 120 volts above ground. As with the black wire, if you touch this conductor, you may get a shock.

White wire is the neutral conductor. It is grounded, so if you touch it you will not get a shock unless you are also touching the red or black. The white wire, however, carries full current, just as the black and red do. Sometimes this wire is color coded gray instead of white.

Green or bare wire is purely a safety conductor. Maintained at ground potential, it is not intended to carry working current, but only to act as a protective ground for equipment frames and metal parts which may be touched by humans. On older electrical appliances the green safety wire may be missing, but on modern gear, made in accordance with best practice, the green wire is seen, connected to the appliance frame.

What is Ground?

In describing "housepower" we use the word *ground* several times; and throughout this book, as in other electrical works, the word will appear many times. Just what is ground?

In the electrical world, ground means many things to many people, so many things, in fact, that its significance is lost unless it is defined as specifically applied. Aerospace engineers talk of ground in an airplane 35,000 feet aloft. Marine architects use the word while referring to a yacht floating in a hundred feet of water. How can this be?

Our earth's moist, conductive soil and the conductive waters of her seas, lakes, and rivers are the real basic ground referred to in building and marina wiring nomenclature. Here, a wire connected to ground is truly "earthed" and is at the earth's ground potential or voltage: The grounded conductor is connected to a water pipe or large-area metal plate buried deep in wet earth. Such a conductor, even though carrying current (as from a source to a motor), will not shock you if you touch it while standing on wet terrain. As mentioned earlier, the white and green wires in the standard AC system are grounded.

Note that a good connection to Mother Earth's ground is essential. Simply touching a wire to dry earth or pushing a metal rod into arid sand will not create an effective electrical ground. The conductor must be in contact with wet earth over a considerable area before constituting a good ground.

It is standard practice to connect one current-carrying conductor to ground in a pair carrying alternating current. Even though the wires alternately are driven positive and negative many times a second, one is always at ground potential. Voltage polarity between them changes constantly; but voltage between the grounded one and earth remains close to zero. This is true all the way from the source to the load.

It's a little hard to visualize how the white wire in a pair of 120 volt current-carrying conductors can remain at ground voltage. What happens is that, with the white wire "tied" to ground, the black wire alternately surges above, then below, ground potential. In short, the black wire is first 120 volts positive, then 120 volts negative with respect to the grounded white wire. (Technically, it swings even farther high and low than 120 volts. But in practical electricity, the nominal, or root mean square—RMS— value is referred to.)

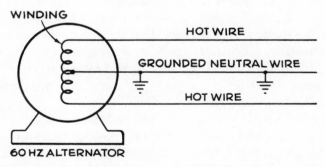

Fig. 4–1 Schematic shows how one wire in an alternating current system can be connected to ground while the other conductors are hot.

In electronics, aircraft, and automotive work, a chassis or frame, where all wires of one polarity are connected, is often called "ground." Strangely enough, this pseudo ground may be floating at some potential other than the earth's. Indeed, it does so in an automobile or airplane where the frame may float at any voltage to which it is driven by outside forces—the most extreme example being during a lightning strike, when the whole thing floats at a million volts above earth ground.

Electronic gear usually has a common ground point, which may or may not be tied to true earth. Obviously that point cannot be earthed in an airplane; but it can be in a boat. Seas, lakes, and rivers are, after all, a part of Mother Earth's ground system.

In this book, unless otherwise specified, the word "ground" refers to a real earth ground of the waterpipe and ground plate variety.

How the AC System Works

In an AC system, such as the one at most marinas, alternating voltage from the black to the white neutral wire is nominally 120 volts. Voltage from the red to the white is also 120. However, voltage from red to black is 240 volts. The higher voltage is often used for on-board stoves, high capacity air-conditioners, and other heavy appliances; but it is not used for hand-held equipment.

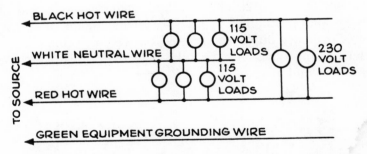

Fig. 4–2 The standard four-wire housepower system has three wires which are current-carrying conductors, and one equipment grounding safety wire.

Common practice is to run three-wire feeder circuits comprising black, red, and white conductors. Half the branch circuits to receptacles are wired black-to-white, the other half are wired red-to-white. This arrangement approximately balances the load on the feeder circuit.

65

Receptacles or power centers along the pier commonly furnish 120 volt power and some also supply 240-volt service. However, physical configuration of the 120- and 240-volt receptacles is different, making it impossible for the boatman to plug into the wrong service. Acceptable types of 120- and 240-volt dock receptacles are shown in the accompanying illustrations.

Dockside Receptacles

Up to the present, there has been confusion concerning pier receptacles and their standardization. Because of this, many cruisers carry an assortment of plugs, adapters, cords, and electrical jury rigs to bring power aboard. Unfortunately, some of these lashups are made from cheap, dime-store fittings coupled to undersized wire; they result in heating of the conductors and loss of voltage aboard the boat.

At this writing, the receptacle picture is improving, and the need for odd-ball plug arrangements should decrease in the future. The latest edition of the National Electrical Code, guide for the electrical industry, pins down what is acceptable. Says the N.E.C.:

"Receptacles which provide shore power for boats shall be rated not less than 20 amperes and shall be single and of the locking and grounding types . . ." This means that for the future, ordinary duplex household outlets are ruled out. Single outlet locking types are the rule. The two kinds are shown in figures 4–3 and 4–4.

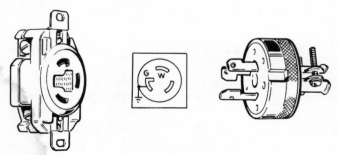

Fig. 4–3 Hubbell Twist-Lock three-wire grounding receptacle rated at 30 amps is suited for use on the pier. Also shown is the type of plug the receptacle accepts. This hardware is rated up to 125 volts.

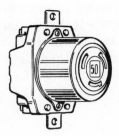

Fig. 4–4 Locking type four-wire, 50 amp, 120/240 volt receptacle is shown. The three radial slots are for the two hot wires and neutral, while the metal shell is the equipment safety ground connection.

Hopefully, more adequate power is on the way, because the new code specifies: "The ampacity for feeder and service conductors supplying power for boats shall be calculated on the basis of a minimum of 25 watts per lineal foot of slip or dock space for boat outlet circuits, plus lighting and other loads." This means that a slip 40 feet long, having a 100 watt light, for example, is required to be wired for 1,100 watts minimum. The code requirements stated above, however, are already becoming inadequate as most cruising boats have one 30-amp service cord, and many have two such lines, or one 50-amp cable.

Specific Improvements

The dim lights aboard your docked boat should get brighter as the new standards are complied with, and as marinas install wiring and receptacles meeting modern requirements. Several electrical hardware companies are now manufacturing 30 amp, 125 volt, two-pole, three-wire grounding, locking receptacles and plugs. Also now available are 50 amp, 125/250 volt, three-pole, four-wire grounding locking devices. This husky, high capacity hardware will appear with increased frequency as marinas switch to the modern equipment.

Where possible, you should always steer clear of the old fashioned two-blade, non-grounding plugs and receptacles. They are "unsafe at any current" because they bring the hot black wire and the white neutral wire aboard your boat; but they leave out the green equipment grounding wire, terminating it ashore, thereby creating a serious shock hazard. Remember, that green wire is a safety grounding wire intended to protect you. Around boats and marinas, it should always be attached to appliances at one end and to a grounding receptacle at the other.

Power Centers

A new convenient method of distributing dockside power is through special "power centers," see Fig. 4–5. These are compact fiberglass or metal enclosures having weatherproof outlets, each individual outlet protected by its own circuit breaker. An advantage to this system is that circuit troubles, overloads or short circuits on one boat will trip the breaker on its own power center only. Other boats on the pier will not be affected. Since the tripped circuit breaker is immediately at dockside, the skipper can easily reset it and reenergize his boat's system without hailing the marina operator.

Power centers are appearing on marina piers with increasing frequency, and should do a lot toward providing adequate power to the cruiser having extensive "household" appliances aboard.

That Power Cord

The importance of a good power cord from boat to pier is hard to overemphasize. The best shoreside power source does the boat little good if the connection is a stringy, undersized shore cable terminated at an inadequate on-board receptacle.

Standard E-8 specifies that a boat's power inlet be a male-type connector fitted with a weatherproof cover, spring-loaded and self-closing. If located in an area subject to flooding or momentary submersion—as on the side of a hull—it must have a threaded, gasketed cover, see Fig. 4–6. Most cables are fitted with neoprene covers at each end to keep the connection dry when plugged in.

This Standard also contains requirements for shore power cables. They must have a grounding wire in addition to the power conductors; they must be of type SO, ST, or STO cord; the shore end must have a locking and grounding cap, and the boat end must have a locking and grounding female-type

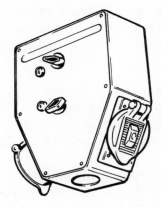

Fig. 4–5

connector to match the boat's power inlet. Cables rated at 30 amps must have #10 gauge conductors; those for 50-amp service require #6 wires. There is a set of different configurations for power connectors of varying ampere capacity to prevent mis-matching of cables and loads. Boat owners are urged to use high quality, corrosion resistant, marine type plugs and receptacles. Ordinary, housecat hardware is inadequate: Through corrosion of its metal and deterioration of the plastic, it will cause unwanted voltage drop as it ages, and will become dangerous to handle. Worse, it may fail completely after a few months of use.

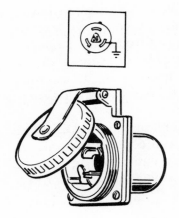

Fig. 4–6 An approved type shore power inlet receptacle has watertight cap, and a blade for equipment grounding.

AC Wiring Aboard the Boat

The wiring arrangement aboard your boat should meet three principal requirements. To be satisfactory, it must:

1. Present minimum shock hazard.
2. Cause no electrolytic corrosion.
3. Be useful and efficient, offering minimum voltage drop between shoreside receptacle and the appliance it feeds.

To meet the three primary requirements, the on-board AC electrical system must be adequately insulated and correctly grounded. Coded wires must be connected to specified terminals; protective devices and switches must be circuited correctly; and above all, the wiring must be workmanlike.

Grounding of AC Wiring

Because grounding technique is important in AC wiring, ABYC defines exactly what it means by the elusive word *ground*, as follows:

"Ground applies to the potential of the earth's surface . . . including any conductive part of the wetted surface of a hull." This definition eliminates any thought of a "pseudo-ground," floating above earth potential, as found on an automobile frame.

Note carefully ABYC's defined difference between the white or gray coded *grounded* conductor, and the green coded equipment *grounding* wire. "Grounded conductor is a current-carrying conductor connected to the side of the source which is intentionally maintained at ground potential. Grounding conductor (on the other hand) is a normally *non-current-carrying* conductor provided to connect the exposed metallic enclosures of electrical equipment to ground. Its purpose is to minimize shock hazard to personnel."

ABYC, the safety agency, insists that all the boat's AC system be constructed and installed so that it can cope with vibration, shock, and a corrosive atmosphere. The entire system must be permanently installed and designed to provide maximum protection against shock for:

- The crew aboard the boat.
- Swimmers or people in a dinghy or other boat who touch the boat.
- People transferring from boat to shore, touching both simultaneously.

Furthermore, your boat's AC system must be designed so that on-board AC generators and shore power cannot simultaneously feed the same circuit.

A feature that is not specified in the ABYC Safety Standard is an AC voltmeter mounted in a readily visible location and connected so that it will indicate the voltage supplied from shore or generated on board. When connecting to an unfamiliar source, turn off *all* branch circuits and read the voltage *before* they are switched on—this may save you from the loss of valuable equipment from over- or under-voltage. This meter can also monitor the output of your on-board generator when it is in use. Also desirable is an AC ammeter for each power inlet. This, if properly watched, will show the current being drawn through the cable at any given time and will aid in preventing damage to the conductors, or more likely, to the connectors. System frequency and nominal voltage should be clearly written on the main AC switchboard. Typical marking would be 120 volts, 60 Hz. The plate is to help prevent the boat from being plugged into the wrong power.

Standard power in the United States, Canada, and most of Mexico, alternates at 60 Hertz (cycles per second). However, almost half the world uses 50 Hz power. If at some distant place in the world, such as Bridgetown, Barbados, you plug into 50 Hz power, some of your on-board appliances will operate the same as on 60 Hz: Toasters, heaters, light bulbs and other resistive appliances will operate ok. But induction motors will run almost 20% slower than at home. Induction motors are the kind used in refrigerators, electric clocks, deep freezers, washing machines, and the like.

Many induction motors designed for 60 Hz, 120 volt power will run satisfactorily on 50 Hz, 120 volts without overheating. However, others will overheat unless, on 50 Hz power, the voltage is reduced to 95 or 100 volts. But as one engineer laughingly put it, "You're lucky to get as much as 95 volts on the stringy end of the line in many 'developing' countries."

If you are lucky enough to be planning an extended cruise away from United States waters, you might buy a copy of *Electric Current Abroad,* latest edition. Listing type and frequency, nominal voltage, types of plugs used, and other data, the book is published by the U.S. Department of Commerce and is for sale by the Superintendent of Documents, U.S. Government Printing Office, Washington, D.C. 20402.

AC Switches Aboard the Boat

It is desirable that switches wired into the boat's AC system be the kind that simultaneously disconnect both current-carrying conductors: the black and the white. This eliminates the use of ordinary hardware switches of the type found in home and office. In shoreside domestic, 120 volt electrical work, single pole switches are used, wired in the black (hot) conductor only.

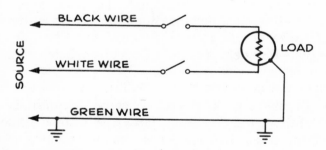

Fig. 4–7 Aboard the boat, switches should be wired to interrupt both the hot and neutral conductors. The equipment ground is never switched.

Switch gear aboard the boat is different. Double pole switches are recommended, one pole breaking the black, the other breaking the white. There is a reason for breaking the connection in both wires when the switch is off: Even though the boat itself is correctly wired, the white neutral wire being grounded, there is a possibility of the system being plugged into dock power with white and black wires reversed. There is also the possibility that incoming shore power may be wired with reversed polarity—the white wire hot, the black grounded. Electricians, particularly amateur ones, can make mistakes. In that case, aboard the boat if there were single pole switches, wired in the black conductor circuit only, you would open the ground circuit, leaving the white wire hot. That is not safe, and is why both wires should be switched on board.

Where single pole switches have been used in AC systems aboard older boats, they should be wired in the black conductor only. The white neutral wire must not be switched, nor must the green or bare equipment grounding wire. Naturally, when the single pole switch system is used, it is most important that the boat be plugged into dockside power with correct polarity: Black wire hot, and white wire grounded.

Testing Polarity

If you are ever in doubt as to correct polarity of incoming power, make a simple, quick check as follows: Using an inexpensive miniature neon-light circuit tester, touch one test prod to the black conductor, the other prod to an earth ground such as the engine block or a below-waterline, metal, thru-hull fitting. The light should glow. Touch the test prod to the white conductor; the light should not glow. Polarity is correct. However, if the light remains dark when you touch the black, but glows when you touch the white, polarity is backward. Reverse the shore connection. Built-in polarity indicators are used on many craft.

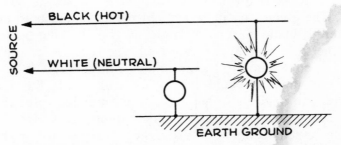

Fig. 4–8 A test light between black wire and ground should glow, but between white and ground it should not—if polarity is correct.

Suppose both shore plug and on-board receptacle are of the correct, polarized, 3-blade, non-reversible type, but you find that the marina receptacle is wired backward? If yours is a one-night tie-up, you will have to live with it, or alternately, make up a temporary cord that will restore correct polarity aboard. If the reversed situation exists at the marina where you "live," urge the operator to have the wiring corrected.

Receptacles Aboard the Boat

Power receptacles located on deck, in cockpits, or other areas exposed to the elements must be watertight and incorporate a self-closing, water tight, cap. Receptacles for attachment to the shore cable must be the reverse service grounding type. All other AC receptacles on the boat must be grounding type with specific provision for the green equipment grounding wire.

FIBERGLASS

Fig. 4–9 Corrosion resistant receptacles with tight fitting protective covers are required in exposed locations.

We keep emphasizing that green grounding wire for a reason. Its purpose is not to conduct electricity when the situation is normal. But it *is* there to conduct current and protect humans against shock in the event the appliance it serves develops a fault. The green wire in an appliance cord connects to the third (centered) blade on a modern electrical plug. That blade mates with the third hole in the approved type receptacle, and in that hole is a connection to the grounding conductor.

In the unhappy event that a hot wire inside the appliance touches the device's frame or exposed metallic case, that case will become electrically "hot" unless tightly grounded. Purpose of the green equipment grounding wire is to ground the appliance and to conduct fault currents to earth, preventing them from passing through a human to ground.

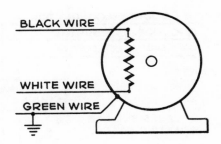

Fig. 4–10 The black and white current-carrying conductors connect inside the appliance to its working windings. The green equipment grounding wire simply attaches to the frame.

Shock Hazard

Because of the inevitable dampness around a boat, shock hazard is naturally greater than in a home living room. That's why the protective grounding green wire is so important on floating equipment. But the green wire cannot do its job unless plugs are the three blade type, and receptacles have three holes to accept the plugs.

In the name of safety, boats fitted with the old fashioned two blade receptacles should be refurbished with the modern three blade type. And the third (green) connection should be securely grounded.

Fig. 4–11 The modern "pansy face" receptacle can accommodate the mating plug's grounding blade.

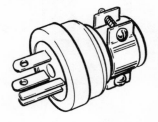

Fig. 4–12 The equipment grounding blade is prominent on an approved type of straight blade appliance plug.

The On-Board 120 Volt System

Shown in Figure 4–13, this system may be used on any non-metallic boat. It may also be used on a metal boat having protection against galvanic corrosion. (More about corrosion protection is found in Chapter 13.)

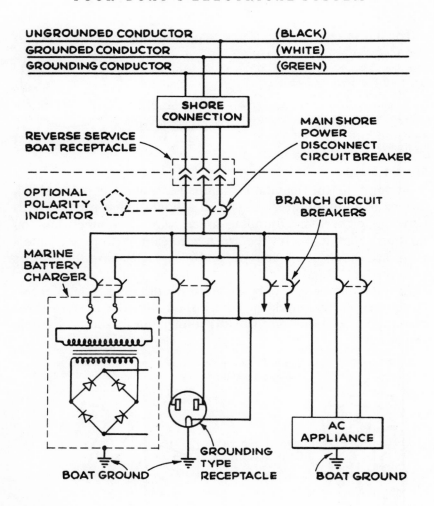

UNGROUNDED CONDUCTOR	(BLACK)
GROUNDED CONDUCTOR	(WHITE)
GROUNDING CONDUCTOR	(GREEN)

Fig. 4–13 Standard 120 volt AC wiring uses a three wire system and receptacle.

The ground (white) and ungrounded (black) shore current wires are connected via the cable to the boat's AC circuit through a main disconnect circuit breaker. This main breaker, when tripped on overload or manually opened, breaks the circuit to both on-board current-carrying conductors, white and black. Neither current-carrying conductor is ever grounded to the boat at any point whatever.

The shore equipment grounding conductor, green or bare, is connected directly to all non-current carrying parts of the AC system. These are the power panel, junction boxes, and the like. The protective grounding wire is also connected to the boat's common ground point. Breakers, fuses, and switches are never placed in the grounding conductor. Its integrity must never be violated.

The On-Board 120/240 Volt System

Similar to the 120 volt system, and shown in Figure 4–14, this

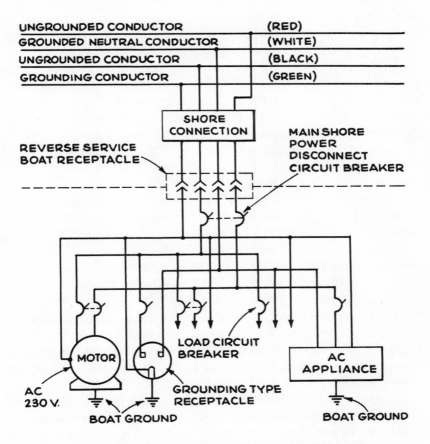

Fig. 4–14 Standard 120/240 volt AC wiring has four wires and receptacle.

system is used on larger boats, particularly those having high capacity air-conditioners and electric galleys. ABYC rates this system as ok on any non-metallic boat or on a metal boat having protection against galvanic corrosion.

In this arrangement, the shore grounded neutral conductor (white) is connected directly to the neutral white wires aboard the boat. No circuit breaker is required in the white. An acceptable alternate is to provide a breaker in the white neutral wire, *provided* it simultaneously opens all white, black, and red conductors when it trips.

In the standard system, red and black ungrounded shore conductors are each connected to the boat's system through a single pole circuit breaker. None of the three current-carrying wires is ever grounded on the boat.

On the 120/240 volt system, as with the plain 120 volt one, the green equipment grounding conductor is connected directly to all non-current-carrying parts of the AC system. It is also tied to the boat's common ground point. Because it is intended to protect the crew against electrocution, the green wire is never switched or overload protected in any manner.

The On-Board Isolation System

Recommended by ABYC as an excellent AC electrical system for most boats, the isolation transformer circuit reduces shock hazard. It also reduces the possibility that the floating AC system will cause galvanic corrosion. Because of the latter, it is recommended for use aboard steel and aluminum craft.

Heart of the isolation system is an on-board isolation transformer. Electrically, it offers complete separation of shore power from the boat's circuits. Shore generated electricity flows through the transformer's primary winding and back to shore. Its energy is transferred to the boat's system magnetically. But there is no direct electrical connection between shore juice and the boat's circuits.

An isolation transformer allows the boat's current-carrying conductors to float completely free of ground. They behave, in a sense, as though they were "dead" wires with respect to earth; but there is voltage *between* them. Because it circulates in its own

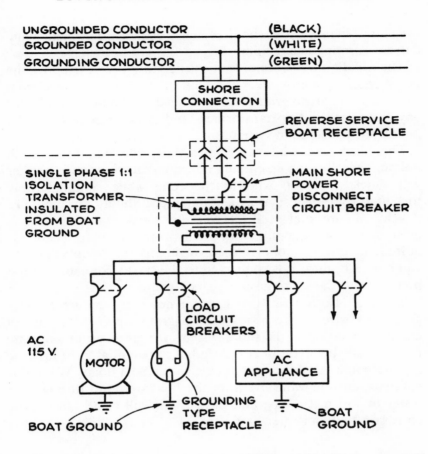

UNGROUNDED CONDUCTOR — (BLACK)
GROUNDED CONDUCTOR — (WHITE)
GROUNDING CONDUCTOR — (GREEN)

SHORE CONNECTION

REVERSE SERVICE BOAT RECEPTACLE

SINGLE PHASE 1:1 ISOLATION TRANSFORMER INSULATED FROM BOAT GROUND

MAIN SHORE POWER DISCONNECT CIRCUIT BREAKER

LOAD CIRCUIT BREAKERS

AC 115 V.

MOTOR

AC APPLIANCE

BOAT GROUND

GROUNDING TYPE RECEPTACLE

BOAT GROUND

Fig. 4–15 In the isolation system, current-carrying conductors make no direct connection to the boat's distribution wiring. The equipment grounding conductor from shore terminates at the transformer shell.

closed circuit, electricity from the isolated system does not try to flow through people or other conductors to true earth ground. It is, therefore, safer for sailors and gentler on boats from a corrosion standpoint.

Figure 4–15 shows an isolation transformer system for 120 volts AC; and a similar system is used where 120/240 volts is brought on board via an isolation transformer. In all cases, the transformer is insulated from the boat. Its primary winding is energized from shore power through circuit breakers; these breakers, when tripped, simultaneously open the black and white current-carrying conductors.

The isolation transformer frame is tied to shore "earth" via the green equipment grounding wire; but the frame is insulated from the boat. The green grounding wire need not be brought aboard any farther than the transformer, and is not run through the boat's AC distribution system.

The black and white current-carrying conductors are both floating free, having essentially no potential to ground; neither will shock a person who touches one while simultaneously touching a ground, such as a water pipe. Should an appliance develop an internal fault, it will not shock the user who is grounded. Consequently, the green protective wire is not required; if however, one is used on board for receptacles and equipment frames, it is connected to the boat's common ground point, *not* to the shore grounding conductor.

There is also a positive reason for not tying the green shore grounding wire to the boat's central ground point. Because of circuit unbalances in the shore system, the green grounding wire may actually be a volt or two different in potential from the true ground potential of the water in which the boat floats. When this happens, current will flow from the boat's ground through the water in which it floats; and the current will cause electrolytic corrosion to underwater hardware.

Protection for On-Board AC Circuits

Your home is protected against fire caused by electric overload or short circuit. Fuses or circuit breakers are the protection; the same kind of devices protect your boat. As back-up, certain switches and disconnects are also needed.

Trip-free circuit breakers are a recommended protective component for on-board application. These are designed so that the reset handle cannot be manually held to override the current interrupting mechanism. "Cheating" on the breaker is impossible.

Two types of breaker are available for on-board use; Magnetic breakers convert current to a magnetic field; and when the field becomes too strong it operates a mechanism, opening the protective switch. Thermal breakers convert current to heat; and when temperature rises beyond predetermined setpoint, the heat operates a bi-metal or other switch mechanism. Many marine electricians, and men at marinas, prefer the magnetic type because it does not derate itself in the hot sun or when cabin temperatures get torrid. Advantage of the thermal breaker is that it offers a time lag before tripping, thus allowing motors to overload the line momentarily while starting.

Correct size fuses offer safe on-board circuit protection. However, fuses have several disadvantages as compared to circuit breakers:

- When a fuse blows, it is more difficult to replace it than simply to re-set a circuit breaker.
- It is dangerously easy to replace a blown fuse with an improper one of excess current-carrying capacity.
- If a fuse blows and no replacement is handy, there is the temptation to shunt it with a length of wire, a practice which leads to fire.
- In damp corrosive atmospheres, fuse clips tend to corrode, offering a high resistance connection which results in voltage drop.

Where fuses are used aboard the boat, the skipper is urged to carry plenty of spares, and to store them close to the active fuse. It is certainly not unrealistic to carry a half dozen spares for each size fuse used on the boat.

Feeder Protection

Feeders from shore power to the boat should be protected with a circuit breaker as specified in ABYC Safety Standard E-8. This device should open each load carrying conductor in the shore power cable; the grounding (green) conductor should *not* be opened. The circuit breaker must be of the trip-free, manually-reset type, UL approved, and of a current rating not to exceed the maximum current-carrying capacity of the wires to be protected.

As mentioned earlier, all current-carrying conductors in

branch circuits must have fuses or trip-free breakers. Also, each circuit serving an AC motor must be protected by a device rated not more than 125 percent of the motor's full load rated current.

Shore Power Disconnect

A safe on-board AC electric system must have a shore power disconnect switch which simultaneously shuts off all current-carrying conductors from shore to boat; the main circuit breaker can be used for this purpose.

A very desirable safety device is a "ground fault circuit interrupter (GFCI)." These units can be installed for the main feeders or for individual circuits; see pages 230–234.

Full Power with Safety

If the boat is to have full voltage through all circuits, and if wiring is to operate cool and safe, AC conductors must be of adequate size. This is a basic rule in wiring. For common wire types, with not more than three conductors cabled or bunched in a raceway, the National Electric Code allows the following ampacities for insulated conductors. This table also indicates the approximate voltage drop per ampere per 100 feet:

From the table, it is apparent that the voltage drop at 15 amps through 100 feet of 14 gauge wire is approximately 7.2 volts; but the same current passing through 100 feet of 10 gauge wire suffers a voltage drop of only 3 volts. Heavy boat wiring pays, especially because it is possible that voltage from the marina and through the power cord may be low to start with.

Gauge Awg	Ampacity	Voltage Drop
14	15	.48
12	20	.31
10	30	.20
8	40	.13
6	55	.08

When inspecting old wiring or installing new, make sure that your boat's AC wiring is as heavy as or heavier than specified by the code. Lighter wire is not only risky but also makes appliances sluggish.

When you're in doubt about the current a circuit handles, energize the circuit, placing on it all the loads it will be asked to carry; then measure the flow of current with a clip-on AC ammeter. If the current is greater than the ampacity rating of the wire, rework the circuit with heavier wire. Alternately, lighten the circuit's load; and run a new circuit for part of the equipment it served.

Regarding wire gauge, a good rule is: "Where there's doubt, use the next heavier gauge." This is particularly true in cabins and bilges baked by the sun where heat increases conductor resistance while decreasing insulation durability.

SYNOPSIS
The housepower AC system coming aboard the boat is the same kind of 4-wire circuitry found in households, but with modifications. Both current-carrying conductors are switched and fused, whereas in household electricity, only one current-carrying conductor is ever "opened." One current-carrying conductor is grounded ashore, but not on the boat. The protective green equipment grounding wire is grounded ashore, and may be grounded on the boat; but it is never switched or fused. Shore outlets must be at least 20-amp size and locking type. An AC system is particularly safe, and contributes to corrosion reduction. All on-board systems should be fitted with trip-free circuit breakers, and must have a shore power disconnect switch.

CHAPTER 5

Boats, Like Bankers, Must Be Bonded

A HUSKY, low resistance bonding system is a *must* on inboard powered non-metallic boats. It is, in fact, required by the American Boat and Yacht Council on boats meeting ABYC's high standards.

What is Bonding?

Bonding comprises a heavy electrical conducting system which electrially "ties together" the entire boat. It acts somewhat the same as the guard grounding conductor in household wiring, but its functions are even more important. In both cases, all exposed metallic enclosures for electrical equipment are held close to ground potential in the event wiring develops a fault.

ABYC cites four important reasons for requiring electrical bonding on non-metallic boats. These are:

1. Bonding provides a low resistance electrical path between otherwise isolated metallic objects, reducing the possibility of electrolytic corrosion due to stray currents between objects.
2. Bonding prevents the possibility of above-ground electrical potential on exposed metallic cases and parts of electrical equipment should a fault develop in such a device.

3. Bonding provides a low-resistance path to ground for voltages higher than system potential, as, for example, during a lightning strike.

4. Bonding minimizes radio interference.

Bonding is Independent

It is important to know that the bonding system is definitely *not* intended to function as the current-carrying conductor in the boat's AC or DC electrical system. For example, it must not be used as the ground return conductor in the DC system; and it must not be used *in place* of the equipment ground conductor in the AC system. In short, the bonding network is intended to act as a heavy electrical back-up, but is not to be intentionally used as a current-carry circuit. You don't intentionally hook circuits to the bonding network for it to conduct working currents.

Details

Where a bonding system is installed aboard a boat having a grounded electrical system, both the bonding system and the electrical system's grounded conductor must connect to a common ground point. Notice that the two systems come together *only* at this one point; they are not interconnected at several points throughout the boat.

ABYC Safety Standard E-1 defines a bonding system as consisting of a "common bonding conductor" and "individual bonding conductors" (also called "bonding jumpers") to the common point and to the metallic parts of electrical equipment.

The bonding conductors must be permanent, continuous, and of sufficient size to conduct safely any currents likely to be imposed on them due to stray currents or short circuits.

Usually running from bow to stern, the common bonding conductor should be uninsulated copper or bronze strip, or copper tubing. The kind of tubing used for refrigeration and plumbing work is good for the purpose. Also acceptable is bare copper or tinned copper wire of heavy gauge. Wire, tubing, or strip must be of thick gauge, not only to provide heavy current-carrying capacity, but to offer ease of accepting low resistance connections. Copper braid, sometimes used to bond aircraft or electronic gear, is not recommended for use in bonding boats. It is difficult to connect to, and is subject to deterioration by corrosion.

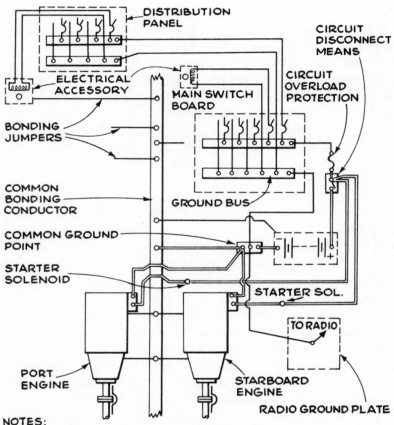

Fig. 5–1 Schematic shows a bonding system on a boat having a grounded direct current electrical system.

Common bonding conductors made of copper or bronze strips

must be no less than 1/32" thick, and no less than 1/2" wide. As a matter of fact, on well constructed yachts it is not uncommon to see the main fore-and-aft bonding strip 1/32" thick and 2" to 5" wide, laid right down the centerline of the boat.

If wire is used as the common bonding conductor, it must be #8 gauge or larger; and if insulated, green. Where tubing is

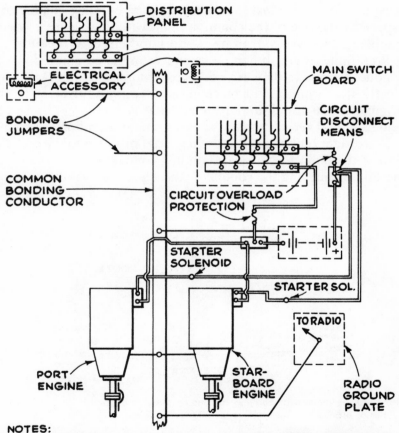

NOTES:
1. ALL ELECTRICAL EQUIPMENT WITHOUT INTERNAL GROUNDS.
2. SWITCH BOARD AND DISTRIBUTION-PANEL CABINETS, IF CONSTRUCTED OF METAL, SHALL BE BONDED.

Fig. 5–2 Schematic shows a bonding system on a boat having an ungrounded direct current electrical system.

used, it must, of course, have conductivity equal to or greater than #8 wire. Standard ¾" or 1" copper refrigeration or plumbing tubing serves well as a common bonding conductor. It is easy to handle, convenient to connect to, and has adequate conductivity.

The Master Conductor

The common bonding conductor is installed in a fore-and-aft direction and so that it will not be submerged in bilge water. It must also be located so that the individual bonding conductors, especially the one to the common point with the negative side of the boat's DC system, can be as short and direct as possible.

Preferably, there should be no splices in the common bonding conductor. Where they are necessary, connections must provide electrical continuity and mechanical strength equivalent to the original conductor. Joint laps must be at least 2" long, brazed or soldered, and secured against failure due to vibration or strain.

Watertight bulkheads present a special problem to the installation of the main fore-and-aft bonding conductor. An acceptable method of carrying the conductor through a bulkhead is to use a

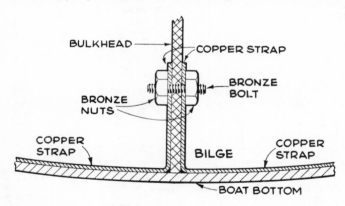

Fig. 5–3 One method of carrying a bonding strap through a bulkhead by heavy copper or bronze hardware above the bilge water level.

very heavy through-bolt of bronze or copper, the through-bolt or bolts, being heavier in electrical cross-section than the bonding strip itself. When through-bolts are used, they should attach to the bonding conductor and pass through the bulkhead well above maximum bilge water level. Also, where possible, it is a good idea to sweat the connections after tightening the through-bolts firmly.

Fastenings used to secure the common bonding conductor to the hull or other surfaces must be of a metal equal to or more noble than the copper conductor. Thus, screws, nuts and bolts of copper silicon bronze, Inconel, or 18–8 type 304 passive stainless steel are fine, but "household" brass screws will corrode, and are no good for the purpose.

A bonding system is similar to a backbone with many ribs—hence there are quite a number of connections. The ABYC Safety Standard requires that all connections at the main bonding conductor and at the bonded items be accessible for inspection and maintenance. (It would be wise to also apply this to splices, if any.) This means that when a bonding system is installed, there should be some kind of removable floorboards or cover plates at the points cited above. Makes sense.

Naval architects say that the main bonding conductor should preferably be routed as close to the centerline of the boat as is practical. However, they say, "On small boats where the electrical components are predominantly on the side of the hull, the common conductor may be routed in a manner to minimize length of the bonding jumpers."

Bonding Jumpers

Shorter than the fore-and-aft main bonding conductor, the bonding jumpers form the ribs of the system. They connect the metal non-current-carrying parts of the boat to the common bond. Naturally, they must be tightly connected at each end with corrosion and vibration resistant fastenings. Where the bonding jumpers attach to the common bonding conductor, strain relief must be provided so the connections remain secure.

The jumpers, like the common bond, need not be insulated. One exception might be where the jumper is close to current-carrying wires, and where chafing might possibly cause a short circuit. Size of wire must be more than great enough to handle maximum expected current, and in no case should be smaller than #8 AWG wire or the equivalent in copper strip or tubing.

Things You Should Bond

If you are installing a bonding system or inspecting an existing one, see to it that all large metal blobs are attached to the boat's system. Include such items as:

• The propulsion engine or engines on a motorboat, and the auxiliary motor on a sailboat are bonded. If the boat has an auxiliary electric generating plant, that, too, must be bonded. To make sure that the prop shaft is well bonded, install a brush or rubbing contact adjacent to it as described in Chapter 13, "Taming Electrolytic Corrosion."
• Electric motor and generator or alternator frames are included. However, where the motor or generator is attached firmly to a bonded engine, as the starter and alternator are, separate bonding is not needed; the engine's bond will serve very nicely.
• Larger cabinets and control boxes housing either DC or AC power components are connected to a jumper. However, it is not necessary to run a heavy bond to every small switch plate or receptacle. These are individually grounded on AC circuits by the equipment grounding conductor, the bare or green wire.
• The cabinets and enclosures of electronic gear must be included in the bonding arrangement. Good bonding protects the electronics against damage from lightning, meanwhile reducing their pick-up of static, spurious signals, and electrical noise. Bonding also acts as a backup in protecting the user against electrical shock hazard from the gear which is energized from the 120 volt AC line.
• Where metallic sheath or conduit is used to carry conductors, it should be connected to the bonding.
• Heavy cables, tubes, pipes or rods comprising part of the rudder or clutch control arrangement should be bonded.
• It is most important that fuel pumps, fuel-fill deck fittings, fuel feed lines, electrically operated fuel pumps and valves be tied to the bonding system. Good bonding of the entire fuel system is a step toward preventing fires caused by static discharge or lightning side flashes.
• Bonding should include metal or lead lined battery trays, and also water tanks and their connecting fill hardware on deck.

Things You Need Not Bond

The ABYC Safety Standard lists two types of items that are not required to be connected to the bonding system. Included are all electrically isolated thru-hull fittings, except that if a zinc block is used for galvanic action protection on a non-metallic hull, then it and all thru-hull fittings should be tied in to the common bonding conductor.

Electrically isolated metallic items not listed in the preceding section are not required to be connected to the bonding system except as a part of a lightning protection system; see Chapter 15.

Metal Boats

Aluminum and steel boats need not be bonded, provided good electrical continuity is maintained between all the items which normally require bonding. A tight electrical connection to the hull will usually more than suffice.

There are two points to watch carefully when using the metal hull as a common conductor.

1. Underwater hardware which might create a galvanic couple with the hull should not be electrically attached to it. In this case, the hardware should be completely insulated from the hull. For example, a copper or silicon bronze underwater fitting should be insulated from the hull. Otherwise, the hull would try to "protect" the fitting, and the hull would corrode.

2. In order to avoid galvanic action between a through-hull fitting and the metal hull, the following should be done with electric pumps: The sea water connection must be insulated from the hull, and an insulating rubber hose placed between fitting and pump. The pump casing and motor frame may be grounded as long as there is no electrical connection between pump assembly and through-hull fitting.

SYNOPSIS

The bonding system is a heavy set of conductors used to electrically "tie the boat together." Bonding is normally non-current-carrying, and completely separate from either the boat's DC or AC system. It is never used as the ground return wire for electric circuits; and those circuits are attached to it at one point only: The boat's common ground point.

CHAPTER 6

The Charging Circuits

THIS CHAPTER applies to the generator and alternator charging circuits driven by the propulsion engine, serving the engine and auxiliary batteries. "Plug-in" chargers, deriving their energy from the 120 volt AC line are discussed in Chapter 7.

The System

Heart of any charging circuit is the generator or alternator, with secondary components comprising the regulator, ammeter, and (in some circuits) a protective device such as a fuse or circuit breaker.

Conventional Generator

The "old fashioned" conventional generator is replaced by the modern alternator on the majority of newer marine engines. However, the older type is still very much alive, being found on some diesels, numerous imports, and on many older engines still in service. It has one advantage over the newer alternator in that it can stand more electrical abuse and still come back fighting.

How the Generator Works

Shown schematically in Figure 6–1, the conventional generator closely resembles a shunt-wound, direct-current motor. So close is it electrically, that if connected to a direct-current power source it will run as a motor.

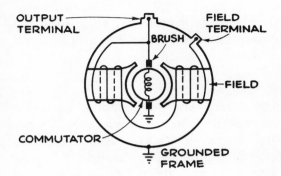

Fig. 6–1 Electrical schematic of two-brush generator shows that armature furnishes output current via the brushes. One end of the field wiring is connected to the hot brush, the other end to the external field terminal.

The field or stationary windings, excited by feed-back of direct current, create a strong magnetic field in which the armature rotates. Driven by the engine via a V-belt, the generator's armature and its integral coils spin through the magnetic field; and electricity is generated in the armature windings. At one end, the armature carries a commutator against which stationary brushes ride or slip, as in a direct-current motor (See Page 245). In the most popular circuits, one brush is grounded to the machine's frame; the other is insulated and connected to the generator hot output terminal.

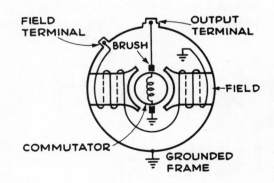

Fig. 6–2 Less frequently used than the circuit in Fig. 6–1, this circuit has the field grounded inside the generator frame. Field excitation is from the output terminal through external resistance to the field terminal.

Heavy Current Commutated

Since the current which is induced inside the generator

originates in the armature or rotor, it must all pass through the brushes and commutator to reach the output terminals. This means that in an ordinary size generator, the brush-commutator combo must handle as much as 40 or more amperes. Both the brushes and commutator must be heavy, clean, and well adjusted or unwanted arc will eat away both assemblies.

Start-Up

When the engine is first started, and the generator begins to spin, its field coils are deenergized, and it would seem that it could not start generating. However, it chain-reacts itself into operation because of residual magnetism in the field coil pole pieces. When the generator is at rest, there remains a trace of magnetism in the field iron. This residual magnetism generates a weak current which, fed to the armature, quickly builds up to many amperes, and the machine is in full swing within split seconds.

Output Control

The generator's output is conveniently controlled by varying the magnetic strength of the field. Since field strength depends upon the current in the windings, if we weaken that current we will reduce generator output. That's the way it is done in practice. An external resistance is inserted in the field circuit. As the external resistance is increased, field current and resulting magnetic strength decreases, and generator output falls.

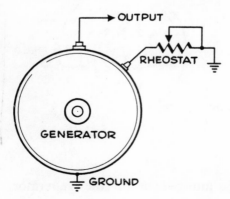

Fig. 6–3 A variable resistance between field terminal and ground adjusts generator output.

On a few larger generators field modulation is via a simple hand-adjusted rheostat of perhaps 10 ohms overall resistance. But most propulsion-engine-driven generators have a voltage control relay in a regulator box that automatically varies resistance in the field circuit to maintain generator output within the desired range. This is described in more detail later.

"Shorting" the Field

Since inserting an external resistance in the generator's field winding decreases output, it would seem that removing all resistance should increase the output. And it does. One internal field winding connection is hot, being fed by the armature. The external connection is normally open. Therefore, if the external connection is grounded or shorted to the generator frame, the machine will put out its absolute maximum charge. This is one way to test a generator, isolating a trouble to either the generator or its external control. The field is shorted to frame by a jumper. If output soars, the generator is ok, and the trouble probably lies in the control circuit.

A word of warning: Don't operate the generator more than a short period with shorted field connection or it will overheat and may be destroyed.

"Flashing" the Field

On occasion, particularly after a generator has been laid up for the winter, its field poles will lose all residual magnetism, and the generator will not put out, no matter how fast it is spun. In this case, you can flash the field, restoring the lost residual magnetism.

Using a piece of heavy wire, make a jump circuit from the battery's hot, ungrounded, terminal direct to the output terminal on the generator. Energize this jumper for only a brief instant, and be careful. Don't get burned: a lot of current will flow. The high current will remagnetize the field poles, and the generator should then operate satisfactorily.

Reversed Polarity

If a generator has been wired into a circuit backward, and its

95

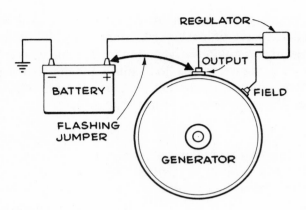

Fig. 6–4 A jumper from battery hot terminal to the generator's output connection flashes the field.

field is magnetized in reverse, it will charge with reversed polarity, *discharging* the battery more and more severely as the engine is accelerated. To cure this rare trouble, simply flash the field with correct polarity, as described above.

Open Circuit is Harmful

Never operate a generator-equipped engine with the generator load circuit open. That is, don't run without a battery in the circuit, or with the wire between generator and battery disconnected. To do so may damage the generator, its regulator, or both.

The Generator Regulator

Three individual units, looking like wire wound relays, comprise the generator regulator. They control reverse current, voltage, and current limit. Operation of a typical regulator is shown schematically in Figures 6–5, 6–6, 6–7.

Reverse Current Cutout

If the generator's output terminal were wired directly to the battery, all would be well while the generator charged. But when the engine was shut down, current would flow back from the battery to the generator, discharging the battery. The reverse current cutout is simply a relay, preventing current from flowing back from the battery to the generator. So simple is its function that it is sometimes replaced by a single diode rectifier which allows current to flow from generator to battery, but not backward.

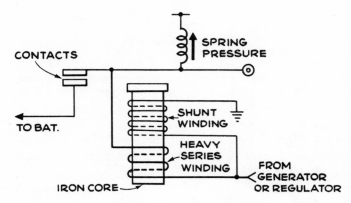

Fig. 6–5 Schematic of reverse current relay shows series and shunt windings around a common soft iron core.

Figure 6–5 shows a reverse current relay schematically. Around its magnetic core, two coils are wound: A shunt winding with many turns of fine wire, and a series winding comprising only a dozen turns of heavy wire. Close to the core pole, urged open by a spring, is the relay contact arm. When the core is magnetized by the windings, the contact arm is pulled down, making a connection from generator to battery.

The shunt winding is designed to pull down the relay arm, closing the contacts, when generator voltage slightly exceeds battery voltage. As the contacts close, current starts flowing through the heavy series winding, adding to the magnetism holding the contacts closed.

When the generator slows or stops, current commences flowing from battery to generator, reversing the direction of flow through the series winding, but not through the shunt. This makes the coils buck magnetically, all but destroying magnetic attraction. Immediately, the relay opens, disconnecting battery from generator.

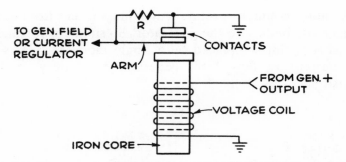

Fig. 6–6 When increased generator voltage is impressed on the coil, the contacts are magnetically pulled apart, inserting resistance R in the generator field circuit.

Voltage Regulator

Shown in Figure 6–6, the voltage regulator is essentially a heavy duty voltmeter which senses generator potential and increases the generator field resistance when output voltage exceeds its setpoint.

Around the iron core is a voltage coil comprising many turns of fine wire. This coil is connected across the generator output; and the higher the generator voltage the stronger the pull of the electromagnet against the relay arm. When generator potential reaches regulator setpoint, the voltage coil urges the contacts apart against spring restraint.

The generator external field circuit is grounded, essentially without resistance when the contacts are closed, but when the contacts open, resistor R is added to field circuit resistance.

It was seen earlier that when field circuit resistance to ground is increased, generator output drops. In the present circuit, resistance is negligible when the contacts are closed. Therefore, when resistor R is thrown in the circuit, in series, generator output potential drops, voltage coil attraction decreases, and the contacts close. Instantly, voltage rises. The cycle is repeated many times a second, as the contacts vibrate to maintain setpoint voltage in the charging circuit.

More sophisticated regulators use two sets of contacts and two steps of resistance to give wide range control throughout the span of generator output. But in all electro-mechanical instruments, the general principle is as described for the regulator in

Figure 6–6. And in most instruments, a current limiter is included in the circuit, working together with the voltage regulator, as described below.

Current Limiter

Located between the voltage regulator and reverse current cutout, the current limiter protects the generator from overheating or burning when the battery is badly discharged or the load very heavy. In that event, the voltage regulator keeps the field grounded, calling for absolute maximum charge rate, and at substantial generator speed, current must be limited.

A simple current limiter is shown in Figure 6–7. Wound on an iron core, pole piece, the current coil is a few turns of very heavy wire, transmitting full charging current from generator to reverse current cutout. The contact set is normally closed, urged shut by a spring; and current in the coil creates a magnetic field tending to pull the contacts open. The contacts are in the generator field circuit, between the voltage regulator and generator field terminal.

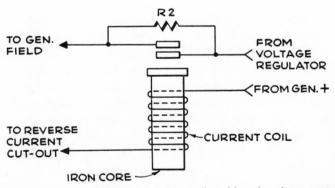

Fig. 6–7 As generator current reaches maximum allowable value, the current winding pulls the contacts apart, increasing generator field resistance, and lowering output.

Assume that the voltage regulator has grounded the field, making the generator work hard. When current flowing through the limiter's current coil exceeds setpoint, say for example 35 amperes, the contacts are pulled apart by magnetic force. Then resistor R2 is inserted in the field circuit, and generator output falls. So does the current coil's pull; and the contacts close. Current rises; and the cycle is repeated many times a second, as the vibrating contacts limit current to a safe value.

Effect of Spring Tension

Spring tension opposes elctro-magnetic attraction operating the contacts in each of the devices: reverse-current cutout, voltage regulator, and current limiter. It is apparent, then, that magnitude of spring force has considerable influence on regulation.

Spring tension is adjustable. In expensive regulator assemblies, it is adjusted by set screws, and in less costly units by bending the spring hanger. In regulators operating on the principles described earlier, effect of *increasing* spring tension is as follows:

a. Reverse current cutout: Cut-in voltage is raised, meaning that the generator must spin faster before being able to charge the battery. On a nominal 12-volt system, typical cut-in voltage is 12.8 volts.

b. Voltage regulator: Operating voltage is raised, meaning the generator will charge harder, other parameters being equal. On a nominal 12-volt system, the usual voltage setting is about 14.3 volts. On an infrequently used weekend auxiliary, it can be raised to almost 15 volts for faster charging.

c. Current limiter: Maximum current is raised, meaning that when heavily loaded, the generator will deliver more current. Adjustment is dictated entirely by generator maximum rating. For a generator rated 20 amperes, the regulator would be set to that value with the generator working into an extremely heavy load.

ALTERNATORS

Doing the same job as the conventional generator, described in earlier pages of this chapter, the alternator looks and works quite differently. For a given output, it is generally more compact and its regulation is simpler. Also, it can be spun at faster ratios to engine speed, offering superior charge rate at engine idling speeds. Generally, the alternator requires less maintenance than the older type generator.

Alternator Function

In some ways, the alternator is just the reverse of the generator: In the alternator, the armature is the stationary member, called the stator; while the field rotates, and is called the rotor. Such "backward" circuit arrangements allow the high output current from the stator windings to be conducted directly to the battery circuit without being transmitted through commutator and brushes. The concept eliminates arc, spark, burning, and the maintenance which results.

Granted, the alternator has two brushes running on slip rings. But the brushes handle only two to four amps, and the rings are smooth, not segmented as in a conventional commutator; therefore, arc and wear are negligible.

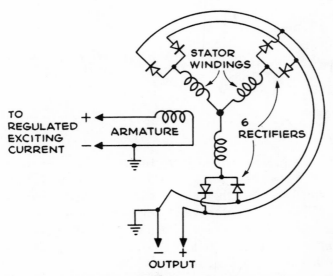

Fig. 6–8 The alternator has three individual stator windings, each terminating at a pair of rectifier diodes which convert AC to DC.

Stator Windings

The alternator shown in Figure 6–8 incorporates a three-phase stator winding, star connected, with the common point of the windings at a neutral terminal which "floats" and is not grounded. Contrasted to a single set of windings, use of three-phase or individual windings increase the number of pulses generated by the alternator, resulting in an electrically smoother output. Three individual phases also reduce the required ampacity of the rectifier diodes, discussed later.

Rotor

The alternator's rotor is much different from the armature in a conventional generator. The rotor has but a single winding, wrapped around the center of the shaft, each end of the winding terminating at a copper slip ring. The winding is wrapped around the shaft, not formed in lengthwise hanks as in the ordinary generator. This gives the rotor winding terrific strength to resist centrifugal force, allowing alternator speeds of 10,000 rpm and more without danger that the rotating member will "throw a winding."

Fig. 6–9 Interleafing iron fingers encompass the rotor coil which gives alternate magnetic polarity to the rotating "spokes."

Iron pole pieces radiate from the center of the rotor, six at each end. They curve and parallel the shaft at their outer ends, interlacing like bent fingers, presenting twelve surfaces to the stator. When the center rotor coil is energized or excited by direct current, the pole pieces become powerful electro-magnets, spinning about inside the stator, inducing three-phase alternating current in the stator windings.

Rings and Brushes

The rotor coil must be energized with a few amperes of feedback exciting current from the battery. Since the rotor spins, the coil cannot be energized by direct conductors; therefore, it is fitted with two smooth copper slip rings at which the winding terminates. The slip rings pick up their exciting current from two small graphite conducting brushes, one brush being grounded, the other being connected to the voltage regulator which modulates rotor excitation current. Since the rings and brushes carry only a few amps of exciting current, they are subject to little wear or pitting, usually lasting the life of the alternator.

Rectifiers

Each of the three phases in the stator terminates its hot end in a pair of diode rectifiers. These are solid state components which pass electricity in one direction only, rectifying alternating current to pulsating direct current. Without moving, they perform the function of the conventional generator's commutator, brushes, and reverse current cutout. As indicated in Figure 6–10, three diodes are connected to the positive alternator terminal; and three are connected to ground, which is the alternator's negative termination.

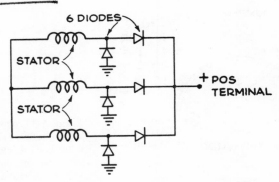

Fig. 6–10 In most popular alternators, six diodes rectify three phase alternating current to direct current suitable for battery charging.

Reverse Polarity

A little study of Figure 6–10 will show why alternator manufacturers put on red tags with big letters saying, "Don't connect to wrong polarity!" If a battery is connected backward, positive post to alternator ground, negative post to alternator output terminal, there will be fireworks. The diodes, rated for perhaps

40 amps, will try to conduct battery short circuit current, hundreds of amps, and will blow like so many fuses. A diode's weakness is that a short circuit will blow it faster than any ordinary fuse.

The moral is: "Don't ever, but ever, connect an alternator with reverse battery polarity."

Rotation

Most alternators are symmetrical both mechanically and electrically and could be rotated in either direction. Usually there is, however, a fan on one end that must be turned in one specific direction only to *pull* cooling air *through* the alternator.

Effect of Dead Battery

The alternator has a weakness. It will not charge an absolutely dead battery. A modest feed-back of current from battery to rotor is required to excite the alternator. If the battery is

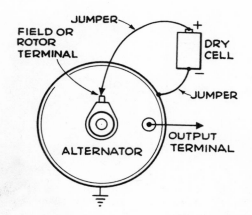

Fig. 6–11 When the boat's storage battery is dead, the alternator can be tickled into operating by exciting the rotor with a dry battery, as shown. A lantern battery or several flashlight cells in series will do it.

completely dead, unable to deliver so little as an ampere (a rarity), the alternator is unable to charge, since excitation is unavailable.

There is an emergency procedure that you can use when the battery is absolutely flat. A lantern battery, or even a half dozen flashlight batteries, in series, can be used to tickle the rotor. The emergency exciting source is connected between ground and the "field" terminal which is the hot brush. Then, when the alternator starts putting out, the regular battery can take over.

Alternator Regulation

The conventional generator control box has a reverse current cutout, voltage regulator, and current limiter. But most alternators use only a voltage regulator.

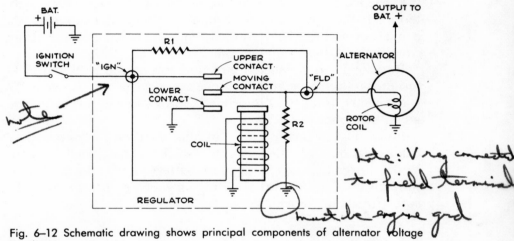

Fig. 6–12 Schematic drawing shows principal components of alternator voltage regulator.

Voltage Regulation

A good voltage regulator is a definite necessity since, if unregulated, the alternator will go wild, grossly over-charging the battery. The voltage regulator senses battery system voltage, and controls flow of exciter current to the rotor so as to maintain system voltage within tolerance.

Figure 6–12 is a schematic drawing of an electro-mechanical voltage regulator used on many popular engines. Mounted on or near the engine, the regulator is connected in the rotor circuit between alternator and the battery's hot terminal. One regulator terminal is marked IGN, the other FLD. The IGN terminal is connected to the ignition switch, allowing the rotor circuit to be energized only when the ignition switch is turned on. A third connection to the regulator is made from its frame to ground: the engine block. On diesel engines, the IGN (or BAT) terminal may be connected to the key-switch controlling the starter circuit, or to the battery through an oil-pressure-sensitive switch.

Inside the Regulator

Heart of the regulator is a relay having two fixed contacts, and one movable double-faced contact. The arrangement is shown in the schematic. The upper fixed contact is connected to the IGN terminal; the lower one is grounded. The center contacts are connected to the FLD terminal, and are urged upward, away from the coil, by spring tension.

Resistor R1 is connected directly between the IGN and FLD terminals, shunted across the upper set of contacts. Resistor R2 is connected from FLD to ground; and its function is to reduce arc at the contacts.

Consisting of many turns of fine wire, a voltage coil is connected between the ignition switch terminal and ground. When the ignition switch is closed, battery voltage forces current through the coil; and the resulting magnetic pull from the coil's core attracts the moving contact.

Low Voltage Mode

When battery voltage is low, current flowing through the voltage coil is proportionately low; and magnetic attraction of the coil's pole piece is insufficient to overcome spring tension holding the moving contact against the upper stationary contact. In this mode, battery voltage pushes current through the upper contacts, through the rotor coil to ground. Since the rotor circuit resistance is now low, maximum current flows through the rotor coil. On a 35 or 40 ampere alternator, full rotor current is on the order of 2.5 amps. Rotor magnetic field strength is now high, and alternator output is maximum for given rotor rpm.

Higher Voltage Mode

When battery voltage rises, magnetic attraction of the voltage coil assembly overcomes moving point spring tension, opening the upper contacts. Now, the moving contact floats, touching neither the upper or lower stationary contact. Battery current now flows through resistor R1 to the rotor, thence to ground.

Resistor R1, in series with the rotor coil, reduces rotor magnetic strength, correspondingly lowering the alternator's output for a given rotational speed. Because potential falls, the voltage coil's magnetic pull is weakened: Spring tension then overcomes the weaker magnetic pull, reclosing the upper contacts. The sequence is repeated many times a second.

Heavy Load

When the electrical load is relatively high, the moving contact oscillates, making and breaking with the upper contact. This alternately modulates rotor circuit resistance, limiting alternator output voltage.

Light Load

When engine speed is high and electrical load low, alternator output voltage tries to increase. Battery voltage, now higher, induces the voltage coil magnetic force to pull the moving contact against the lower stationary contact which is grounded. Current now completely ceases flowing through the rotor since both ends of its coil are grounded.

Bypassing the rotor coil causes alternator output to cease momentarily: The coil loses magnetic pull, and the moving point returns to the neutral or no-contact position, floating between the upper and lower stationary contacts. Now, current flows through resistor R1 to the rotor; and alternator output rises. Consequently, at high rpm and low electrical load, the moving contact oscillates between floating position and the lower contact, thus limiting charging voltage.

Reverse Current

No electro-mechanical reverse current cutout is required in the charging circuit since the diode rectifiers inside the alternator prevent the backward flow of current from battery to alternator stator. However, excitation current must be prevented from flowing to the rotor when the engine is shut down. This is done by connecting the exciter circuit to the ignition keyswitch. On diesel engines, a switch sensitive to oil pressure is often used.

Current Limiting

Most alternators require no current limiter since their inherent impedance restricts current output to a safe value. Therefore, no external limiting device is used.

Charging Rate

In discussing generator and alternator controls, we have described voltage modulation and current limiting. The reader may wonder, "What determines the charging rate indicated on the ammeter?"

The voltage control determines charging rate, increasing rate when the battery is low or heavily loaded, decreasing rate when the battery is fully charged. By maintaining (or trying to maintain) generator output voltage at exactly one level, the voltage regulator creates a "constant potential" charging system. As explained in Chapter 7, if a given voltage, above nominal, is applied to a dead battery, that voltage will force a high charge rate; if the voltage is maintained unchanged as the battery comes up to charge, the identical potential will charge the battery at a much slower rate.

Voltage regulators are usually set so that, when the battery is fully charged, the residual charging rate will be but 3 or 4 amps. On a nominal 12-volt system, this dictates that the regulator be set at approximately 14 volts.

Ammeter

Ammeter A2 is wired into the battery circuit as shown in Figure 6–13 and indicates the net current flowing into or out of the battery, excluding the current furnished for engine starting. The starter circuit is not wired through the ammeter because starting current is a hundred amperes or more, whereas most dashboard ammeters are rated for only 30 to 40 amps.

As shown in the diagram, generator current flowing to the

battery passes through the ammeter, deflecting its pointer in one direction. On the other hand, battery current flowing to the accessory load flows through the ammeter oppositely, deflecting its pointer in the reverse direction. However, if generator output exactly matches accessory demand, no current flows through the ammeter, even though the generator may be delivering heavy current to the load.

On a few larger installations a separate uni-directional amme-ter, A1 in Fig. 6–13, is wired in the circuit at the output terminal. This extra meter helps the boatkeeper monitor generator/ alternator performance, separating it from the "net effect" reading of the conventional, center-zero ammeter.

Voltmeter

Shown in Figure 6–13, a direct-current voltmeter, wired from the hot load terminal to ground, is a fine system-monitoring and trouble-shooting instrument. It is not standard, but is found as an extra on better DC systems.

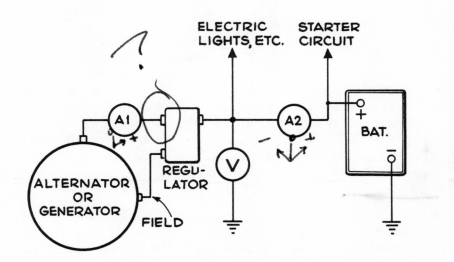

Fig. 6–13 The customary ammeter A2 responds to new current flowing to and from the battery. Meter A1 indicates generator current only; while the voltmeter monitors system voltage.

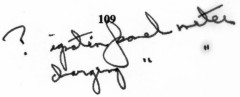

For a nominal 12-volt system, the best kind of voltmeter is one with suppressed zero and expanded scale. The face of this type instrument indicates from about nine to 16 volts, yielding desirable resolution for the important part of the voltage scale. On this meter, a change of less than half a volt is readily apparent, and movement as little as tenth of a volt is readable.

The experienced boatman learns to interpret the readout from his voltmeter particularly after he has lived with it for a few weeks and become accustomed to its behavior. Low voltage after the system has been idle indicates loss of charge due to leakage or aged battery cells. Abnormally high voltage indicates that the alternator voltage regulator is set too high. Low voltage while the alternator operates signifies that the regulator is adjusted too low, or that system load is beyond the generator's capacity.

Wiring

The conductor from generator or alternator output terminal to its feed point must be of heavy gauge because considerable current flows when the generator is working hard. Resistance in this circuit cuts generator charging ability, adds load to the generator and creates dangerous heat. A 30 ampere machine should be wired with #10 gauge wire or heavier; and #8 gauge should be used for currents of 40 to 45 amperes.

Since the generator or alternator's frame is commonly the ground conductor, it must be well connected to the engine. On occasion, the pivot point, used for V-belt tightening, has been known to offer a high resistance connection, electrically noisy. For this reason, it is a good boatkeeping procedure to ground the generator or alternator frame to the engine via a flexible cable or wire strap.

Protection

Generator and alternator output circuits are usually unprotected by fuses or circuit breakers because if this circuit is opened, source voltage will rise to a magnitude damaging to the machine. However, it is perfectly good practice to protect the circuitry, *provided* a two-pole circuit breaker is installed. The breaker senses charging current, one of its poles being in the generator or alternator output conductor, the other pole wired in the field or rotor circuit. With this arrangement, as shown in Figure 6–14, when the breaker trips on overload, it not only opens the charging circuit, but also opens the control circuit. Because both circuits are open, the generator or alternator can spin without harm.

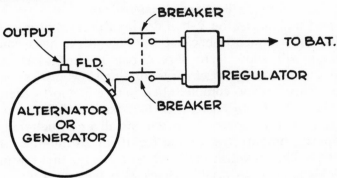

Fig. 6–14 If the alternator or generator output circuit is protected by a circuit breaker, another pole of that same breaker should be wired in the field circuit.

Master Switch

If there is a master switch in the battery system, as dictated by

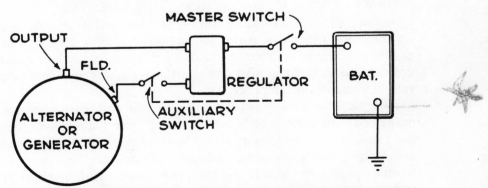

Fig. 6–15 Ganged with the master switch, an auxiliary switch must open the field circuit when the charging circuit is opened.

111

safest practice, it should have an auxiliary switch for the generator or alternator control circuit. Much smaller than the master, the auxiliary switch opens the field or rotor circuit when the master is open circuited. Ganged double switching, as shown in Figure 6–15, prevents generator voltage from surging wildly should the master switch be open circuited while the engine is running.

Boatkeeper Maintenance

Inspect and adjust the V-belt driving the alternator or generator. Do this frequently because the belt works hard, and slight looseness will allow it to slip. When it slips wear increases quickly, and soon the machine is running slowly, with decreased output. This leads to complete belt failure in short order.

Replace the driving belt when it looks the slightest bit worn; and always carry a spare. After you install a new belt and tighten it properly, operate the engine for 10 to 20 minutes, then retighten the belt. It will stretch and "seat" in the first few minutes. Good idea, also, to double check belt tension after a day of operation.

Generators and alternators have ball bearings at the drive pulley end, and require no lubrication there. But a few have an oil cup at the other end, where a sleeve bearing is used. Put a few drops of oil in this cup about twice a season.

Once a month or so, give the wiring a quick once over, making sure that all connections to the generator and regulator are secure. Also inspect the wiring to the battery. Loose connections or faulty wiring in the charging circuit can not only result in a run down battery, but can also damage the regulator and generate radio frequency interference.

After several seasons of hard use, a conventional generator may need commutator or brush service. Remove the cover from the brush section and, using a flashlight, inspect the brushes and commutator. If the copper commutator segments appear burned, worn or pitted, the unit is due for a trip to the overhaul shop. If the brushes are worn down to short nibs, they need replacing, because when they wear too short they cause arc, and will ruin the commutator. They'll also cause radio noise.

Shooting Alternator Trouble

The following are alternator troubles and possible causes:

- Alternator will not charge, even into a low battery:
  1. Drive belt very loose or broken.
  2. Badly worn brushes or slip rings on rotor.
  3. One or both brushes stuck out of contact with slip ring.
  4. Open rotor circuit inside or outside alternator.
  5. Open stator (charging) circuit inside or outside alternator.
  6. Blown rectifiers.
- Low, Unsteady Charge:
  1. Loose drive V-belt.
  2. High resistance in the charging circuit wiring or connections.
  3. High resistance in the alternator-to-engine winding.
  4. Open or poor connection in the stator winding.
- Low Charge and Low Battery:
  1. High resistance in the charging circuit.
  2. Low voltage regulator adjustment.
  3. Shorted rectifier or open rectifier.
  4. Grounded stator winding.
- Excessive Charge to a Charged Battery:
  1. Voltage regulator adjusted too high.
  2. Regulator contacts stuck shut.
  3. Voltage regulator coil open circuited.
  4. Regulator not properly grounded.
- Noisy Alternator:
  1. Alternator loose in its mount.
  2. Worn, frayed, "lumpy" drive V-belt.
  3. Worn ball bearings.
  4. Bent drive pulley or cooling fan.
  5. Open or shorted rectifier (causes singing).
  6. Open or shorted stator winding.
- Excessive Ammeter Fluctuation:
  1. High resistance in the rotor circuit.
  2. Defective regulator.
  3. Loose wiring in charging or control circuit.

Shooting Generator Trouble

- Generator will not charge, even into a low battery.
  1. Drive belt very loose or broken.
  2. Badly burned brushes or commutator.

3. Weak brush springs, or brushes out of contact with commutator.
4. Open circuit to the field winding.
5. Spring tension on reverse current cutout too tight.
6. Voltage regulator adjusted for lower than battery voltage.
7. Open wiring or connections in the charging circuit.
- Low, Unsteady Charge:
  1. Loose drive V-belt.
  2. High resistance in the charging circuit.
  3. High resistance in the generator-to-engine mount.
  4. Poor connection or high resistance in the field circuit.
  5. Worn brushes, dirty commutator.
  6. Spring too loose on the current limiter.
  7. Dirty, pitted contact in the reverse current cutout.
- Low Charge and Low Battery:
  1. High resistance in charging circuit.
  2. Voltage regulator spring too tight.
  3. Worn brushes, dirty commutator.
  4. Open circuit or very high resistance in field circuit.
- Excessive Charge to a Charged Battery:
  1. Spring too tight on voltage regulator.
  2. Voltage regulator contacts stuck shut.
  3. Open circuited voltage regulator.coil.
  4. Grounded field circuit between generator and regulator.
  5. Grounded field coil inside generator.
- Noisy Generator:
  1. Generator loose in its mounts.
  2. Worn, frayed, "lumpy" drive V-belt.
  3. Worn ball bearings.
  4. Bent drive pulley or cooling impeller on generator.
- Excessive Ammeter Fluctuation:
  1. High resistance in the field circuit.
  2. Defective regulator.
  3. Loose wiring in charging or control circuit.
- Generator Discharges Battery with Dead Engine:
  1. Contacts stuck shut in reverse current cutout.
- Generator Discharges Battery when Running Fast:
  1. Polarity is reversed. Field must be flashed for correct polarity.

SYNOPSIS

The conventional generator delivers direct current to the

load via its armature, commutator, and brushes; while the alternator does the job from its fixed stator coils via diode rectifiers. The generator commonly has a three-element regulator, controlling field current, but the alternator usually has a voltage regulator alone, to control rotor current. Advantage of the generator is that it can stand more abuse than the alternator. But the alternator offers the advantages of higher capacity, better low speed performance, and reduced routine maintenance.

Charging rate is controlled by maintaining voltage nearly constant, and is indicated on an ammeter between generator and battery. A voltmeter is a good indicator, supplementing the ammeter. When a master disconnect switch is wired in the battery charging circuit, it should have an auxiliary switch which opens the control circuit simultaneously with the charging circuit.

CHAPTER 7

The Boat's Battery Charger

THE BATTERY CHARGER, sometimes referred to as a rectifier unit, is the crossover or connecting link between the boat's AC and DC systems. Energized from 120 volt alternating current, from dockside or onboard AC generator, the charger keeps the boat's batteries charged when the engine-driven alternator is not operating.

Function

The charger's function is first to transform 120 volt housepower to lower battery voltage, then to *rectify* the reduced voltage from alternating (AC) to direct (DC) current. Additional functions in some chargers include voltage and current regula-

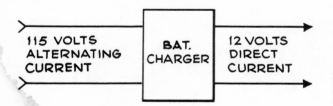

115 VOLTS ALTERNATING CURRENT — BAT. CHARGER — 12 VOLTS DIRECT CURRENT

Fig. 7–1 The charger is a connecting link between the boat's 120 volt housepower system and the battery. However, the AC is isolated from the battery, there being no direct connection between the two.

116

tion, automatic line compensation, automatic turn-on and turn-off, and remote control. Better types of chargers also include fuses, circuit breakers, and output instrumentation.

Automatic Control

Modern charging units having solid state or magnetic control are particularly suited to boats with many battery-powered accessories. This kind of unit maintains constant voltage on the DC system and its batteries; an automatically controlled charger does not constantly trickle charge: On the contrary, upon detecting falling DC voltage, the unit charges the system bringing voltage back to normal. The rectifier will automatically charge whether falling potential results from slow "shelf life" discharge or from the current drained by an active load such as an automatic direct-current operated refrigerator.

Hum and Ripple

Low level of hum or ripple in a charger's DC output is a desirable characteristic in a unit used aboard a boat fitted with extensive electronic equipment. Electrical hum ensues when a high percentage of alternating current leaks through the charging circuit and is superimposed on the direct current. Then the direct-current circuits are said to have high AC ripple. A reasonable percentage of ripple is tolerable for most purposes; but when too much is imposed on the DC lines, it causes unpleasant hum in radios and can adversely effect other DC gear.

Better chargers use full-wave rectification to minimize ripple, rectifying both sides of the AC cycle, rather than just one. Some more expensive units incorporate filters to still further reduce the hum component. As a matter of fact, the battery itself acts as something of a filter. The reader will notice less alternating current hum on the boat's line when the battery is connected than when the system is energized by charger alone, the battery being removed.

Direct Operation

It is feasible with some chargers to operate direct-current

motors or lights directly from the rectifier without a battery in the system. However, this is not advisable unless the charging unit is rated for this specific service. In some circumstances, it is hard on the charger; and unless the rectifier is filtered, ripple and hum level will be objectionably high, with voltage regulation poor. Instructions accompanying each individual unit will tell whether or not it is rated as a power pack for direct operation without a battery in the circuit.

Chargers rated to be used as a direct source of energy, without a battery floated in the circuit, are often called battery-eliminators. A typical unit is the Heathkit Model PS-1175 which furnishes a well-filtered, closely-regulated DC output adjustable from 12.0 to 14.5 volts at 5 amperes continuously and up to 10 amperes intermittently (for up to 10 minutes).

A Simple Charger

The basic battery charger is not complex; and a simple one is diagrammed in Figure 7–2. Incoming 120-volt alternating current power is dropped in transformer T1 to battery charging voltage and fed to the rectifier. Then, rectifier diode D1, either a vacuum tube or solid state device, passes half wave pulses of current to the battery, 60 times a second. This circuit, found on inexpensive chargers, was typically used on the old Tungar chargers; and its output is rich in hum and ripple.

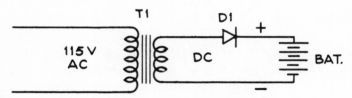

Fig. 7–2 Simple battery charger is a transformer and single rectifier.

An Improvement

A better charger is that in Figure 7–3. In it, the transformer's low voltage winding is center-tapped for negative return, and the two sides of the winding feed two rectifiers D2 and D3 to give full-wave rectification. Output is 120 pulses a second, ripple being lower than from the charger in Figure 7–2.

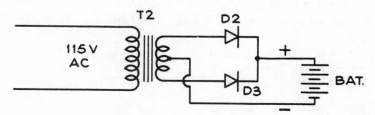

Fig. 7–3 A center-tapped secondary winding and two diodes feed direct current to the battery in this full-wave charger.

More Versatile

Varying input voltage or different charging rates, or both, may be selected manually in the charger shown schematically in Figure 7–4. The low voltage secondary transformer winding in T3 is tapped for selected voltages. Switch SW1 selects the desired voltage, feeding the full-wave bridge rectifier having four rectifiers D4, D5, D6, D7.

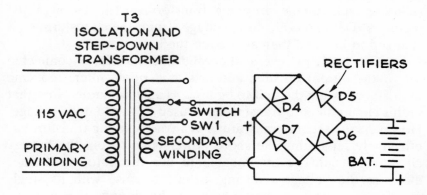

Fig. 7–4 The selector switch in this charger allows several rates of charge to be chosen manually.

Infinitely Variable

The charger shown in Figure 7–5 accommodates a wide variety of input voltages and charging rates. Intelligently used and monitored, it can be used to energize DC equipment directly, because its output voltage can be adjusted to match the load, provided, of course, that the load is not beyond its capability.

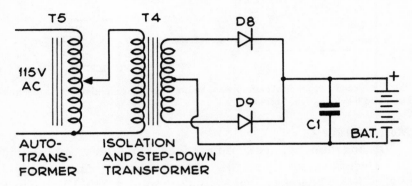

Fig. 7–5 A manually adjustable auto transformer gives this charger/eliminator wide charging rates.

A manual, almost infinitely variable auto-transformer such as a Powerstat or Variac, selectably reduces line voltage fed to the isolating and voltage dropping transformer T4. Through the rectifiers D8 and D9, low voltage from the transformer is changed to DC and then applied to the battery.

Capacitor C1, of several thousand microfarads, is connected across the output circuits, and acts as a ripple filter, reducing hum and allowing the unit to be used as an eliminator. Note that in this circuit an auto-transformer is used to vary output voltage. However, the second transformer is a true isolating transformer, effectively separating the shore power circuit from the battery circuit. It would be unthinkable to use the auto-transformer alone as the voltage reducing means, because with its single winding it offers no isolation between the circuits. For more on the theory of the isolation transformer, see Chapters 4 and 13.

Fully Automatic

The charger circuit shown schematically in Figure 7–6 is used in one of those sophisticated types capable of charging the battery to the equivalent of full voltage and then shutting itself off. When circuit voltage drops, due to sagging battery voltage or appliance demand, the charger turns itself on.

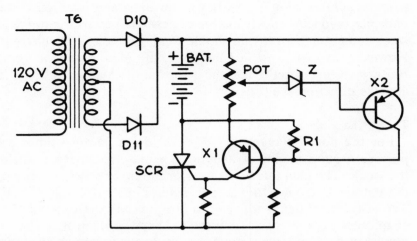

Fig. 7–6 Schematic diagram shows one type of automatic charger having the ability to turn itself off when charging is complete.

Transformer T6 and full-wave rectifiers D10 and D11, deliver charging current to the battery through silicon controlled rectifier SCR in the negative or ground return line. The SCR is a solid state electrical trigger or gate, very much like a relay. Transistor X2 compares battery voltage with zener diode Z voltage. A zener diode provides reference voltage much as a laboratory standard cell does. When battery voltage falls, transistor X2 is cut off. Immediately a positive voltage is developed across resistor R1 and between the emitter and base of transistor X1. Promptly, X1 conducts, firing or triggering the SCR just as though it were a relay being closed; and, of course, the SCR conducts like a closed switch, applying charging current to the battery.

Charging current slowly forces battery voltage to rise; then when battery voltage reaches nominal, X2 again commences to conduct, cutting off X1, and killing the gate signal to the SCR. Charging now ceases completely. The manually variable resistor POT allows the operator to adjust the voltage at which charging starts and stops.

Trickle Charging

Because many pleasure boats are used on weekends only, it

would seem a simple, workable arrangement to leave the batteries on a slow trickle charge of perhaps a quarter ampere all week long. In theory, this should keep the cells fully charged. However, as explained in Chapter 2, the idea is not too good. Battery experts don't like the constant trickle because of its adverse effect on the cells.

Timed Charging

For the boat "plugged in" at dockside, a 24-hour timer can provide a good means of keeping the batteries charged during the week. The charger, in series with the timer's switch, charges the battery at from 3 to 6 amperes per 75 ampere-hour battery. Typically, the timer is adjusted to turn on the charger from 15 to 45 minutes per day, or as required to keep the electrolyte specific gravity at peak reading. General purpose timers may be used for this purpose, and are available in many hardware stores and electrical supply houses carrying lamps, intrusions alarms, and the like. An excellent model of timer for this job is one that can be set in increments of from 15 minutes to 24 hours.

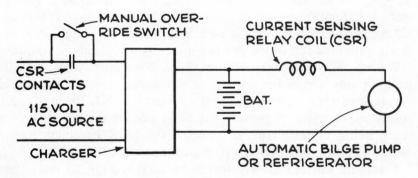

Fig. 7–7 With this simple rig, the bilge pump or refrigerator automatically energizes the charger when current is demanded.

Demand Charging

A circuit the author has used successfully on a boat with automatic bilge pumps incorporates a current-sensing relay. Wired in series with the battery conductor serving the bilge pumps, the sensing relay "feels" when the pumps draw power from the battery, and immediately turns on the charger which forces more DC into the battery than the pumps draw.

The demand charging circuit is shown in Figure 7–7 in which CSR is the coil of the current-sensing relay in series with the bilge pump's automatic float switch. The reader with ingenuity, who is also a reasonable electrician, can construct a rig similar to the one shown. It takes a little experimenting to adjust the current-sensing relay to close at the desired valve, and open smartly when the load is removed. A reverse-current relay from a conventional generator may be modified for the job, or an ordinary general-purpose relay may be stripped and rewound with a dozen turns of heavy wire, converting it to a current-sensing relay.

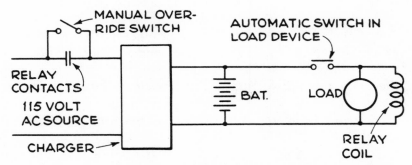

Fig. 7–8 An ordinary across-the-line relay energizes the charger when the load is turned on.

Another approach to automatic charger activation is shown in Figure 7–8. An ordinary general-purpose, direct-current relay is wired across the line on the appliance side of the automatic switch, such as the float switch handling a bilge pump. The practical difficulty is that in most bilge pump or refrigerator switches it is difficult to get at the cold connection between switch and motor.

For safety and neatness, the relay and switch are fastened inside a small metal enclosure, and the wires lead out through neatly fitting grommets. Purpose of the manual override switch is to permit normal operation of the charger regardless of commands from the current-sensing relay.

Isolation Required

Code-making bodies insist that a marine charger have electrical isolation between the 120 volt AC service and battery circuit. There must be no direct electrical connection, all power being transferred magnetically through a two-winding transformer.

The isolation requirement rules out the auto-transformer because it has but a single winding, more like a single winding reactor than true transformer. Note that where the auto-transformer is used in Figure 7–5, it is followed electrically by an isolation transformer, so that through-leakage is blocked.

Isolation Test

Should the reader want to check his charger for isolation between AC input and DC output, he may do as follows:

1. Locate the charger near a water pipe or other good earth ground and plug it into a 120 volt receptacle. Turn it on.

2. Connect a small dashboard size six- or 12-volt test light to the charger's positive output lead. Touch the other test lead to the grounded pipe. The bulb should not glow.

3. Using the charger's negative lead, perform the same test; and the bulb should not glow.

4. Reverse the 120 volt AC plug in its receptacle, and repeat the tests with positive and negative. The bulb must remain dark.

If the bulb glows in the tests, there is electrical leakage between the AC lines and DC circuits, and the charger should not be used aboard the boat.

Charge While Starting?

When you hit the starter switch to crank the engine, battery voltage may be momentarily dragged down to seven or eight volts on a 12-volt system. Will low voltage, resulting in high charge demand, damage the charger? That depends. Some chargers will blow a fuse or open a breaker, others are designed to cope with the load. Check the manual for your charger, but it is always safer just to turn it off before hitting the starter switch.

Technical Requirements

The American Boat and Yacht Council has a standard for marine chargers or rectifiers. The following suggestions, useful to the owner in judging a charger, are based upon the ABYC standards:

1. Automatic chargers should have a type of control which will properly charge at rates generally acceptable to battery manufacturers. As a guide, automatic units should be designed to maintain voltage of between 2.15 and 2.35 volts per cell. This applies under no-load conditions with the batteries fully charged, and the electrolyte at 77°F.

2. Input voltage or voltage range should be clearly marked on the unit's nameplate. This is important because some chargers also have taps or adjustments which must be manipulated to match the rectifier to its input.

3. Rectifier circuits should be full wave, or filtered, or both, to minimize objectionable ripple and hum in the output.

4. Cabinets, supporting brackets, and other structural parts, if made from corrodable metals, must be well galvanized, coated, or otherwise well protected against rust and corrosion.

5. Grommets, bushings, etc., should be provided to prevent chafing of wires passing through metal cabinets. Clamps or other means should be used to relieve any strains on these wires.

6. Transformers must be the isolating type, well doped, treated, or coated for use in damp, salty environments.

7. All marine chargers should have an ammeter to indicate output current. More sophisticated units should also have a voltmeter; this is particularly true of chargers having adjustable input or output.

Installation

ABYC specifies that chargers be installed in a dry accessible location, well removed from engine exhaust piping or other heat radiating surfaces. Specifically, chargers should not be located where the ambient temperature exceeds 122°F, or where they are exposed to direct radiant heat.

Chargers should never be located directly above batteries where they will be bathed in rising electrolyte vapor, nor should they be exposed to drips from cowl openings, ports, or ventilators. Best location is at least two feet above normal bilge water, and protected against splash. Many good installations are made with the charger mounted well up on a machinery compartment fire wall or bulkhead. The unit should not be buried under other machinery because controls and meters must be readily available and visible.

Electrical Protection

The rectifier's circuits must be protected, of course, and there must also be means of disconnecting the 120 volt AC power as well as the DC output power. Specifically, standards making bodies require the following:

1. An easily accessible manual disconnect switch should be provided in the AC power leads to the charger; and this switch should open the "hot" AC lead, or both sides, and there should also be a fuse or circuit breaker that opens both leads.

2. The charger's output must have a fuse or circuit breaker in the ungrounded lead for overload protection.

Shore Power Connections

A good charger has three internal terminals to receive shore power. Two terminals are for the black and white hot and neutral wires, the third is for the equipment grounding conductor. Terminations are clearly marked, with input and output connection points well separated.

Parallel Connections

The Constavolt marine charger is one of the better known makes; and its manufacturer, LaMarche Manufacturing Co., makes the following suggestions regarding parallel installation. The instructions are typical, applying in most instances to other makes of chargers:

"A Constavolt charger can be used across sets of batteries connected in parallel. For each additional parallel battery across the charger output, an additional 5 amperes of charge must be used for charging current."

Twin-Engine Connections

Twin-engine cruiser installations require a special switching arrangement. LaMarche advises as follows for this kind of circuitry:

"When a charger is used with double-battery systems in a twin-engine cruiser, the two-battery systems are connected across the output of the charger in parallel so that both sets of batteries are maintained at full charge. However, when both engines are running, the batteries should be disconnected from each other or an unbalance between the separate alternator systems might develop.

"In order to electrically separate the batteries when both engines are running, a 200 ampere vapor-proof switch must be installed between the two battery sets in the ungrounded conductors. One set of batteries remains connected to the charger; the other set is disconnected. However, the switch can be closed for starting one engine on both sets of batteries, or for charging both sets of batteries from one engine, the other engine being shut down."

A more modern solution, however, is to use a charger that has a "charger divider." This feature is now found on most chargers of medium or greater current rating. Separate DC outputs are provided for two or more batteries; these outputs are isolated from each other with diodes so as to prevent a weak or defective battery from dragging down a good one. Charge dividers are also available as separate units to permit chargers without this feature to be safely used on multiple-battery installations. See Chapter 24.

SYNOPSIS

The charger converts AC dock power to DC battery power, charging the boat's batteries under fixed, automatic, or manual rate control. Battery chargers use full-wave rectification or incorporate some kind of filtering to reduce ripple and hum. Some chargers may be used to operate DC appliances directly; but this is not true of all. True marine chargers must incorporate isolating transformers rather than auto-transformers. Constant trickle charging is undesirable, and to eliminate it, fully automatic, timed, or demand charging is suggested. Rectifiers should be installed high above the bilge water, must have overload protection, and should have switches in both AC and DC connections.

CHAPTER 8

Alternating Current Generating Plants

An on-board alternating current power generator, gasoline- or diesel-engine driven, offers several advantages for the cruising boat of roughly 30 feet or more length.

1. The generator frees the boat from dependence on a shore power cord.

2. It allows the boat to be cruised anywhere, and to moor or anchor where its skipper pleases, without regard to shore power availability.

3. Self-provided power allows the use of electric cooking, baking, heating, and air conditioning, all of which draw more current than is available at some marinas.

4. A generating plant can be selected which provides 240 volts as well as 120, the higher voltage being demanded by larger appliances, particularly the man-sized galley stoves.

5. Battery charging is always available on the boat having a generating plant. Should the main-engine starting battery get too low, it can be recharged from the on-board power station (if that has its own separate starting battery).

Size and Weight

The following table is averaged from several kinds of power

plant, and is intended to show the magnitude of size and weight to be expected for a given wattage output.

Output Watts	Weight Lbs.	Width	Length
3,000 D	365	21"	29"
4,000 G	330	22"	29"
7,500 D	500	19"	33"
10,000 D	770	20"	46"
15,000 D	925	21"	47"
D = Diesel		G = Gasoline	

First Cost

Purchase price varies considerably depending upon the accessories such as fresh water cooling, type of starting, silencing arrangement, and whether the engine is gasoline or diesel. However, a ballpark idea of cost can be gleaned from the following list prices averaged from quotes made in mid 1980 on basic models:

Output Watts	List Price
3,000 D	$2,800
4,000 G	$2,400
7,500 D	$4,500
10,000 D	$5,000
15,000 D	$5,700

The above approximate prices are for true marine, water-cooled units of high quality. Complete radio shielding adds about $175 to the cost and top-quality silencing adds about $300. Automatic "demand starting" costs something like $350. Installation costs are additional and will vary with the complexity of the job.

What Capacity Required

How large a generating plant do you need on your cruiser? That depends upon how many accessories and appliances you have on board, and upon how many are likely to be operated at any one time. The size of the largest electric motor has a bearing on the matter, too, since alternating current induction motors draw 4 to 5 times more current when starting than when running.

The following tabulation gives an idea of the wattage demand by various 120 volt appliances. It is not specific, but is intended to give the magnitude of demand for planning and estimating:

Item	Approximate Watts
Air conditioner (¾ HP)	800
Electric blanket	50-200
Coffee maker	550-700
Electric stove	550-1500 per element
Fan	25-75
Electric fry pan	1200
Space heater	1000-1500
Battery charger	up to 800
Toaster	800-1150
Vacuum cleaner	360-520
Water heater	1000-1500
Refrigerator	200-300
Television set	75-300

Estimate the Demand

Should you turn on all those appliances at once, the load on the generator would exceed 10,000 watts. Fortunately, you will probably never have more than 40% to 60% of the stuff on the generator at any one instant; and therefore an electric plant of 4,000 to 6,000 watts capacity will handle the job. It's up to you to appraise the situation and make an intelligent selection depending upon your and your crew's habits.

From the table we can see that an electric stove may demand 1000 watts per element. If such a stove has four burners all energized at once, it will load a 4,000 watt generator to the gunwales with nothing else turned on. Keep the cooking habits in mind when choosing a power plant.

Watch those Induction Motors

Remember that it is skating on thin ice to talk about the

wattage demand of alternating-current induction motors, the kind used on refrigerators and air-conditioners. Although we may estimate that a ¾ HP motor draws 775 watts from the system, its *current* demand may be closer to that drawn by a 1,500 watt heater. The difference is due to the low power factor of the induction motor. (See Page 244). The point is, when estimating the capacity of generator required, you can about double the wattage for induction motors to arrive at required current.

Volt-Amperes are Better than Watts

A still better approach is to think in terms of volt-amperes. Add up the total of amperes required, then specify the size of power plant you need in this term. Generator manufacturers tend to think more in volt-amperes than in watts. For the current demand of various size induction motors. (See Page 277.) For the current demands of light bulbs, heaters, stoves, toasters, and other resistive loads on 120 volts, obtain current by dividing wattage by 120. Thus, a resistive device rated 1,000 watts demands 8.3 amperes approximately. Fluorescent lights have a poor power factor; and before you compute their current demand, double the published wattage. Your answer will be in the ballpark.

Fuel Cost

Since most generating plants are operated but a few hours a day, and at partial load, fuel consumption represents a small fraction of that burned by the propulsion engines. The following published figures give an indication of fuel consumption in gallons per hour for several sizes of power generators at partial and full load:

Output & Type	50% Load	Full Load
3,000 watt diesel	.26 Gal/Hr.	.41 Gal/Hr.
4,000 watt gasoline	.55	.96
7,500 watt diesel	.54	.83
10,000 watt diesel	.65	1.0
15,000 watt diesel	.90	1.4

The above figures indicate that the 4,000-watt plant, when delivering 2,000 watts, burns about 0.55 gallons per hour. Using gasoline at $1.30 per gallon, this results in a cost per thousand watt hours (kWh) of about 36¢. Assuming that the 10 kW diesel unit uses fuel costing $1.15 per gallon, it delivers a kWh of power for about 15¢ at half-load.

Installation

The best place for a generating plant is in the engine compartment. That enclosure has ventilation for the propulsion

Fig. 8–1 Installation of a small generating plant. Note the good features:
1. Seacock in water line
2. Water filter
3. Heavy mounting base that distributes weight evenly.
4. Vibration isolation pads
5. Fuel shut-off valve at engine
6. Flexible exhaust section

engines, is often sound insulated, and has stringers capable of carrying the generator plant's weight.

Regarding position, the manufacturer of Kohler electric plants has the following recommendations:

"We recommend that if the plant is mounted parallel to the keel, the engine be located forward of the generator or in such a manner as to facilitate minor servicing. Remember that oil changing, filter element changing, and carburetor adjustments occur more frequently than do changing the generator brushes.

"Maintain as much space as possible around the engine portion of the electric plant. If possible, a removable hatch should be placed above the electric plant engine. Sufficient space should be allowed for regular maintenance needs; and be sure that easy access is allowed to the seacock on the water intake."

Mounting

The plant should be mounted on stringers which distribute its weight over many frames, or on a platform which distributes its weight evenly over a fiberglass boat. It should be mounted high enough to be out of bilge splash and low lying vapors, and high enough so the exhaust line can pitch downward from its engine. Where the assembly is located close to or below the waterline, the exhaust must be arranged as shown in Figures 8–5 and 8–6.

Vibration Elimination

To prevent vibration transmission through the hull, the electric plant should be mounted on first-class vibration eliminators, resilient pads, or springs. When mounted in this way, the assembly has no rigid connection to the hull or superstructure and is free to vibrate and shake independently. No part of the plant must touch deck supports, bulkheads, or hull. All connecting lines, such as water, fuel, exhaust, and electric must be flexible. Should any one of these be rigid, not only will it telegraph noise to the boat, but will soon fracture due to fatigue.

Cooling

Whether cooled by direct circulation of raw water, or by a heat exchanger system, the motor should be connected as prescribed by its manufacturer. A seacock must be fitted at intake on the hull, and this seacock should be turned off when the boat is left unattended. A water filter or strainer is desirable, and it is a good idea to have some kind of automatic alarm or shut-down which operates if the engine should overheat. Where the generator installation is below the flotation waterline, it is extremely important that all connections have the highest integrity, that flexible hoses be of top quality, and all hose connections be double-clamped. If the cooling system should spring a leak while the boat is unattended, the boat may go to the bottom.

Water pick-up scoops or scuppers in the hull bottom should not be in line with those for the propulsion engine or immediately aft of any projection which might make the water turbulent. Also, the scupper should have some kind of strainer grill to keep twigs and other debris from entering.

Fuel Supply

The electric plant should use the same fuel as the boat's propulsion engines, and can draw from the same tanks, if that is desired.

Safety is the key word in fuel system installation and inspection; and every inch of the way, the fuel system should conform to the requirements of American Boat and Yacht Council and National Fire Prevention Association. If the reader plans to install an electric plant himself, or to have one installed (which he will inspect), he is urged to first get the following publications which are safety guides: *NFPA #302.* or *Safety Standards For Small Craft.* Addresses for NFPA and ABYC are found on Pages 486, 487.

Highlights of a safe fuel system are these:
• The fuel tank must be secured against shifting by means which are beyond possible reproach.
• Tank must be vented overboard so spill and vapors never enter the boat.
• Tank, fill plate, and fuel lines must be electrically connected to the boat's bonding system.
• Fuel must be drawn from the top of the tank via a dip tube. No outlet must ever be made in the side or bottom of a tank.

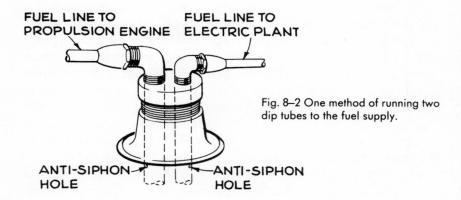

Fig. 8–2 One method of running two dip tubes to the fuel supply.

• An anti-siphon orifice inside the tank in the dip tube must prevent siphoning of fuel after the engine stops. Also, there must be a shut-off valve in the fuel line close to the tank. Preferably the shut-off should be an approved solenoid actuated valve which will block the fuel flow when the engine is shut down.

• The carburetor float must *never* be depended upon to shut off fuel flow when the engine stops. On an installation where the carburetor is below the fuel tank, it is suicidal to do so.

• In addition to the mandatory fuel shut-off at the tank, an additional valve may be installed near the carburetor, allowing engine work to be done without the contents of the fuel line being drained, and also acting as an added safety.

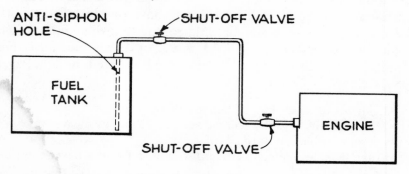

Fig. 8–3 Generating plant engine must have a fuel shut-off valve close to the fuel tank, and should have one near the carburetor.

• The use of a T fitting in the propulsion engine fuel line is discouraged. If the generator's engine feeds on the same line as the big engine, the smaller one may be starved when the boat is underway.

Exhaust System

A quiet exhaust arrangement is more important on a generating plant than on the main propulsion machinery because the

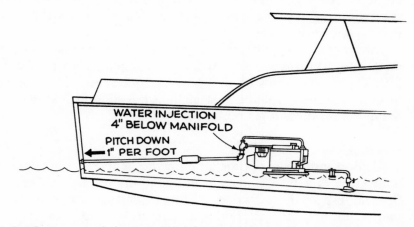

Fig. 8–4 Getting enough downward pitch for the exhaust is relatively easy on a power boat installation.

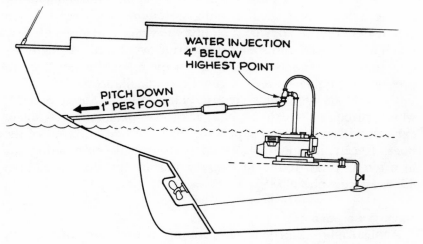

Fig. 8–5 One method of handling exhaust on a sailboat installation where the generating plant is below the waterline.

generator often operates at night when the crew (and neighbors) are trying to relax. The exhaust must do its job without allowing water to flow back into the engine. It must form a flexible, not rigid, connection between generating plants and the hull; and it must be adequately water cooled. As shown in Figures 8–4 and 8–5, the exhaust line must pitch down about 1″ per foot from the point of cooling water injection to its termination. Naturally, special arrangements are made for installations below the waterline, as shown in Figure 8–5.

Exhaust lines must be of adequate size to keep back pressure moderate. 1½″ pipe is recommended for plants up to about 3 kW; 2″ pipe for plants up to 7.5 kW; and 2½″ pipe for plants up to 15 kW. Runs should be as straight as possible, with long radius bends where turns must be made.

Silencing

A good muffler is appreciated on the generator, not only by your crew, but by yachtsmen on boats moored or tied nearby. Several especially effective muffling systems are offered by marine electric power plant manufacturers; and these are designed specifically for the application.

Onan's Aqualift is a tank-like muffling system into which both engine exhaust and spent cooling water are discharged. Using exhaust energy, the device then lifts the water and gases up to as much as four feet, and spews the matter overboard. Aqualift not only quiets the exhaust; it also solves the cooling water disposal problem for below-waterline generator installations.

The makers of Kohler electric plants offer a Super Silencer which, fitted in the exhaust line, also cools exhaust gases, mixes exhaust with water, and expels the water-gas mixture out of the boat. It can lift spent water up to four feet, eliminating the inverted U often found in below-waterline installations. Super Silencers cost about $85.

Sound Absorption

Acoustically absorbent conforming covers are offered by several electric plant manufacturers under such names as Hush Cover and Sound Shield Enclosure. Provided with convenient

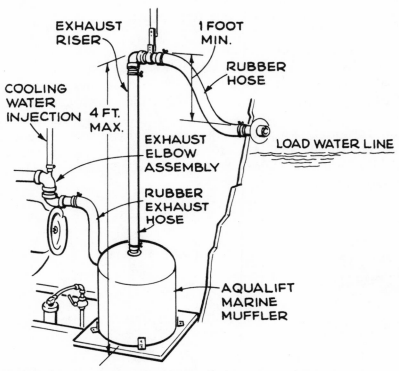

Fig. 8–6 Onan's Aqualift muffler silences engine and lifts cooling water above the waterline.

snap or clip openings for maintenance, these covers soak up a great deal of airborne sound, and contribute substantially to a mute generator complex. One of these muffling covers is well worth installing on a plant which is operated late into the night. The cost of a cover is in the $300-$700 area for most sizes of unit.

Wiring

Battery wiring follows the same principles as discussed in Chapters 2 and 9. Heavy cables are required to handle starting currents; and battery polarity must match that of the generating plant where battery current is used not only for starting but for alternator excitation.

Alternating current wiring for the "housepower" is made as

described in Chapter 4, and, in most cases, is the same wiring as used for the shore power. See Chapter 22.

Ship to Shore Transfer Switch

An absolute *must* where shore power is also connected to the boat's AC system, the shore transfer switch is double throw. As shown in Figure 8–7, in one position the switch connects the boat's conductors to the generating plant, in the other, it connects shore power. Simultaneously, it disconnects the unused system. This is vital, because if both systems are on the line together, there will surely be fireworks as one system bucks the other. Cost range is $60-$200.

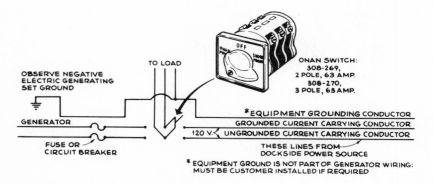

Fig. 8–7 The load transfer switch is wired to prevent simultaneous connection of generator and shore power to the boat's housepower circuits.

Notice that the transfer switch opens the current-carrying conductors, but does not open the equipment grounding conductor. The latter is the green "safety" wire discussed in Chapter 1.

Starting

Several starting systems are found on generating plants:

1. Conventional starter motor with manual control.
2. Starter windings in the generator with manual control.
3. Starter windings in generator with automatic demand control.

Conventional Starting

Found most often on larger generating plants, particularly on diesels, the conventional starter is identical to that used on propulsion engines. This kind of starter is discussed at some length in Chapter 9.

Manual Generator Starting

By adding starting windings to the alternating current generator, the machine is converted to a powerful direct-current motor, operating from battery power fed through a commutator and set of brushes. This type of starting is simple, quiet, and fast spinning, eliminating the mechanical drive found in the conventional starter. With this system, the operator throws a switch located anywhere in the boat, and the engine starts. Several switches may be installed so that the generator can be started from, say, the galley, head, and main cabin. When power is no longer needed, the switch is simply opened, and the driving engine stops.

Demand Starting

An electric control box replaces the simple manual switch in such systems as the Onan Control-O-Matic and others. On the control console is a switch offering Run, Automatic, and Off. In the Run position, the switch eliminates the automatic start feature and simply locks the generator on. In Automatic selection, the controls function as follows:

1. Direct-current battery voltage is conducted on the 120-volt AC power lines. Little or no current flows since there is no load on the line.

2. Someone turns on a light or appliance, causing a little direct current to flow. A control relay senses the current, flips, and starts a chain reaction. First, it turns on the bilge blower, if the system includes the blower feature. Then, after a time delay, the controller energizes a contactor, cranking the engine and getting it up to speed.

3. When AC voltage rises close to normal, a main contactor applies AC voltage to the lines and locks the generator on.

4. When the load is removed, as by the light being turned off, a current transformer senses the open circuit, and "pulls the switch" opening the contactor, and shutting down the generator. Battery voltage is reapplied to the lines, awaiting another load signal.

Safety devices are included in automatic starting. If the engine fails to start in 45 seconds, the starting power is shut off, and the system must then be manually reset. Should oil pressure fail to rise, the engine is shut down; and if the engine overheats, it is also shut down.

Frequency Control

Line frequency is directly related to speed; and the faster an alternator rotates, the higher the frequency. 60 Hertz generating plants commonly spin either 1,200, 1,800, or, in a few cases, 3,600 rpm. To keep revolutions at design speed, the driving engine is fitted with a mechanical governor; and this is adjustable.

A simple way to check on your generator's speed and frequency is with an ordinary synchronous electric clock having a sweep second hand. Use the clock and a watch or stopwatch. Plug in the clock, run the power plant, and compare the electric clock with the watch. If the electric clock runs fast, slow the generator as required to make the clock "keep time." If the clock lags, speed up the engine via governor adjustment. Without much difficulty, you should be able to make the clock keep time within a second per minute.

AC from the Propulsion Engine

Because the boat's propulsion engine runs at speeds varying over a range of 4 to 1 or more, in the past it was almost impossible to use it to drive a 60 Hertz alternator. Obviously, as the skipper maneuvered, the frequency would vary all over the lot. However, several new approaches have made it possible to use the propulsion engine to run a 60 Hertz power plant. One method is mechanical, the other hydraulic, and both incorporate constant speed drives.

Mechanical Drive

Named Auto-Gen, an engine mounted and driven alternator is made by Mercantile Manufacturing Co. It delivers 120 volts at 4,250 watts intermittent, 3,750 constant load, at 60 Hertz, plus or minus about three cycles per minute. Heart of the assembly is a V-belt constant speed drive. Through a governor, the mechanism senses engine speed, then varies the diameter ratio between two V-pulleys to maintain alternator speed synchronous. One end of the constant speed drive is propulsion engine driven, the other end connects to the alternator.

Auto-Gen can be mounted directly on the propulsion engine, or placed near when it can be belt driven. The drive includes a magnetic clutch, similar to those on air-conditioner compressors, allowing the unit to be shut down when not needed. Weight is just under 100 pounds; and the alternator uses battery power for excitation.

Hydraulic Drive

Constant frequency and installation flexibility are achieved by a hydraulic pump-and-motor combination with interconnecting lines. The system is easy to understand. The propulsion engine drives a hydraulic pump; the pump, via connecting tubing, energizes a constant speed hydraulic motor, and that motor drives the alternator at synchronous speed for 60 Hertz.

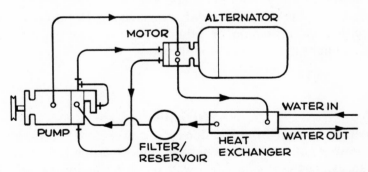

Fig. 8–8 Plumbing schematic shows how engine-driven pump transmits high pressure fluid to hydraulic motor. In turn, the constant-speed hydraulic motor spins the 60 Hertz alternator.

143

The hydraulic pump is belt driven, and may be mounted on the engine or near it. The alternator can be tucked anywhere that offers a dry location and enough ventilation, making the unit ideal for auxiliary sailboats. Frequency regulation is plus or minus about three Hertz with the hydraulic pump varying between 1,300 to 4,000 rpm.

Off Season Layup

If the electric plant is to be decommissioned for any length of time, proper storage is essential. The following is based on recommendations made by Kohler Company for gasoline powered equipment:

1. Drain crankcase oil while engine is hot. Flush with clean oil, then refill.

2. Shut off the fuel valve and run the engine until it starves.

3. Remove the spark plugs; then pour a teaspoon of oil into each cylinder. Rotate the engine by hand several times, then install the plugs.

4. Drain the cooling system, including engine block and seawater pump. On closed-cooling systems, fill completely with clean water and anti-freeze.

5. Clean the exterior and wipe it down with light oil.

6. Disconnect and remove the batteries to where they can be stored in a dry, cool place and kept charged.

7. Cover the entire unit with a dust cover. But do not cover it with a polyethylene or other non-breathing plastic sheet which might make it sweat and rust.

SYNOPSIS

Freeing the boat from the dockside power cord, an on-board housepower generator can energize almost unlimited electrical appliances. The cost of a 7,500-watt plant is roughly $4,500 plus accessories and installation. The cost of a kWh of power will vary with the type and price of fuel—in mid–1980, from 14¢ to 36¢ The power plant should be vibration- and sound-proofed, and special attention should be given to its exhaust system. A ship-to-shore transfer switch is essential. Several varieties of propulsion-engine-driven alternators are now available.

CHAPTER 9

Engine Starting Circuits

ONE CHARACTERISTIC of engine cranking circuits is that most of the components are electrically and mechanically rugged. The circuits are basically simple, but their husky construction springs from the work they perform, involving up to several hundred amperes of current, and more than a horsepower in work. Another characteristic is that the heavy components are, in the main, designed for short duty cycles: They work very hard for brief intervals, but tire easily:

Components

Principal components in the standard engine starting system are:

1. Starter motor
2. Mechanical drive
3. Solenoid relay
4. Neutral safety switch
5. Starter switch
6. Heavy cables and control wiring
7. Battery

The Motor
Energized by battery current, most engine-starting motors are

shunt-wound, 4-pole, 4-brush, high-current machines using very heavy windings in both field and armature. Because of the high currents flowing, the windings appear more as bus bar than ordinary magnet wire. Figure 9–1 shows the internal connections and circuit arrangement in a starter.

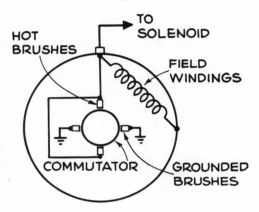

Fig. 9–1 Starter wiring schematic shows field windings, with two brushes grounded, and two hot. All windings are very heavy wire.

Both mechanically and electrically, the starter resembles the conventional DC charging generator, except that its windings are much heavier, its brushes and commutator conduct more current, and it ordinarily has plain shaft bearings. Because of its extraordinary power, coupled with limited efficiency, the motor heats up quickly when working at capacity. After 10 or 15 seconds of full load output, the motor windings are usually up to fully allowable temperature, and the motor must be given a short rest before being worked again. A representative duty cycle might be 5 seconds on, 15 seconds off, or thereabouts.

The Mechanical Drive

Several different kinds of mechanical drive are used to transmit starter motor high-speed rotation to the slower turning engine; and all incorporate reduction gearing of some kind. In addition to reducing armature-to-engine speed by a ratio as high as 50 to 1, the mechanical drive also provides means to engage and disengage the starter from the engine. Three types of drive are common: helical shaft, shifter fork, and double reduction.

Helical Shaft Drives

Often called a "Bendix Drive," the helical variety of drive is found on older engines, and on some modern auxiliary motors. This drive automatically engages the starter's small pinion gear with a large-diameter ring gear on the flywheel. It does so by inertia.

The small starter gear is carried on a spirally-threaded shaft, the shaft comprising an extension of the armature. Free to rotate several revolutions, the pinion can screw itself along the helical shaft for about an inch. When electric power hits the starter, the armature shaft suddenly accelerates, but the weighted pinion gear, because of inertia, stands still for a brief instant. Since the shaft is spinning and the gear is not, the gear screws itself forward and into mesh with the engine flywheel ring gear. There, its fore-and-aft motion ceases against a stop, and the pinion rotates the engine flywheel.

The engine starts. Now, the flywheel spins faster than the pinion, kicking it back out of engagement, where it remains as the engine continues operating. Because the pinion gear assembly is counterweighted out-of-balance, it cannot idly drift back into engagement with the flywheel ring gear.

To absorb the crashing shock when the little pinion hits the flywheel gear, and to help it recoil from that gear when it has finished its job, the pinion assembly incorporates a heavy, tough helical spring. The spring is between the spiral drive and small gear, carrying full starter-motor torque. If the spring breaks, as it may on occasion, the drive is rendered useless.

Advantage of the helical shaft drive is its simplicity and lack of external mechanical parts. Disadvantage is the heavy mechanical shock it delivers when it slams its pinion into the engine's flywheel. Compared to other drives, it is also slightly more susceptible to troubles created by rust.

Shifter Fork Drive

Used extensively on modern engines, the shifter drive positively engages the starter pinion with the flywheel ring gear before the starter motor starts to spin. In this device, the pinion is carried by the armature shaft extension, and the extension is splined, allowing the pinion to slide freely fore-and-aft while transmitting torque. A shift fork or yoke slides the pinion along the shaft; and an overrunning clutch integral with the pinion allows the starter motor to crank the engine, but prevents the engine from spinning the starter.

As a refinement, between the shifter fork and pinion, there is a spring connection offering "snap" to the pinion's sliding motion. If the pinion should fail to mesh with the flywheel ring gear at first, but should engage tooth-on-tooth, the spring will snap it home the first split second that the starter motor rotates. Unlike the heavy spring in the helical shaft drive, the pinion "snap" spring carries no starter torque, is less subject to breakage.

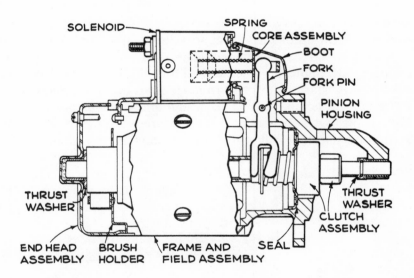

Fig. 9-2 Cutaway side view shows how shifter fork slides the pinion fore and aft to engage flywheel ring gear. The flywheel is not shown.

When the engine is to be cranked, the shifter mechanism first slides the pinion into mesh with the flywheel gear; then immediately power is applied to the starter motor, spinning the assembly. When the engine fires and runs, the operator releases the shifter, disengaging the pinion from flywheel. Simultaneously, the starter motor is deenergized.

Should the operator hesitate and not immediately release the pinion from the engine ring gear, the overrunning clutch will prevent the engine from accelerating the starter to explosive revolutions. Since some engines may quickly climb to 4,000 rpm, and since gearing of 20 to 1 between starter and engine is common, without the overrunning clutch the engine might try to spin the starter 80,000 rpm. Naturally, at this absurd speed, the starter would explode centrifugally, spraying its parts over the boat. But the one-way clutch prevents this catastrophe.

The most common method of synchronizing shifter actuation with starter motor electric switching is via a solenoid relay. This device is discussed below.

Double Reduction Drive

A modification of the shifter fork drive, the reduction variety is found on larger gasoline engines and diesels. The flywheel engaging mechanism is as described for the shifter fork drive; but between the starter motor's armature shaft and the pinion shaft, there is a reduction gear. The design allows reduction ratios as high as 50 to 1 between starter armature and engine, obviously giving the starter terrific torque at the engine crankshaft.

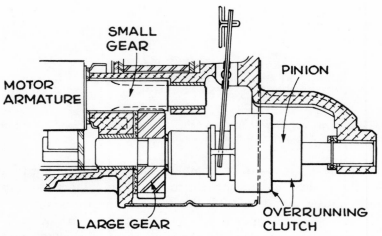

Fig. 9–3 Reduction gear drive gives this starter almost twice the cranking torque of the direct drive starter.

Solenoid Relays

Electromagnetic relays or solenoid starting switches perform one or more of three functions: 1. Close the heavy current circuit between battery and starter; 2. Shift the starter drive; 3. Apply extra voltage to the ignition circuit. Being heavy duty, special purpose relays, starter solenoids comprise a magnet winding, plunger, heavy current contacts, and special accessories tailored to the application. Battery voltage to actuate the solenoid comes via a control circuit in which we find the manual starter switch or button, and possibly a safety device to prevent starting "in gear."

Solenoid Switching Function

When control current from the manual starter switch flows through the solenoid winding, it generates a strong magnetic field, pulling a soft iron plunger against spring pressure. Near the end of its travel, the plunger closes a heavy-current switch, usually a copper disc and two rugged contacts. When the disc is pressed against the contacts, it conducts battery current from one heavy terminal to the other. Externally, one terminal is connected to the hot battery cable, the other to the starter.

Solenoid Shifting Function

When serving starters which have a shifter fork drive, the solenoid plunger invariably does the work of sliding the pinion into mesh with the flywheel gear. Linkage connects the solenoid plunger to a shift lever arranged that when the solenoid is energized, plunger travel throws the pinion into mesh during the first part of its travel. After engaging the gears, the plunger closes the starter switch, the sequence preventing the starter from spinning and stripping its gears before engagement.

Because it requires substantial force to move the shifter smartly, the solenoid coil is of heavy wire and draws appreciable current. On some larger solenoid packages, current is reduced through use of two windings: A heavy, high-current winding and auxiliary winding are both energized momentarily to throw the plunger home with force. But at the end of its travel, at the point where it energizes the starter motor switch, the plunger opens the circuit to the high-current winding, leaving the lighter auxiliary winding to hold the switch closed. The dual circuit reduces battery drain during the interval when the starter is cranking the engine.

An unusual pseudo solenoid is used on one make of starter. One of the starter motor's field poles is hinged to move farther and closer to the armature. When the starter is energized, the pole-piece is drawn down magnetically, and a linkage from the pole-piece engages the starter device.

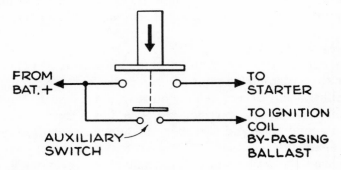

Fig. 9–4 Small auxiliary switch in starter solenoid assembly furnishes battery voltage to ignition coil while starter is energized.

Solenoid Ignition Function

Numerous starter solenoid switches feature an auxiliary switch, wired into the ignition circuit; see Fig. 9–4. Movement of the solenoid plunger actuates this switch; consequently, it is closed during the interval the starter motor is drawing battery current. The auxiliary switch shunts the ballast resistor (see page 159) out of the ignition coil's primary circuit, thereby increasing primary voltage and intensifying spark while the engine cranks. The idea is to make the engine start more easily.

The Neutral Safety Switch

On many engine installations there is a switch on the marine transmission, actuated by the shift lever. When the lever is in other than the neutral position, the switch is open circuited preventing the engine from cranking by opening the control circuit between manual starter switch and solenoid; see Fig. 9–5.

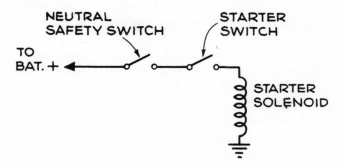

Fig. 9–5 Neutral safety switch in starter control circuit is closed only while marine transmission is in neutral. It is wired in series with the manual switch.

The purpose of the safety switch is, of course, to prevent the boat from starting "in gear" and charging ahead or astern, out of control.

If yours is an older boat, not equipped with a neutral safety, you might want to make a morning's project of installing one. Kits are available for many models of transmissions. However, if you cannot locate a kit, you might apply a little ingenuity and rig a Microswitch on the transmission or manual control, wiring it into the solenoid control circuit to prevent starting in forward or reverse.

The Manual Starter Switch

Often combined with the ignition switch, the manual starter switch handles only the moderate current demanded by the starter solenoid relay control circuit, not the heavy current demanded by the starter. Some starter switches are also wired to furnish battery voltage directly to the ignition coil, by-passing the ballast resistor during the short interval when the engine is being cranked.

Cables and Wiring

Those heavy cables connected from battery to ground, battery to solenoid, and solenoid to starter, are an important part of the starting complex. Even the slightest excess resistance in these cables will deteriorate starting performance unbelievably.

Consider a cranking circuit with 100 amperes flowing from battery to starter. Unwanted additional resistance as tiny as 1/100th ohm will decrease starting voltage by a volt. If the original condition was 100 amperes at 10 volts, adding the mere 1/100th ohm will reduce voltage to nine and current to 90. This means that instead of being able to draw 1,000 watts, the starter motor can only demand 810 watts. Surprisingly enough, that added 1/100th ohm reduced starting capacity by almost 20%.

The example points up the attractive feature of 32-volt starting for diesels, which are tough to crank. In a 32-volt system, cable resistance has much less than half the effect that it has on a 12-volt system, because for a given power, current is only 3/8th as much. (Voltage drop equals current times resistance.)

The surface where the starter assembly mounts to the engine is just as much a part of the heavy current system as the battery cables. Battery juice flows to the starter through the cables but returns to the battery via the starter frame, engine block, and ground strap. For this reason, it is important that the starter flange and engine housing to which it attaches both be shiny-clean when a starter is mounted. Rust, dirt, or loose fastenings offer high resistance, preventing the starter from performing well.

The above paragraph shows why it is a good idea to connect a substantial ground strap directly to the starter's mounting bolts or cap screws. Ground circuit resistance is minimized. Furthermore, heavy starter currents, a potential cause of corrosion, need not be conducted by the engine's cast iron block.

Control wiring is of much smaller gauge than that of the battery cables, since it carries but a few amps, compared to a possible several hundred in the cables. Nevertheless, control wiring must be heavy enough to carry solenoid current, on the order of 15 amps, and must be free of shaky connections which will cause chatter in the solenoid and difficult starting.

The Battery

The battery's role in the starter circuit is vital, obviously; and the all-important storage battery is treated in some depth in Chapter 2.

Starter Trouble Diagnosis

Troubles relating to a hard-starting engine are discussed in Chapter 12. Additional specific troubles found in the starter itself are pinpointed in the analysis that follows here, where common malfunctions are cited.

Starter Motor Will Not Operate

Where the starter motor acts completely dead, not struggling or attempting to operate, look into the following:

1. Dead battery
2. Loose, broken, or disconnected battery cable
3. Starter very loose on its mount
4. Open circuit in manual starter switch or wiring
5. Burned contacts in solenoid relay
6. Open coil in solenoid relay

Starter Struggles, Won't Crank

If the starter draws current, hums, growls and seems to be drawing appreciable amps, investigate the following:

1. Weak battery
2. Loose connection or corrosion on cables
3. Starter loose in mount
4. Internal ground in starter motor windings
5. Armature rubbing on field poles inside motor
6. Damaged, jammed, or rusty drive
7. Water in engine cylinders causing hydrostatic lock

Starter Spins Smartly; Engine Does Not

1. Broken overrunning clutch
2. Pinion and shaft rusted, dirty, sticky
3. Broken Bendix spring on helical shaft drive
4. Broken linkage or spring in solenoid shifter mechanism
5. Broken teeth on engine ring gear

Solenoid Plunger Clicks and Chatters

1. Discharged battery; Weak battery will pull in the solenoid

plunger, but when solenoid connects starter to battery, added load drops voltage, dropping out the plunger. This sequence continues, causing chatter.
2. Corroded solenoid contacts
3. High resistance in battery cables or connections

Starter will not Disengage
1. Broken solenoid plunger spring
2. Faulty manual starter switch; won't open
3. Rust or dirt on drive mechanism

SYNOPSIS

The starter, a short-duty-cycle motor, draws high currents from the system, necessitating the use of heavy components and wiring throughout. Mechanical drives are either the helical shaft or shifter fork type, and sometimes incorporate a reduction gear. A heavy solenoid relay switches starter current on, and in the shifter fork drive it also meshes the starter pinion with flywheel ring gear. In some designs an auxiliary switch shunts the ballast resistor during the starting cycle. The manual starter switch, often ganged with the ignition switch handles the moderate current required by the solenoid.

CHAPTER 10

Ignition—How It Works

A BOOK on marine electricity would be incomplete without good coverage of power plant ignition. Certainly the marine engine's ignition system is the most vital and hard-working electrical system on board a gasoline-powered boat; and it's also the system which causes the most acute embarrassment when it fails.

Because of ignition's importance, and its vulnerability to attack by the marine environment, two chapters are devoted to the subject. This chapter describes ignition systems, telling how the components work together to generate spark; the following chapter covers ignition trouble-shooting and tune-up.

Starting with the ignition switch, let us look into the system's components one by one as an aid to understanding the entire complex:

The Switch

Usually provided with a key lock, the ignition switch is connected in the circuit between the battery hot terminal and the ignition coil hot primary winding terminal. Terminals on both switch and coil are usually identified by the marks "Bat" or "Ign." Many ignition switches incorporate secondary contacts and extra terminals energizing the starter when the key is turned against spring pressure to its extreme position. Due to the dual function you must remember, when servicing the ignition switch, to observe correct connections when attaching wires. It's a good plan to tag all wires before unhooking them from the switch; then you will know what's what when making new connections.

Switch Troubles

Mechanics seem to ignore the ignition switch when trouble-shooting, yet you should keep in mind that it can be a troublemaker. Because of the damp marine environment, this is true to a greater extent aboard a boat than in a car or truck. A switch making poor or intermittent contact can cause the engine to start hard, miss, and quit completely just when it is needed the most. Many a diagnosis of "bad coil" or "wet plug wires" has in reality been a faulty ignition switch.

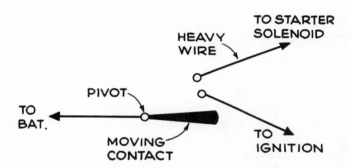

Fig. 10-1 Schematic of ignition switch shows that when the moving blade touches both starter and ignition contacts, starter is energized. Partial motion of blade energizes ignition only.

The Wire from Switch-to-Coil

The low voltage wire running from the ignition switch to coil, carries from two to five amperes, and the conductor may be ordinary copper, or in a few instances it may be alloy resistance wire. Resistance wire is occasionally used as a substitute for a ballast resistor, the function of which is described in subsequent paragraphs.

If the wire from switch-to-coil is resistance conductor, it must never be used to furnish juice for another accessory. Voltage drop through the resistance is computed on the basis of ignition coil only. If you add an additional load at the coil end of the wire, you will reduce the coil's primary winding voltage; this, in turn, will lower spark voltage. Even if the switch-to-coil wire is copper, it is best not to hang any new accessory on it since that will load the switch circuit, possibly reducing spark intensity.

The Ballast

Roughly half an ohm in resistance, the ballast resistor is connected in the circuit between the ignition key switch and the coil's primary winding. Ballast function is to drop battery voltage to a lower potential allowing favorable ignition coil design without excessively high current in the primary winding. The ballast increases resistance as it warms, automatically furnishing higher voltage for cold engine starts, then reducing voltage and resulting current demand as the engine warms to its job and the ballast follows suit. On most marine engines the ballast resistor is a wirewound component, coiled in a ceramic case. However, in a

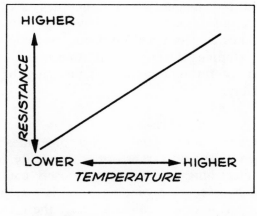

Fig. 10-2 Ballast resistor drops voltage to coil's primary winding, reducing voltage more when the ballast element heats.

few installations, it may be a simple length of alloy wire connecting the ignition switch to the coil. This arrangement was described in the preceeding paragraph.

In some circuits, the voltage-reducing ballast is by-passed and switched out of the system while the engine is being cranked by the starter. Here, a shunt is actuated by the starter circuit, usually by the starter solenoid, shorting out the ballast while the engine cranks. Purpose of the shunt is to maximize primary voltage and generate hot spark during the starting period, when battery voltage is severely decreased by the starter motor's enormous current demand. Several by-pass systems are found: One uses an auxiliary contact in the starter solenoid; another employs an extra contact in the starter key switch; yet a third consists of a relay which is closed by energy from the starter switch.

Ballast Problems.

Like all electrical components, ballast resistors are subject to trouble. Corrosion is a menace which sometimes eats away at the windings, increasing resistance and lowering primary circuit voltage. Sometimes a ballast will burn out, opening the circuit completely, and stopping the engine. At other times its terminals corrode, making intermittent contact, and causing the engine to misbehave horribly.

The Coil

A rose is not always a rose, and a coil is sometimes not a coil, particularly when it is really a transformer. In reality, an ignition "coil" is what electronic people call a "loosely coupled transformer." It has two separate windings, and is a step-up transformer. But since it has been called a "coil" these many years, we will follow suit in our nomenclature, knowing down deep that the thing is a transformer.

Inside the Coil

The coil's primary winding of several score turns of heavy wire is wrapped around a magnetically-soft iron core. Energized by the battery, several amperes flow through the primary, which has only a few ohms resistance. Much different is the secondary winding which is also wound around the same soft iron core. The secondary is the high-voltage spark winding, comprising several thousand turns of fine gauge insulated wire, and offering a resistance of perhaps 10,000 ohms. How different the windings are, even in terminations: The primary winding terminates at two ordinary screw-type low voltage terminals, but the high voltage secondary terminates in a high voltage, highly insulated tower into which the distributor wire fits. The cold end of the high voltage secondary simply fastens to ground or to the primary winding terminal.

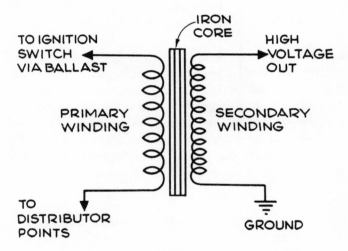

Fig. 10-3 The ignition coil is actually a step-up transformer of high ratio. Primary winding is a few turns of heavy wire; secondary wiring is comprised of thousands of turns of hair-like wire.

Magnetic Activity

Current flows through the primary winding, generating a healthy magnetic field around the iron core. Then, when primary current flow is suddenly interrupted by opening of the breaker points, the magnetic field rapidly collapses. The contracting magnetic lines of force now slice across the multi-thousand turn secondary winding, inducing potential of 10,000 volts or more. Intense spark voltage is then conducted to the special high voltage termination on the coil's tower.

Causes of Trouble

High voltage leaks, invited by moisture, dirt, salt, and small cracks in the coil's high voltage insulation cause most secondary circuit troubles. On the other hand, corrosion and poor connections generate most primary circuit grief. Seldom does a coil's voltage slowly weaken with age. More often, the unit will quit stone cold all of a sudden because a connection has broken, because of a drenching, or because one of the windings has open circuited, and the component has failed outright.

RFI Suppressor

To suppress radio frequency interference, many ignition coils are fitted with a suppression capacitor, wired between the hot primary coil terminal to ground. Do not confuse this capacitor with the similar-appearing ignition condenser. The suppressor unit must always be connected to the coil's battery or ignition key terminal, *never* to the coil terminal which is connected to the distributor. If you connect the RFI suppressing capacitor to the

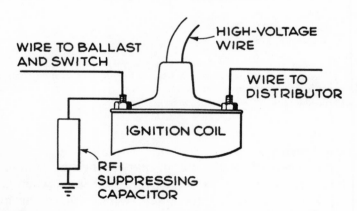

Fig. 10-4 Radio interference suppressing capacitor is connected between battery terminal and ground.

coil terminal which is connected to the distributor, it will fail in its job. Worse, it may degrade ignition performance.

High Voltage Wires

The main high-voltage ignition wire transmits spark voltage from the ignition coil to the center terminal in the distributor cap, thence to the rotor. Radiating from the distributor are similar heavily insulated wires carrying high voltage to the spark plugs. This set of wires, the ignition *harness,* may have stranded copper conductor or a resistance conductor made of carbon impregnated string or resistance alloy. Where used, resistance conductors are intended to suppress radio frequency interference.

Possible Trouble

High-voltage wire problems usually originate with cracked insulation, broken wire, or a widely separated connection at coil, distributor or plug. If the circuit between coil and distributor is broken, the engine dies. If, however, continuity to just one plug is interrupted, the engine (if multi-cylinder) will continue to run; but it will miss with an even cadence.

High-voltage plug wires, particularly on high-compression engines, must never be closely harnessed, bunched, or paralleled in a tube or raceway. As far as practicable, high-voltage wires should be separately dressed, spaced from one another, and also kept away from ground. Tight bunching of ignition wires can induce misfiring and cross-firing.

Cross-firing of spark plugs is where two plugs are fired at the same time, or where the intended plug misfires, and another does fire. Tight bunching of adjacent plug wires causes a pair to respond as a capacitor. When the surging pulse of voltage appears in one wire, it is capacitively coupled to the next wire, both wires then carrying spark, when only one is intended to do so. The moral is to keep the wires neatly separated.

Distributor

The distributor and all its inner workings "times" the spark and sequentially directs high voltage to each spark plug in a predetermined firing order. It is the engine's nervous system, subject to no end of ills in the marine environment. Comprising the complete conventional unit are the points, condenser, cap, rotor, and advance mechanism. These will be described individually.

Breaker Points

Inside the distributor housing, the breaker points determine the exact time at which each spark discharge is generated as the engine rotates. The points are a high-speed switch. When closed, they complete a circuit from the battery, through the coil's primary winding to ground. "Ground" in this case is the distributor housing.

The magic moment is when the points separate, breaking the primary circuit, and inducing spark. Ignition timing is dependent on the exact split second that the points "break" and they must open crisply, at exactly the right time in the engine's cycle.

Clearance and Dwell

Driven by the engine camshaft, the distributor shaft rotates, and its lobes or cams, one for each cylinder, push the points open against spring pressure. The distance which the points are forced apart is called "point clearance," and the angular degrees of

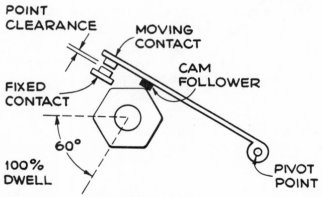

Fig. 10-5 Point clearance is measured with cam follower at top of a cam lobe. On the six-cylinder distributor shown, dwell must be less than 60°, since that angle represents 100% dwell.

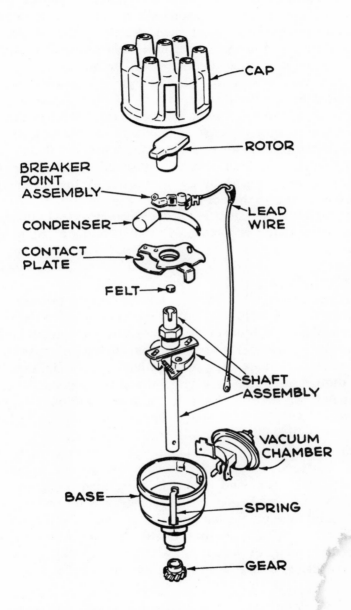

CAP

ROTOR

BREAKER POINT ASSEMBLY

CONDENSER

CONTACT PLATE

FELT

LEAD WIRE

SHAFT ASSEMBLY

VACUUM CHAMBER

BASE

SPRING

GEAR

Fig. 10-6 Exploded view of a distributor.

shaft rotation during which they remain closed is termed "dwell." The dwell can be defined in angular degrees or percent; and dwell increases as point clearance decreases. If clearance were decreased until the points no longer opened at all, dwell would be infinitely great, defined 100% or 360° dwell.

Correct dwell is seen to be a function of point clearance, and determines the length of time, at a given engine speed, that the ignition coil's primary winding can magnetically energize the iron core. It takes a finite time to magnetically "saturate" the core. If points are adjusted with excessive clearance, dwell time is too short to saturate the iron, and, at high speed, spark will be weak.

On the other hand, long dwell, caused by insufficient point clearance, results in the points being "scraped" open rather than being snapped open smartly. Spark becomes weak, indeterminate, and sour; the engine tends to stall, and starting becomes sluggish.

Breaker Point Springs

So much attention is ordinarily lavished on the points that the springs are sometimes overlooked as a source of good or bad ignition. Since the breaker points are urged toward the closed position by a spring, it is apparent that the spring must be very much alive to actuate the points at high speed. Because of its mass, though small, the moving point resists following the cam at high speed. If the spring is weak, the points will bounce (racing men call it "float") at high speed. Performance then deteriorates as the engine develops a surging high-speed miss.

There is however, a practical limit to how much force the point spring can exert. Heavy spring pressure can act as a drag on the advance mechanism, and may distort or even break the point arm. Distributor makers publish specifications for correct spring tension; and tune-up mechanics often consult these data, adjusting tension accordingly. In most distributors, adjustment is made by careful bending of the spring, which is a flat leaf, or, in some cases, by selection of appropriate shims or washers.

Double-Point System

On opening the distributor on some eight-cylinder marine

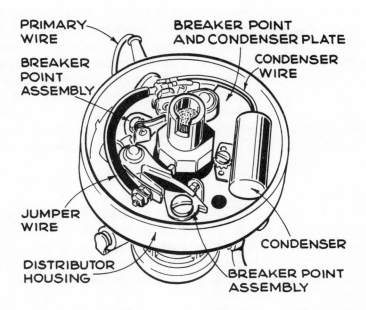

PRIMARY WIRE

BREAKER POINT AND CONDENSER PLATE

CONDENSER WIRE

BREAKER POINT ASSEMBLY

JUMPER WIRE

CONDENSER

DISTRIBUTOR HOUSING

BREAKER POINT ASSEMBLY

Fig. 10-7 Shown is a distributor with two sets of breaker points. One set breaks the primary circuit; the other makes it.

engines you will see two sets of breaker points. Dual sets are used to give maximum possible dwell while retaining reasonable clearnace and reducing the possibility of point bounce. The points are angularly arranged so that one set breaks the circuit; then the other set closes it almost immediately.

In single point-set distributors, the greatest dwell practical in an eight-cylinder machine is on the order of 28° to perhaps 32°. But in a distributor having two point-sets, dwell can be raised to 35° or even 38°. The theoretical maximum dwell is something less than 45°, since that is the total angle between adjacent cam peaks in the distributor shaft.

Double Points, Two Coils

Usually offered as a custom option for high-speed, high-performance marine engines, the dual-point coil system is excellent ignition. In effect, it is two almost completely separate systems, each system firing 4 cylinders of an eight-cylinder power plant.

A four lobe, rather than eight lobe, cam is used in the 8-cylinder dual rig. The point-sets are disposed so that one set handles four cylinders, the other set handles the other 4 in alternate firing order. One big advantage is that dwell (and coil saturation) can be as high as 60°, whereas in the conventional distributor it is seldom higher than 30°, as explained in earlier paragraphs. The system functions beautifully at the highest speeds. Another advantage is that point life is extended because each point-set shares the work with the other, each assuming half the total load.

Point Troubles

Points spawn just about every kind of ignition trouble imaginable: Corroded points cause missing; wide point clearance can cause knock; insufficient clearance generates back-firing through the carburetor air horn; excess dwell makes the engine hard to start; weak spring "breaks up" the engine at high speed; pitted points stall the machine; and a broken point kills it entirely. Obviously, points must be serviced and adjusted frequently.

The Rotor

Perched on top of the distributor shaft, the rotor is a high speed rotating switch. It picks up spark voltage pulses from the ignition coil, sequentially distributing the spark to the plugs in correct firing order. It is made of insulating material and has a metal conductor carrying ignition voltage from its center pivot point to its tip.

Rotor Troubles

Since the rotor handles very high voltage, its insulation must be excellent. If resistance breaks down, or if the rotor develops small cracks, becoming electrically leaky, spark hotness suffers. An electrically leaky rotor can cause hard-to-trace loss of spark, even when all other ignition components check out correctly.

Condenser Function

A condenser and capacitor are the same thing, and the word "capacitor" is more often used in electronic work. However, since "condenser" has been popular in distributor work for years, we will use it here.

Physically, the condenser is most often located inside the distributor, close to the points, although sometimes it is fastened to the ignition coil. Electrically, it is connected across the points as a shunt, from the hot point to ground. Its function is to provide a high-frequency path from the coil primary winding to ground. At the instant the points open, collapsing the magnetic field in the coil, the condenser, in series with the primary winding, resonantly "rings" the coil. This increases spark voltage. Lacking a condenser, the circuit will generate only the most anemic spark, with voltage too puny to fire the spark plugs, even under favorable conditions.

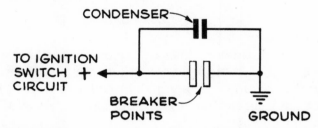

Fig. 10-8 This electrical schematic shows relationship of distributor breaker points to condensor.

Condenser Ills

It does not wear out, and, unlike the points, the condenser is a relatively trouble-free component. On occasion, because of the damp marine environment, a condenser will become electrically defective and inefficient. However, as a rule, if a condenser gives trouble at all, it fails completely due to an internal short circuit or an external open lead.

Distributor Cap

More than just a top closure for the distributor, the cap performs an important function, and on better distributors it is made of a superior quality plastic. Imbedded in the plastic are conductors carrying high voltage from the coil's secondary winding to the distributor rotor, and from rotor to the plug wires. Continuity and insulation for the high voltage are essential in the cap, or ignition will be interrupted.

Cap Defects

More marine ignition trouble is generated by defective distributor caps than is sometimes suspected. As the plastic ages, it sometimes develops hairline cracks. These fill with invisible traces of a salt which attracts moisture and spawns a spark grounding network, killing spark during damp weather. Unhappy mechanics have traced hot spark all the way through to the distributor, but have then found no spark at the plug wires. Later, after considerable trouble-shooting, they determine that the spark is leaking away to ground via a defective distributor cap.

Centrifugal Advance

In the lower distributor housing, underneath the breaker points, is a set of centrifugal governor weights. These are attached to the rotating distributor shaft and spin with it, flying out farther and farther as the engine accelerates. Moving

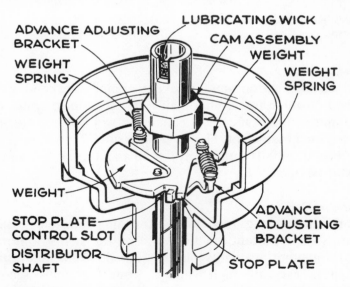

Fig. 10-9 Centrifugal advance mechanism, showing weights and springs.

centrifugally against restraining springs, the weights, through cam action, advance the distributor lobes ahead in phase relationship to the engine crankshaft. At speed, the points break earlier in the cycle, advancing spark timing as required for optimum performance. Pulling the weights in, the restraining springs retard the spark for easy starting and smooth idling.

Centrifugal Defects

In the marine distributor, the centrifugal advance mechanism and its springs sometimes rust, sticking in one position, or responding in a limited range to speed changes. Such trouble is occasionally overlooked by the mechanic accustomed to working on auto and truck engines where, because of kinder environment, the advance seldom malfunctions. Most frequently, the advance rusts into the retarded position, giving the engine a smooth idle, but forcing it to lose power, overheat, and sometimes pop back through the carburetor at high speed. The cure is to disassemble the distributor and clean the mechanism.

Vacuum Advance

Supplementing centrifugal advance in some distributors is a vacuum-actuated timing control which modifies ignition advance in response to the magnitude of mainfold intake vacuum. Intake vacuum is largely a function of engine loading. Therefore, the vacuum advance modifies ignition timing largely in accordance with load and throttle setting.

High vacuum in the intake manifold signifies light load. Sensing this, the device advances spark farther than the mechanical weights have already done. Low or weak vacuum indicates acceleration and heavy load on the engine. On detecting low vacuum, the device retards timing relative to that which would be given mechanically.

Many vacuum advance mechanisms detect intake vacuum at an accurately positioned, small-diameter, rifle-drilled hole in the carburetor. The little hole is located so that it is exposed to vacuum beneath the throttle butterfly valve when that valve is open more than for idle.But the little hole is blocked off and cannot feel vacuum when the throttle is closed for idling. This design directs virtually no vacuum to the advance actuator during idle. Response is retarded spark, a parameter contributing to smooth idling. But as the throttle is advanced to a position faster than idle, it exposes the hole to vacuum on the manifold side of the butterfly valve, and the vacuum mechanism responds by advancing spark timing.

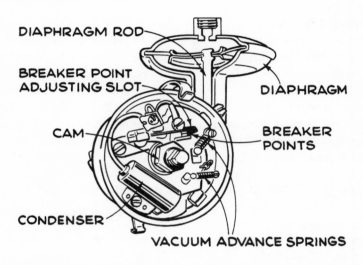

DIAPHRAGM ROD

BREAKER POINT ADJUSTING SLOT

DIAPHRAGM

CAM

BREAKER POINTS

CONDENSER

VACUUM ADVANCE SPRINGS

Fig. 10-10 Cutaway shows how vacuum acts on diaphragm to modify ignition timing.

Vacuum Control Defects

A diaphragm is ordinarily the device used to measure vacuum and to position the timing mechanism: From the diaphragm come most of the troubles associated with vacuum advance. After cracking or perforating with age, the diaphragm leaks. Slowly, it ceases functioning, and to compound the trouble, it bleeds air back into the manifold, where unwanted air upsets idle performance and reduces acceleration. Best cure, of course, is to renew the diaphragm assembly.

Spark Plugs

In this book, our interest in the spark plug is as an electrical component, not so much as a member of the engine's thermo-dynamic team. Electrically, the spark plug is simplicity itself: It comprises a center electrode separated from the side electrode by a ceramic insulator. Inside the cylinder high-voltage spark leaps from the center electrode to the one on the screw shell, and that is that. For good ignition, the plug must be of the correct heat range, must have proper threads, and a tight gasket.

Plug Troubles

Spark plugs are subject to many ills as anyone knows who has tinkered with engines. If the plug operates too cool, or is subjected to rich mixtures, it will gather black soot and misfire. If the ceramic cracks, the plug may short, particularly during damp weather or when the engine is heavily loaded. Undersized electrode gap causes uncertain ignition, accompanied by sluggish high speed performance. An oversized gap may cause high speed miss, and contributes to hard starting. Too wide a gap forces ignition voltage to rise above normal, and may damage the coil.

Surface-Gap Plugs

Inside the combustion chamber, the tip of a surface-gap spark plug appears as two concentric rings in the same plane, separated by a ceramic ring between them. When the plug fires, high voltage travels from the small center ring, across the ceramic surface to the outer ring. Advantage of the plug is that it operates cool, having no projections to gather incandescent points of carbon. This feature makes the surface gap particularly suitable for use in outboard motors where fouling is a persistent problem.

Particularly suited for use in motors having capacitor discharge ignition, surface-gap spark plugs usually don't do too well with conventional spark. Consequently, if your engine has the conventional system, you will do well to stick with the type plug recommended by the manufacturer.

However, if your engine has capacitor-discharge ignition, the story is different. In fact, the surface gap plug was developed in response to the spark characteristics of CD ignition. It takes full advantage of CD's lightning-like, ultra-fast spark discharge. But when married to ordinary ignition, the surface-gap plug tends to slowly bleed away the charge before an arc can flash across the electrodes, and this is particularly true after the plug becomes a little sooty.

Capacitor-Discharge Ignition

Electronic capacitor-discharge ignition is quite different from the conventional variety, and in some respects it is an opposite. The following highlights indicate basic differences:

1. In the CD system, energy is stored in a capacitor and released at the crucial moment. In standard ignition, energy storage is magnetic.

2. Spark can be triggered in the CD system when the points make, or when they break; or points can be eliminated completely. The point-break system is almost universal with standard systems.

3. The "coil" in a CD system is a pulse transformer of low primary impedance, sometimes using a ferrite core. It generates spark on current inrush. The conventional coil, iron cored, throws its spark on current outrush.

4. CD spark is hotter, lasts for a shorter interval than conventional spark. CD voltage hits the spark plugs with more of an electrical hammer blow, giving it the ability to fire dirty plugs.

Figure 10-11 is a block diagram of a typical capacitor discharge ignition system. It shows the workings as follows:

The Inverter

Energized by the boat's battery, the inverter changes direct current to alternating current at hundreds of cycles a second. The inverter is a transistorized power oscillator, similar to an audio signal generator, and it furnishes all the power required by the CD ignition system.

Step-Up Transformer

Usually part of the power pack incorporating the inverter, the step-up transformer has its primary winding energized by high

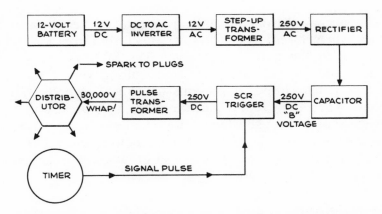

Fig. 10-11 Block diagram shows functions in a capacitive discharge ignition system.

frequency alternating current from the DC to AC inverter. Output from the secondary winding is on the order of 150 to 300 volts; and, of course, that output is AC.

Rectifier

Solid state rectifiers, usually the silicon variety, convert medium voltage high frequency current from the step-up transformer to direct "B" current of approximately the same voltage. In effect, all of the components thus far described could be replaced by a single "B" battery of, say, 250 volts. Function of the inverter, transformer, and rectifier are simply to convert 12-volt battery current to direct current some 20 times higher in voltage.

Capacitor

As the system name implies, the energy storage capacitor is the heart of the CD ignition. It soaks up "B" power from the rectifier power supply and stores it at the 150 to 300 volt level, ready to be shot forward to the next component on demand. Usually, the capacitor is a bank of two capacitors, one having 5 to 10 times the capacity of the other. The large one is kept highly charged all the time, acting as a reservoir of power. The smaller one discharges its energy on demand, is then immediately recharged by the big one.

SCR Trigger

The silicon-controlled-rectifier is a gate or electronic switch which, when closed, blocks flow of "B" current from the storage capacitor to the pulse transformer. The SCR switch is easily opened and closed, its operation requiring very little signal energy. When closed, it presents an almost completely open circuit. When triggered, it flips the other way, presenting a low resistance path through which power can flow. It can be thought of as a relay, operable with little signal power, and able to open and close incredibly fast. As a matter of fact, in modern circuits of other kinds, SCRs often replace relays.

Pulse Transformer

Replacing the ordinary ignition coil (and usually called a "coil" itself) the pulse transformer converts "B" voltage to extremely high ignition potential. When the SCR, acting as a trigger, snaps shut the circuit between capacitor and pulse transformer, there is a surge of current. Hitting the pulse transformer's primary winding like an electric hammer, the rush of current from the capacitor induces a blast of hot spark from the secondary winding. Compared to ordinary spark, the whap of voltage from the pulse transformer builds up much faster, and decays quicker. The sudden intensity of spark gives the system its ability to fire fouled-up spark plugs. Because the standard system's voltage builds up more slowly, it can leak across the fouling before it has time to jump. The CD system's quick rise time, however, forces the spark to jump before there is time for leak-off of voltage.

The Timer

Breaker points comprise the timer in the standard system. In the CD circuitry, the timer may be a point-set, a rotating magnet, a light beam and photo-cell, or a proximity switch.

In the capacitor-discharge system, the points, or whatever timing device is selected, handle only a weak current, it being in the milliampere range as contrasted with the several amperes which the conventional point-set interrupts. Result of low current in the CD's timer is extended life and reduction in required maintenance.

The small timing signal generated by the timer, breaker points, magnetics, or whatever, is transmitted to the "grid" or trigger in the SCR, and the SCR fires allowing the capacitor charge to surge into the coil's primary as described. The timer is advanced and retarded by mechanical or vacuum means, the same as in the conventional ignition system.

A popular "pointless" timing system uses a magnet, slotted disc, and a pick-up coil. The disc, with a slot for each engine cylinder, rotates at half crankshaft speed, in a 4-cycle engine, and is interposed between the magnet and coil. As one of the slots rotates into position between the magnet and winding, the latter senses the lines of force and generates a blip of current. The blip is transmitted to the silicon controlled rectifier, the SCR triggers, and a rush of "B" voltage is thrust into the pulse transformer. Spark flashes immediately.

In the capacitor discharge ignition system, the distributor proper, rotor and cap, are relatively conventional. Often they are manufactured of a higher grade plastic than is customary in standard units because they must withstand the electrical stress generated by fierce voltage spikes.

An Interesting Experiment

The reader, having a little shop and an interest in electrical puttering, can simulate a capacitor discharge ignition system from his junk box. Figure 10-12 shows the principle of the thing.

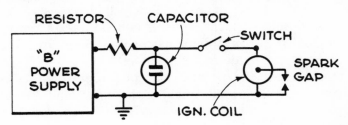

Fig. 10-12 Mock-up of CD ignition will throw a spark when switch is closed. The switch simulates timing points.

Use any conventional ignition coil for the demonstration, a capacitor rated to match or exceed the "B" voltage, and some kind of "B" voltage supply, preferably between 100 and 250 volts. The resistor between the power supply and capacitor simply protects the supply against surges, and might be something like 500 ohms. Value of capacitor can be experimented with. You can try anything from 0.5 to 25 microfarads.

With the rig set up as shown, energize the "B" supply; then close the switch which simulates the SCR in a real system. You will get a whap of spark across the gap. For fun, experiment with various size capacitors. But a word of caution: Don't get bitten by the spark. And always give the spark a gap through which to jump to ground. Should you open-circuit the high voltage termination, the hot spark may arc-over inside the coil, and ruin the coil in doing so.

SYNOPSIS

Starting with the switch, and continuing through the ballast and coil's primary winding to the points, the ignition primary circuit is energized by battery voltage. When the points "break," interrupting primary current flow, high spark voltage is induced in the coil's secondary winding. The "coil" is actually a transformer.

High voltage from the secondary winding is conducted to the center of the distributor cap. From there it flows to the rotor which distributes timed high-voltage spurts of spark to the plugs in correct sequence.

Point clearance determines dwell, which increases as clearance decreases. Dwell, in turn, controls coil saturation time at any given engine speed. In systems having dual-point arrangements, dwell interval can be desirably extended.

Shunted across the points, the condenser provides a low-impedance path to ground, making the coil "ring" or resonate when the points suddenly open. Without a condenser in the system, spark will be very feeble.

As the engine speeds up, spark is automatically advanced to fire earlier in the cycle. Advance may be effected centrifugally, or by vacuum, or both.

Capacitor-discharge ignition converts battery voltage to "B" voltage and stores this in a capacitor. Acting as a gate or trigger, a silicon-controlled-rectifier, on signal from the points or other kind of timer, dumps a charge of capacitor energy into the "coil" or pulse transformer which generates high voltage. The high voltage is then distributed to the plugs in correct firing order.

CHAPTER 11

Tuning the Ignition

WHEN A marine engine loses power, accelerates grudgingly, starts with difficulty, and generally acts tired, chances are its ignition needs tuning. With a grasp of ignition fundamentals, the specifications, a few parts and tools, you can do a very respectable tuning job yourself. Rounding up and enticing a really good ignition mechanic aboard your boat is often a tougher job than doing the tune-up yourself. So why not try your hand at this most frequently needed electrical job?

Fundamentals

Ignition fundamentals were discussed at some length in the previous chapter. Review them, if you like, keeping in mind the function of each component: switch, ballast, coil, points, condenser, rotor, distributor cap, and spark plugs. These are the parts you will be manicuring.

Specifications

Before tackling the ignition, try very hard to get the specs on spark plug tightening torque, initial timing, point clearance, plug electrode gap clearance, and point dwell. If you find it impossible to get these data on your marine engine, attempt to find out on what automobile or truck engine the marine unit is based. Then see if you can get the specs on that machine. Lacking the specs, it is possible to do a reasonably good tune, provided you use some ingenuity and employ your "engine-ear." But on the whole it is most rewarding to work according to the good book.

Parts

Get everything on hand before tackling the ignition's innards. To do a really complete job, purchase new points, condenser, distributor cap, rotor, and high-voltage wiring harness. There's a possibility you may need a new ballast resistor, too, if the old one is corroded and seedy looking.

Tools

The right tools make otherwise difficult jobs easy. For ignition tune-up, you should have the following implements:

- Set of miniature "ignition" wrenches.
- Pair of long-nosed pliers.
- Several small screwdrivers.
- Set of feeler thickness gauges.
- Spark plug adjusting tool with gauges.
- Point file.
- Torque wrench.
- Dwell meter.
- Timing light.

The reader may throw up his hands and say, "I can't afford to buy a dwell meter and timing light for the few tune-ups I do per year; that's extravagant!"

But it is not extravagant. Consider that you pay from $25 to $50 for the labor on a thorough ignition tune-up for each occurrence. You can buy a good dwell meter under $35, and a timing light under $30. After your second tune-up, you are ahead of the game. What's more, having the tuning tools on hand, you are undoubtedly going to check on the ignition more frequently, and will tune more often. You will find that your dwell meter and timing light will be among your most frequently borrowed tools, proving, sir, that most boatmen should own these important instruments. (A side issue is that you'll probably end up tuning your automobile, as well—saving more money.)

Incidentally, the Heath Company, Benton Harbor, Michigan, sells engine tuning instruments in kit form, and they are excellent tools at a modest price.

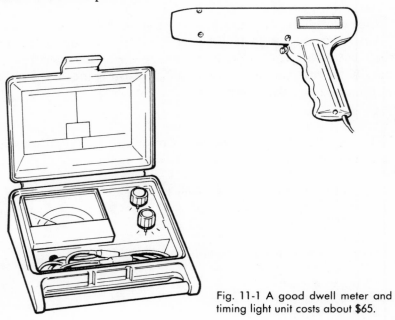

Fig. 11-1 A good dwell meter and timing light unit costs about $65.

Inspect the Switch

While you are puttering around the switch, trace the wires, making sure they are secure, well insulated, and free of fraying. Replace conductors which appear ratty; and trace through to the ballast.

Look at the Ballast Resistor

Wired between the ignition switch and coil in the primary circuit, the ballast must be fresh looking and free of corrosion. Its terminals must be clean and tight. If it fails to meet these criteria, best plan is to replace it. It is not a costly item.

182

After checking through the wiring, switch, and ballast, run the engine a short time to be sure all's well. As a matter of procedure, it is smart to run the engine after each adjustment or replacement. Then, should the machine refuse to start or if it runs poorly, you will know what particular part or adjustment causes the trouble; and you will not have to go trouble-shooting the entire system to find the root of the malfunction.

Change the Plugs

You have been working through the primary system toward the distributor. Now, before you attack the distributor's innards, turn to the spark plugs a few minutes.

Fig. 11-2 Measuring spark plug gap is done with a wire-type feeler gauge.

Brush, blow, or vacuum all the dust and dirt out of the spark plug recesses. Remove the old plugs. Using a feeler gauge, gap the new spark plugs to specification; don't simply install them fresh from the carton without adjustment. If you do not have the specification, adjust the gaps to 0.030". Put a little oil or grease on the new threads, and install the plugs, being careful not to start them cross-threaded. Use your torque wrench and tighten them to the specified tightness. If you don't know the specification, tighten to 25 pound-feet.

Start and run the engine.

183

Install New Points and Condenser

Carefully open up the distributor by removing the cap. Many caps are held in place with spring clips; some are fastened with two screws.

Take out the rotor. Some simply push on to the distributor shaft, others, shaped more like a wheel, are retained by two screws. In either case, removal is easy; but be careful not to drop the screws down in the bottom of the distributor where you will have a devil of a time retrieving them.

Note exactly how the point-set is installed, and how it is wired. Then remove both the points and condenser. Install the fresh components exactly as the old ones came out. Work carefully,

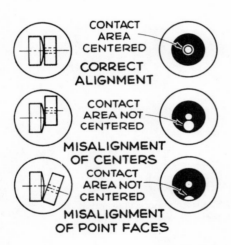

CONTACT AREA CENTERED
CORRECT ALIGNMENT

CONTACT AREA NOT CENTERED
MISALIGNMENT OF CENTERS

CONTACT AREA NOT CENTERED
MISALIGNMENT OF POINT FACES

Fig. 11-3 Correctly installed, the breaker points "kiss" at centers.

being alert not to bend or distort the moving point arm. After installing the points, examine the way they seat together. The two contact surfaces should be concentric and square with each other. If there is a misalignment, very carefully bend the pivoted point, as required, to bring the points into true relationship. You want the centers of the contacts to kiss straight-on; see Fig. 11-3.

Adjust Point Clearance

With the new points correctly in place, you will set the clearance. This is the spacing between the point contact surfaces when the points are wide open; and this spacing directly effects dwell and timing.

Slowly rotate the engine by hand or by bumping with the starter until the point's cam follower is on top of a cam lobe. The points are now open to their widest possible position. You will see that the fixed contact is adjustable in some manner, allowing it to be shifted to increase or decrease the point clearance. Using a feeler gauge, carefully adjust the points until the clearance is as specified in engine specs. Then tighten the set screw, if one is provided.

Calculating Point Clearance

By far, it is best to adjust to the clearance specified by the engine manufacturer. However, if, despite your best efforts, you can't find the specification, you can hit it fairly closely by the following procedure:

1. Nudge the engine over until the breaker point cam follower is centered on a flat between two cam lobes. The points are now closed.

2. Without moving the cam, adjust the points to exactly zero clearance. Now, the points are just kissing, and the cam follower is also touching a flat on the cam. The most minute rotation of the shaft will start to open the points.

3. Slowly rotate the engine until the points are wide open, the cam follower being on top of a lobe. You have now opened the points to absolute maximum possible clearance.

4. Use a feeler gauge, measure the maximum clearance. On a typical eight-cylinder distributor it might be, say, 0.028".

5. Select *half,* or a little more than half, of absolute maximum as your operating clearance. For the eight-cylinder distributor cited in (4) above, this would be from 0.014" to 0.017".

Set the Dwell

Button up the distributor, not forgetting to install the new rotor. Run the engine. Hook up your dwell meter in accordance with its instructions. Idle the engine and watch the dwell.

- If dwell is too great, increase point clearance.
- If dwell is too small, decrease point clearance.

Dwell by Rule of Thumb

Naturally, you will set the dwell to that recommended by the engine maker. However, if it is impossible to find the specification, you can proceed by a general rule; chances are you will be fairly close to home base. For conventional four-stroke-cycle engines, use the following dwells:

Four-cylinders: 54°
Six-cylinders: 36°
Eight-cylinders: 27°

The suggested dwell angles are based upon the points remaining closed for saturation 60% of the time, and open for 40%. If the distributor has a dual-point, single-coil, system, the eight-cylinder dwell may be increased to 34°. At any rate, there is nothing sacred about these exact dwells because different cam shapes demand modified dwells. But the given angles should make the engine well and happy.

Closed Time	Dwell exposed in degrees		
	4-Cyl	6-Cyl	8-Cyl
100%	90°	60°	45°
90%	81°	54°	40.5°
80%	72°	48°	36°
70%	63°	42°	31.5°
60%	54°	36°	27°
50%	45°	30°	22.5°
40%	36°	24°	18°
30%	27°	18°	13.5°
20%	18°	12°	9°
10%	9°	6°	4.5°

Fig. 11-4 Table shows relationship of percentage dwell time to dwell, in degrees.

In custom distributors having two point sets and two ignition coils, each set firing four cylinders, the dwell is adjusted as for a 4-cylinder engine. Each point set is given dwell of 50° to 60°.

Re-Time the Engine

After the points are replaced and adjusted, the engine must be re-timed. This is so because any change in point clearance and dwell alters the timing.

The initial (idling speed) timing on modern engines is usually somewhere between top-center and 10° before top-center; and this adjustment is one of the most critical that you will make in your tuning program. Set the timing "by the book," avoiding the temptation to wander too far from the specifications. Should you advance the spark excessively, cylinder pressures will be overly high, the engine may knock, will run rough, and may well be damaged. If you adjust the spark in retard, on the other hand, the engine will lose pep, may overheat, and may burn its exhaust valves.

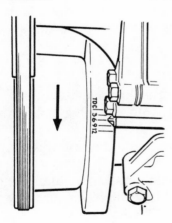

Fig. 11-5 These are typical timing marks on belt drive of engine. Timing is shown five degrees before top center.

Run the engine at idle, pointing the timing light at the appropriate marks on the rotating member and stationary pointer. Considering the direction of rotation, if the rotating mark appears "early," retard the spark by rotating the distributor in the direction of its shaft rotation. Do the opposite if the spark is "late." Once you're hooked up and ready, re-timing of the engine is the work of but a few minutes. However, avoid using the timing light in bright sunlight. Doing so obscures the strobe effect, making it difficult to see the spinning timing marks. Work in a subdued light, and scribe a thin white chalk line on the timing marks before starting the engine.

Check the Advance

After you are satisfied with the adjustment of the initial timing, determined at idle speed, test the advance. With the strobe light directed at the timing marks, speed up the engine. The light should show ignition timing advancing with speed. Usually, the advance will start at about 1,000 rpm, and continue until the engine has accelerated, reaching some 2,000 to 2,500 rpm, at which speed full advance will be achieved.

Finding Top-Center

On a few marine engines, particularly older ones, you will search in vain for any indication of timing marks either on the flywheel, vibration damper, or generator drive pulley where they are customarily found. If this happens, create your own top-center mark as follows:

1. Remove the spark plugs.
2. Carefully insert some kind of straight feeler such as a pencil, screwdriver, or piece of rod into the plug hole of number 1 cylinder.
3. Crank the engine slowly clockwise until the piston is felt to be at its highest rise in the cylinder.
4. Now, rotate the engine, continuing clockwise, until the piston descends about one half inch. Mark the feeler carefully at a point exactly flush with the spark plug hole boss.
5. Mark the flywheel or crankshaft-mounted V-belt pulley at some point in alignment with a fixed pointer on the engine block.
6. Rotate the engine counterclockwise to where the piston is at highest rise, and *continue* going counterclockwise slowly until the piston descends to where the feeler mark is exactly flush with the spark plug boss, (at one half inch descent).

7. Mark the flywheel at the fixed pointer on the engine block.

8. You now have two marks. Halfway between those marks is top-dead center of number 1 piston. Mark that point carefully; then repeat the routine several times for increased accuracy.

Install New Cap and High Voltage Wires

Before removing the old distributor cap and spark plug wires, note carefully which distributor wire goes to what plug. Make a simple sketch to help you reassemble the wires correctly. Now, remove the old distributor cap and all the plug wires. Before installing the new cap, spray a mist of ignition moisture repellent, such as CRC, in the cap. Install the cap and wires; spray the exterior with moisture repellent; spray the high voltage wires, the plugs, and the ignition coil. A thin coat of moisture inhibitor coating the entire high voltage system will help a great deal toward easy starts on damp mornings when moisture tends to condense on the cool engine.

Run the engine.

General Suggestions

• After completing the tune-up, recheck every nut, bolt, screw, and adjustment, making sure that all is secure.

• Following the tune job, and after the engine has operated something like 15 hours, give the dwell and timing a follow-up test. Sometimes, in the first few hours of use, while the point's cam follower is seating itself, the clearance will decrease, dwell will increase, and, as a result, ignition timing will become retarded. If you readjust dwell and timing after the first 15 hours, the adjustments should remain in spec for the following one or two hundred hours.

• When working on a powerful engine, one difficult to crank, remove the spark plugs, relieving compression and making the engine easier to rotate while you are working on the points.

• Adjust new spark plug gaps on the small side of specification tolerance. As the plugs are used, the gap will grow.

• If, after the engine is re-timed, it knocks or pings at advanced throttle, retard the spark just enough to eliminate the trouble. Do so while using the kind and brand of gasoline you customarily buy.

• Should the engine idle rough, hard, and fast, after it is re-timed, try retarding the spark a little. However, do not retard the spark too much or the engine will be lazy at high speed, and may suffer from overheated exhaust valves.

For Your Log Book

Cruisers maintained Bristol fashion sometimes have an engine room log, having entries kept up-to-date by the boatkeeper. If you are one of those keeping a technical log, you might want to enter all or part of the following data in the book. It will be most useful for future tuning jobs or for trouble-shooting, should that unpleasant chore ever become necessary.

1. Date, engine-hours, and jobs done during tune-up.
2. Dwell and point clearance.
3. Plug gap and tightening torque.
4. Initial timing at idle.
5. Engine rpm required to give full advance.
6. Primary current flow, key on, points closed, engine stopped.
7. Primary current flow at fast idle.
8. Resistance of the ballast when cold.
9. Resistance of coil primary, and coil secondary when cold.

SYNOPSIS

Having the correct specifications, parts, and tools is important; and a timing light and dwell meter are a great help. Engine electrical tune-up includes inspection and adjustment of ignition switch, ballast, plugs, points, condenser, and wiring, as well as the distributor cap and rotor. Work includes installation of new parts, plus adjustment of timing, dwell, and advance.

CHAPTER 12

Electrical Trouble-Shooting on the Engine

ALAS, DESPITE the best maintenance and most loving tune-up, the gasoline marine engine is known sometimes to quit, run rough, or refuse to start at all. Electrical troubles are more common in the marine power plant than in the auto engine because the yacht's machinery is beset by nature's tougher opposition.

The most obvious enemy is the wet environment in which the marine engine lives, and we all know that electrons and dampness simply don't cotton to each other. The second adversary is lack of use. Most recreational small craft are used only on weekends, except during the owner's vacation, and are laid up when the season is over, decommissioned for months on end. Infrequent use, supplemented by periods of idleness, invites rust, corrosion, and dampness penetration, all three of which attack the electrical system.

When a marine engine fails to perk, simply refusing to start, chances are nine to one that the trouble is electrical, and not in the fuel or compression system. Once running, but performing badly, the chances are still 7 to 1 that electrical malfunction is at the seat of the trouble. Consequently, if you flush out the electrical gremlins, odds are that you will cure the malady.

In this chapter are found a variety of electrical engine troubles.

In some cases, there is a simple listing of possible causes, the cures being obvious. In other instances, commentary is intended to be helpful in pointing up the cure for a specific trouble.

Starter Will Not Try to Rotate

If the starter refuses to struggle, hum, or show any sign of trying to rotate when you close the starter switch, do these things, stopping when you locate the trouble:

1. With starter switch closed, test for battery voltage on the battery terminals with test light or voltmeter.

2. Clean the battery posts and cable clamps. Test for voltage at the solenoid switch. Make sure the ground strap is ok.

3. Test for voltage on the starter side of the solenoid.

4. Test for voltage at the starter terminal.

5. If there is voltage all the way to the starter terminal, between terminal and engine block, make sure the starter is tightly mounted to the engine. Its ground-return connection is through its hold-down bolts and flange.

6. If starter still fails to respond, remove it for bench repair.

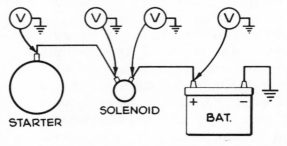

Fig. 12-1 With start switch closed, voltmeter or test light should indicate adequate voltage at the points shown.

Starter Struggles; Won't Rotate

1. If the starter won't crank the engine, or does so very slowly and with protest, test battery voltage with meter or test light while the starter struggles. Dim test light probably means battery needs attention. On a 12-volt system, potential below seven volts spells trouble.

2. If battery seems ok, check all cable connections: clean posts and clamps.

3. If voltage at starter terminals is almost equal to that at battery terminals, and if this voltage is seven to eight volts or more on a 12-volt system, while the starter struggles, the starter is probably defective. But before taking action, be sure there is no mechanical problem. Try this: Remove the spark plugs and see if the engine will then crank. If it has a cylinder locked with water, this procedure will clear it.

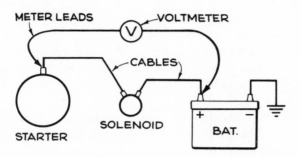

Fig. 12-2 When the starter operates, voltage drop from battery hot terminal to starter terminal should be but a fraction of a volt.

Engine Starts; Immediately Quits

If the engine fires, runs a few seconds, but stops as soon as you release the starter switch, look to the ballast resistor. If the ballast is open circuited, the ignition may be energized by an auxiliary starting shunt during the start period, but will be killed as soon as the start switch is opened.

Engine Cranks but Won't Fire

This is the most common of all troubles. When the engine fails to start after a few seconds of cranking, stop and find the trouble before wearing down the battery with fruitless grinding of the starter.

1. Find if the coil is throwing spark. Hold the high-voltage wire from the coil about a quarter of an inch from the engine block. Crank the engine. There should be spark.

2. Assuming there is no spark. Do as follows: Unbutton the distributor and make sure the points are opening and closing with shaft rotation. Close the points. Open and close the points with your finger. Each time they open, there should be a spark from the coil's high-voltage wire to ground. If there is no spark, check:

a. The moving point for being short-circuited to ground, or corroded.

b. The condenser, by substitution.

c. All primary circuit wiring, by inspection and trouble light.

d. The ignition coil by substitution.

[Now, let's backtrack. Suppose that in Step 1 you found hot spark coming from the coil. Then proceed as follows to assure that this spark from the coil is conducted to the spark plugs:]

3. After rehooking the main high-voltage wire to the distributor's hot connection, remove a wire from one spark plug, holding the end a quarter of an inch from the ground. With the ignition switch on, crank the engine. Spark should jump from wire to ground.

a. If spark *does* jump, remove and service the spark plugs; the trouble may be there.

b. If spark *does not* jump, you have determined that there is high voltage from the coil to distributor, but no voltage from distributor to plugs. Therefore, the spark is being grounded on either the distributor cap or rotor.

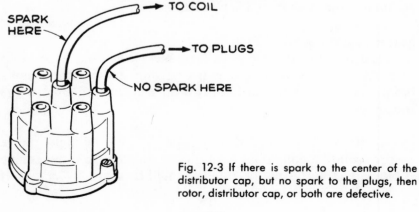

Fig. 12-3 If there is spark to the center of the distributor cap, but no spark to the plugs, then rotor, distributor cap, or both are defective.

4. Open the distributor; remove the rotor and cap. Inspect both for cracks, breaks or chips. Wipe them dry, or, if possible, bake them in an oven at about 200°F for a quarter of an hour. Make sure they are bone dry. Spray them both with moisture repellent such as CRC, misting the cap both inside and out.

5. Try the spark test at the plugs again. If there is still no spark, and if the plug wires are bone dry, you are due to install a new cap and rotor.

Starter Spins; Won't Crank Engine

Some starter drives require sudden acceleration to force the small starter pinion into mesh with the flywheel ring gear. This kind of starter will sometimes wind up to speed, but fail to engage for any one of the following reasons:

1. Low battery voltage.

2. Dirty, corroded connections to battery cables at one or both ends.

3. Poor contact in starter solenoid.

4. Poor contact between starter mounting flanges and engine block.

5. Rusted, dirty pinion gear drive mechanism, preventing pinion from advancing on its shaft.

Stalling at Idle

This kind of stall has nothing to do with carburetion. As the ignition system "ages," and the point clearance decreases, there comes a state where at idle the points no longer completely open. The engine quits when the throttle is closed. The remedy is to tune the ignition, adjusting points to correct dwell.

Popping-Back

Backfiring through the carburetor, especially when the engine is cool and is being accelerated, is caused by retarded ignition timing. Remedy is to advance the spark.

Spark-Knock

Detonation, or pinging, sometimes called "knock," is invited by overly-advanced ignition timing. Cure is to retard the spark. The assumption is made that the engine is not overheated, overloaded, or being operated on poor gasoline.

High-Speed Miss
Look into the following:

1. Improper dwell.
2. Fouled or improperly adjusted spark plugs.
3. Cracked ceramic insulator on one or more plugs.
4. Weak spring in the ignition point-set.
5. Cross-firing due to high voltage ignition wires being tightly bunched or having poor insulation.
6. Loose wiring, poor connections in the primary or secondary circuits, or an intermittent ignition switch.

No Generator Output
If generator or alternator output is weak or non-existent, look into the following:

1. Broken or very loose V-belt.
2. Disconnected field or battery wires.
3. Defective regulator.
4. Defective diodes in the alternator.
5. Burned brushes in the conventional generator.

One way to isolate generator output trouble to the voltage regulator or generator is as follows:

a. On a conventional generator, disconnect the wire from regulator to generator field terminal. Run the engine at fast idle; then short-circuit the generator's field terminal to the grounded frame. If the generator is good, it will immediately put out, indicating that the regulator is defective. Don't run the generator for long with grounded field, however, or it will overheat.

b. On an alternator, disconnect the voltage regulator from the alternator. Use a jumper, and hook this in series between the battery hot (not ground) terminal and the rotor terminal frequently marked F, for field. This is the terminal which excites the alternator's rotor. If the alternator is good, it should put out when the rotor is excited, and the alternator is spinning at a good speed.

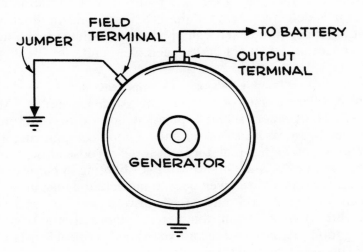

Fig. 12-4 Temporary jumper from field terminal to ground tests for output.

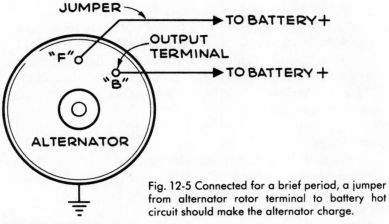

Fig. 12-5 Connected for a brief period, a jumper from alternator rotor terminal to battery hot circuit should make the alternator charge.

Reduced Alternator Output

If alternator output is somewhat low even when there are demands on the electrical system, one or more diode rectifiers may be open. If output is only half what it should be, there may be a short-circuited diode. An alternator with a shorted diode usually whines; and the singing is more noticeable at idle speed.

If trouble-shooting tests indicate that either the generator or alternator is defective, remove the offender from the boat and have it overhauled in a well-equipped shop. Voltage regulators, however, are usually replaced as a complete unit.

Trouble-Shooting of Components

Here is where a mite of foresight helps immeasurably. As a dedicated boatkeeper, spend a pleasant hour with your ohmmeter, making measurements on known good components. The information you gather may turn out to be a godsend next time the chips are down, and you are trouble-shooting in earnest.

Typical resistances are given here to indicate the magnitude of resistance expected, and may be a help when you are in a real pinch. But to make your ohmmeter a more useful trouble-shooting tool, measure and record your boat's critical resistances before you are in the heat of battle.

Always make your resistance measurements with the component disconnected from its circuits, and at room temperature.

Ignition Coil

Measure resistance between the two primary terminals: one to two ohms. Resistance between either primary terminal to the metal case should be infinite. Resistance of high-voltage winding, measured from "hot" terminal to either primary terminal will be between 5,000 and 10,000 ohms. Resistance from hot terminal to case should be infinite.

Spark Plugs

Resistance from hot terminal to shell: infinite. If there is any appreciable conductance, the plug is fouled.

Condenser

Set the ohmmeter on a high range such as X1,000 or X10,000. Touch one ohmmeter prod to the condenser's metal case, the other to the pigtail lead. As the test leads touch, the needle

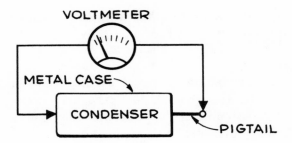

Fig. 12-6 A good distributor condenser will kick the voltmeter needle up-scale several minutes after the condenser has been charged to 100 volts.

should kick, then fall back to infinte. Reverse the leads. The needle should do the same, with an even greater kick. If the meter fails to kick, the condenser is open. If the meter shows a finite steady resistance, the condenser is leaky. Replace it.

If you have a source of 100 to 150 volts direct current, you can give the condenser a real acid test: Charge the condenser to that voltage by touching the case to one power source terminal, the pigtail to the other. Careful! Don't get bit. Set your volt ohmmeter to a voltage scale equal to, or higher than the charging voltage. Wait half a minute; then touch the meter test leads to the condenser's case and pigtail. The needle should kick up scale almost to the charged voltage. In fact, a good, dry, clean condenser will show a snappy voltage even after sitting idle for half an hour after charging.

Ballast Resistor

Be particularly careful to measure the ballast when it is at room temperature; its resistance increases with heat. Use the X1 scale, and the resistance should be barely readable, being on the order of 0.5 to two ohms for a 12-volt component.

Points

Resistance across the closed points should be zero, and across the open points should be infinite. Values from the grounded point to engine block must be zero, and from the hot, pivoted point to engine block, infinite. Wiggle the pivoted point with your finger when making that last test, and be sure all wiring is disconnected from the distributor.

Starter Relay

Solenoid coil in the starter relay, usually connected between the starter switch and ground, has extremely small resistance. Tested with an ohmmeter, a good solenoid coil will show a fraction of an ohm resistance.

Alternator

Beware the validity of resistance readings made on an alternator unless you have made the same measurements on the unit when in good condition. Various alternator designs have different internal hook-ups, making resistance quite different. So, make those measurements on a good unit while you can.

Typical resistance taken on a good Leece-Neville, 40 amp, 14-volt alternator, look something like this on the X1 scale of a common ohmmeter:

Battery (plus) terminal to ground is 40 ohms with meter test leads in one polarity, infinite resistance with test leads reversed. This shows the effect of the rectifier diodes. Field (rotor) terminal to ground is six ohms, showing the rotor winding and slip ring assembly is intact and terminate in the rectifiers.

However, when measurements are made in diode circuits, readings will change greatly from scale to scale on the ohmmeter. This is because a diode changes its conductivity with applied effective voltage. So, remember to use the same scale for all measurements, using the results only for a rough guide.

A 12-volt active test light, as described in Chapter 19, is useful for quick trouble-shooting of an alternator. Connected in one polarity between output (battery) terminal and ground, the light should glow. Connected in reversed polarity, it should extinguish. The same applies to the connections between output terminal and neutral. Connected in either polarity between ground and rotor (field) the light should glow.

SYNOPSIS

Because of the corrosive environment in which it lives, the

marine engine is subject to more ills than the auto engine. Many of those troubles are, of course, electrical.

Starter troubles can originate in the battery, cables, or switch. Hard starting is frequently traceable to ignition; and troubles at all speeds often originate with trouble in the points. Knock is eliminated by retarding the spark; high-speed miss frequently starts with bad plugs or crossfiring. Generator and alternator troubles can be separated from those spawned in the regulator by isolating the two systems. Each component can be tested with an ohmmeter as an aid to trouble-shooting.

CHAPTER 13

Taming Electrolytic Corrosion

BOATMEN OFTEN refer to galvanic corrosion as "electrolysis corrosion" or more often simply as "electrolysis." This old terminology is technically incorrect and is being phased out by such bodies as the American Boat and Yacht Council. There are two reasons for improving the terminology:

1. Electrolysis refers to chemical or electro-chemical changes in a liquid solution or electrolyte due to the passage of electricity. By inference alone does the word describe the effect of electrolysis on a metal submerged in the electrolyte.
2. Incorrectly used, the loose word "electrolysis" gets applied to matters related to stray-current corrosion; but the meaning is not specific. It is desirable, therefore, to adhere to the terminology adopted by standards making bodies.

Galvanic Corrision
Most boatmen are familiar with galvanic corrosion: It occurs when dissimilar metals are immersed in an electrolyte and are touching each other or are electrically connected by a conductor. Boating waters, both fresh and salt, are electrolytes, salt being the stronger of the two. Simply tie a strip of aluminum and a strip of copper together by wire, dunk the pair in your local waters,

and two things will happen: Electricity will flow through the wire; and the aluminum will corrode. By your experiment, you have both created a weak electric cell and generated corrosion.

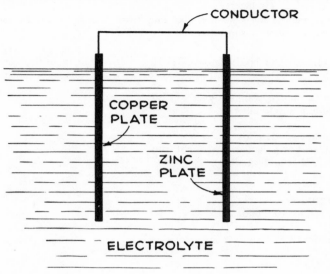

CONDUCTOR

COPPER
PLATE

ZINC
PLATE

ELECTROLYTE

Fig. 13-1 Electric current flows from plate to plate through the electrolyte, returning via the conductor. In the electrolytic process, the zinc plate is corroded.

In the above demonstration, the two metal plates are called electrodes, and the boating water is the electrolyte. Of the two metals, the least noble (aluminum) corrodes, while the more noble (copper) resists corrosion; and in the process, water is subjected to electrolysis.

Those Noble Metals

The least noble metals are active ones; and they corrode easily. Magnesium, aluminum, zinc are typical examples. These are called anodic and are electrically positive in polarity. The most noble metals are passive; they are electrically negative, said to be *cathodic* and having high corrosion resistance. Nickel, Inconel, and 18-8 stainless steel are popular examples of noble metals. The table in Figure 13-2 lists a series of maritime metals,

203

giving their relative order in the galvanic series in sea water. Least noble metals are at the top, most noble at the bottom in this tabulation made by the American Boat and Yacht Council.

Fig. 13-2 Prepared by the American Boat and Yacht Council, this table gives the galvanic series of metals in seawater.

ANODIC OR LEAST NOBLE—ACTIVE

Magnesium and magnesium alloys
CB75 aluminum anode alloy
Zinc
B605 aluminum anode alloy
Galvanized steel or galvanized wrought iron
Aluminum 7072 (cladding alloy)
Aluminum 5456
Aluminum 5086
Aluminum 5052
Aluminum 3003, 1100, 6061, 356
Cadmium
2117 aluminum rivet alloy
Mild steel
Wrought iron
Cast Iron
Ni-Resist
13% chromium stainless steel, type 410 (active)
50-50 lead tin solder
18-8 stainless steel, type 304 (active)
18-83% NO stainless steel, type 316 (active)
Lead
Tin
Muntz metal
Manganese bronze
Naval brass (60% copper—39% zinc)
Nickel (active)
78% Ni.-13.5% Cr.-6% Fe. (Inconel) (Active)
Yellow brass (65% copper—35% zinc)
Admiralty brass
Aluminum bronze
Red brass (85% copper—15% zinc)
Copper
Silicon bronze
   5% Zn.—20% Ni—75% Cu.
   90% Cu.—10% Ni.
   70% Cu.—30% Ni.
   88% CU. 27. Zn.—10% Sn. (composition G-bronze)
   88% Cu.—3% Zn.—6.5% Sn.—1.5% Pb (composition M-bronze)

Nickel (passive)
   78% Ni.—13.5% Cr.—6% Fe. (Inconel) (Passive)
   70% Ni.—30% Cu.
18-8 stainless steel type 304 (passive)
18-8 3% Mo. stainless steel, type 316 (passive)
Hastelloy C
Titanium
Platinum

CATHODIC OR MOST NOBLE—PASSIVE

Self-Corrosion
   In some instances, galvanic corrosion occurs in a single piece of hardware immersed in sea water and not in contact with a more noble item. Common red brass household screws offer an example. Non-marine brass is an alloy of zinc and copper, and the two are combined metallurgically in flake or crystal formation. When put in sea water, such brass corrodes rapidly: Electric current flows internally, near the surface, between the tiny bits of zinc and copper. Because it is less noble, the zinc is eaten away, and the remaining object is reduced to spongy copper.

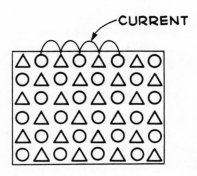

Fig. 13-3 Corrosion can occur when current flows between bits of copper and zinc in common yellow or red brass immersed in an electrolyte.

O = ZINC BIT

△ = COPPER BIT

   The above explains why you must not use ordinary land-lubber brass bolts and screws as marine fastenings. Monel, stainless steel, or copper are much better. Even good, hot-galvanized iron fittings will inevitably outlast kitchenware brass ones.

Environmental Effects

Increase in either water temperature or salinity increases the rate and severity of galvanic corrosion. Deterioration also increases as water pollution gets worse and as the adjacent metals are more dissimilar on the galvanic scale. Not surprisingly, corrosion abates when water temperature, salinity, and pollution decrease. It is also reduced when the metals are galvanically similar, when they are insulated from each other, and when they are physically separated to the maximum possible distance.

Prevention

There are four important ways the boatkeeper can prevent or reduce galvanic corrosion:

1. Fasten underwater hardware with screws, nuts and bolts of the most noble metal practicable. Join underwater parts with fastenings equal to or more noble than the basic part. Should electrolysis now occur, the fastening will be protected at the possible expense of the heavier hardware; but the boat will not suffer because of hardware failure. A fraction of an ounce of metal eaten away from the heavy hardware probably won't hurt anything. But that same weight of metal corroded from a smaller, more highly stressed fastening, may spell major trouble.

2. Paint underwater hardware with vinyl or other plastic, non-metallic paint. Acting as an insulator, paint will suppress current flow and reduce galvanic action. Avoid brushing metallic-base, anti-foul paints on underwater hardware such as propellers, rudders, and struts. Usually, the metal in the paint will react with the base metal, and the paint will not adhere well, nor will it act as an anti-foulant.

3. Insulate dissimilar underwater metals where possible so no current can flow from one to the other except through the water. This is usually difficult because of conductivity inside the wet hull. In that event, take the opposite tack and bond all underwater fittings with heavy wire (#8 gauge or heavier) and protect the entire system cathodically as later described.

4. Offer cathodic protection to all underwater fittings, both individually and collectively. This suggestion is made last because it is important and warrants considerable expansion.

Cathodic Protection

Galvanic anodes, usually zinc, or battery operated impressed current systems should be installed on any boat having underwater hardware. A possible exception is the trailered boat, used but a few hours a week, and stored dry. But on moored boats, good cathodic protection, intelligently installed, will reduce galvanic corrosion to the vanishing point. It will not, however, eliminate *stray-current corrosion;* but we will discuss that in later paragraphs.

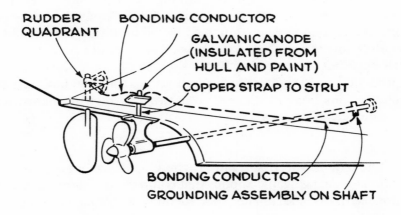

Fig. 13-4 ABYC suggests this anode arrangement on a non-metallic hull. Note that the anode is unpainted.

When you fasten a mass of zinc to a plate of copper or bronze and immerse the assembly in boating water, electric current flows from one metal to the other through the water, returning to the first metal through the metal. In this example, because zinc is the less noble, it will assume positive polarity and become the circuit's anode. The copper plate will become negative, forming a cathode to which the current flows through the water. Here we have an electric cell in which the zinc will corrode and deteriorate while the copper will be protected.

The practical effect of attaching zinc to a copper or bronze plate is that we sacrifice the zinc and protect the plate. This is a typical way of protecting a metal rudder.

But note carefully: If the zinc is to protect the plate, it must make good electric contact with it, and must be dunked in the same body of water.

For example, to protect a propeller strut, the zinc can be firmly attached to the hardware making secure electrical contact. Alternatively, but not as desirable, the zinc anode can be attached to the fiberglass or wood hull, a wire or strap electrically connecting it to the strut. The electrical circuit between the zinc anode and the hardware it is supposed to protect must be complete or the zinc will do nothing. You can attach as many anodes as you like to the bottom of your boat, but they will protect nothing unless connected to the hardware electrically.

Probably the easiest way to protect underwater gear, is to tie it all together electrically: Bond such items as rudders, struts, propeller, prop shaft, through-hull fittings, and the hull's ground plate. Thus bonded, the entire network is then protected with adequate zinc masses.

Anodes

The American Boat and Yacht Council suggests that you purchase zinc galvanic anodes that conform to Military Specification MIL-A-18001. The spec defines a balanced alloy that corrodes at a relatively uniform rate without forming a crust which would reduce efficiency in later life.

Attaching Anodes

The best anode is of limited efficiency if not correctly attached to the metal it is supposed to protect. Herein lies the weak point of many commercial anodes: These simply have holes through which the mechanic passes screws and attaches the anode to the hardware. This is satisfactory when the anode is new; but after some weeks of corroding, the drilled holes are eaten away. They expand, and, as a result, the fastening becomes loose and sloppy.

Obviously, electrical resistance is increased between anode and hardware, with resulting reduction in protection. Better zincs are made with a cast-in galvanized iron or steel insert. Making intimate contact with the anode, this insert is tightened to the hardware, assuring longer useful anode life.

Anode Area

What area of anode is required to protect specific hardware? That depends upon composition of the underwater metal, water temperature, salinity, and paint condition. However, a good general rule is given in Military Specification MIL-A-818001:

One square inch of quality zinc anode will protect 800 square inches of freshly-painted steel, or 250 square inches of bare steel or bare aluminum alloy. A square inch of good anode will protect about 100 square inches of copper or copper marine alloy. However, when the boat is underway, the protection ratio is reduced; more anode area is required to maintain the same degree of protection. For this reason, it is wise, where feasible, to use a somewhat greater area than indicated by the general rule. Anodes are not that expensive.

Don't Paint

"Protect the zinc and ruin the hardware," might be a way to state it: Never paint the boat's anodes, because paint will act as an insulator, substantially reducing the zinc's efficiency. Each time you paint your boat's bottom, install fresh anodes. If you have the work done by a yard, specify what anodes you want installed; and inspect the job before the hull goes overboard. Make particularly sure about how the anodes are fastened, and, naturally, see that they are bright and unpainted.

Extra Dockside Protection

Most boats spend a great percentage of their time tied to the pier or resting at a mooring; consequently, most corrosion takes place while the boat is idle. Fortunately, it is easy and cheap to increase dockside protection against corrosion; and several marine suppliers sell portable anodes for the purpose. One of these, called "Guppy," is fashioned of zinc, in the shape of a fish:

Fastened to a heavy wire, the anode is dangled over the boat's side and into the water while the boat lies idle. At the other end of the conducting cable there is a clamp, and this is gripped onto the boat's power plant or other component of the bonded system. The portable anode then does yeoman's duty protecting the boat's underwater hardware, propeller, rudder, and the like. Not only does the extra anode protect the underpinnings, but it also greatly extends the useful life of the permanently installed zincs.

Protecting the Prop

By all means, protect the propeller against corrosion; but avoid fastening shaft collar anodes around the propeller shaft close ahead of the wheel itself. Zinc shaft collars disturb the water's laminar flow, may decrease prop efficiency or even create cavitation. If you do use a collar-type anode, fasten it on the prop shaft, as far forward as possible, close to where the shaft emerges from the hull.

In arrangements where you protect the propeller and shaft by a remote anode, you must provide special bonding between anode and shaft. It is not safe to depend on the electrical conductivity between the power plant, flange couplings, and prop shaft. Conductivity between engine and shaft is unreliable. The way to overcome this is to install a brush, wiper, or sliding contact to bear on the rotating shaft. Then, using adequate size wire, electrically connect the sliding contact to the boat's bonding system. The propeller and its shaft will now be at the same electrical potential as the remainder of the bonded system.

Bottom Paints

Many bottom anti-foul paints contain copper or mercury and are electrically conductive. Regarding the interaction between such paints and anti-corrosion anodes, ABYC states:

"Where galvanic anodes are mounted on bottom paints that may have conductive elements, or where there is a possibility of paint damage in the anode area due to high current density, the anodes should be insulated from direct contact with the paint by a suitable nonconductive coating or gasket." Insulation of the anode from the paint should not interrupt the electrical continuity of the anode with the metals being protected.

Steel Boats

Boats with steel hulls may be protected by zinc, aluminum or magnesium anodes attached tightly against the steel bottom. ABYC points out that steel hulls should usually have anode protection both forward and aft. Non-metallic hulls, with most of the exposed hardware aft, usually require protection aft only.

Aluminum Boats

Corrosion protection of aluminum boats presents a special case where the protection must be more carefully controlled than on boats of other materials. Aluminum is unusual, being amphoteric,—having both acid and basic properties. It must be neither under nor overprotected, whereas other metals can be overprotected and suffer little harm.

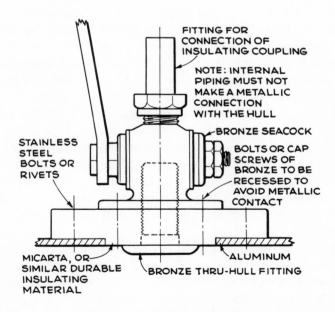

Fig. 13-5 Sketch shows suggested method of attaching bronze seacock to an aluminum hull to minimize corrosion. The fitting is insulated from the hull.

For boats with aluminum hulls, cathodic protection must be controlled more closely than for hulls of other metals. ABYC suggests the use of aluminum or zinc sacrificial anodes. Magnesium anodes are not normally recommended. The underlying thought is that magnesium, improperly applied, may overprotect the aluminum hull and damage it.

Underwater parts of bronze or of other metal more noble than aluminum must be well insulated from electrical contact with the aluminum hull; otherwise the hull will be sacrificed to the hardware. Insulation of bronze parts minimizes galvanic activity between hull and hardware. Through-hull fittings such as seacocks may be mounted through insulating ferrules or washers of nonconducting material. Shafts and rudder posts should be insulated from the hull; then these may be protected separately from the aluminum hull.

Impressed Current Systems

Protective systems of the kind described, using metal anodes, generate their own current, and in a sense are passive. These systems work well, within limits, provided the anodes are replaced regularly and are kept clean.

Impressed current systems, as the name implies, use an outside source of current, doing the same or a better job, and requiring no anode replacement.

One, two, or even more anodes are attached to the hull below the waterline. The anodes, however, instead of being easily corroded zinc or magnesium, are platinum coated. They are very noble, indeed, and do not corrode. The anode needs not be chemically active, and does not have to corrode, because the boat's battery raises its potential, more than simulating the activity of a freely-corroding anode, and protecting the boat's hardware.

A typical impressed current system comprises three principal components: controller, anode, and reference sensor or electrode. Sensing corrosion potential in the water, the reference electrode transmits this information electrically to the controller. Then the controller, drawing power from the boat's battery, applies required current to the anode. In response, current

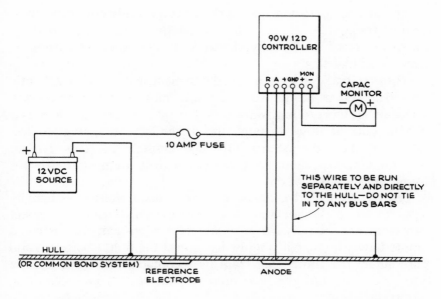

Fig. 13-6 Impressed current system uses battery voltage to protect hull and hardware against corrosion. Reference electrode senses current amplitude for protection. In response, controller applies positive voltage to the anode, making hull and hardware cathodic, immune from rust and corrosion. The monitor indicates system condition.

flows from the anode, through the water, to the otherwise unprotected underwater hardware, which is cathodic.

On boats of ordinary size, battery drain is all but negligible, being on the order of a few hundredths of an ampere. Anode corrosion is practically nil because of platinum's great corrosion resistance. Most impressed current systems are designed for negatively grounded boats because that is the standard grounding system. While this type system is for sizable inboard boats, in the main, several of the outboard and outdrive manufacturers are offering impressed current systems to protect the lower units of sterndrives and larger outboard motors.

STRAY-CURRENT CORROSION

Referring to stray-current corrosion, an engineer recently said, "It is a real hardware wrecker. It is the black beast that can ruin a boat from the waterline down, in nothing flat. A severe case of stray current corrosion makes ordinary galvanic corrosion look almost friendly."

Strong talk? Not really; because stray-current corrosion is generated like this:

Through bad design or a mistake in electrical wiring, the boat's electrical system has its wires crossed. Impressed voltage on one piece of submerged hardware is higher than on another; and as a result, current flows through the water from one item to the other. If the circumstances are bad enough, currents can be several amperes, and an otherwise sturdy item of hardware ruined in a matter of days.

Stray-current corrosion is scary; but fortunately it is usually easy to trouble-shoot and cure. If you have reason to suspect stray-current activity in a boat, corrosion can be arrested immediately if you will simply disconnect the boat's batteries and disconnect the shore plug from its receptacle. This will kill the stray currents and give you time to plan your trouble-shooting program.

Crossed grounds, voltage drop in a circuit, and alternating current leakage from the "housecurrent system" to ground are the most frequent offenders causing stray-current corrosion.

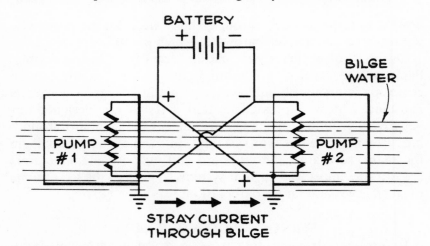

Fig. 13-7 Crossed grounds, giving opposite polarity to the grounded frames, forces stray current through the bilge water separating pump #1 from pump #2. Severe corrosion results.

Consider crossed direct current grounds first; Suppose that a boat has two bilge pumps, one forward, another aft. One pump is grounded in the standard negative ground polarity; the other, alas, is grounded to the positive side of the system: This spells trouble. Current will flow from one pump frame to the other; and the resulting electrolytic corrosion will surely wreck one pump.

Another example: Consider a bilge pump and a bait tank permanently installed: Assume that the bait tank is wired properly and grounded to your boat's negative ground; but assume that the pump has positive ground, which is backward. This spells trouble. Current is going to flow from one to the other; and the resulting corrosion will ruin one of the items.

Don't Cross Grounds

Watch polarity. Always ground accessories to the same polarity. Make sure there is one continuous, integral, heavy ground conductor serving all appliances; and be sure all electrical accessories are connected tightly to this system.

Watch New Installations

When installing new DC appliances or checking old ones, make sure that switches, circuit breakers or fuses are in the hot (positive, as standard) side of the line. The ground side must never have a switch or fuse, because if that side of the line opens electrically, current will flow through water or dampness from appliance to battery, and corrosion will be invited to do its worst.

Check on Voltage Drop

Loss of voltage between battery and accessory is termed line voltage drop, and is a cause of stray-current corrosion. For example: Assume that battery voltage is 12.6 volts. But there is a drop of 0.6 volts in the ground wire feeding the radio transmitter. If the radiophone is tied directly to its ground plate, the plate, in the water, will take on a voltage 0.6 volts lower than that of the battery and its negative ground system. The prop shaft and propeller are electrically tied to the ground system; therefore, these will be 0.6 volts positive with respect to the radio ground

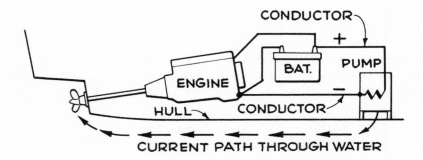

Fig. 13-8 Where conductors to the pump are insufficiently heavy, the pump will be at a different voltage than the engine and its propeller. Current will travel through the water between pump and prop, inviting corrosion.

plate. They will corrode. (Note: This apples to single-sideband radios; VHF sets to not use ground pates.)

The remedy for this is to electrically connect the radio telephone's ground plate to the boat's common ground point, which is usually close to the battery. The radiotelephone system is then tied to the same ground point, and the underwater metals are at the same potential, with corrosion stopped.

This same technique, that of tying all accessory grounds by individual heavy wire to the common ground point, is an important step toward eliminating stray-current corrosion.

Well-designed modern boats usually have electrical systems with a common ground point close to the battery or batteries. In the interest of reducing corrosion, the following are usually connected to this common ground:

- Negative battery strap.
- Bonding system conductor.
- Main switchboard ground return conductor.
- Radio ground plate lead.
- Auxiliary generator ground.

Bonding is Important

A tight bonding system is definitely needed on inboard powered boats. As a matter of fact, it is *required* on boats meeting ABYC standards. Bonding is discussed in some depth in

Chapter 5, and the reader may want to review the chapter, noting the importance of bonding in corrosion prevention. One of the prime objects of bonding in a boat is to provide a low resistance electrical path between otherwise isolated metallic objects. This, to reduce the possibility of electrolytic corrosion due to stray currents.

Corrosion from Shore Power

When plugging into the pier receptacle to bring 60 Hertz AC housepower aboard, you may unknowingly bring an uninvited guest as well: stray-current corrosion. Aboard a boat with a well designed AC system it is not likely, but on a craft with haywire circuits, it is a good possibility.

Make dead sure there is no electrical connection of any kind between the black or white current-carrying wires and the boat's ground. That is a prime rule in preventing corrosion from the 60 Hz system. The entire housepower system must float at its own potential; because if power wires are connected to the boat's ground, current will flow from underwater appendages to earth: The current can be of considerable magnitude, and will cause severe corrosion.

The green or bare equipment grounding conductor in the AC system can be connected to the boat's common ground point. This conductor ties the boat's ground network to shore ground, bringing both to the same potential. However, only the equipment grounding conductor may be connected to the boat's ground. Never attach the white neutral wire to the boat ground, or you will have corrosion rampant should the shore plug be reversed, or if the local feeder is wired incorrectly, with the white wire hot, and the black neutral. Such things are known to happen.

Isolation Helps

The isolation-transformer AC system, described in Chapter 4, helps greatly in blocking the cause of stray current corrosion. In this arrangement, land furnished current flows through the transformer's primary winding only. Transformer core and frame are insulated from the hull.

Shielded and insulated from the primary, the secondary winding furnishes AC power to the boat, and the boat's system floats completely free of shore current. Correctly designed and installed, the isolation transformer system completely eliminates AC stray current between boat and water, and is strongly recommended for steel and aluminum boats.

Frequent Causes

Three frequent causes of AC stray-current corrosion are:

1. Leaky insulation on the hot (black or red) AC wire.
2. Defective battery chargers.
3. Shore-power polarity devices.

Leaks from the Hot Wire

Damaging leakage currents are created by poorly insulated wires in wet locations, also in circuits in which the hot (black or red) wire is energized while the neutral (white) is open. Both wires should be switched on and off in a marine system, because if the shore plug is reversed in a system where only one wire is switched, it may be the neutral. That leaves the hot wire hot; and nowhere for the juice to go except to be a potential trouble maker.

Some older boats have switches in one wire only, supposedly the hot (black) conductor. If yours is such a system, always plug into the dock so that the black wire is hot. A quick check with a neon tester will tell you immediately if polarity is ok. Touched to an energized black wire and earth ground, it should glow. Touched to the white wire and ground, it should remain extinguished.

Battery Chargers

A few garage-type battery chargers are built around auto-transformers and are not suited to marine work. An auto-transformer is one where the primary and secondary windings are electrically connected, usually being one winding with taps. This kind of transformer offers no true isolation of AC power line and the DC charging circuit. It can create strong stray currents.

You can check your charger for stray leakage with this simple test: Clip a low watt, 12 volt, automobile light bulb in series between one battery clip and a good ground, such as a water pipe. Energize the charger; and the bulb must not glow. Reverse the power cord; again, the bulb must not glow. Repeat the two tests on the other battery clip. If the bulb remains cold, the charger is OK.

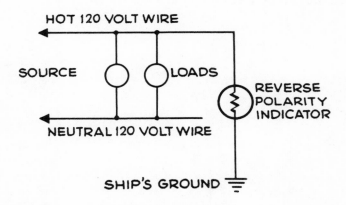

Fig. 13-9 A reverse-polarity indicator, where used, must have very high resistance or it will leak current to the boat's ground, generating corrosion.

Polarity Devices

Some shore power polarity indicators or polarity reversing devices cause mild stray current corrosion because they have insufficient resistance between AC power connection and the boat's ground system. If you have a polarity device on board, it is desirable to have one that can be switched on only momentarily for testing and is not normally in the circuit. ABYC Standard E-8 now allows the installation of a polarity indicator provided that it has a resistance of at least 100,000 ohms at 120 volts, 60 Hz.

SYNOPSIS

Electrolytic corrosion, incorrectly called electrolysis, eats away at underwater hardware which is not at the same electrical potential. Least noble metals are active and are eaten away when in contact with more noble ones. Some metals can galvanically corrode themselves. Corrosion is accelerated by higher temperature or salinity of the water, by close proximity of dissimilar metals, and by the extent to which the metals are dissimilar on the galvanic scale. Protection is provided by applying anodes, such as zinc, to hardware, by installing an active battery-powered system, by adequate bonding, and by eliminating stray currents which may come from the boat's electrical system.

CHAPTER 14

How Shocking

MOST READERS of this book realize that 120 or 240 volt alternating current "housepower" presents more of a shock hazard aboard the cruiser than in the home. The extension cord is also more of a potential killer on the damp pier and adjacent wet terrain than it is in the dry surroundings of the typical kitchen or bedroom. Electricity and wet locations mixed, spell danger.

No One is Safe

You face danger when standing on a wet deck, pier, or on marina ground, using or touching an electric tool. If the appliance develops a fault internally, current can surge from it through you to ground; and the resulting shock can be lethal.

Current Does It

It is not voltage, but current, which kills people. Naturally, the two are related, and higher voltage can force more current through a man. But don't ever believe the foolhardy fellow who says 120 volt house current can't hurt. Properly (or improperly!) directed through your chest, it is lethal.

How Much Current?

According to medical experts, a healthy adult can be killed by a current as small as 0.06 ampere, 60 milliamperes, surging across his chest. Surprising thing is that 60 mills represent the current drawn by an ordinary flashlight bulb; and that is not very much power. Even less is required to kill a child or a grownup suffering from a heart condition, say authorities.

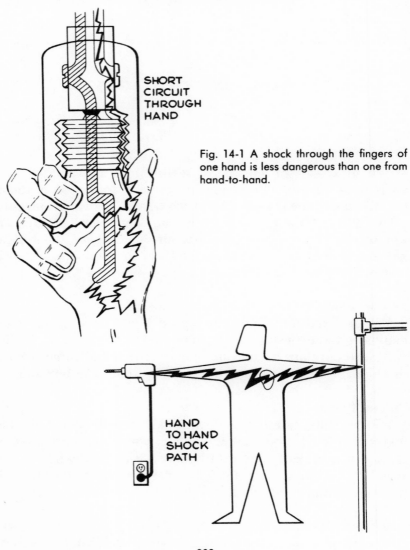

SHORT
CIRCUIT
THROUGH
HAND

Fig. 14-1 A shock through the fingers of one hand is less dangerous than one from hand-to-hand.

HAND
TO HAND
SHOCK
PATH

The Case of the Wet Sailor

Drenching wet with salt water, a boatman might have as little as a thousand ohms resistance between his hands or on other points across his body. Consequently, it appears that wires carrying as little as 60 volts may be dangerous; certainly those carrying twice that voltage *are* to be more than respected! Since dockside power runs from 110 to 125 volts above ground potential, it certainly can be classed as dangerous.

Electricity is Quick

Lethal shocks happen in mere seconds, often too fast for you to save yourself by dropping the offending wire. Technicians who've studied the matter say that in one second, less than a tenth of an amp can kill; and a third of an amp takes only a third of a second. That does not give you much time to take remedial action after you have grasped a hot conductor. What is worse, sometimes the current makes your grasp tighten in an involuntary vise-like grip. Then, unless help arrives *fast,* it may be curtains for you.

The Stage is Set

The standard shorepower 120/240 volt AC system was explained in Chapter 4. However, with emphasis on how shock hazard is created, we will review it here quickly:

Power is transmitted by a three-wire system wherein the conductors function as follows:

1. A black coded wire is 120 volts "hot" above ground or earth potential.
2. A white coded wire, called neutral, is at or close to safe ground or earth potential.
3. A red coded wire, like the black, is 120 volts "hot" above ground.

Remember that the red and black wires are 120 volts hot relative to the white neutral, which is grounded in the manner of a lightning rod or water pipe. Should you touch the white

223

conductor while simultaneously grasping the black or red, you'll get a nasty shock. Similarly, if you ground yourself, as by touching a water pipe or standing on a wet pier, while at the same time touching a live wire, you will be shocked.

Aboard a boat or in the dockside area, most electrical accidents occur when someone with wet hands completes a circuit between a hot conductor and damp grounded surface. Frequently, the accident is through no negligence on the part of the victim. It's not a bare wire, obviously dangerous, which he touches; it is a defective appliance, tool, or a badly wired receptacle.

A typical accident is where a diligent boatkeeper is working in a wet bilge. While handling an electric power tool, he grabs a through-hull fitting or other metal hardware connected to the bonding network which is grounded. The electrical tool has an internal fault, there being a connection between its motor's field winding and the metal frame. Completing the circuit between the tool's "hot" frame and ground, the worker gets a frightful shock.

Another typical accident happens in the galley where the cook reaches to the electric frying pan, at the same time touching the galley sink, which is electrically tied to ground. If the electric fryer has an internal fault, the cook will receive a jolting shock straight across the chest, where the danger is greatest.

There's Safety in the Green

The most basic prevention against electric shock is the green equipment-grounding wire which runs through modern power cords. Terminating on the third, or round, blade of newer appliance plugs, the green wire is a safety ground, specifically intended to eliminate or substantially reduce shock hazard. Attached to the appliance frame, outer casing, or exposed chassis, the green equipment-grounding wire protects the appliance user from shock. It does so by diverting to ground most of the voltage surging in the item when it develops an internal fault. The most typical fault is where the hot wire in the power cord touches the frame internally.

224

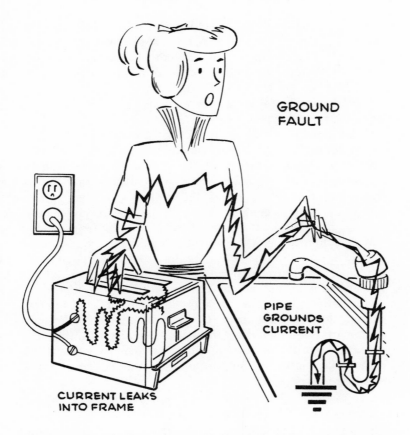

GROUND
FAULT

PIPE
GROUNDS
CURRENT

CURRENT LEAKS
INTO FRAME

Fig. 14-2 If its green equipment-grounding wire is missing or defective, a galley toaster can be a lethal instrument.

But Even the Green Can Fail

It is apparent from the above that the green equipment-grounding wire improves tool and appliance safety manyfold. But unfortunately it does not offer completely foolproof protection, as pointed up by the following examples:

• Sometimes, unknown to the appliance user, there is a defective connection, or high resistance in the equipment grounding conductor. The electrical connection may be defective in the appliance or at

225

the plug, or the plug's grounding blade may be corroded. The receptacle may be wired incorrectly, or wired without the grounding conductor. Possibly the marina or yard's feeder wiring is improperly arranged, with the grounding conductor missing, designed with high resistance, or simply not grounded. Worst of all, the supposed equipment grounding wire may even be hot: This is rare, but has been known to happen.

• Older, non-grounding receptacles will not accept the modern three-prong grounding type. An adapter must be used between the appliance plug and the receptacle; this has a pigtail lead from the green wire of the appliance cord. The catch is that the user will frequently neglect to screw the pigtail grounding wire to the receptacle plate to complete the ground. Alas, even when he does, he must pray blindly that the old receptacle plate is grounded.

• Well grounded, as when touching a galley faucet, the sailor is an excellent current conductor. In the event he handles a faulty appliance while grounded, and if the green conductor offers even a moderate resistance, he may be shocked: The high-fault current can divide, with most flowing through the green wire, but the remainder surging through the human. Contrary to popular belief, current in conductors does not *all* flow through the easiest path. It divides, most going through the easy path, but the remainder going through the higher resistance, in proportion (see the equation for parallel resistance on page 482).

Breakers Don't Protect You

Circuit breakers and fuses in the AC wiring protect the conductors and appliances against harm due to overcurrent; but they in now way offer protection against shock hazard. Circuit protective devices are rated at much too high a current to reduce shock. In the housepower AC circuits, typical circuit breakers are sized to trip at from 5 to 20 amperes. However, we have seen that it takes but a fraction of an ampere to kill; therefore, fuses and breakers offer no protection against electrocution.

How about changing to circuit breakers or fuses sized small enough to offer protection against shock hazard? This approach will not work: Breakers or fuses sensitive enough to protect against shock danger would be far too delicate to energize even the tiniest bulb or motor.

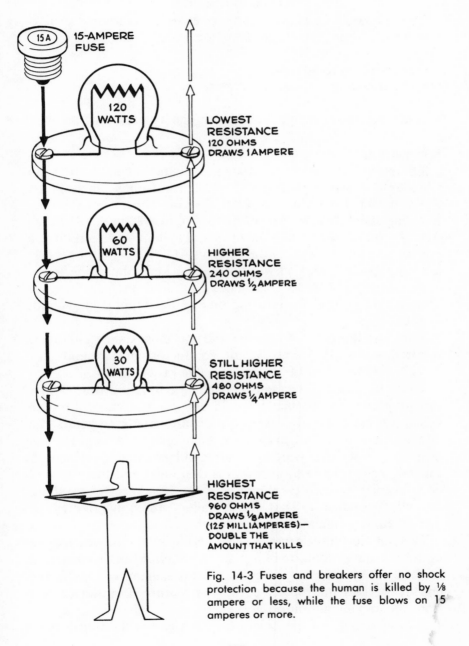

15-AMPERE FUSE

120 WATTS

LOWEST RESISTANCE
120 OHMS
DRAWS 1 AMPERE

60 WATTS

HIGHER RESISTANCE
240 OHMS
DRAWS ½ AMPERE

30 WATTS

STILL HIGHER RESISTANCE
480 OHMS
DRAWS ¼ AMPERE

HIGHEST RESISTANCE
960 OHMS
DRAWS ⅛ AMPERE
(125 MILLIAMPERES)—
DOUBLE THE
AMOUNT THAT KILLS

Fig. 14-3 Fuses and breakers offer no shock protection because the human is killed by ⅛ ampere or less, while the fuse blows on 15 amperes or more.

Additional Protection

Two electrical devices offer themselves as additional protection against shock hazard in damp locations:

- The isolation transformer.
- The ground fault circuit interrupter.

Each has its advantages and limitations, as explained below:

Isolation Helps

The on-board isolation system is explained and illustrated in Chapter 4, starting on Page 62. The transformer, in isolating shore power from the on-board system, enhances safety by reducing shock hazard. Since the on-board system is "floating" free of ground, almost like the electrical system on an airplane, a person may touch either of the 120 volt AC wires, simultaneously touching ground, and he will not be shocked. Should he touch *both* wires, he'll receive a shock, because there is voltage between them; but on touching one or the other and ground, he'll be safe.

Since the majority of shocks, and the most dangerous ones, result from contact with a hot conductor and ground, the isolation transformer offers considerable protection.

To do its shock protection job well, the isolation transformer should preferably be made specifically for the marine job to which it is assigned. Autotransformers are strictly no good. The onboard isolation unit must have high resistance between the primary (shore side) winding and secondary (boat side) one. A capacity shield between windings is desirable; and there should be convenient means for connecting the iron core to the shore grounding conductor. That, incidentally, is the only point where the system is grounded in any manner.

The isolation transformer's secondary winding may be tapped up to provide on-board voltage slightly higher than provided at dockside. The idea is to compensate for sagging voltage at the end of the pier and power cord. The feature does not detract from the unit's main purpose.

A disadvantage of the isolation system is that the transformer is heavy and bulky, and is usually located low in the boat where it is subject to rust. An obvious minor drawback is its cost which, for a 5,000 volt-ampere (approximately 5,000 watts) unit, is about $275. A partial drawback is that, because of inevitable slight electrical leakage, isolation may not be absolute. And in the event of a serious internal fault inside the transformer, isolation will be completely lost.

Searching for Leaks

It is simple to search for loss of transformer isolation. A sensitive test is to connect a neon test light between either of the secondary winding connections (the boat's wiring) and the ground. In this case, ground is represented by the boat's engine, or other component attached to the grounded bonding system and underwater hardware. Thus connected, when contacting either of the AC conductors, the test light should not glow.

Even in a relatively secure isolation system, a sensitive miniature light may glow slightly, but the system might still be safe since many glow lamps will indicate current as slight as 2 to 3 milliamperes (0.003 ampere) and this magnitude of current is relatively safe from the shock standpoint.

A less sensitive test is made with an ordinary 120 volt parallel strung Christmas tree lamp of the indoor tree variety. These bulbs will glow gimly on a current of 20 to 30 milliamperes, and shine at full brilliance, passing about 60 milliamperes. Consequently, when connected between ground and either of the boat's powerwires, if the Christmas tree lamp glows, the system is too "leaky" to be safe.

The two tests described, one with neon, the other with a miniature incandescent bulb, are not infallible. The results depend to some extent upon where the electrical leak is located. If it is a short circuit between one power wire and ground, voltage between that wire and ground will be zero; between the other and ground it will be 120 volts. If the leak or short is at the center of the isolation transformer's secondary winding, voltage from each of the boat's two power wires to ground will be half of circuit voltage, and measured leakage current from each will be the same.

If there is serious worry about current leakage, it can be measured from each circuit wire to ground with an AC ammeter, and the readings will help determine the nature of the trouble. Only difficulty is that sensitive AC ammeters are expensive and not readily available.

One point for safety: Test lamps, meters, or other leakage-to-ground devices should be removed from the circuits after tests are made. Left in place, they constitute a leak themselves, partially destroying the very safety they are intended to reveal.

The GFCI

Old in theory, but newly popularized through the use of modern electrical components, the *ground fault circuit interrupter* is a safety device which can replace the isolation transformer in some instances. It can also do some jobs that the isolation unit can't; and in many versions it is light and portable.

About the size of a small adding machine, the portable ground-fault circuit interrupter instantly and automatically opens the AC circuit when a grownup or child touches a hot conductor or the farme of an appliance having an internal fault. Working almost magically, the GFCI is such a life saver that it is required in certain areas of a boat to meet ABYC standards—a 120-volt outlet in a head must have a GFCI. In addition to plug-in and portable GFCI's, this feature can also be incorporated into regular circuit breakers to provide protection for entire circuits.

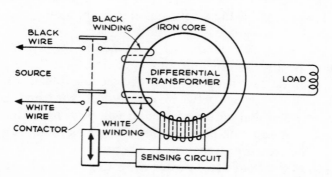

Fig. 14-4 When the load pulls more current through black winding than white, sensing circuit trips the contactor, opening the circuit in mere milliseconds.

Inside the GFCI

Connected in the circuit between source and appliance, or between source and receptacle, the ground-fault interrupter, in a sensitive circuit, compares the exact current flowing in both the hot wire and neutral. When both currents are identical, indicating an "all's well" balance, the interrupter leaves its gate open, allowing juice to flow to the load.

Upon sensing even a slight unbalance in current between the hot and neutral wires, the GFCI flips to alarm condition. Immediately, it chops off the flow of current to its protected circuit. In effect, the GFCI's brain has told it that someone or something is connected between the hot wire and ground. "Shut off the switch!" it says. And that is just what the interrupter does. Promptly.

Fast and Sensitive

Acting with incredible speed, a typical ground fault circuit interrupter will trip as fast as 0.125 second after sensing a fault. And so sensitive is it that it will trip upon detecting a fault as tiny as 0.005 ampere, which is only 5 milliamperes, current far less than that required to hurt a normal human, or even a frail child.

Limitations of the GFCI

When a person touches *both* the conductors in an extension cord coming from the GFCI, the device cannot protect him. Fortunately, this kind of shock poses less danger than the kind received when that person touches the hot wire with one hand while completing the circuit to ground with his other hand or feet or both.

When a child sticks his finger in a light socket, the little digit completes a circuit between shell and center conductor. The kid yells bloody murder. His finger burns; but no current has flowed through his chest area, and he is unharmed except for lost pride, which his mother can restore. However, when the little future sailor stands in water, or sits in a bath, and then grabs a "hot" appliance or live wire, he receives a jolt across his body which may be lethal.

It's that kind of body shock that the GFCI protects against.

Using the GFCI

At the present state-of-the-art, the best GFCI around boat and pier is the portable variety. Aboard your boat you may protect yourself by using the fault interrupter when working with electric tools in damp locations. In the galley, plug appliances into it. In the head, use it to power hair driers, electric razors, and space heaters. Always keep it between your hand-held tools and the power source when working around the pier or in the boatyard. You simply plug the power cord from the portable interrupter into any 120 volt AC receptacle; then plug the appliance into the GFCI. You are safe from shock.

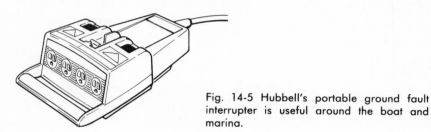

Fig. 14-5 Hubbell's portable ground fault interrupter is useful around the boat and marina.

GFCI Limitations

Plugged into dockside, and feeding all the boat's AC receptacles, the GFCI usually flunks out. In theory, it should be able to protect the entire boat against ground fault; but actually it can't make the grade. Boat environment, including the wiring, is so damp and electrically leaky that the current leakage to ground through the hull appears to the GFCI's brain as a dangerous fault. Not being able to tell whether the leakage is through something inert, or a human, the instrument transfers to alarm condition, shutting off the power.

It is feasible to protect individual appliances or a limited number of cabin receptacles with one GFCI. But, because of extensive electrical leakage, it is impractical to guard the entire boat with one instrument.

Not for Overcurrent

The GFCI must not be relied upon as an overcurrent protective device, replacing circuit breakers. It is not intended as a working current limiter, and should be used in addition to ordinary overcurrent protection, not in place of it.

Where to Buy

GFCI's are increasing in popularity; and better electrical supply houses carry them, particularly suppliers in areas having swimming pools and boats. One popular GFCI is named *Circuit Guard*. It's a portable, compact interrupter made by Harvey Hubbell, Inc., Model GFP-221, with four receptacles, rated 20 amps at 120 volts, trips to safe condition on detecting a fault current of 6 milliamperes. List price, at this writing, is about $290. Hubbell has a smaller model rated 15 amps which simply plugs into a wall socket, fitting over the existing receptacle plate. Price is just under $70.

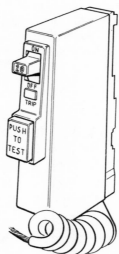

Fig. 14-6 Square D company now offers its Quik-Gard series of circuit breakers, incorporating a ground fault interrupter.

An extensive line of fault interrupters is offered by Pass and Seymour, Inc., which manufactures units rated from 15 to 100 amperes. Model 91 is of interest to yachtsmen. Priced at about $185, its current rating is 30 amps at 120 volts, and trip current is five milliamperes.

The Square D Company has introduced a new series of circuit breakers incorporating ground-fault protection. Selling under

$60 list price at this writing, the breakers named "Quick-Gard," are available in 15, 20, 25, and 30 ampere ratings for 120 volt service. They fit Square D QO load centers of NQO panel boards, directly interchangeable with ordinary breakers. Rated fault trip current is five milliamperes, assuring that the breakers comply with National Electrical Code requirements.

SYNOPSIS

Dockside "housepower" of 120/140 volts is definitely a serious shock hazard, more so around damp boating locations than about the house or apartment. As little as six hundredths of an ampere can kill in less than a second.

Suggested means of protection against shock hazard are:

• Make sure only three-blade, approved, grounding receptacles are used onboard and on the pier.
• Fit the boat with an isolation transformer "floating" system, making sure it is as "leak free" as possible.
• Use a ground-fault circuit interrupter to feed tools and appliances in wet locations.

CHAPTER 15

Protect Your Boat
Against Lightning

IN OTHER chapters we have seen how to secure the boat against fire and persons against shock created by relatively tame AC and DC on-board voltages. Now we turn our attention to protection against the very real dangers created by high voltage from outside the boat—hazards created by lightning bolts.

Bonded and correctly wired, with attention to the squelching of lightning strikes, your boat is a safe, secure place to be during a thunderstorm. Statistics bear this out. Rare, indeed, are cases where boatmen have been hurt by lightning striking a boat which is properly protected as described in this chapter.

Securing your boat against lightning is not difficult; we will be specific how to do it in a moment. But first a few words about lightning itself. Understanding the frightening phenomenon helps make clear the reasons for the steps we will take.

What is Lightning?

Many years ago, Ben Franklin theorized and then proved that lightning is ultra high voltage elctricity. In later years, scientists learned that there is always a space charge over the earth; but that during storms the charge increases in voltage until there is arc-over between earth and sky, or between clouds of opposite potential.

The earth is negatively charged, the upper atmosphere

positively charged. Thus, say experts, the earth, the atmosphere, and the ionosphere form a vast capacitor, through the dielectric of which there is a constant leakage resulting from ionization. What maintains the charge against the leakage is not well understood. Apparently, magnetic phenomena, radiation, and bombardment from space keep the atmosphere charged, counteracting the electron leakage from earth to sky.

During a Storm

Even during the early stages of a lightning storm, the space charge increases; voltage difference between clouds and ground rises. Leakage current multiplies by several orders of magnitude, and becomes measurable on ordinary instruments. As a storm approaches, a voltmeter connected between a high antenna and earth will indicate an erratic, rising potential. And sometimes, when the storm is near, voltage gradients between earth and sky become so intense that sharp points, as at the top of a mast, glow with an eerie flame-like corona.

During a violent storm accompanied by rapid vertical build-up, theory states that clouds become charged positive at the top, negative below. Some experts say that charging results from the differential falling rate of large and small water drops.

Falling through rapidly rising air currents, larger water droplets acquire a positive electric charge, smaller ones take a negative charge. At the tops of rising air currents, great thunderclouds form. In the clouds, large drops, falling through the rapid upward currents, split upon reaching a critical size, and an electrical as well as physical separation takes place: Large drops take a positive charge while continuing to fall; smaller particles assume a negative charge, and are carried upward by the vertical wind. Particles may unite again, then drop and reseparate; consequently, charging is a continuing process.

Lightning

The great clouds we have described operate as an enormous electric generator, increasing the potential until something just *has* to give. Finally, a lightning bolt flashes out, temporarily reducing voltage and relieving the stress. The lightning may jump between two surfaces in the same cloud, may flash between two clouds, or between clouds and the earth or sea below.

The arc between cloud and earth is sometimes more than a mile long, packing many millions of volts. According to some experts, lightning between clouds may be as much as twenty miles long! However, discharges between clouds do not worry boatmen. But lightning between clouds and earth is dangerous; and that is the variety against which we must protect our boats.

Protection

We take several relatively simple steps to secure our yacht against the ravages of lightning. All measures are designed to intercept the lightning bolt, conducting its massive voltage to ground with as little electrical resistance as possible. The two principal steps in marine lightning protection are to short circuit the high voltage before it can do harm, and to bond the boat together so all parts will be safe. Bonding was discussed earlier in this book; but its lightning squelching aspects will be amplified here.

Guidelines

The American Boat and Yacht Council offers recommendations and sets standards for marine lightning protection. It is upon ABYC standards that our suggestions are based.

A Safety Check

Inspect your boat, checking point by point, reassuring yourself that she is fully protected from lightning. If you find equipment or wiring not to your liking, have corrections made in accordance with the recommendations that follow:

The Grounded Mast

Primary lightning protection is a well-grounded vertical conductor, a mast, serving as a high-rise lightning rod. A conducting mast or rod attracts to itself direct lighting hits which might otherwise strike within a cone shaped space. The apex of this cone is the top of the rod or mast; and the base is a circle at the surface of the water, the circle having a radius approximately twice mast height. A sharp-pointed spike extending at least six inches above the mast increases its effectiveness.

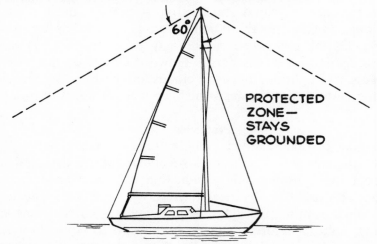

Fig. 15-1 An invisible umbrella of lightning protection is offered by a properly grounded and bonded mast or antenna.

The Circle of Protection

Lightning authorities say that protection is 99% for the 60 degree angle shown in Figure 15-1. They also say that the probability of protection can be increased to 99.9% by extending the mast height sufficient to reduce the 60 degree angle to 45 degrees. This means that if you have a good conducting rod or mast located about equidistant from bow and stern, and if it has a height about half the boat's length, you are extremely safe. This points up that the conventional sailboat having a well-grounded aluminum mast, enjoys an excellent cone of protection, which should bring justifiable peace of mind to her skipper.

Securing the Mast

The lightning arrester or protective mast is bonded from top to ground with #8 gauge or heavier copper wire. When doing this job, keep the conductor as straight as possible, because sometimes a lightning strike will leap from a sharply bent conductor to an adjacent surface. A sailboat's aluminum mast need not be fitted with a heavy copper conductor since aluminum has splendid electrical conductivity. However, the aluminum mast together with its rigging must be electrically connected to ground as described in the following paragraphs.

Large Metal Objects

Avoid placing bulky metal objects close to the grounding conductor if you can possibly make other arrangements. There is a strong tendency for sparks or side flashes of lightning to leap from the grounding conductor to adjacent metal objects. A method of preventing damage from such side flashes is by electrically bonding large metal objects to the grounding conductor.

Using heavy wire, electrically interconnect large metal masses within the hull. This would include stoves, machinery, refrigerators, and the like. Connect these masses electrically to the lightning protective system and to the boat's bonding network which was described in Chapter 5. Proper interconnection will prevent the objects from "attracting" side flashes of lightning.

Workmanship

Don't skimp on the mechanical construction of a protective system; and make all electrical connections tight. Use noncorroding materials and heavy conductors. You will expect your lightning grounding system to remain effective for many years, yet you are likely to give it little attention after it is installed.

Use the Antenna

Your boat's radio antenna can be used for lightning protection if it is the proper type (not many are!) and has a means of being grounded during electrical storms or is fitted with a transmitting-type lightning arrester. A fiberglass antenna with a spirally-wound conductor, or one with an internal loading coil, is not acceptable. Even if the wire in a fiberglass antenna is straight, it is usually too small to serve effectively for lightning protection. Thus *no* fiberglass antenna can be trusted for lightning protection unless it has been inspected and approved by a *qualified* technician—and very few such antennas can be expected to pass.

An antenna that does offer the possibility of lightning protection is a masthead VHF unit consisting of a roughly 34″ stainless steel whip rising out of a loading coil case about 3″ in diameter and 3″ high. The base of the loading coil, and the outer conductor (braid) of the antenna coax cable, can be grounded; this puts the entire antenna at DC ground without affecting its radio performance. The base coil case should be bolted to a grounded metal mast; if the mast is of wood, the case should have a heavy, #8 or larger, grounding wire run to an underwater ground plate tied into the bonding system.

Antennas for single-sideband radios can be expected to contribute little to lightning protection because of their fiberglass construction, even though the installation may include a ground plate.

Corrosion Resistance

Your lighting protective system must use materials that are highly corrosion resistant. Never use a combination of metals that are basically different and form a galvanic couple in the presence of moisture. Always use copper for a conductor except for conducting materials which are otherwise part of the boat (rigging and spars, for example).

Conductor Defined

The American Boat and Yacht Council advises the following in regard to copper conductor used in the lighting arresting system:

Copper conductor should weigh at least 50 pounds per thousand feet. Cable conductors should be of a diameter not less than #8 AWG. The size of any individual wire strand in a cable should be not less than #17 AWG. (For #8 wire, this means Type 1 stranding with only 7 strands, *not more*.) Thickness of any copper ribbon or strip should be not less than #20 AWG (0.032″). Where other materials than copper are used, the gauge should be large enogh to give conductivity equal to or greater than #8 AWG copper cable.

Connections and joints in the lightning squelching system must be mechanically strong and made so they have no measurable electrical resistance. The reason for using heavy electrical conductors and for making perfect connections in the lightning grounding system is that powerful electric currents flow at the instant of a direct strike. Should the conductor be too small, it may fuse. Fire could result from the arc-over. Connections must be excellent because high resistance junctions will heat up, or may fuse, flash, and start a fire.

Electrical Togetherness

It is particularly important to tie your boat together electrically. Interconnection is part of the lightning protection plan devised by engineers in the ultra high voltage field. All sizeable metal objects are made a part of the lightning conductor system through interconnection with it. An alternate plan, where tying together is impractical, is to independently ground each large metal mass. As mentioned earlier, the object of tying all major parts firmly to ground is to prevent side flashes.

Both interior and exterior metal bodies are interconnected in the network. Such masses as horizontal hand rails on decks and cabin tops, vents and stacks from heaters or galley stoves, dinghy davits, metal masts, and the like must be electrically "welded" together. An air-conditioner, extending through the cabin wall, must not be neglected.

Sizeable inboard metal objects should be electrically interconnected; aboard a well-designed boat, the basic bonding system (described in Chapter 5) will suffice. However, be safe: Inspect your boat. Bonded together with heavy conductor should be the engine, water and gasoline tanks, auxiliary generator and, if used, the control rods serving clutch and rudder. There is little need to ground small metal objects such as clocks, instruments, medicine chests, or compasses, but you can do so if you are inclined.

Pointed Objects

Metal projections through the boat's deck, cabin top, or sides above the sheer line should receive your attention. Be sure to bond these items to the nearest bonding conductor. Where possible, also ground them at their lower extreme ends within the boat. Be particularly careful to ground spotlights and other projecting hardware that can be touched by the crew.

Ground Revisited

Ben Franklin grounded his early lightning rods directly to Mother Earth; but you cannot do that aboard your boat, obviously. Consequently, you "ground" the entire lightning conductor system to the water in which the boat floats. According to lightning rod men, final ground can be almost any metal surface which is normally submerged in the water, and has an area of at least one square foot. Metal rudders, propellers, and keels may be used for grounding, but this may not be enough. The external ground plate often necessary for medium- and high-frequency single-sideband transmitters is usually adequate. Obviously, if the boat has a metal hull, its bottom presents a superior grounding surface, and no further ground need be provided.

Sailboats

Adequate protection is offered by a sailboat's wood mast *provided* it has metal standing rigging with all rigging well grounded. Simply depending upon the shroud's partly submerged chain plates is not enough for a safe ground. There must be at least a full square foot of grounding surface in the water: This, regardless of heel angle. In addition, experts say that all stays, sail tracks, and other metal rigging should be grounded.

Dinghys

Dinks, canoes, launches, and the like can be made safe by a temporary lightning protective mast which may be rigged before an electric storm. The mast, unless of sturdy metal, must be fitted with a heavy conductor all the way to the top. Grounding may be a heavy gauge, flexible, copper wire attached to a submerged metal ground plate one square foot in area or larger. A metal centerboard might serve as a good ground plate on a small sailboat so equipped, provided the board is down in sailing position.

Protect Yourself

Safety people suggest you do the following to protect yourself during an electric storm:

1. Remain in the cabin of a closed boat when at all possible.
2. Don't swim. Stay out of the water until the storm passes.
3. Avoid contact with any components connected to a lightning conductive system. Never act as a bridge between items. For example, don't touch the clutch lever and spotlight control handle simultaneously.
4. If you're caught on the beach, exposed and lacking protection, lie low. Remain close to the ground until the worst of the electric storm passes.
5. Do not touch radio receiving or transmitting antennas or lead-in wires during a storm. Avoid touching on-board electrical appliances.

After a Close Shave

Protected as described in this chapter, a boat will come through any number of strikes with complete safety. However, if your boat is struck, and you are aware of it, give the electrical system an inspection, and also swing the compass, re-correcting it for deviation if necessary. Lightning strikes on a boat have been known to alter the magnetic characteristics of a boat and its machinery.

SYNOPSIS

Lightning is a bolt of ultra-high voltage lashing from sky to earth; and to protect against its ravages, we direct it to a first class electrical ground before it can cause trouble. On the boat, the greatest protection comes from a grounded conducting mast, while secondary effects are suppressed by bonding of all metal on the craft. Heavy conductors are used for all lightning protection work, and sharp bends are avoided in all the related wiring.

CHAPTER 16

Electric Motors
Aboard the Boat

THIS CHAPTER concerns electric motors both large and small, so commonly found aboard the cruiser, houseboat, or larger auxiliary. These busy little armature spinners range all the way from the miniature unit of a windshield wiper to the big jobs found in anchor winches and refrigerators.

Basic Types

Both direct-current and alternating-current motors are found aboard most cruisers. Looking much alike, they perform similar tasks; but internally they are quite different, both physically and electrically. Direct-current motors incorporate brushes, a commutator, and wire-wound rotor. Most AC motors, on the other hand, lack brushes, and have a simple inert-looking rotor.

AC Motors

Usually operating on 120 volt, 60 Hertz power, alternating-current motors draw their energy from dockside or an on-board AC generating set. An induction motor, the kind commonly used on refrigerators and most fans, simply has no urge to rotate when connected to direct current, even though the voltage be appropriate. Occasionally, small AC motors are operated from DC to AC inverters which derive their power from the boat's batteries; but here, the motors see AC, not DC.

Refrigerators, air-conditioners, power tools, galley appliances, clocks, and tape recorders comprise just a few of the applications for AC motors. On-board AC motors range from ⅓₀₀ hp for clocks and timers, to several horsepower for large air-conditioners.

DC Motors

Aboard moderate-sized boats, direct-current motors are 12 volt, drawing power from the craft's storage battery. Some types of DC motor will operate reasonably well on alternating current provided voltage is matched to the motor; but others will be ruined by AC. Popular applications for DC motors are in engine starters, windshield wipers, fans and blowers, bilge pumps, power tilt for outdrives, pressure water systems, electric toilets, and winches. Powers range from over a horsepower for engine starters and winches down to perhaps ⅕₀ hp for small fans.

Special Motors

The universal-type motor is special in that it will run satisfactorily on either AC or DC. Electric hand tools and vacuum cleaners usually use this kind of inherently high speed motor, where armature speed is from 5,000 to 25,000 rpm. Contrast this speed to that of the induction motor, the most common variety of which spins 1,750 rpm!

Universal motors will run on either kind of juice; however, in order to do their rated work, they must be connected to the correct voltage. They are universal as to frequency, but not as to voltage; and a 120-volt universal motor will barely rotate on 12 volts. Reduced voltage will not damage the universal motor, however, whereas prolonged low voltage applied to an induction motor, as used in a refrigerator, may burn it out.

DC Motors

Fastened to the inside of the cylindrical motor frame and placed 180 degrees apart are two wire-wound electromagnets. These are the fixed-field poles in a two-pole motor. On the motor's rotating member is another group of electromagnetic windings, usually numbering between four and 30, depending upon motor design. The stationary electromagnets or poles comprise the field structure, the rotating ones are the armature; and it is the armature which delivers the useful work.

How it Works

Immediately the DC motor is switched on, the field magnets become steadily energized by a flow of current from the source, such as the battery. However, the rotating electromagnets on the armature are energized only in timed sequence, determined by their angular relationship to the field magnets. Each rotating pole is momentarily energized and attracted to a field magnet just forward of it in its rotational path. Magnetic attraction pulls the armature magnet ahead in orbit. Then, when it is pulled around into alignment with the field magnet, the armature magnet is deenergized. Immediately, the pole following behind it is energized, and so on, in rapid succession.

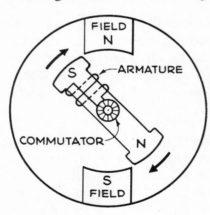

Fig. 16-1 The commutator feeds current to rotating armature poles so they are magnetically attracted to field poles. When rotating poles align with fixed ones, they are de-energized, and a following set is energized. The function is repeated many times for each revolution of the armature. Only two rotating poles are shown; actually there are many.

The Commutator

The radially-arranged spinning armature electromagnets or poles are electrically connected to a matching radial series of copper contacts. These constitute the commutator. Fixed to the motor frame, insulated, and sliding against the commutator segments are spring-loaded, current-carrying brushes, usually

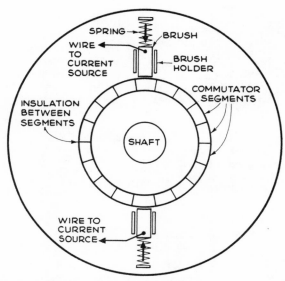

Fig. 16-2 Springs gently urge conducting brushes against commutator segments, transmitting current to armature windings sequentially as the shaft rotates.

two, sometimes four. The brushes are graphite or metallic bars forming electrical contacts that energize the appropriate armature poles in correct sequence as the armature rotates.

Series DC Motors

Field and armature windings are series connected (like series Christmas tree lights) in a series-wound motor. Direct current flows through one field winding, across a brush a commutator, through the armature windings, then through the other brush to the opposite field winding and back to the source. Very high speed characterizes this motor, rpm of from 5,000 to 20,000 being common.

The series-wound DC motor has indeterminate speed regulations: unlike most other kinds of electric motors, its rpm does not inherently level off at some relatively moderate speed; the series motor's armature spins increasingly faster as load decreases. In fact, on full voltage, some series motors will centrifugally throw their armature windings if operated load free.

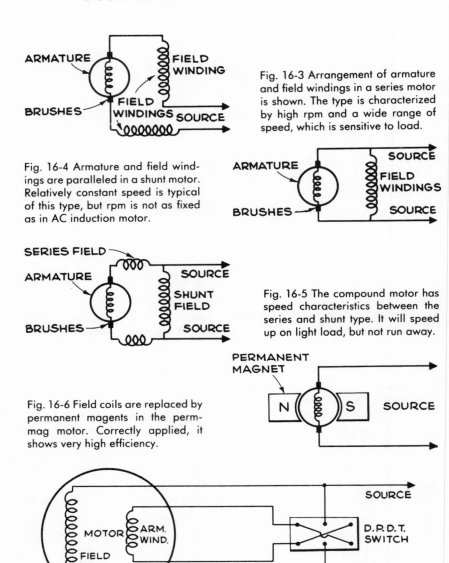

Fig. 16-3 Arrangement of armature and field windings in a series motor is shown. The type is characterized by high rpm and a wide range of speed, which is sensitive to load.

Fig. 16-4 Armature and field windings are paralleled in a shunt motor. Relatively constant speed is typical of this type, but rpm is not as fixed as in AC induction motor.

Fig. 16-5 The compound motor has speed characteristics between the series and shunt type. It will speed up on light load, but not run away.

Fig. 16-6 Field coils are replaced by permanent magents in the perm-mag motor. Correctly applied, it shows very high efficiency.

Fig. 16-7 Schematic shows switch arrangement used to reverse direct current motor. Switch is double pole, double throw. Note that the switch reverses the motor, but does not shut it off. A separate switch is required for shut-down.

Shunt Motors

Windings in the armature and field are parallel connected in a shunt-wound motor, each set of coils being fed from a common pair of terminals. Applied voltage flows directly across the field windings, which are attached to the motor terminals. The brushes are also direct connected to the terminals, energizing the armature through the commutator.

Characteristically, the shunt-wound motor has better speed regulation and operates more slowly than the series motor; and it will not run away if operated without load. The shunt type is typically found on marine engine starters, anchor winches, and some direct-current refrigerators.

Compound Motors

Something of a hybrid between the series and shunt motor, the compound type has two sets of field windings. One set, through the brushes, is in series with the armature coils; the other set is connected directly to the motor terminals. Frequently designed for a specific application, the motor has good speed characteristics, and is sometimes found on direct-current appliances rated between ⅛ hp and ½ hp.

Permanent-Magnet DC Motors

A relative newcomer to the motor family, the permanent-magnet variety owes its growing popularity to the recent development of super-power permanent magnets. Made of new alloys, these magnets pack a terrifically strong field into small space, permitting compact, powerful motors to be designed around them. The perm-mag motor is characteristically efficient because it has no field winding with attendant resistive losses. The rotating armature is conventional, but the field poles are permanent magnets; therefore, current flows via brushes through the armature only.

Originally manufactured in flea sizes only, for toy and small instrument application, the perm-mag motor is growing constantly. Units of ⅓ horsepower are available for 12-volt DC circuits, with more powerful motors, up to 1 hp, for higher voltages. This kind of motor apparently has a bright future aboard ship, particularly becuase of its inherent high efficiency.

Reversing DC Motors

The easiest motor to reverse is the permanent magnet one. To reverse it, you simply interchange battery connections to opposite polarity at its terminals. Because the magnetic polarity of the field poles is fixed, reversing the polarity of supply voltage to the armature, through the brushes, inverts armature polarity, making the motor run backward.

The majority of conventional direct-current motors can be reversed, operating satisfactorily with right or left-hand rotation. But this is not true of all motors: If the manufacturer wants his motor to be field-reversible, he brings four numbered leads to the connection box. Two leads come from the brushes, and two from the field windings. To reverse the motor, the two field conductors are left in position while the two armature leads are interchanged. This reverses the polarity relationship between the two internal circuits, and the motor rotates in the opposite direction.

Shaft Bearings

Plain sleeve bearings are used a great deal on intermittent duty motors, and on some constant duty units. Heavy or long duty motors often have ball bearings, needing little or no lubrication. If the reader plans on buying a motor for continuous duty, or if it is to be installed in an inaccessible location, it is wise to buy a ball bearing motor. Such a motor is also best if the motor is mounted with its shaft vertical, or if there is an imposed end thrust load.

How Much On-Time?

Some DC motors are intended strictly for intermittent duty. An example is the marine engine starter motor, many of which are designed for a duty cycle of 15 to 30 seconds on, followed by several minutes off, during which to cool. A heavily loaded starter motor will roast if operated more than a few minutes without a following lengthy cooling off period.

Of course, there are DC motors designed for continuous duty; others are designed for continuous duty only when used in fan service where they are externally cooled. In buying a motor for some specific service, you must always consult the nameplate for ratings, or refer to the technical bulletin describing the motor.

DC Current Demand

The size conductor you must use when wiring a new DC motor depends on its current demand. Textbook theory states that a motor will demand 746 watts per theoretical horsepower. That assumes 100% efficiency. But because of losses, and for added safety, it is better to compute current assuming about 1,800 watts per horse for small, low voltage motors. To determine approximate motor watt demand of small motors, multiply hp times 1,800. To derive amperes, divide watts by supply voltage.

Example

A 12-volt ⅛ hp, direct-current motor will consume about 225 watts, with current demand just under 19 amps. Therefore, if the motor is fed by 20 feet of wire, the conductor size should be a pair of #10 AWG, assuming a 10% voltage drop is acceptable. See Figure 3-7 on Page 56 for required wire sizes for given currents and voltage drops.

Effect of Light Load

The above example assumed the DC motor to be fully loaded. However, if the motor is lightly loaded, it will draw less than full rated current. Current diminution, however, will not be proportional to load reduction, because the motor loses efficiency as its load is reduced. Simply "fanning the breeze" at no load, the motor still draws enough current to overcome friction, windage, and electrical losses.

Speed Control

Direct-current motors, particularly those driving windshield wipers, fans, and blowers, can have their speed varied by a variable resistance in the hot conductor. A rheostat or stepped resistance is usually used; and one is selected that will cut motor current to about half: This will reduce motor output to one quarter of full power, usually sufficient reduction.

Calculating a Rheostat

No great precision is required in selecting a rheostat to control the speed of a simple appliance such as, for example, a windshield wiper or blower: The following method will come close enough:

    1. Energize the subject motor with full voltage and, using a DC ammeter, measure the current demand. For this example, assume it is 4 amperes. Also assume the voltage is 12.

    2. Divide the voltage 12 by current 4 to obtain resistance 3 ohms. $R = E/I$. This resistance will cut current in half to 2 amps, and motor power to about a quarter. Consequently, you will buy a rheostat having resistance span from 0 to 3 ohms or thereabouts.

    3. Rheostats are generally sized according to watts dissipation. To determine the wattage you will require, square the "cut" or reduced amperes 2, obtaining 4. Multiply rheostat resistance 3 by squared current 4 (I^2R), obtaining watts 12. You will buy a rheostat rated 12 watts or higher: The higher the wattage rating of the control, the cooler it will operate.

It is well to buy a rheostat of larger than theoretical wattage not only for cool operation, but to assure the slider can handle maximum current. When you turn the control to high motor speed position, the rheostat winding need dissipate little wattage, but the slider will be carrying close to full motor current. For this reason, you may want to purchase your rheostat by specifying overall resistance and maximum current, rather than wattage.

Another approach, one eliminating the rheostat slider, is shown in Figure 16-8. Several resistances are wired in series; and a switch selectively energizes the motor with full battery voltage, or with one or more resistors, in series. The switch must, of course, be capable of handling full motor current.

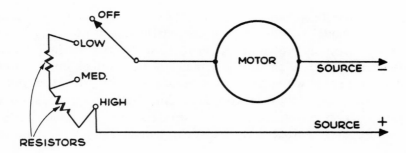

Fig. 16-8 Two resistors and four-position tap switch offer three speeds and "off."

Figure 16-9 tabulates the resistance required to reduce 12-volt DC motor power to 1/4 of full value, and indicates the wattage size of rheostat to use. The tabulated values can be used for dimming lights, also, where light current is substituted for motor current.

Approximate H.P.	Amperes Original Current	Ohms External Resistance	Wattage Rating Required
1/4	38	0.31	114
1/8	19	0.63	57
1/10	15	0.8	45
1/25	6	2.0	18
1/50	3	4.0	9
1/100	1.5	8.0	4.5

Fig. 16-9 External resistance required to reduce motor (or lamp) output to one quarter of original value. Table is for 12 volt circuits. Currents shown for motor horsepowers are very approximate since current demand varies with motor type.

Watch for Voltage Drop

It is obvious that since a rheostat of few ohms will reduce motor power markedly, resistance in the boat's wiring will do the same thing. This emphasizes the importance of heavy DC wiring in motor circuits. Inadequate wiring not only causes power-robbing voltage drop, but may also be dangerous, since undersize conductors get hot due to resistance losses.

Two-Position Drop Test

Using a DC voltmeter, you can easily test motor circuits for voltage drop, as shown in Figure 16-10. First, run the motor with its normal load, then carefully measure the voltage immediately at its terminals while the motor operates. Then, with the motor still operating, measure voltage at the battery terminals. The difference in voltage is the line drop. It should not exceed 10%, because even a 10% potential drop causes 20% loss of motor power.

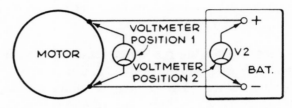

Fig. 16-10 With motor operating at load, voltage is measured at the motor terminals, then at battery posts. Voltage difference indicates circuit voltage drop.

One-Position Drop Test

A simple but slightly less accurate method of measuring line drop to the motor may be used without significant error on small motors: The connections are shown in Figure 16-11. Energize the motor; run it with normal load; measure the voltage at its terminals. With the voltmeter still connected, close to the motor terminals but on the hot side of the switch, shut off the motor. Watch the voltage rise. Difference between "on" and "off"

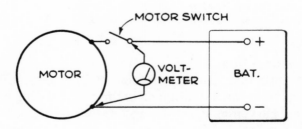

Fig. 16-11 Closing of motor switch causes voltage drop; and voltmeter indicates effect of circuit resistance, including that in the battery.

voltages is the drop. The reason this method is less accurate than the first is that it includes the battery's voltage with and without load. However, on a small motor, that change should be slight, particularly if there are other loads simultaneously on the battery.

Direct-Drop Test

A third method measures drop directly, and it is shown in Figure 16-12. This method is good where current is very heavy, and where you do not want to leave the motor running for more than a relatively few seconds. Typical application is to measure the voltage drop to an engine starter, eliminating the effect of battery voltage drop, which will be considerable.

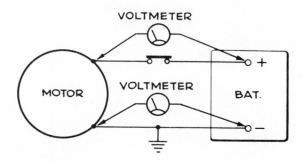

Fig. 16-12 Connected direct from motor terminal to battery post, the voltmeter will read voltage drop in the cable which it shunts. Switch must not be opened in test, or full battery potential will appear across the voltmeter in the hot cable.

Use a voltmeter with full-scale calibration less than motor voltage. For example, on 12-volt system, use a meter scale of something like 3 to 5 volts. Proceed as follows:

1. Energize the motor.
2. Measure the voltage between positive battery post and positive motor terminal.
3. Remove the meter from the circuit.
4. Shut off the motor.
5. Repeat the procedure in the negative conductor.

The reason for taking the voltmeter out of the circuit *before* opening the motor switch, is that if the switch is between meter connections, the meter will see full battery voltage; that would be hard on the instrument unless its full scale matched or exceeded bettery voltage. However, a high-reading voltmeter makes the test less sensitive since such a meter has less resolution.

Inside the AC Motor

We have explored the DC motor; now let us look into the AC motors aboard the boat.

Although the theory of its internal modus operandi is fraught with mystery, the common AC induction motor is electrically and mechanically simple. Many induction motors, such as those used on blowers and other appliances, have but a single moving part, the armature. Modern induction motors have no armature windings, brushes, or commutator; some have starting switches or external capacitors, but all are simple.

Poles vs. Speed

In the AC machine, the stator or field windings are arranged around the motor frame, much as in a DC motor. Motors rated 3,450 rpm or thereabouts have two poles; motors of approximately 1,725 rpm have four poles, and motors rated around 1,150 rpm have six poles. Speed on 60 Hertz usually equals a little less than 7,200 divided by the number of poles, and within the motor's load rating is fairly independent of that load.

Stator "run" windings are connected directly across the 120- or

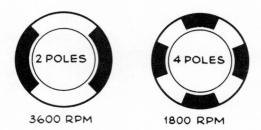

Fig. 16-13 60-Herz induction motors seek a synchronous speed of 3,600 rpm if two-pole, and 1,800 rpm if four-pole. However, the motors operate slightly slower than the synchronous speed.

240-volt AC power source. As the alternating current surges 60 times a second through the pole windings, magnetic fields follow suit, rising and falling rhythmically inside the motor.

The Armature

Called a squirrel cage rotor, the induction motor's armature is similar in general appearance to that in a DC motor; but the squirrel cage rotor is simpler: Instead of windings, it has simple, straight individual copper bars buried in slots parallel to the motor shaft. Each bar is short circuited to the others at its ends, and there is no commutator, hence the motor has no brushes.

Since there are no brushes, how does the rotor become energized? As follows: Magnetic fields are induced in the armature through induction, similar to the way one transformer winding induces current in another winding. As the undulating magnetic lines of force from the stator windings surge across the rotor's copper bar conductors, they induce strong currents therein. In turn, the induced currents create new magnetic fields, and these, acting with the stator magnets, give the rotor its torque.

No Inherent Starting Torque

Unlike the direct-current motor, the AC induction motor has

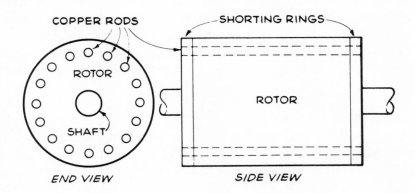

Fig. 16-14 An induction motor is simple, having no commutator. The rotor is comprised of iron laminations encasing lengthwise copper bars, and the bars are short-circuited at each end by metal rings.

no starting torque unless separate electrical means are provided to "get it going." As long as the rotor remains stationary in the pulsating magnetic field, it feels no urge to rotate. Think of it as compared to a surfboard, sitting still in the water, allowing waves to pass under. But once the rotor is nudged to rotate, however, slowly, it is urged by the magnetic waves to follow, just as the surfboard, once started, is carried shoreward by the waves.

Good Speed Regulation

Because the induction motor's armature "rides" the electromagnetic waves created by the 60 Hertz electricity, it has superior speed regulation. It cannot go faster than the waves, and unless it is overloaded, it will not fall far behind. Therefore, line frequency, usually 60 Hertz, and number of poles, as explained on Page 244, determine the motor's speed. Special motors have provision for speed variation through switching the number of effective poles, or varying the amount of "slip" behind the waves. But the majority of induction motors are pretty well married to their one design speed.

Synchronous AC Motors

Synchronous motors are a special breed that run at *exactly* one speed, commonly 1,800 rpm. Properly loaded, the synchronous motor's rotor locks in on power line frequency and stays there with zero zlip. Most common use is for clock and timer power. Some of these have a permanent magnet armature shaped like a star wheel, and the magnets spin around like wagon spokes following the magnetic field as it chases around the many-pole stator.

Getting the Motor Started

It was explained earlier that the armature, stalled in the pulsating magnetic field, generates no torque. But once urged in either direction, quickly accelerates to normal speed, continuing in the direction in which it was started. Alternating-current motors are frequently classed by the means giving them their starting impulses.

Resistance Starting

Commonly called a "split-phase" motor, this variety is probably the most common AC type of all, and because it is inexpensive, it is used on numerous appliances not requiring high starting torque. A centrifugal pump often uses a resistance split-phase motor.

If two groups of waves or "phases" chase themselves around the motor stator, the armature will try to follow; and making the phases revolve is how the split-phase motor is given its starting torque. A set of "phase" windings is added to the "run" windings on the stator. The phase or starting windings are displaced ninety degrees from the run windings, and are wound with higher electrical resistance—more ohms.

The start or phase windings generate a second magnetic field, displaced from the run winding field because of higher resistance. Now, there are two phases of waves chasing in a definite direction around the motor; and the rotor is pulled around with the phases.

The Starter Switch

Start or phase windings are energized only during the brief moments that the AC motor accelerates to speed. As it approaches rated rpm, a starter switch deenergizes the start wind-

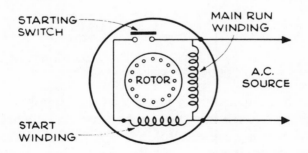

Fig. 16-15 In most induction motors, the starting switch is centifugally operated, cutting out the starting winding as the motor approaches speed. In hermetically sealed galley refrigerator motors, the switch may be operated by a current-sensing coil.

ings with a click. In some motors the switch is internal, being actuated centrifugally by governor weights. On other units, particularly hermetically sealed galley refrigerator motors, the switch is actuated by a current sensing coil. In series with the power feed wires, the sensing coil is part of a relay, and when it feels the current decrease, as the motor reaches speed, it releases the contacts which feed the start windings.

Capacitor Starting

Resistance starting and capacitor starting are almost the same. The important difference is that the phase or start windings are energized during the start interval via an electrolytic capacitor in series between starter switch and winding. Electrical size of the capacitor is typically between 50 and 160 microfarads, and physically it is often seen as a black cylinder mounted on or near the motor.

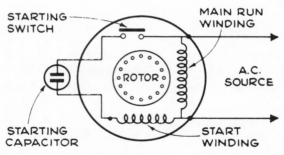

Fig. 16-16 In the capacitor-start motor, a high value capacitor is switched in series with the starting winding until the motor approaches running speed.

The capacitor creates better phase shift than simple resistance start windings, increasing the motor's starting ability while reducing its starting current for a given torque. Its reduced current demand and increased efficiency make the capacitor-start motor attractive for on-board appliances, such as galley refrigerators, because getting enough current from the shore power cord is always a problem. Where the skipper has a choice between ordinary "split phase" or capacitor-start motor, he should always choose the latter.

Two-Capacitor Motor

Starting of the two-capacitor motor is as described for the capacitor start unit. The difference is that after the high value electrolytic capacitor has started the motor and been switched out of the circuit, a capacitor of smaller electrical value, typically 10 to 30 μF, continues to energize the start windings. As long as the motor continues operating, the "run" capacitor keeps feeding a moderate current to the start windings. This improves efficiency while reducing hum. The two-capacitor motor approaches the polyphase industrial unit in smoothness and ability to hang on to a load. One might compare it to a plain resistance-start motor as comparing a diesel to a gas engine.

Permanent Capacitor Motor

On board the boat, this simple, efficient AC motor is fine for easy starting loads such as fans, blowers and centrifugal pumps. It has no starting switch, a single moderate-size capacitor being permanently wired in the phase or start windings. With a capacitor sized somewhere between one and 15 microfarads, the unit is sometimes provided with special tapped stator windings, allowing its speed to be externally varied within the limits. The tapped stator capacitor motor is used a great deal on blowers.

Shaded Pole Motor

Extremely popular for cabin fans, blowers, and other light duties, requiring to perhaps 1/10 hp. the shaded pole motor virtually sweeps the board in the flypower category. The motor is simple, inexpensive, and not particularly efficient; but efficiency is of secondary importance in very small AC motors and simplicity has its blessings. This type motor has the usual run windings of two or four poles, and each pole has a shading winding biased to one side of the pole piece. The shading winding is a single turn of heavy bus-bar or copper strap, and is short circuited. Current induced in the shading coil creates a secondary magnetic field displaced in phase from the main field. This acts as a phase winding, giving the motor its urge to rotate. No starter switch, capacitor, or current relay is required since the shading coil remains active whenever the motor is energized.

Reversing

Except for the shaded-pole motor, all the types of AC motors described are potentially reversible. To reverse the motor, you interchange connections of the start winding leads with respect to the run windings. Motors intended to be reversed have all four leads led to a terminal box.

How Much Current?

Figure 16-17 shows the values of full-load motor current for induction motors running at usual speeds and motors of normal torque characteristics. Specific motor current may vary from the given values, but for planning purposes, these figures are most

Horsepower	120 V.	240 V.
1/6	4.4	2.2
1/4	5.8	2.9
1/3	7.2	3.6
1/2	9.8	4.9
3/4	13.8	6.9
1	16	8
1 1/2	20	10
2	24	12

Fig. 16-17 Full-load currents in amperes for alternating-current motors are shown in this table.

useful. Some hermetically sealed refrigeration motors demand much more current than indicated in the table. These are electrically of low efficiency, depending upon refrigerant for cooling. However, the appliance nameplate will indicate current rating.

Effect of Light Load

Induction motors draw somewhat less than full-load current when lightly loaded; but the decrease in current demand is not proportional to the reduction of load. This is true in the AC motor to a greater extent than in the DC machine. For example, one split-phase motor which draws 10 amps at full load, demands

8.7 amps at half-load; and will still soak up eight amps with no load at all.

Because current demand of an AC motor decreases less than linearly with load reduction, it is unwise on board a boat to be overconservative in sizing a motor to a load. A 1/6 hp motor working full load, draws much less than a 1/3 hp motor loafing at half load. The picture can be improved somewhat with power factor correction, as explained in Chapter 17, but it is still best to select on-board induction motors sized to work hard rather than motors too big for the assigned job.

Speed Control

The AC induction motor is by nature a constant speed animal, and controlling its speed over a wide range is all but impossible. Unless the motor is designed for external speed changing, it should be operated at nameplate rpm. Note that this does not apply to the universal motor which, with its wound armature, commutator, and brushes, closely resembles the DC motor. Speed of the universal motor, commonly found in hand drills, may be varied by reduced voltage from transformer or rheostat, or may be controlled by a "light dimming" Triac or Powerstat.

Some AC fan motors are wound so that a different number of poles may be switched in and out of the circuit, giving two or more finite speed ranges. For example, when switched to four poles, fan speed is about 1,725, but when six poles are switched in, speed drops to about 1,100 rpm.

Watch the Voltage

Induction motors are sometimes damaged by dropping voltage from the shore power cord. Because they are constant speed devices, they will hang onto the load as long as they can, despite low voltage. Finally, however, if supply voltage sags too low, the motor will "stall" off its run windings and fall back on the start windings. After a short interval, the machine will either burn out or trip a protective device.

Sometimes an AC induction motor, such as one driving a pump, will cycle on and off in response to low voltage. Here, a thermal protector, sensing that the motor has fallen back to its start windings and is drawing excessive current, "pulls the switch." After the motor cools, the protector reenergizes it, and the struggle is repeated, until finally the motor roasts for good.

Voltage at the Pier

Aboard a boat having an AC appliance such as a refrigerator, supply voltage measured at the appliance cord, with the motor running, should be 105 volts or more *minimum*. Otherwise, the motor may not be able to carry its load. In addition, during a brief interval when the motor starts, voltage must not drop lower than 95 volts; otherwise, there may be trouble ahead. Where voltage is low due to excess demand at the marina, current demand may be reduced by some of the means suggested in Chapter 17.

SYNOPSIS

Direct and alternating-current motors are outwardly similar, but electrically quite different. The DC motor has a wound rotor, commutator, and brushes. The AC induction motor has a simple "shorting bar" rotor, with no brushes or commutator. The universal motor, operating on either AC or DC, closely resembles the standard DC motor, and operates at very high speed. Direct-current permanent magnet motors are highly efficient and are commonly found in small fractional horsepower units. The synchronous motor, operating on AC runs at exactly one speed, is used to power clocks and timers. Many motors both AC and DC are reversible by interchange of external leads. Motors draw less current when lightly loaded, but current reduction is not proportional to load reduction. This is particularly true of AC induction motors.

CHAPTER 17

Hold Down
That Current Demand

GONE ARE the days when metropolitan power companies, such as Con Ed in New York, advertised the beauties of heating homes by electricity, and "living totally by electricity." Now is the day of the blackout, brownout, and plea to turn off the air-conditioner.

The honeymoon of unlimited electrical power appears to be cooling.

Reasons for Conservation

Aboard the boat tied to the marina's pier, there is another good reason for conserving watts and reducing current demand. Watts and current, as we shall see, are closely related, but aren't the same thing, even at the same AC voltage. Conservation on the boat is more important than in house or apartment because the entire marine supply system is generally weaker.

Consider a typical older marina and its AC power system. Piers have been added in the past few years; the electrical system has been extended, but not necessarily beefed up. By the time AC power leaves the pole transformer and is distributed over the yard's sprawling network, there's little reserve at the last receptacle down the line.

Another thing: With more families week-ending aboard the boat in its slip, and with the boat wife demanding all the conveniences to which she is accustomed, power demand has been amplified. Electric stoves, space heaters, air-conditioners, refrigerators, and deep freezers take a lot of power from the line. And the more power that's taken, the lower the voltage drops, until, at best, appliances refuse to operate properly, and, at worst, something burns.

Yet another reason for being careful about on-board current demand is that in many installations the power cord or boat's wiring, or both, are inadequate. This is particularly true on older boats on which the electrical system has grown haphazardly.

Four Ways to Conserve

To cool the fevered cord connecting boat to pier, and to ease the load on the marina's system, four approaches come to mind. Used individually or together, they work wonders toward chopping down current sucked through the power cord.

1. Use existing equipment with care.
2. Choose new appliances wisely.
3. Generate power with an on-board generator set.
4. Improve power factor of AC appliances.

Use Equipment with Care

Follow the old fashioned advice, "Turn it off when you're not using it." This applies to lights as well as appliances. Why burn a 200-watt reading lamp in one cabin, sucking almost two amps from the system, while you are elsewhere watching the TV, drawing another three amps? By killing the unneeded light, you've cut current demand by 40%. At home it may not mean much; but aboard the boat, saving two amperes might help a lot.

When possible, select "low" or moderate heat when cooking on an electric galley stove which is energized by dock power. Try to use one burner at a time, and, of course, use the oven as little as possible. A plan used by some boat wives is to do the heavy cooking at home, then use the boat stove for reheating. Smart girls use pressure cookers, too, because with this kind of utensil, less electric energy is required to cook anything from a simple vegetable to a complete meal.

Keep electric refrigerators and deep freezers closed as much as possible. Use moderate settings for both. Don't turn them as cold as they will go. Also, if either the refrigerator or freezer seems to cycle on and off with unwarranted frequency, have it checked by a refrigeration mechanic: Starting current for these devices is five times greater than running current, and each time one starts, it loads the line something awful.

Choose New Gear Wisely

Where a 60-watt bulb is perfectly adequate, don't install a 100. If a little two-slice toaster takes care of breakfast, don't be tempted to set up to a four holer. Rough it a little; leave the electric hair drier off the boat. Want TV aboard? Then buy one of the new all (or nearly all) transistorized sets. They draw less current, and heat the cabin less than the tube models.

You plan to air-condition the cabin. This takes a lot of juice, so don't overdo it. Buy the smallest that will do an adequate job. You might also favor an air-conditioner incorporating a water-cooled condensing unit. For equal cooling capacity, it should draw less current than one with air-cooled condenser, and in many instances it will be quieter, since it needs no condenser fan or blower.

For on-board use, a top-opening deep freeze is much better than a front-opening one since the top-opening freezer does not lose its volume of icy air each time the door is opened. Holding its cold air better, the top-opener uses less electricity. It also is less liable to dump its contents on the cabin deck in a seaway.

The smallest electric refrigerator that will handle your needs comfortably is the best from a conservation standpoint. Its location can effect the refrigerator and its relative on-time. If the box has an integral condensing-unit machinery compartment, the entire unit must be installed where there is adequate ventilation behind and around the cabinet. Otherwise, the condenser coil can't shed its heat; compressor head pressure will be excessive;

the motor will work harder; and the refrigerator will be "on" more than required. This wastes power.

The same theory applies to boxes having remote condensing units connected to the cabinet by tubing. Either the condensing unit should be water cooled, or if air cooled, must be well ventilated so it can get rid of its heat.

Electric space heaters are nice to have aboard, breaking the chill on brisk mornings and cool fall evenings. But electric heaters draw lots of current: When buying one, look at the nameplate rating; you will find that most heaters are rated between 1,200 and 1,700 watts, which on 120 volts, means they draw from 10 to 14 amperes, admittedly a lot of current by boat standards.

Choose an electric cabin heater which has two "speeds" or a thermostat or both. With this unit, you can conserve by selecting the lower heat after initial heat-up, and can hold down total demand by adjusting the thermostat to the lowest setting commensurate with reasonable comfort.

Generate Your Own

On board the boat of, say, 30 feet or more, there is a lot to recommend an on-board AC generating set, where the AC demand is great. With your own little powerhouse, you're free forever from the dock's supply of power, except perhaps for battery charging while you're away from the boat.

With your own engine-driven generating set, you can cruise where and how you like and still have all the AC power demanded by the crew. The generator makes it possible to anchor in remote places, far from the apartment house atmosphere of the crowded marina. The set, properly selected, and wired, also assures you of almost unlimited power for electric ranges, heaters, and other power sucking devices.

For example, a 12,000 watt AC generating plant, powered by a modest four-cylinder motor of 16 to 20 hp, can deliver 100 amperes of juice at 120 volts. That's a lot of current. How many marinas can you waltz into, plug in, and blithely demand 100 amperes? Mighty few! Their facilities simply can't handle it, and, in addition, the dockside power cord would have to be the size of a fire hose.

A discussion of AC power plants is found in Chapter 8.

Improve the Power Factor

Power factor is a slightly mysterious parameter affecting the current demand of many AC power consuming accessories. It forces the item to draw more current from the line than indicated by wattage. In extreme cases, for example, an appliance with exceptionally low power factor, running on 120 volts, and rated 100 watts will draw 2 amps rather than 0.83 amps. The lower figure is that expected when power factor does not enter the picture.

It is apparent, then, that if you can improve power factor of certain accessories, you will reduce AC current demand.

A Little Theory

In direct-current circuits, volts times amps equals watts. But in AC circuits, volts times amps times *power factor* equals watts. If P.F. is 100%, as in an incandescent light bulb, then AC volts times amps equals watts. But if power factor is 50%, as in many flourescent fixtures, then watts equals volts times amperes times P.F., and instead of drawing, say, 1 amp from the line, the fixture will draw 2 amps.

The Villains

Low-power-factor electrical items found aboard the cruiser include appliances driven by induction motors, transformers, fluorescent lights, and battery chargers. Depending upon motor loading, voltage, and design, power factor of the named accessories will fall somewhere between 40% and 80%, indicating that they demand 250% to 125% of the current than indicated by their wattage rating. These are inductive components.

The Heroes

Toasters, hair driers, space heaters, galley stoves, water heaters, and incandescent lights are resistive loads, have high power factor, and require no correction. These are resistive (not inductive) components.

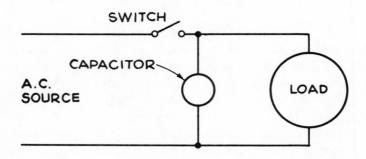

Fig. 17-1 The capacitor is wired in parallel with the load on load side of switch.

How to Correct

Connecting the correct value of capacitor across the power input terminals of low power factor components will raise P.F. and reduce current demand. If the exact value of capacitor (sometimes called a condenser) is connected across the appliance terminals, power factor may be raised to a hundred percent. To automatically switch the capacitor across the line at the same time as the inductive load, the capacitor is connected to the load side of the switch. This is shown in Figure 17-1.

Determining Capacity

How many microfarads of capacity are required to reduce current to its lowest value? The simplest way to determine is as follows: Run the appliance without correction, measuring its current demand. Start connecting capacitors across the line, incrementally increasing the number of units in parallel until current is brought to a minimum.

It will be obvious when enough capacity has been stacked across the line. When you reach optimum capacity, additional capacity will have an adverse affect, increasing, rather than decreasing current. Because capacitors are expensive, it is customary to slightly undercorrect the P.F., picking a capacitor of the nearest handy lower value.

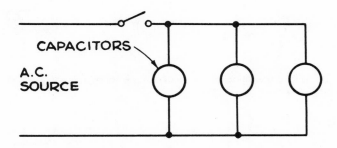

Fig. 17-2 For increased capacity, units may be connected in parallel across line.

Typical Results

Figure 17-3 shows the effects of power factor correction on a sampling of typical on-board appliances. Except for the big 240 volt cabin air-conditioner, all are 120 volt. The examples are given only to indicate the magnitude of improvement possible through P.F. correction. The reader must not automatically assume that the same capacity will be required for similar units. As described earlier, the best way to determine the microfarads for correction is by experiment.

Appliance	Uncorrected Current Amperes	Corrected Current Amperes	Current Reduction	Required Capacity μF
1/6 hp split phase motor running light	2.5	0.7	72%	55
1/25 hp fan motor running light	1.2	0.5	58%	20
Cabin fan	0.56	0.4	29%	8
Fluroescent light	1.1	0.54	51%	17
Battery charger light load	0.82	0.35	57%	18
Cabin dehumidifier	3.5	1.9	46%	60
240 volt cabin air conditioner	5.5	3.8	31%	48

Fig. 17-3 Table shows reduction in current demand with power factor correction.

271

Fig. 17-4 This oval case capacitor is typical of the kind used for power factor correction.

Capacitor Specifics

Not every kind of capacitor will perform satisfactorily in power correction work. The kind that do the job, lasting for years, are impregnated film, oil filled, with names such as Dykanol, Askarel, Clorinol, and manufactured by Sprague, General Electric, Dayton, and Cornell Dubilier. When you buy capacitors, specify that they are for continued across-the-line application: These are the type used for motor *run* capacitors. Electrolytic capacitors used for motor *start* are no good for correction work. Electrolytics will fail after a few moments of across-the-line connection.

Where to Buy Them

Electrical supply houses, lighting contractor suppliers, and industrial electronic mail-order suppliers, as well as electric motor repair shops are sources of capacitors for P.F. correction. If you need help in finding a source, look in the Yellow Pages.

Suitable capacitors are found in catalogs from electronic supply houses such as Allied and Lafayette. One such catalog lists Cornell Dubilier hermetically sealed AC Dykanol capacitors in drawn oval street cases, and having 370 volt rating. The rating is adequate for any possible on-board use. An idea of capacitor costs is given by the following list prices (as of mid-1980):

Microfarads	Price
4	$ 7.40
10	11.40
15	16.70
25	24.15

If you can manage to buy capacitors through wholesale supply houses, such as W. W. Granger, the prices will be some 30% less than those indicated above.

How do you Measure Current?

Ordinary volt-ohm meters do not have a scale for measuring AC amperes; and the best instrument is a clip-on AC ammeter, opened like a pincher, and snapped around one insulated conductor. There is no contact with the conductor, current being measured magnetically, by transformer action.

Fig. 17-5 The Amprove is typical of good snap-on AC ammeters so useful for measuring appliance current demand.

The reader seriously interested in general AC system maintenance and power factor correction will do well to get a snap-on ammeter. If not abused, it will last a lifetime. Amprobe is a well known AC ammeter, and the junior model sells for under $50.

Correction Strategy

With a limited number of capacitors, it is possible to make parallel combinations yielding many values of effective capacity. Using jumpers and clips, combinations of capacitors can be connected across the line to determine the capacity necessary to make the desired degree of P.F. correction. Suggested values to buy are the following, expressed in microfarads: two, four, eight, 16, and 32. Figure 17-6 shows the values of effective capacity that can be obtained by paralleling these. Should you want to extend the test possibilities to 126 microfarads in the same two step sequence, add one 64 μF capacitor to the kit.

Desired Microfarads	Parallel Combination	Desired Microfarads	Parallel Combination
2G	2	34	32-2
4G	4	36	32-4
6G	4-2	38	32-4-2
8G	8	40	32-8
10	8-2	42	32-8-2
12	8-4	44	32-8-4
14	8-4-2	46	32-8-4-2
16	16	48	32-16
18	16-2	50	32-16-2
20	16-4	52	32-16-4
22	16-4-2	54	32-16-4-2
24	16-8	56	32-16-8
26	16-8-2	58	32-16-8-2
28	16-8-4	60	32-16-8-4
30	16-8-4-2	62	32-16-8-4-2
32	32		

Fig. 17-6 Five selected capacitors can be arranged in parallel combinations yielding 31 equivalent values.

Make up a dozen test leads, about a foot long, with alligator clips on each end. Using these and your snap-on AC ammeter, you can experimentally determine how much capacity is required for each accessory; it's really an interesting and educational project. After noting the required value for each, make permanent, neat capacitor installations using the test capacitors or additional ones as required.

You will have one of the few cruisers in the world with power factor correction.

Safety Precautions

Don't ever put your fingers across capacitor terminals after disconnecting from the power line. The highly efficient kind of capacitor you are using can store a shocking amount of energy, and can release it like lightning, giving you a nasty jolt, and perhaps a burn.

Avoid leaving charged capacitors around where children might play with them. After using one experimentally, discharge the capacitor through a light bulb to tame it. Otherwise it may sit innocently for several hours, still packing a punch.

Whether or not the capacitor will be charged depends upon the split second it was removed from the line. Occasionally, you will happen to remove it at "zero voltage crossover" during the cycle. Then it will be discharged. But if you remove it from the 120-volt line at exactly the "wrong" instant, it may be charged to as much as 170 volts.

Do not discharge a charged capacitor with a screwdriver or other metal tool. Doing so is hard on both the tool and capacitor. Use a light bulb with test prods, or a resistor of several hundred ohms.

SYNOPSIS

Current conservation aboard the boat is far more important than in home or shop because on the boat the source is limited even if an on-board generating plant is installed. Ways to conserve are to use existing equipment with care, choose new appliances wisely, and improve power factor on some appliances.

Power factor is improved through capacitors connected in the circuit and energized when the appliance is switched on. Typical items requiring correction are refrigerators, pumps with induction motors, deep freezers, chargers, and fluorescent lights. Required capacity is determined by experiment, current being measured with a snap-on ammeter.

CHAPTER 18

Saving Soaked Equipment

ON-BOARD electrical gear sometimes gets thoroughly soaked, either by being drowned in sea water (or lake, or river water) or by being left out in a downpour. Of the two varieties of soaking, immersion is the worst, because flotation water carries dirt, silt and muck into the accessory. Furthermore, if the water is saline, it impregnates the item's innards with salt, an enemy of all electrical equipment.

Salt, the Foe
When you're cleaning up a drowned electrical assembly, it is particularly important to get out all salt, because remaining salt will cause future trouble in two ways: It is hygroscopic, attracting moisture from the air, causing corrosion. Furthermore, it converts virtually nonconductive, clear dew-point or atmospheric moisture into highly conductive electrolyte, causing all kinds of internal faults in electrical machinery. Even the trace of salts in brackish or fresh lake water can do this.

Salvation is Universal
Almost any kind of electrical accessory can be saved after a dunking. No matter how sad it looks after you have recovered it, there is a strong possibility you can restore the appliance to service. In his shop, the author has recovered items as diverse as

an air conditioner, pump, air drier, electric drill, toaster, battery charger, distributor, generator, and starter.

Patience is Important

Drying, cleaning, and refurbishing drenched equipment, and putting it back into service involves a simple technique; but it requires patience. The prime rule is: Don't apply power to it until you are sure it's bone dry. The higher the operating voltage, the more applicable the rule. Obviously, the insulation resistance in damp 120-volt fiber insulator is more severely stressed than that on one handling only 12 volts.

Should you plug in a unit, such as a 120-volt motor, while it is still soaked, current will flow across moisture paths where it shouldn't go. Soon, the electricity heats the wet insulation; and that material chars, quickly losing resistance. Current increases through the fault; and finally the entire circuit burns up.

Equipment

Simple kitchen and home workshop equipment is adequate for drying and cleaning drowned marine gear:

- A gas or electric baking oven with a thermostat that is reasonably trustworthy, and a thermometer. The thermometer can be the familiar meat-cooking kind.
- A hair drier, or electric bathroom heater with blower.
- Spray can of CRC or other moisture inhibitor.
- Oil can.
- Plenty of clean fresh water.
- Patience.

Not commonly available, but most useful, is a supply of compressed air. High velocity air, blowing from a compressed air gun, has a fast drying effect in tough-to-get-at labyrinthian passages inside the electrical equipment. The air's low dew point, combined with its speed, does a fast drying job which can then be topped off with a little heat. Small compressed-air rigs intended for paint spraying are readily available from tool rental houses. You might consider leasing one of those for your next drying-out session.

Take it Home

Where at all possible, take the soaked electrical equipment from the boat and transport it to your home or shop. Granted, you cannot easily remove fixed wiring and switchboards; these must be dried in place. Motors, generators, heaters, electric tools, and appliances, however, should be taken ashore for drying.

Rinse it Well

In a tub, laundry sink, or any available watering place, rinse the accessory thoroughly with warm, clean, fresh water. Use a little soap, if you desire. The bath will flush out silt, dirt, and salt; and the rinse is obviously more important if the accessory was immersed in salt water than in fresh.

After washing and rinsing the motor, or whatever it is you are recovering, shake it out. Position it every which way; and if you have a compressed air source, blow out as much water as possible. The exhaust blown from a vacuum cleaner is of help, because its air stream is warm and dry. Set the item down on a table in front of an electric fan for a while, as an alternate. If possible, do this out in the sunshine.

Bake It

Warm the electric or gas baking oven to about 185°F, and allow the temperature to stabilize. Many ovens overshoot to temperature hotter than thermostat setpoint when first started; and such heat might damage your item. So, check temperature with an oven thermometer before baking out the electrical widget on which you are operating.

Place the electrical item on an open grid-shelf, and bake it gently. Shift its position occasionally; and give it plenty of time. On an ordinary starter motor, for example, two to three hours at 185°F is satisfactory. But at all costs, avoid trying to speed the process with higher temperature which might damage the insulation or a plastic feedthrough bushing.

Spray It

After you are sure the accessory is bone dry, use hot pads,

unload it from the oven, and let it cool. When it is just a little warmer than room temperature, spray its insides with a mist of moisture inhibitor such as CRC. If the item has rotating parts, oil or grease its bearings.

Try It

After cleaning, rinsing, baking and spraying, you are ready to give the components a try. Hook it up to its normal power supply and run it a while. If it looks, sounds, and smells okay, put it back in service.

On-Board Components

It is all but impossible to remove some components from the boat, short of doing a rebuilding job. How about drying out those things which must remain on board? Here, you must bring the required tools and equipment to dockside: fans, heaters, heat lamps, blowers, hair driers, moisture repellent, and, when available, a rented compressed-air source with blow gun.

Clean It

Using a fresh-water hose, watering can or bucket, rinse out the item. Drive out as much of the silt, salt, and dirt as you possibly can.

Dry It

If you have a compressed-air supply, put it to work blasting air through all the waterlogged passages and starting to dry out the innards. If you do not have compressed air, try a vacuum cleaner with hose reversed. Then aim electric heaters at the component to start dehydrating it. Help the electric heater with a fan to keep the air moving and assist the drying. Be careful, however: Watch the temperature; and never leave the make-shift rig unattended. You don't want to ruin the accessory or start a fire. Repeatedly feel the thing you're drying. When it feels too hot to hold, move the heat source farther away, or reduce heating power.

Maintain the item good and warm all day. If it is a motor that you are reclaiming, rotate the shaft occasionally. Move the heater to different angles, too, making the bake-out as uniform as possible. When you are sure things are completely dry, allow the temperature to return just warmer than ambient; then spray with moisture repellent. Now, the equipment is ready to try.

Tricks of the Trade

Alternating-current induction motors can be dried slowly through the application of low voltage DC to the windings. The author has had success with this method, using a 12-volt battery charger with adjustable output. The motor is first washed, rinsed, and blown clear of as much water as possible. Then, on a typical quarter horsepower AC motor, about six amps DC is flowed through the windings via the motor's power cord. After a few hours, the motor frame will become uncomfortably warm to the touch, and current may have to be reduced. If the charger has but one fixed rate, current can be cut back through the insertion of a resistance in the leads.

Low-voltage direct-current applied all day will do no harm to the motor's insulation, but will dry it out. Moderate-voltage DC can force appreciable amperage through the windings in an induction motor because the motor's reactance does not impede direct current.

It is a good idea to remove the capacitor from a capacitor-start motor before baking it. And it is not a bad idea to replace a start capacitor that has been submerged any length of time; because even though it functions at first, internal seepage may condemn it to failure after a few days.

Resistance heater elements often found in toasters and electric space heaters, usually gather grass, weed, or bilge dirt after a dunking. Such resistance elements need brushing, blowing, and cleaning while being dried. If they are left contaminated, the remnants may catch fire when the heater is first energized.

Heater banks positioned by ceramic ferrules must be especially well dried before the elements are energized to full heat. If you attempt drying them with their own heat at full power, the wet ceramics will crack. However, you can dry this kind of heater assembly by applying greatly reduced voltage for a prolonged period.

Testing

As pointed out in Chapter 1, an ohmmeter is a most useful electrical trouble-shooting tool. You can make use of it here, testing for short-circuits or electrical faults to ground in appliance or motors.

When you believe the accessory is well dried and ready to use, test it: Set your ohmmeter on the X100 scale, and measure the resistance between the unit's terminals and its frame. The resistance should be close to infinity. If it is not, and if additional drying does not bring resistance up, the appliance may be risky to put back in service.

SYNOPSIS

Most drowned electrical gear can be saved through a program of cleaning, rinsing, air drying, and baking, followed by a spray of inhibitor and a resistance test. Bake-drying should be at moderate temperature; and no electrical item should be placed back in service until it is thoroughly dried.

CHAPTER 19

Shooting Faults
With a Dual-Purpose Light

THE TROUBLE light and the methods of using it described here, will help you a great deal in finding trouble in the 120-volt AC system and the DC system on board.

A trouble light, particularly the two-mode, self-powered type used in this chapter, is just about the most useful, practical electrical tool you can have on the boat. It can be used almost anywhere, at any time; and when its signals are understood, it is a gem of a trouble spotter. For some trouble-shooting work, this test light is equal to or even more useful than a voltmeter or ohmmeter because:

- The light is cheap, rugged, and requires no adjustment.
- Its indication is instantly apparent.
- The light is electrically less sensitive than a voltmeter or ohmmeter. It places a small but useful load on the circuit under scrutiny, and is less likely to give false readings. This is particularly true when it is used to test the diodes in an alternator.
- The test light refuses to glow to full brightness unless the circuit has at least reasonable integrity and low resistance. An ohmmeter, on the other hand, deflects measurably on stray leakage currents through the damp hull or poor insulation.
- Having its own battery power, the test light will quickly check out components which are disconnected from their circuits. It will glow if they have continuity, remain dark if they are open-circuited.

The Test Light

If your boat has a 12-volt direct-current system, you can construct your dual purpose tester from readily available, inexpensive parts. Use some kind of box or case, a single-pole double-throw switch, eight flashlight batteries in series, a small 12-volt bulb and socket, and a pair of test leads, preferably terminated with small alligator clips.

Suitable for the tester, and available in most gas stations, a #57 bulb, (or equivalent) is the miniature instrument dashboard type. It draws about one-quarter of an ampere at 12 volts, which is just about right for your purpose.

Wiring Arrangement

Figure 19-1 shows how the components are wired. As arranged, when the test prods are touched together, they make a circuit through the batteries and switch to the bulb; that's the arrangement in "internal" mode. In "external" mode, the test leads make a circuit through the switch directly to the bulb. In this configuration, the test prods energize the bulb only when touched to a live 12-volt source, such as the boat's battery.

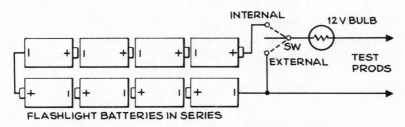

Fig. 19-1 Switch SW selects internal or external mode for trouble light.

Longevity

With the suggested #57 bulb and a set of fresh flashlight cells, the batteries should last a full season. This is especially true since you only energize the bulb for brief periods while troubleshooting or testing. When storing the instrument, always throw the selector switch to "external." Then, if the test prods accidentally are in contact while the light rig is stored, the cells will not be discharged.

Usable on 120-Volt Circuits

An attractive feature of this type light is that it can be used to wring out 120-volt AC circuits as well as battery voltage ones. When used for work on AC housepower, the circuits *must be deenergized* during the tests.

Be Careful about Selection

When trouble-shooting, do not throw the selector switch to "internal" while touching the test clips to a 12-volt live circuit. If you touch the leads with one polarity, no harm, the light won't light. But if you connect with opposite polarity, the bulb will be subjected to double voltage, and may burn out. A close look at the electrical schematic in Figure 19-1 will show why.

Using the Tester

The following are tests you can make on specific accessories, components, and systems:

Boat's 120-Volt Standard System

Select "internal."

Make *certain* that every switch in the 120-volt AC system is open, and that non-switched items such as electric clocks and refrigerators are unplugged. All fuses should be intact and in place. Unplug the dockside power cord, and carry out the tests on the cord's plug blades. When the test light is hooked as indicated, you should have the following response:

   a. Black wire to white wire: No glow.
   b. Black wire to green wire: No glow.
   c. White wire to green wire: No glow.
   d. Either black or white to boat's common ground: No glow.
   e. Green wire to boat's common ground: Glow.

If the test bulb glows when it should not, in (a.) to (d.) above, or if it does not glow, in (e.), here's what is signaled:

   a. Continuity between black and white (hot and neutral) indicates a load on one of the circuits, or a bad insulation leak between wires. You can locate the offending circuit, by pulling all branch circuit fuses, or opening all circuit breakers. Then close one breaker or fuse at a time, testing until you find the loaded circuit.

b. There should never be continuity between the black (hot) and green (grounding) wire. Conductance here indicates a dangerous condition, and you must trace individual circuits until you locate and correct the fault. Glowing of the light on black to green connection indicates a shock hazard.

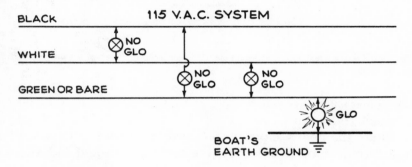

Fig. 19-2 Desired test light responses on standard 120-volt AC system un-plugged from shore power.

c. A current path from white (neutral) to green (grounding) wires aboard the boat defeats the safety feature of the grounding conductor. Both of these wires should be grounded at some place *on shore,* but not on your boat. If your light tells that they are connected on the boat, find out where and untie them. Only the green or bare wire can be earthed on the boat.

d. Test d. is made touching one test light clip to an earthed metal such as the engine block. Glowing of the light indicates there is a ground fault. It should be traced and eliminated since such a fault can cause severe electrolytic corrosion.

e. In the standard system, the green (grounding) wire is tied to the boat's common ground. Failure of the light to glow tells that this connection has not been made. However, note the remarks under "Isolation System" below.

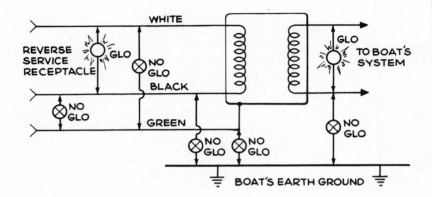

Fig. 19-3 Desired test light response on 120 volt isolation system un-plugged from shore power.

120-Volt Isolation System

Select "internal."

Where the boat's shore power cord terminates at an isolation transformer aboard the boat, the test light should indicate as follows when hooked to the shore power cord plug in various blade combinations:

    a. Black wire to white wire: Glow.
    b. Black wire to green wire: No glow.
    c. White wire to green wire: No glow.
    d. Either black or white to common ground: No glow.
    e. Green wire to boat's common ground: No glow.

Here, the light's response is different from that on the standard system: Test (a.) shows continuity through the isolation transformer's primary winding; and test (e.) tells that the grounding conductor is not tied to the boat's common ground.

240-Volt Standard System

Select "internal."

Tests are the same as for the 120-volt standard system with additional checks on the plug blade attached to the red wire. Correct responses are:

a. Black to red: No glow.
b. White to red: No glow.
c. Green to red: No glow.
d. Red to boat's common ground: No glow.

240-Volt Isolation System

Select "internal."

Here again, the red wire enters the picture; and all is okay if the test light responds as follows:

a. Black to red: Glow.
b. White to red: Glow.
c. Green to red: No glow.
d. Red to boat's common ground: No glow.

When making test measurements on red, white, and black conductors in an isolation-transformer system, you may notice the light is slightly less bright than when the test prods are short circuited. This simply indicates the resistance in the transformer's primary winding. One other point: When manipulating the test clips on the shore power plug from the isolation transformer, handle the thing gingerly. If your fingers are across the blades when you break the test connection, the inductive kick from the transformer may give you a startling bite.

12-Volt DC System

Select "external."

Open all switches in the boat; but have all DC breakers and fuses closed and intact. Leave the battery ground strap connected, but remove the hot cable. Be sure the master switch is closed. Connect the test light between the battery's hot post and the disconnected clamp. The light should remain out. If the light glows, connected as described, current is leaking from the battery to some circuit or other in the boat, or to ground. If there is a leak to ground, corrosion is invited, and in any event the current leak is a drain on the battery.

To locate the direct current leak, leave the light connected between battery post and cable clamp. Then disconnect one

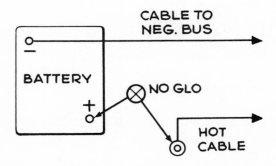

Fig. 19-4 With boat circuits turned off, test light in "external" mode must not glow when connected between hot battery post and its disconnected cable clamp.

circuit after another throughout the boat until the light extinguishes. You will have located the culprit, and can make repairs as needed.

Bonding System

Select "internal."

Clip one test lead to the common bonding conductor, or to some accessory known to be well connected thereto. One at a time, touch the other test lead to all other items which should be bonded. The light should glow, indicating continuity. Try the engine, ground bus, major accessories, refrigerator, fuel and water tanks, radio ground, and lightning protective mast.

Appliances

Select "internal."

Test 120 volt toasters, electric tools, refrigerators, hair driers, and the like for shock hazard. Clip one test lead to the appliance's outer frame or shell. Touch the other lead alternately to one blade, then the other of the appliance power cord plug. The light must not glow. If it does, the item is dangerous and must be repaired. Leave one test clip on the frame. Touch the other lead to the third plug blade found on modern plugs. This is the grounding blade, attached to green wire, and should make the light glow.

Direct-Current Motors

Select "internal."

Connect the test leads to the motor's terminals; and the light should glow. If it does not, rotate the motor shaft. If manual rotation causes the light to blink on and off hesitatingly, it may be signaling badly worn brushes or commutator.

Connect one test prod to the motor frame. Touch the other prod alternately to one, then the other of the motor's terminals. The light must not glow. If it does glow, it is saying that the motor has an internal fault to the frame. Granted, on 12 volts there is no shock hazard, but leakage due to this kind of fault can cause electrolytic corrosion if the motor is used in a damp location. (This test does not apply to an engine starter motor in which the frame is the ground return conductor.)

Alternating-Current Motors

Select "internal."

The same tests as described for direct-current motors may be performed on AC motors. However, manual shaft rotation will have no effect on the continuity response of induction motors. Those are the kind having no commutator or brushes, as opposed to universal motors found in vacuum cleaners and hand tools, which do have brushes.

Fuses

Select "internal."

Connect the two test leads to the fuse, one to each of its terminations. A good fuse will make the light glow; a blown one will leave the light dark.

Circuit Breakers

Select "internal."

Make connections as on a fuse. A tripped breaker will leave the light dark; a closed one will make it glow.

Conductors

Select "internal."

Where the test prods can be brought to the terminations, any wire or other conductor can be checked for continuity. A good conductor makes the light glow; an open circuit leaves it dark.

Condensers/Capacitors

Select "internal."

Ignition condensers and other capacitors are checked by touching one test clip to the pigtail lead, the other to the shell. The light should remain dark. If it glows, the capacitor is internally shorted. Connections to motor start or motor run capacitors are to the two terminals. If the value of capacitance is large, and your bulb small, a good capacitor may make the bulb glow for an instant when you first make contact; but it should then quickly extinguish.

Ignition Ballast Resistor

Select "internal."

Clip the test leads to the resistor terminals; and the light should glow. Designed ballast resistance is insufficient to observably reduce the brightness of your small bulb. Supplementary ballast tests are found on Page 199.

Breaker Points

Select "external."

Turn the ignition on. Clip one test lead to the engine block, the other to the ignition coil terminal which is connected to the distributor. This is the low-voltage primary-winding terminal. Electrically, you are now connected across the breaker points, in series with ignition coil and ballast.

Crank the engine. The light must blink on and off cleanly. With points open it must be bright; with them closed it must turn off. If it fails to respond in this way, see additional trouble-shooting information in Chapter 12.

Engine Timing

Select "external."

Attach the test clips as described in "Breaker Points" above.

Crank the engine ever so slowly until number one cylinder is on compression stroke and the timing marks are approaching alignment. Just as the specified marks match up, the test bulb should glow, indicating that the points have opened.

If the light glows before the moving mark reaches the stationary one, ignition is early. If it does not glow until after the moving mark passes the stationary one, spark is late. Adjustment is made by slight rotation of the distributor body in the direction required for correction. Additional details on timing using a high-speed strobe light are found in Chapter 11.

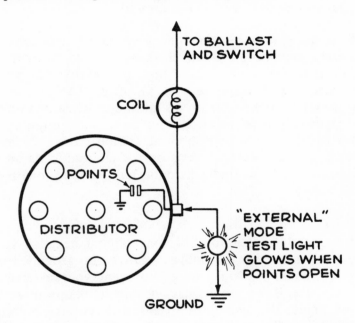

Fig. 19-5 Connected as shown, in "external" mode, glowing of test light indicates that points are open. The hook-up is useful for initial timing adjustments.

Alternator

The following are test light responses on a negative ground Leece-Neville alternator with a star-connected stator. The results are typical for alternators of this kind, where stator windings terminate at a neutral terminal.

Select "internal."

a. Test light's negative lead clipped to alternator ground:
Responses:
Rotor (FLD) to ground: Glow.
Neutral terminal to ground: No glow.
Output (B plus) terminal to ground: No glow.

b. Test light's positive lead clipped to alternator ground:
Responses:
Rotor (FLD) to ground: Glow.
Neutral terminal to ground: Glow.
Output (B plus) terminal to ground: Glow.

Where the reader is in doubt as to internal connections on his particular alternator, he can clear his doubts by performing trouble light tests on a unit of known integrity. He will then know the correct responses on his own. The skipper with foresight might make tests on his alternator when it is functioning properly, jotting down his findings. Such information is invaluable during a trouble-shooting session.

One reminder: Make all tests on the alternator, as on other accessories, with the unit disconnected from its control and output wiring.

Generator

Assuming the generator has conventional negative ground, make your tests with the light's negative clip grounded to the frame of the unit. Doing so will prevent your reversing the magnetic field. If you should inadvertently hook up with reversed polarity, flash the generator's field with correct polarity as explained in "Flashing The Field," Chapter 6.

Select "internal."

Connected between field terminal and ground, the light should glow. Between output terminal and ground it should glow. While it is connected between ground and output, manually rotate the drive pulley: The light may flicker slightly as the commutator slides under the brushes. But if the flicker is pronounced, you may suspect dirty or worn commutator, brushes, or both.

When connected between field and ground, the light may be

slightly dimmer than when between output and ground. This simply indicates higher resistance in the field windings than in the armature. No problem.

SYNOPSIS

The dual-mode, self-powered trouble light is an extremely useful trouble-shooting and tune-up tool, applicable to both the DC and AC circuits aboard the boat. Easily built, it can test almost every kind of component. The instrument flows a moderate current through the circuit under test, thus minimizing false readings as might be offered by a sensitive voltmeter or ohmmeter. Fuses, breakers, conductors, insulators, capacitors, breaker points, and complete circuits are among components which can be tested with the light.

CHAPTER 20

Keeping Electrical Noise Out of the Electronics

ELECTRICAL NOISE generated in the boat's electric circuits can bother electronic equipment in diverse ways. It causes static on radio receivers, fools depth sounders into reporting incorrect depths, takes the fidelity out of sound equipment, and reduces the accuracy of direction finding equipment. It also forces the TV picture to roll or tear and cause "snow" on the picture.

Some varieties of interference are so cantankerous that even the expert electronics technician has difficulty in tracking them down and effecting a cure. But other sources of noise are common to most power boats. It is those common sources with which we are concerned here, and which can be quieted by simple techniques.

Many radiotelephone receivers incorporate a noise limiter circuit which suppresses sharp noise peaks, both those coming from the boat's electrical circuits, and those generated in the atmosphere. Unfortunately, the receiver cannot differentiate between a radio signal and electrical noise. Similarly, depth finders have filters to clean up the returning signal, but here again the circuit cannot always discriminate between a returning blip and noise which has similar characteristics.

There is little trouble when the logic signal is considerably stronger than the noise. However, if the noise is the stronger of the two, the receiver, depth finder, or other device will demodulate and amplify it despite internal filtering. Even the sharpest circuits have a hard time seeking signals mired in a swamp of electrical noise.

Different kinds of man-made electrical noise generated aboard the boat can deteriorate performance of radiophones, portable radios, direction finders, depth sounders, and TV sets. Common on-board creators of electrical noise are:

1. Engine ignition
2. Generators and alternators
3. Voltage regulators
4. Propeller shafts

Each component requires its own kind of noise suppression, to be discussed in the following paragraphs.

A Useful Search Coil

A handy radio-noise-sniffing coil is a useful tool, helping you locate the source of radio frequency electrical disturbance. There is nothing critical about this search coil's design; and you can make it yourself.

Wind about 50 turns of insulated magnet wire, any gauge such as 16, 18, or 20, on a short cardboard or wood form about 2½ inches in diameter. Or, if you prefer, you can simply wind the wire into a trim hank, securing it into a neat coil with strips of tape. Connect the ends of the coil to several feet of television antenna twin lead, preferably making a soldered connection. Attach the other end of the twin lead to a radio receiver's input terminals, one wire to the antenna post, and the other to ground.

Turn on the radio, tuning it between two stations. If it has an automatic volume control switch (AVC) turn it off. Carry the search coil from place to place, putting it close to accessories which you suspect of generating radio noise. As it approaches close to an item which is generating hash, you will hear the volume of that interference increase on the radio.

Junior's low-fidelity pocket-size transistor radio can be a help as a radio noise sniffer, too. Using it as such, tune it between stations, and move it around like a geiger counter, placing it

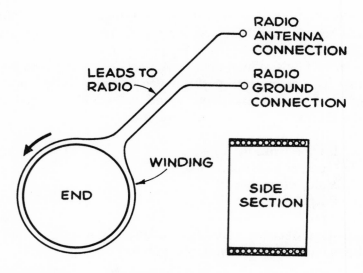

Fig. 20-1 This simple search coil helps locate sources of radio frequency static.

alternately near one suspected component, then another. Keep the volume control low. When the little set comes close to an accessory which is radiating static, you will hear the fuss on the radio speaker.

Ignition Noise

Interference from ignition is easy to identify since it has that characteristic sharp snap, pop, noise each time a plug fires, the staccato keeping time with engine revolutions. As a first step in silencing this, install a suppressor resistor in the high voltage wire between coil and distributor cap.

Install a 1 μF 200 volt capacitor between the ignition coil's hot primary terminal and ground, the best ground in this case being the engine block. It is important that you connect the capacitor to the terminal wired to the ignition key, not the terminal connected to the distributor. Connecting to the wrong coil terminal will do little good toward noise suppression, and may deteriorate engine performance.

If ignition noise is still bothersome, install resistor-type spark plugs or, alternately, replace the copper high-voltage wiring with

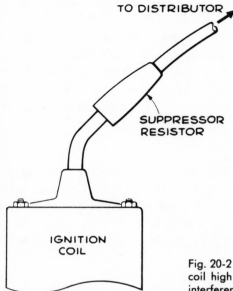

TO DISTRIBUTOR

SUPPRESSOR
RESISTOR

IGNITION
COIL

Fig. 20-2 A suppressor resistor in the ignition coil high voltage cable often reduces radio interference.

suppression resistance wire. It is available at auto parts stores.

Should the above steps fail to reduce ignition noise to a tolerable level, you may have to resort to shielding. Shielding kits are available for many ignition systems from marine electronic shops. Encasing the entire high-voltage system including spark plugs, the distributor, and coil, the conductive shielding effectively grounds radio-frequency signals before they can be radiated from the system.

In lieu of shielding around the ignition components, screening can be tried, although it is usually not as effective. Here, the engine hatch is screened in with copper mesh, and the screen is grounded to the craft's bonding system. In such an arrangement, it is important that the hatch above the engine also be screened and flexibly bonded.

Noisy Spark Plugs

An occasional engine will be found fitted with Champion "U" type spark plugs, one such plug being UJ6. It is all but impossible to eliminate noise caused by these plugs because they have a spark gap near the top of the porcelain; and this gap radiates strong spatter over a wide RF spectrum.

Replace type "U" plugs with resistor types such as Champion XJ6, XJ8 and equivalent. Investigate all spark plug wires for continuity and also that they are making good contact in the distributor cap and at the spark plug terminals. High-voltage discontinuities which cause visible spark are a potential source of radio frequency noise.

Ignition Coil Location

The coil must be mounted on the engine—not on a bulkhead; and its metal container must make good electrical contact with the engine head or block. A few coils are plastic cased rather than being encapsulated in a metal can. Plastic types often radiate excessively, and should be replaced with metal units, or shielded.

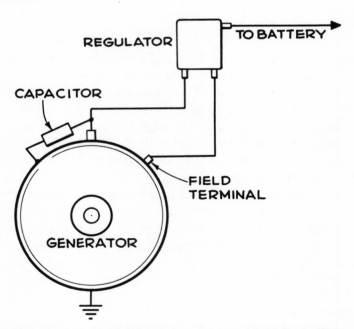

Fig. 20-3 A capacitor connected between generator output and ground helps silence the generator's whine.

Generator and Alternator Noise

The whine and snarl often associated with the conventional generator can be softened or eliminated as follows: Connect a 1 μF 200-volt capacitor between the armature (battery) terminal and ground—ground in this case being the generator frame. Do not install the capacitor on the field (control) terminal; doing so may alter regulator characteristics.

In very bad cases of generator whine, install a 1 μF 200 volt capacitor on each carbon brush holder to ground, using short, stubby leads. This suppresses brush spark and electrical noise close to its source, and is reported especially effective on 32- or 120-volt direct-current generators.

Alternator Hiss

The alternator is inherently quieter than the conventional armature-and-brush generator, its high frequency noise being quieted by an internal capacitor. Most remaining alternator noises can be eliminated or greatly minimized by a 1 μF 200 volt capacitor bewteen the alternator's output (battery) terminal and ground.

Regulator Noise

Generator and alternator voltage regulators generate various kinds of radio frequency noise. Often, the noise is similar to that

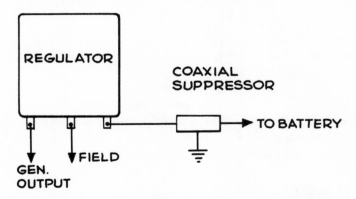

Fig. 20-4 Connected in the lead between the regulator and battery, the coaxial suppressor reduces noise originating in the regulator.

coming from spark plugs; and popping noises are common. In some cases the popping stops as engine speed is reduced to idle.

When suppressing the regulator, put a 1 μF 200 volt capacitor between the regulator's battery connection to ground. Keep all leads short. If the by-pass capacitor reduces the noise, but not enough to satisfy you, purchase a coaxial suppressor capacitor, wiring it in series with the battery lead. You can get a coax suppressor in an electronic parts store.

Electric Motor Noise

Direct-current motors such as those on pumps, fans, and windshield wipers, and also universal AC motors, such as on hand tools, can be filtered. Connect a 1 μF 200 volt capacitor across the line close to the motor. If the motor is still electrically noisy, install a capacitor on each commutating brush holder, connecting the other end of the capacitor to the grounded motor frame. Keep all pigtail leads as short as possible.

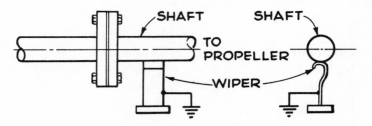

Fig. 20-5 A metal wiper or brush conductively bearing on the propeller shaft is connected to the boat's bonding network for radio noise reduction.

Miscellaneous Noise Sources

There are many other possible minor sources of electrical noise—too many in fact, to list them all—but here are a few that you may encounter:

Propeller Shaft

Should you hear steady noise bursts on the radio when the prop shaft is spinning, but notice that the noises disappear when the clutch is thrown to netural with the engine still running, the prop shaft may be generating static. You can eliminate this source of disturbance by installing a bronze finger or brush that wipes the shaft while maintaining electrical contact with it. Electrically connect this finger or wiper to the boat's common bonding system, using heavy wire.

Electric Tachometer

Some electrical tachometers, those connected to the ignition system, cause electrical noise which can be detected by electronic equipment. If you suspect that interference may be coming from your electric tach, perform a test by disconnecting it while listening for improvement.

One remedy is to shield all the wires associated with the tachometer, and ground the shielding. Also enclose the sending unit in a shielded box, and ground that.

Sailboat Shrouds

An eerie electrical whine may sometimes be heard on sailboat radios despite all other electrical equipment being turned off. This mysterious interference sounds as though an invisible giant is running a knife blade along the antenna wire; it's a static-like noise with no specific pattern.

Such noise is caused by turnbuckles on stays and shrouds. You can eliminate the trouble by installing shorting jumpers across the turnbuckles. The best method is to drill small holes in each half of the turnbuckle, fastening a wire to each half with small screws. Then wrap the entire turnbuckle neatly with plastic tape to protect the connections.

Grounding and Bonding

Many facets of the bonding and grounding were explored in Chapter 5; but the noise reduction aspect is worth reiterating here. Good grounds help minimize electrical noise. When grounding any accessory, use heavy wire or cable, connecting metal enclosures and chassis to the boat's bonding. Don't allow equipment to share one ground wire; and provide an individual grounding conductor for each piece of electrical gear.

VHF Radiotelephone Precautions

Raytheon Company, in its instructions for intalling the RAY-45 VHF/FM Marine Radiotelephone, cautions as follows about bonding:

"All unbonded metalwork in the vicinity of the antenna, such as hand rails, steering cables, permanent halyards, windshield frame, or plumbing can affect the performance of the radio. It is good practice to bond these together and ground to the engine with a heavy conductor and suitable clamps. In some cases, this bonding will be essential, since any unbonded metalwork may act as a parasitic absorber or re-radiator of the antenna transmit signal. These parasitic elements may severely distort an otherwise excellent antenna pattern. *Bond all metalwork!*" (Emphasis is Raytheon's.)

SYNOPSIS

The boat's electrical and mechanical machinery generates radio-frequency noise which can be searched out and suppressed. Ignition crackle can be suppressed or shielded, while the noise from generators, alternators, and motors can be softened by capacitors or shielding. Prop shaft noise can be grounded; and all electrical machinery is less likely to radiate hash when well grounded and bonded.

CHAPTER 21

Electricity and Your Compass

SINCE A current-carrying conductor is encircled by a magnetic field, and since the compass responds to such fields, a conductor close to the compass will deviate the instrument. The stronger the current, the greater the disturbing influence; and the closer the wire is to the binnacle, the greater the effect.

In the spring of 1972, the author conducted a series of experiments to demonstrate the practical effects of boat wiring on compass accuracy; and the results appeared in *Motor Boating & Sailing*. Results of the tests highlight the disturbing effects of conducting wires and electronic equipment on the magnetic compass.

The Method

In the experiments, we placed several types of compass in the center of a turntable, the lazy-susan simulating a boat, able to head in any direction. Sequentially, a current-carrying wire was placed fore-and-aft, then athwartship, at compass level, then above and below the compass.

At each relationship, the wire was dressed at several measured distances from compass center. Then at each of these measured distances, several values of current were sent through the conductor. The wire was 12 gauge. Four feet comprised the straight test length arranged near the compass, the balance being

303

dressed away at right angles, running to the power supply 20 feet away. The power source was kept this distance to make its magnetic effect negligible. The test arrangement is shown in Figure 21-1.

Effect of Latitude

The described experiments were conducted at latitude north 40° 34'. We mentioned latitude because farther north, close to the earth's magnetic poles, the effect of stray currents would be worse. This is because at high latitudes the earth's horizontal magnetic component is weaker. Had the experiments been conducted closer to the equator, the deviating effects of our electric wires would have been less.

Effect of Compass Type

Several yacht compasses and a surveyor's needle type instru-

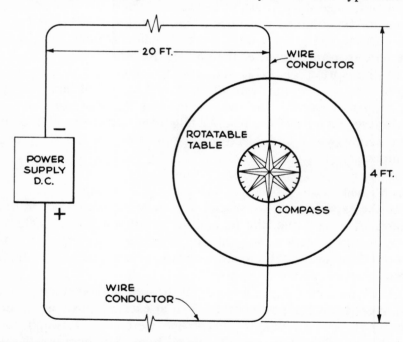

Fig. 21-1 General arrangement of rig for testing effect of electric currents on the magnetic compass.

ment were tested and each seemed to respond about the same. Regardless of damping, each compass would settle, pointing at the magnetic vector resulting from earth's attraction and the field encircling the conductor.

Current is the Enemy

Direct current flowing in a wire close to the compass induces deflection, and the magnitude of deviation is proportional to current intensity. Thus, eight amperes has twice the effect of 4 amperes. *Current,* not voltage, is the important parameter. A wire several hundred volts above ground potential, but carrying no current, bothers the compass not, even though in close proximity to it.

Alternating Current

Wires carrying alternating current have no effect on the directional readout of the compass unless they are carrying exceptionally powerful currents and are very close. In that case they cause the compass magnets to vibrate; and it is conceivable that high density AC currents might damage the compass. But in practical application there seems to be little to fear from AC circuits.

Twisted Pairs

Direct-current wires dressed close to the compass in twisted pairs have little or no effect on the compass, causing no perceptible deviation. This is because the magnetic field around one wire is clockwise, around the other is counter-clockwise, and the two fields cancel. Conversely, the worst situation is where the wires, far from being closely twisted, are actually dressed apart, the positive conductor on one side, the negative on the other side of the binnacle. Here, the two fields, rather than cancelling, double their deviating effect on the compass.

Horizontal Wires

Direct-current wires in the horizontal plane exactly at the level of the compass magnets have no deviating effect. However, as the wire is raised or lowered from the magnet's level, it deviates the compass clockwise at one level, counter-clockwise at the other, depending upon the direction of current in the conductor.

Horizontal direct-current wires running above or below the center of the compass deviate the card. Induced error is greatest when the wire is aligned north-south, and is essentially zero when alignment is east-west.

Vertical Wires

Direct-current conductors arranged vertically in proximity to the compass have a deviating effect. Deviation is greatest when the vertical wire is north or south of the compass needle, and is substantially zero when located east or west.

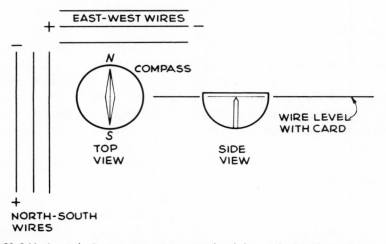

Fig. 21-2 Horizontal wires at compass magnet level do not deviate the instrument.

Effect of Roll and Pitch

Magnitude of deviation from the field around direct-current wires varies as the boat rolls and pitches. For example, a wire positioned horizontally athwartships at compass card level will deviate the card first clockwise, then counterclockwise as the boat pitches.

Effect of Boat's Heading

The boat's magnetic heading modifies the effect that live

direct-current wires have on the compass. Consider a vertical conductor located forward of the compass lubber line. This wire will have maximum deviating effect when the boat heads north or south, will have little influence when the boat is on east or west courses.

Effect of Radios

Virtually all radio receivers, from tiny shirt pocket models to the largest shelf consoles, incorporate permanent magnet speakers. In recent years, technological advances in the magnet art have made these magnets more powerful. The result is that even a small radio in the compass's vicinity can have a profound effect on instrument readout; and, in fact, if the radio is close enough its magnet can even reverse the compass card. Small TV sets and most radio direction finders also have internal permanent magnet speakers, and these instruments can exert an evil influence on the compass, just as a radio receiver does.

The Experiments

The effects of various wire arrangements and of the relative positioning of radio speakers were determined in the experiments described in the following paragraphs. The specific distances and positioning of wires will convey an idea of what to expect from conductors carrying known currents on board your boat.

Wires at Compass Level

The experiments with direct-current wires strung horizontally at compass magnet level are illustrated in Figure 21-2. Currents of 2.5, 5, and 10 amps through the conductors at 6, 12, 24, and 36 inches from the compass center generate no perceptible compass card movement. Immediately the north-south wires were displaced from the compass magnet plane; however, the compass was deflected. For the illustrated polarity, deviation was counterclockwise as the wire was elevated, clockwise as it was depressed below the compass magnet plane. The experiment demonstrates the effect of a boat rolling when on a northerly course, or pitching on a west course. It emphasizes that dressing wires at compass magnet level will not prevent deviation on an actual boat.

Wires Under the Compass

The effect of a wire running directly under the compass is shown in Figure 21-3, where the wire is aligned north and south, parallel to the compass needle. The following table gives the deviation produced by different currents and wire distances from

| | | Distance From Compass | | |
Amperes	6″	12″	18″	36″
10	26°	14°	8°	4°
5	12.5°	7°	4°	2°
2.5	7°	3.5°	2°	1°

Deviation

the compass card. With the polarities shown, the card deflects clockwise in response to current. Reversed polarity reverses the deviation.

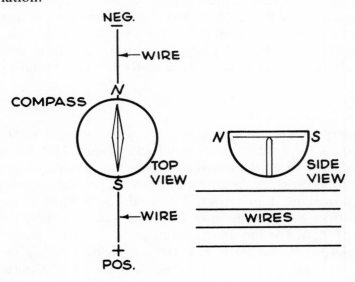

Fig. 21-3 A north-south current-carrying wire under or over the compass has considerable deviating effect.

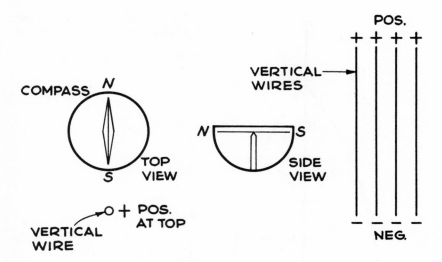

Fig. 21-4 A vertical wire north or south of the compass deviates the card when current flows.

Vertical Wires

Figure 21-4 demonstrates the effect of a wire running vertically, directly south of the compass; and the following table shows the effect of current and distance. With the polarities shown, the needle deflects clockwise when current flows. Reversed polarity gives reverse deviation; and when the wire is east or west of the compass, its effect is zero.

	Distance From Compass				
Amperes	6"	12"	18"	24"	36"
10	23°	10°	5.5°	3°	1°
5	13°	5°	2.5°	1°	
2.5	7°	2.5°	1.7°		

Deviation

Effect of Headings

An experiment simulating the effect of a conductor on the compass aboard a boat placed on several headings, is shown in Figure 21-5. The energized conductor is fore-and-aft, eight inches beneath the compass magnets. The wire is carrying 5

309

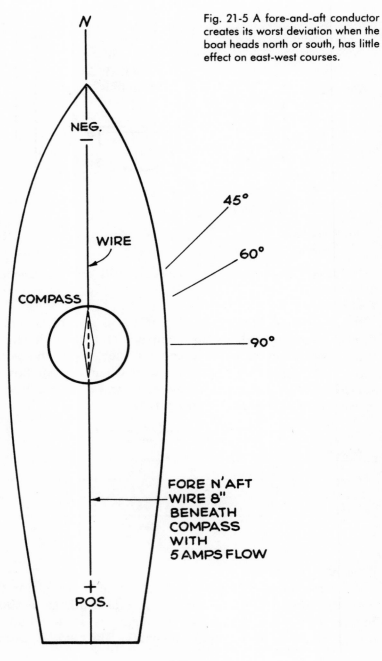

Fig. 21-5 A fore-and-aft conductor creates its worst deviation when the boat heads north or south, has little effect on east-west courses.

N

NEG.
−

45°

WIRE

60°

COMPASS

90°

FORE N'AFT
WIRE 8"
BENEATH
COMPASS
WITH
5 AMPS FLOW

+
POS.

amperes, positive aft, negative forward, creating clockwise deviation with the boat on north headings. The boat's heading versus deviation is tallied in the following table:

Heading	Deviation
000°	14°
045°	12°
060°	9.5°
090°	0°

Specific Components

Wire-wound electrical components having external fields can amplify the deviating effect of direct currents. Such components are typified by relays, solenoids, and ignition coils. The point is illustrated by the following tests made with an ignition coil drawing three amperes, and placed due east or west of the compass:

Distance	Deviation
36″	2°
24″	4°
18″	10°
12″	30°

Radio Speakers

Earlier in the chapter the radio speaker was mentioned as a source of compass error. The following figures indicate just how bad an influence a speaker can be, and are based upon a little three-inch portable radio speaker, having a magnet of but a few ounces. Orientation of speaker is due west of compass:

Distance Of Speaker To Compass	Deviation
6′	Trace
4′	2°
3′	4°
2′	13°
1′	50°

These figures show that any on-board radio with permanent magnet speaker should be in a fixed position if it is closer than some 5 *feet* from the compass. With the radio in a fixed location, the compass can be swung and adjusted; compensation will then include correction for the effect of the speaker.

Checking Your Boat for Deviation

If you would like to check the effect of your boat's electrical systems on the compass, perform this test in calm water: Set the boat on a north-south heading. Watch the compass closely while someone energizes and deenergizes each direct-current circuit. Watch for telltale compass deflection. Repeat the experiment on an east-west heading, and, if you wish, on several intercardinal headings.

Curing Deviation

If you locate a circuit which upsets the compass, you can take one of three tacks, of which the first is best:

1. Rewire any offending circuit, using twisted pairs of wires, and dressing all conductors as far from the compass as practicable. At all costs, avoid running one wire of a pair on one side of the compass, its mate on the other side.

2. If the deviating circuit is one which will be energized part time, as a light circuit, prepare two deviation cards. One will give compass correction with the circuit energized; the other will apply when the circuit is cold.

3. Have the compass swung and corrected with the circuit either energized or cold; thereafter, always navigate with the circuit in that state.

The experiments indicate that when you correct your compass, or have it adjusted by a professional, the boat's electrical circuits should be in the cruising state. Furthermore, the compass should be checked in the normal daytime electrical condition, lights off, and in the nighttime state, lights on. Cruising sailboats should try the compass with the auxiliary engine running, and shut off, and also with the boat reasonably heeled to simulate her attitude on both tacks.

After electrical alterations on the boat, and following the installation of new electrical or electronic equipment, reswing the compass to make sure the compass has not been affected. Also, when doing any wiring, pay particular attention to the dress of conductors in the helm area, assuring they are dressed in twisted pairs.

SYNOPSIS

The magnetic field surrounding direct-current conductors deviates the compass from its earth-induced heading, the error being determined by the amplitude of current and distance of the conductor from the binnacle. The effect is more pronounced at high latitudes; and it is current, not voltage, which induces the error. Alternating current has little effect other than to make the compass vibrate. Both horizontal and vertical wires create error; but if the conductors are dressed in twisted pairs, the error is negligible. Roll, pitch, and boat heading modify the deviation caused by a given conductor; and the same applies to the effect of a magnetic radio speaker. Deviation can be measured and corrected on the boat; and correction tables can be prepared.

Part 2

Manual of Electrical and Electronic Projects

CHAPTER 22

Adding AC Convenience Outlets

THE TERM "duplex convenience outlet" is the technically correct name for the familiar double outlets commonly installed in several places in each room of a house. Almost all cabin cruisers, even the smaller ones, will have several of these about the boat, either as a standard feature or as a factory-added option. But here "Murphy's Law" once more comes into effect—you have enough outlets on your boat, but there's one place where you want to put a 120-volt AC appliance that doesn't have an outlet nearby. (Although the most-commonly used term is "110-volt," the correct designation is 120-volt.) Double sockets and extension cords can be used, but these are unsightly and they can become a safety hazard. The proper answer to meet your need is to install an additional duplex convenience outlet where it can be reached by the appliance's own power cord.

PLANNING

As with almost any boat project, the first step will be to thoroughly study the situation and plan your work.

Can you flush-mount an outlet where you want it? Is there enough depth behind the panel for the fixture and its enclosing box? Is there an access route for the necessary wires?

Or if there is not depth behind the panel, will you accept a surface-

317

mounted box and outlet fixture? If so, is there room behind the panel for the wiring, or must it be surface-mounted also?

What will be the heaviest load you will plug into this outlet? What size wire must you use? Is there capacity on an existing circuit, or will a new one have to be established from the distribution panel?

There must be answers to these questions, and probably others deriving from your particular boat and power needs, *before* you buy any materials or make the first cut. *Think* your project through completely, then—and only then—go to work.

Selection of Materials

The standard duplex convenience outlet as used in your home will be satisfactory for installation on your boat. Make sure that you get the modern type with a third hole for a round *grounding* prong. This type can be used with AC devices having either a

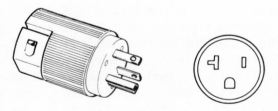

Fig. 22-1 Where somewhat more current is required than can be handled with the standard "household" fixtures, a 20-ampere socket and plug can be used.

two-prong or a three-prong plug, and such will be necessary if your device does have the newer three-prong plug. A standard 15-ampere outlet will normally be satisfactory, (see Figure 4-11) but you should be aware that there are outlets rated for 20 amperes which will accommodate the special 20-ampere male plug on which the two flat blades are not parallel but at right angles to each other. Outlets and their covering plates come in a variety of colors; simulated wood grain patterns are also available for the plates. A box around the fixture is necessary for safety because of the dangers of 120-volt electricity.

Wire Types

The wires you use to connect your new outlet to a source of power should also be specifically selected for use in a marine environment. The ABYC standard for 120-volt wiring on small craft, E-8, lists a number of recommended insulation types. Don't bother with learning what the abbreviations stand for, but do make sure that the wire you use is marked with insulation designation THW, THWN, XHHW, MTW, or AWM; insulation

Fig. 22-2 Heavier gauges of wire will be marked every few feet with the manufacturer's name, insulation type, gauge, and voltage rating, plus UL approval if applicable.

type of TW can be used provided that the wire is not routed through any machinery spaces. Insulation should be rated at a minimum of 600 volts. Conductors should be stranded, not solid; don't use NM cable (Romex) that is widely used in homes. Wires must be of an adequate size to carry the anticipated current; for a standard 15-ampere outlet 14-gauge wire will be satisfactory for the short runs involved and will be economical.

When you buy the wire, make sure that you get enough! Almost always a job takes more than you think it will because of the indirect route that must be taken by the wires from the source to the load. There should be three conductors—black, white, and green—in an overall nonmetallic sheath; don't use armored cable type BX.

INSTALLATION

Having studied the problem, made your plans, and bought your material, you are ready to start the work. Assuming that you are going to mount your added receptacle flush in a panel, and that you have determined that there is adequate clear space

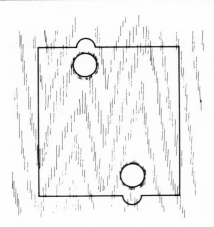

Fig. 22-3 Outlet box was used as template to mark bulkhead for cutting; two smaller holes have been drilled for starting the saw.

behind the panel as well as a route for the wires, take the box that will go around the receptacle and hold it in place on the front of the panel and mark its outline with a pencil. Now put the box aside and drill two holes ½" or more in diameter *within* the marked area near diagonally opposite corners. Next use a saber saw or a hand keyhole saw to cut out the marked area. Be reasonably neat, but any ragged edges of this hole will be hidden by the receptacle cover plate. Punch out one or more of the molded-in or stamped-in "knockouts" in the box so that wires can enter; then mount the box with appropriate fasteners.

Installing the Wires

Loads placed on convenience outlets on boats are usually light enough that wiring can be run from the nearest fixture already installed. In case of doubt, however, the safest procedure is to run the wires all the way back to the fuse or circuit breaker at the distribution panel. Wiring must be installed as high as possible, well above any bilge water level; wires should also be kept well away from exhaust lines or other heat sources. Wires must be routed so as to protect them from any possible physical damage; the use of conduit is not generally desirable as it provides a place for moisture to collect; if its use is necessary, however, provide drainage holes. Where wires pass through bulkheads or structural members, protection from chafing *must* be provided. Wires can be "fished" through inaccessible spaces with a metal tape as used by professional electricians, but I have found that a handy method is to use a short length of soft aluminum wire that can be shaped as needed to go around corners. (This wire is commonly used to ground TV antennas and is available at stores such as Radio Shack.)

Run the wires that you are installing from the source of power to the new receptacle allowing adequate slack enroute to avoid any strains on the wire and enough slack at each end for ease in making connections to terminals. Wires should be supported throughout their length at intervals not exceeding 18 inches. Nonmetallic clamps are best, and these should be of the proper size—not so small as to crimp the insulation on the wire, but not so large that the wire can move back and forth within the clamp. Metal clamps can be used if they are fitted with a nonmetallic liner, but it is much simpler and cheaper to use the plastic clamps.

With stranded wire, it is necessary to use terminal lugs rather than merely shaping the wire around each terminal screw. These should be of the crimp-on type of the proper size for *both* the wire gauge and the terminal screw or stud. The plastic insulating sleeves on the terminals are color-coded for the wire size— yellow for gauges 10 and 12, blue for 14 and 16, and red for 18 to 22. Use the correct crimping tool, and test the strength of your crimp after it is made—#14 wire should withstand a 30-pound pull, and that's a really hard pull.

Connecting the Wires

Make sure that the power is off (it probably is on if you were using an electric drill or saber saw)—the best way is to completely disconnect the shore power cord. Attach the wires to the new receptacle—the black ("hot") wire is attached to the terminal marked B or identified by a darker color such as brass. The white (grounded) wire goes to the terminal marked W or identified by a lighter color such as silver. The green (grounding) wire is attached to the terminal marked G or identified by a bit of green paint.

Next attach each wire at the point at which you are going to get your power, another receptacle or the distribution panel. Make sure that each wire goes to the proper terminal; if you are connecting to another receptacle, check that it was wired correctly when it was installed.

Testing

Now you are ready to test your installation. If you have an ohmmeter, test between the hot and grounded wires and then between the hot and grounding wires (any loads on this circuit must be turned off or disconnected). If you read zero or low resistance, go back over your work and clear up the indicated short-circuit; your tests should show open-circuits. Being very careful because of the exposed terminals, turn the power on and test with an AC volt-meter; you should read 120 volts, or whatever the supply is at that moment. The wires should now be worked back through the knock-out hole or holes so that the receptacle can be pushed back into the box and secured with two screws either to the box or the panel. The cover plate is now put on using a single machine screw at its center.

Miscellaneous Requirements

If your new receptacle is to be installed in a location subject to rain, spray, or splash, it must be fitted with a nonmetallic cover, either individual covers over each socket or one larger cover over both. These must be kept closed except when the outlet is in actual use.

Above-surface Installation

If you are unable to flush-mount a receptacle where you need one, it is possible to do an above-surface installation by mounting the box on the outside of the panel and the fixture in it as before. Wires are then run on the surface of the panel protected by a metal raceway or "wiremold." These are available in small-enough sizes, and in a variety of colors, so that the completed job need not be unattractive. If raceway is not readily available,

½" PVC pipe can be used, secured in place with plastic clamps as used for wire. If desired, the pipe can be lightly sanded and painted to match.

Labeling

Outlets for 120-volts AC should be labeled for positive identification. Small plastic nameplates are available at marine supply stores, but a tape labeler makes a neat, and much less expensive, job. It is very important that any "convenience outlet" for 12-volts DC be of a *completely different* design. The AC receptacles are of a standard type that you will have to use, but you will have a wide variety of types to choose from for any low-voltage DC outlets which must be polarized for positive and negative leads. These, too, should be properly labeled.

CHAPTER 23

Adding to the 12-Volt DC System

ALMOST EVERY boat—even outboards and smaller sailboats—will at sometime be a candidate for an addition to its electrical system. New boats are never delivered with all the electrical and electronic gear that the skipper desires. The new owner of a used boat will probably have some ideas for equipment additions or changes. Such extensions to a craft's 12-volt DC electrical system will sooner or later become one of the owner's projects, and there's no reason that it can't fall into the "do-it-yourself" category.

Possible Projects

Among the various projects that may develop are the installation of additional electrical or electronic equipment, or the relocation of some item. You may want to add another bilge pump or engine compartment blower, a depth sounder or a radio. Perhaps you may not like where the boat manufacturer or previous owner placed an item of equipment and want to re-install it elsewhere. Quite often a boat is delivered with some cabin lights, but not enough, or without one placed where you can lie in your bunk and read. Many boats do not have a light in the engine compartment or in a hanging locker where it would be useful. In Chapter 22 we covered the installation of 120-volt AC "convenience outlets." Often there is a need for comparable outlets for the 12-volt DC electrical system to power tape recorders, calculators, fans, and other items that use such a source of power. Several outlets of this type located at possible points of need throughout the boat will add to convenience and comfort.

Problems to be Considered

In making additions to a boat's DC electrical system the principal problems to be considered are the wiring and the overload protection. Wires must be installed of a gauge suitable to the load to be carried and the distance from source of power to the load, which in turn is determined by the route the wires must take. Overload protection must be provided for the new circuit even though the piece of equipment may have its own built-in or in-line fuse. Protective devices include replaceable fuses and circuit breakers; both have their advantages and disadvantages.

WIRING

Wiring for low-voltage DC circuits presents somewhat different problems from the considerations discussed in Chapter 21 for 120-volt AC outlets. There the load was often unknown and the wire gauge was selected for the maximum rating of the duplex outlet; voltage drop was not significant and the length of the wires was not considered. For 12-volt DC circuits the load is generally fixed and known—an item of equipment or a specific size light bulb or bulbs. Voltage drop (the amount that the voltage at the load is less than the system voltage at the source of power due to current flow along the wires) is important—wire gauge is selected based on load amperes and length so as to keep voltage drop to an acceptable value. Overheating of wires is, of course, a safety concern, but it is not a problem where wires are heavy enough to ensure an acceptably low voltage drop.

Wire Gauges

Wire comes in standard sizes designated by "American Wire Gauge (AWG)" numbers. These are like the number series of drill bit sizes, they vary inversely with the size of the wire—the larger the gauge number, the smaller the wire, and vice versa. The system is established so that a change of three numbers, either up or down, changes the cross-sectional area of the wire by a factor of two; a change of six numbers changes the area by a factor of four which is the same as doubling, or halving, the diameter. Voltage drop is inversely related to cross-sectional

#10   #16
(NOT ACTUAL DIAMETERS)

Fig. 23-1 Wire gauge #10 is twice the diameter of gauge #16, and has one-fourth the resistance for the same length. If there were a #13 size, its resistance would be one-half that of #16, and twice that of #10.

area—for a given current, doubling the cross-sectional area would halve the resistance and halve the voltage drop. (Safe current-carrying capacity—avoiding overheating—is roughly a function of cross-sectional area, but, as noted before, this is not a consideration when selecting wire size for low-voltage DC circuits.) When applying the doubling/halving rule of three gauge numbers in practical applications, however, it must be remembered that for wires smaller than #4AWG (larger gauge numbers) wire is available only in even numbers, 6, 8, 10, etc.

Selecting the Wire Gauge

The proper size of wire for a particular project is selected from tables using values for the system voltage, current, length of wires, and permissable voltage drop expressed in percent of the system voltage. (Voltage enters into the picture since for a given load, higher-voltage circuits will require less current.) Formulas are available for calculating necessary wire size, but tables are available and much easier to use; see pages 56 and 58.

These tables are derived from Standard E-9 published by the American Boat & Yacht Council (ABYC). One set of tables is for use where a voltage drop of 10% is acceptable; typically this includes cabin lights and most motors such as pumps, fans, etc. A separate set of tables is provided for more-critical installations where the voltage drop must not exceed 3%; typical cases involve radios, depth sounders, and other electronic gear. (Although the requirements for navigation lights are stated in terms of visibility range rather than voltage at the lamp, it is a good idea to wire them from the 3%-drop table.)

The current to be carried in the new circuit must be known. Most DC electrical and electronic equipment will have a nameplate giving the amperes drawn from the circuit, or this information will be available on the box in which the gear comes or in its instruction book. (If the load of electronic equipment should be given in milliamperes, divide such figure by 1000 to get amperes.) The current drawn by bulbs used in cabin and other lights can either be determined from catalog tables, or if rated in watts, determined by dividing the voltage into the power rating in watts. Outlets for various different possible uses should be wired for the heaviest anticipated load.

Low-voltage DC circuits on a boat are of the two-wire type with conductors both for the positive—"hot"—lead and for the negative—"return"—lead. This differs from automotive circuits that have a single "hot" wire and use the vehicle's frame for the return circuit. *Caution:* This use of two wires can cause confusion in the use of wire-size tables. Some tables are stated in terms of the distance from the source to the load; others are in terms of total conductor length and since there are two wires this figure is twice the "distance" used in some tables. The tables on Pages 56 and 58 of Part I of this book are based on the sum of the length of the two conductors.

Wire Routing

The route that the new wires will take from the source of power to the load must be carefully considered. The same considerations as for AC wiring in Chapter 22 apply—the wires must be kept clear of bilge water, adequately supported along their length, and protected from chafing of their insulation. Wires should be supported or secured at intervals of not more than 18 inches. Non-metallic clamps are preferred except over engines, moving shafts, or other machinery but clamps of metal may be used if protection is provided so that the insulation of the wires is not damaged. Metallic clamps or straps must be used if wiring is routed over engines, moving shafts, or in other areas if failure of the clamps or straps due to fire could cause an additional hazard. Detailed planning is required as the route to be followed by the wires determines both their length and the required gauge—and once you purchase your wire, you can't change either! At the same time, determine the number of wire clips and cable ties that you will need to support the added wires. If wires must be routed so that they would be visible above decks, appearances can be improved by enclosing them in tubing; see Chapter 22.

Wire Selection

Having developed our project plans to the point of determining the wire gauge and length, we are ready to purchase materials. (Add a couple of feet or so, just to be sure—it will only cost a bit more and there's nothing worse than finding that you need 32 feet of wire just after arriving back at your boat with a purchase of 30 feet.) Use enough length of wire so that there is no mechanical strain on the connection at either end. Wires for use on a boat should be stranded instead of solid because of the vibration that is normal on motorized craft. The type of insulation must be suitable for the marine environment and temperature in the areas of the boat through which the wires will run. Again we turn to ABYC Standard E-9 and guidance in the selection of wire insulation will be found on Page 55 of Part I.

Wire Termination

After the wires have been routed and installed in the manner mentioned above, they must be properly terminated at each end. Crimp-on terminals and connectors are satisfactory and soldering is not necessary. Terminal lugs must be right for *both* the size of wire used and the stud or screw on which they are to be placed. Wire sizes are indicated by the color of the plastic insulating sleeve of the crimp-on terminals—yellow for gauges 10 and 12, blue for 14 and 16, red for 18 to 22. Ring terminals are much preferable to spade terminals although "captive spade" terminals, those with a turned-up lip at each side, may be used if under a screw head, or a flat washer is used between the lug and the nut on a stud terminal. Information from the ABYC standard is covered on Page 53.

If the device to be added has wire leads rather than mechanical terminal screws or studs, the connection will be made with a crimp-on "butt connector." Here a problem of different wire sizes may arise. Quite often the wires that come with a bilge pump or a lamp socket will be of a smaller gauge than the wires that you are running for some distance from the source. Use a butt connector of a size suitable for the larger wire and try doubling back the end of the smaller wire to make it fit the connector. Always test the mechanical strength of such a connection after it is made by giving the wires a good strong pull. If a satisfactory crimped connection cannot be made, you may have to resort to soldering, which will always work. If the added item of equipment is one that you will want to sometimes remove—for security or winter storage—you can use "quick disconnect" terminals in lieu of butt connectors if the circuit carries not more than 6 amperes; these can be repeatedly pulled apart and rejoined easily.

Wiring Color Codes

If your boat is only a few years old, it is likely that its factory-installed wiring is all the colors of a rainbow—in accordance with ABYC Standard E-3. This color coding is a great help and should be followed when adding to your boat's electrical system. Negative (return) leads should be white although black is permitted and is sometimes used. Positive (hot) leads are coded according to their use as follows:

Pumps—dark gray
Cabin and instrument lights—dark blue
Bilge blowers—yellow
Gauges—tachometer, dark gray; oil pressure, light blue; fuel, pink; water temperature—tan.

Coding for other uses, ones less likely to be involved in a do-it-yourself project, can be found in ABYC Safety Standard E-3. It should be noted that some colors are used for more than one purpose, but these will be so different that confusion is unlikely; for example, dark gray is used for both electric tachometers and for navigation lights.

SWITCHES

Often the newly-added device, such as a cabin light will have its own integral switch and no other will be needed. In other instances, such as the addition of a bilge pump or windshield wiper, a new switch must be installed. Sometimes if the overload protection (see a later section of this chapter) is in the form of a circuit breaker, that unit can also serve as the off-on switch for the new circuit.

If a new switch is to be installed it must be of a suitable type—adequate current-carrying capacity and usable in a marine environment. It can have either screw terminals or short wire leads and be connected into the circuit accordingly. It is not necessary to open both sides of the two-wire circuit and the switch may be of the "single-pole, single-throw (SPST)" type *provided* it is placed in the positive lead—never put a switch solely in the negative lead. Any switch placed in an engine or fuel tank compartment on a boat using gasoline as its fuel must be "ignition protected" and approved by Underwriters Laboratories (UL).

OUTLETS

Convenience outlets at several points on the boat can be very useful for powering fans, tape recorders, calculators, electric games, etc. Some boatmen use outlets in the form of a cigarette lighter socket as plugs with attached cords are readily available at

Fig. 23-2 A convenient type of 12-volt DC outlet for a boat is a panel-mounted "cigarette lighter" socket. Many accessories come with a matching plug, and separate plugs, or plugs with cords (shown), can be purchased.

stores; Radio Shack item #270-021. Sockets can be purchased already mounted in a standard plate that fits a wall box like an AC outlet, Radio Shack item #270-1539. A two-outlet Y-adapter (#270-1535) and an extension cord (#270-1536) are also available.

Alternatively, small female receptacles can be used but these must be polarized and distinctively different from any 120-volt AC convenience outlets. DC outlets should also be properly labeled except for those of the cigarette-lighter type.

OVERLOAD PROTECTION

Electrical circuits on boats can become overloaded in either of two ways—by a defect in the load equipment or device, or from a short-circuit in the wiring at the load or along the length of the wires. Many items of electronic equipment, and some electrical gear, will have a fuse built into the device or inserted in the positive lead just outside the case. While this will serve to protect from an overload or short-circuit *within* the device, protection is still needed at the source to open the circuit in the event of a wiring fault. This protection is most often achieved by use of a fuse or circuit breaker that is a part of the boat's electrical distribution panel. The rating of the protective device should not be greater than the safe current-carrying capacity of the circuit wiring.

Fuses are less expensive than circuit breakers, but are also less convenient. The small cylindrical glass fuses usually used on branch circuits on boat—Type 3AG or AGC—are installed in holders in such a way that a blown fuse is not readily apparent. There is also the problem of maintaining on board an adequate stock of replacements (at least three) in each size and type used.

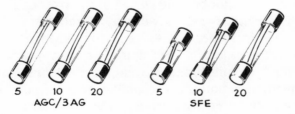

Fig. 23-3 Type 3AG/AGC fuses are all of the same length regardless of rating. Type SPE fuses vary in length, longer for higher current ratings.

A special slow-blowing type of fuse must be used with motors to handle the heavy initial surge of current without going to so large a size that the unit would not really be protected. Another major problem of fuses on boats is the corrosion that can develop at the fuse holder. This can slowly build up as a result of the marine environment and ultimately increase resistance until the circuit is broken. Fuse holders are often out of sight and out of mind; maintenance is neglected and failures come without warning. If you do use fuses, be sure to avoid automotive-type SFE fuses in which the length varies with the current rating; the varying physical sizes makes for problems with fuse-holder panels.

A circuit breaker, on the other hand, is much more expensive, but no spares are required and it can also serve as the off-on switch for that particular load. Breakers will carry 100% of rated

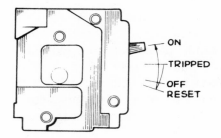

ON
TRIPPED
OFF
RESET

Fig. 23-4 A circuit breaker is more expensive than a fuse, but no spares need be carried and the unit also can be used as an on-off switch.

load indefinitely and small continuing overloads up to about 130% of rating for brief periods that decrease with increasing severity of the overload. Circuit breakers must be of the "trip-free" type that cannot be held closed under overload conditions. For motor starting, breakers will stay closed for a brief—10-20 seconds—current surge, but will open if the high current continues, as in the case of a mechanically-stalled motor. So-called "self-healing" circuit breakers that reset themselves without external manual action are acceptable only as part of a device that is on a circuit otherwise protected by a fuse or breaker at the source.

If there is an unused fuse or circuit breaker on the distribution panel, it is wise to use this for the new circuit if feasible—the size of a fuse can be easily changed; a circuit breaker can be replaced with one of a different rating but such is less easy and is more expensive. If there is no spare position available, it is permissible to add the new circuit to an existing fuse or breaker if the total load or circuit wire rating will not be exceeded.

CAUTION

Special caution must be used if the wires of the circuit you are adding come within 3 or 4 feet of a magnetic compass. The flow of electricity in a pair of wires can create a magnetic field capable of seriously changing the compass' deviation. This undesirable effect can be avoided if the two wires are run together and tightly twisted, the magnetic field around one wire cancelling out that around the other. In any event, after such a circuit has been completely installed, observe the compass closely as the current is slowly switched on and off; these tests should be made twice with the boat securely motionless at a pier, once the boat is on a heading nearly north or south, and again on a heading nearly east or west. If the compass card is observed to move, re-route the wires, or increase the twisting, or both, and recheck. For further details, see Chapter 21.

An electric light that is added to an engine room, forepeak, or other area where it might be struck and broken must be given mechanical protection. A broken bulb may well result in a short-circuit and possible fire hazard. You can use a small bulb in a nearly flush fixture—much like the "dome light" in a car. Or you can use a regular house-type bulb—but one for 12-volts—with a protective wire cage around it.

CHAPTER 24

Batteries and Battery Chargers

BASIC INFORMATION on storage batteries, alternators (generators) and their regulators, and battery chargers was presented in Chapters 2, 6, and 7 of Part 1 of this book. Here we will consider some additional aspects of these topics, plus others not touched on there; much of this relates to recent developments in this field.

STORAGE BATTERIES

There are a number of terms that must be understood if you are to select, use, and care for the lead-acid storage battery or batteries in your boat properly. There are several different battery types, which are described below.

Battery Types

We are all familiar with "automotive" batteries as found in our cars and trucks; we are perhaps less familiar with the term "marine battery." This is a lead-acid battery, as described in Chapter 2. It is very much like the automotive type, but it includes construction features that recognize the environment in which it will live and work; these features add to the cost if it is a true marine battery and not just one with a different pasted-on label. A genuine marine battery is much more rugged in many ways. The molded rubber case is thicker and stronger, with reinforcement added at its corners to reduce the possibility of breakage. Terminal posts are molded into the rubber in a manner that minimizes any possibility of leakage; see Figure 24-1.

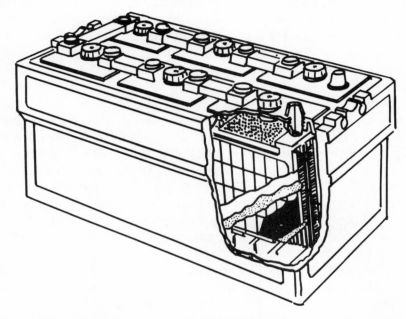

Fig. 24-1 Sketch of a marine-type storage battery; see text for special construction features.

Although you will not be able to look inside to check them, a true marine battery should have special internal construction features. Positive plates should be made of active material of high density to provide longer life; the plates may also be thicker, with fewer but heavier grids to hold the active material in place. Separators in ordinary automotive batteries are often chemically treated paper. This material tends to break down when subjected to overcharging or continuous-duty service. A heavy-duty marine battery should have thick fiberglass mats as separators. Another satisfactory separator material is Dynel, and microporous rubber may be used in conjunction with either fiberglass or Dynel. Negative plates must match the quality of construction of the positive plates.

Marine batteries will often have lug terminals either in lieu of or in addition to automotive-style tapered post terminals. These batteries will also provide for easier handling by having molded-in carrying handles or loops of synthetic rope. Despite the better construction features, the warranty on marine batteries will often be considerably less than on batteries for use in cars and trucks because of the harsher environment and the probability that they will get less regular servicing (but this latter needn't be so!).

Other terms now used to describe storage batteries include "low maintenance" and "maintenance-free." Conventional batteries, as described in Chapter 2, use grids of lead alloyed with antimony to provide stiffness. That characteristic is achieved, but the antimony is a prime factor in "gassing" when the battery is charged. The bubbles carry off water, so the battery must be periodically serviced. A conventional battery can eventually run dry and be ruined. The caps on such batteries have vent holes to let the gas escape, a possible explosion hazard if proper safety precautions are not taken.

A "low maintenance" battery is one whose grids are made with the smallest possible amount of antimony. Gassing is considerably reduced but still occurs with some loss of water. These batteries have conventional vented caps and do require some maintenance, but at longer intervals.

A more recent development is the "maintenance-free" battery, in which antimony has been replaced with calcium in the lead used to form the grids. Gassing is reduced to a very small percentage of that found in conventional batteries. Small, inconspicuous vents are provided to prevent pressure buildup, but water is not lost; with no need to replace water, the conventional filler cap is eliminated. As there are almost no gas fumes coming from the battery, the explosion hazard is greatly reduced, as is corrosion at the terminals. The very small amount of gas that does escape carries only a tiny amount of electrolyte, and this is compensated for by providing a somewhat greater amount initially. A maintenance-free battery that is fully discharged may not recover to its full capacity; if this happens several times, the battery may become too damaged for any further useful service. A low-maintenance battery can handle deep discharges better than a maintenance-free battery, but such hard service is better met by a battery specifically designed for such use as described below.

Deep-Cycle Batteries

To get the most reliable service and longest life from the storage batteries on your boat, you must understand the two very different types of use to which they are put. One type of load is that of starting the engine. Here a very heavy current—in the hundreds of amperes for inboard engines—is drawn, but only briefly, usually just a few seconds. The battery is, in most instances, only discharged from near 100% of capacity down to roughly 80%, or if the engine is warm, perhaps down to only about 90% of capacity. The battery is then immediately recharged by the engine-driven alternator; see Figure 24-2.

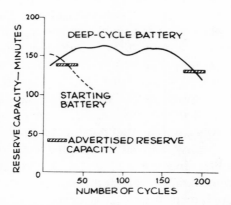

Fig. 24-2 Comparison of battery life in terms of deep discharge-recharge cycles for two types of storage batteries. "Reserve capacity" is the time in minutes that a fully-charged battery can produce current at 25 amperes before the voltage falls to 10.5 volts.

The other type of load on the batteries in your boat is quite a different matter. Current is drawn from the battery for lights, pumps, radios, and other electronic equipment, refrigeration, etc. Here the individual drains are relatively light, from a small fraction of 1 ampere up to perhaps 5 or 6 amperes, and intermittent. Under way with an engine running, these loads are carried by the alternator; but at anchor or on a boat under sail, they are fully carried by the battery, subject to periods of recharging when the engine is run. On a long day's sail, or at anchor for overnight or longer, the battery carrying these loads—typically called the "ship's service" or "house" battery to distinguish it from the "starting" or "engine" battery—may approach conditions of full discharge. This series of major changes, from fully charged to nearly discharged, and back again, has led to the development of specially designed "deep cycle" batteries.

A conventional battery rated at, say, 100 ampere-hours (AH) can typically go through 20 to 40 near-complete discharge/recharge cycles before its capacity begins to diminish. It then becomes a 90 AH battery, then 80 AH, and so on down; it can no longer be restored to its initial capacity no matter how long it is recharged.

Deep-cycle batteries use good marine-type construction of high-density positive plates, which are additionally reinforced with an interlocking structure of fiberglass mat. Greater plate area is important for very heavy loads such as engine starting, but for deep-cycling the desirable characteristic is greater active material in thicker plates. This thicker structure locks in the positive plate's active material and prevents excess shedding, the ultimate "cause of death" for lead-acid storage batteries. As a result of this construction, deep-cycle batteries are capable of retaining full recharge capacity through 150 to 200 cycles before starting to decline. In a controlled test of two batteries of similar rating, a conventional battery fell below its rated capacity after 28 deep cycles, but its counterpart designed for such service retained its capacity until 187 deep discharge-recharge cycles had been completed.

A deep-cycle battery can be used for engine starting, but it is less effective in such service. It can start an engine if all is well, although it may not turn the engine over as fast as a regular battery, as it will produce a somewhat weaker current. Under difficult conditions it may not be able to start the engine at all. Starting service will not damage a deep-cycle battery; deep-cycling can, however, shorten the life of a starting-type battery.

Battery Selection

The two types of service are illustrated in Figure 24-3. One word of caution in selecting a "ship's service" battery for your boat. Be sure to get one with an adequate ampere-hour rating. Compute your various loads and their running time, then add a

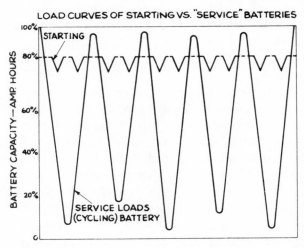

Fig. 24-3 Under normal conditions, a starting battery is only very slightly discharged before it is recharged by the alternator. A "service" battery, however, may be very deeply discharged overnight by the use of lights, pumps, radios, etc. with the engine not running.

generous safety factor. Even a deep-cycle battery will last longer if it is kept farther from the full-discharge point on each "deep" cycle. A battery of higher capacity is also advantageous for the additional hours of electrical power it can provide in an emergency when the engine has failed and there's no recharging to be had. Pay the few dollars more to get a genuine marine battery—even if you treat your battery with care and protect it from physical abuse, the stronger construction will result in added years of reliable service. On all but the smallest of boats, consider having two batteries, one regular-style for starting and one of "deep cycle" design for miscellaneous lighting, pumps, radio, etc., loads. Match your needs to the proper type and size of battery.

A further development in lead-acid storage battery design promises both increased efficiency and reduced weight. Traditionally the grids that were the support structure for the active material have been made of lead (alloyed with antimony or calcium). A manufacturing process has been perfected that makes possible the use of lightweight thermoplastic materials for grids. Although there is less lead in the battery, its ability to store electrical energy is not diminished. Cells are less prone to shorting out from material shed by plates, as the grid edges and feet are of nonconductive polypropylene.

Battery Maintenance

Your batteries should be maintained as stated in Chapter 2 and checked periodically with a hydrometer. Be aware, however, that a hydrometer will not show you anything about the internal condition of the battery's plates. The specific gravity can be pushed up by charging, but if the negative plates have become overly "sulphated" and/or too much active material has been shed from the positive plates, the battery will have little real capacity regardless of the hydrometer reading.

A battery should be tested by taking a hydrometer reading for every cell. The hydrometer must be clean inside and out. Draw up only enough liquid to float the indicator—tapping may be necessary; too much liquid and the indicator will rise until it hits up against the top stopper, and a false reading will result. Always measure specific gravity before adding water. The indicator should be read at eye level, but if possible keep the hydrometer in the battery to avoid dripping electrolyte. When squeezing the bulb to empty the hydrometer, be sure to put the liquid back into the same cell it was taken from. To be safe, always wear glasses or goggles when testing or working with batteries. Ideally, all readings would be the same, but minor variations should be expected. If, however, any cell reads 50 "points"—0.050— less than the rough average of the other cells, then you have, or soon will have, troubles, and the battery should be replaced. Never add acid to a battery to raise the specific gravity reading. (Another indication of trouble is when one cell consistently takes more water than the others on routine servicing of a conventional battery.) If a battery shows adequate specific gravity but still will not crank an engine, it may have a bad cell. This is best determined by a "high discharge rate" or "breakdown" test performed at a battery shop.

When adding water—after your hydrometer tests—check each cap (except on maintenance-free batteries) to ensure that the vent is clear; this may prevent an explosion. Then check that the terminal connections are clean and tight. Spraying with a compound designed for this use will prevent the buildup of corrosion; the older procedure of smearing on a coat of petroleum jelly will do some good, but it does not penetrate into smaller spaces that are reached by the spray.

Batteries can be more conveniently "tested" by installing a voltmeter of the expanded-scale, suppressed-zero type described in Chapter 6. These readings should not be taken while the battery is being charged, or for about 15 minutes after charging ceases; readings should be taken when there is no load turned on and when discharging the battery. Voltmeter readings, however, are not a substitute for periodic hydrometer checks of each cell, tests that may give you warning of potential failure of cells.

BATTERY CHARGING

The batteries on your boat are charged from the engine-driven alternator or from a 120-volt AC-powered battery charger, as described in Chapters 6 and 7. Charging should start at a rate in amperes equal to about 20% of the capacity in ampere-hours. Within 15 to 20 minutes, however, this rate should have been reduced automatically by the voltage regulator to about a 10% value and this current continued until reaching the "finish rate" as described in Chapter 2. If your voltage regulator does not control the rate of charge in this general manner, it may need adjustment; see Chapter 6. Provision must be made for venting away from batteries the hydrogen gas that is produced by the charging process; the faster the rate of charge, the greater the hazard from gassing. "Fast" or "boost" charging at rates of 40 to 60 amperes is permissible for a half hour or so, but the gas problem is such that the battery should be removed from the boat and charged onshore.

Charging Multiple Batteries

Earlier in this chapter you were advised to have two batteries. But if you have only one source for recharging them, what do you do? You can connect the batteries in parallel across the output of the charger (the term "charger" is used here for the source of energy, whether it is the engine-driven alternator under way or a 120-volt AC shore-powered rectifier). This will work as long as the charger is active—the battery at the lower level of charge will take a greater share of the charger's output, and both batteries will eventually come up to full charge. But if the charger is inactive and one battery is "weaker" than the other—or worse yet, if one should develop an internal flaw— then your "good" battery will go down trying to bring the "bad" one up, and you could be left with two batteries both too low to do the job you have for them.

Battery Isolation

To prevent the above from happening, you can install separate switches for each battery, or a rotary selector switch, if your boat does not already have one. This, however, requires you be present, and remember, to take the necessary action to parallel the batteries for charging and separate them for use. A simpler, foolproof method is to connect the batteries in parallel through "isolating diodes." These are simple, solid-state electrical components that function as an electrical checkvalve—electricity can flow through a diode in one direction but not in reverse. Two diodes connected as an isolating unit are shown in Figure 24-4a; the complete circuit with charger, isolator, and batteries is shown in Figure 24-4b. You can buy the diodes at a store such as Radio Shack and make your own isolator, but it is perhaps simpler to purchase an assembled battery isolator at a marine or recreational vehicle supply store. The reason for this is that there is a small voltage drop across each diode—about 0.7 volt—and this drop at the quite considerable charging current produces significant heat. To radiate this heat, the diodes must be mounted on a finned metal block called a "heat sink." If you are going to make your own, get silicon diodes that are rated for at least the maximum charging current per battery at 25 volts or

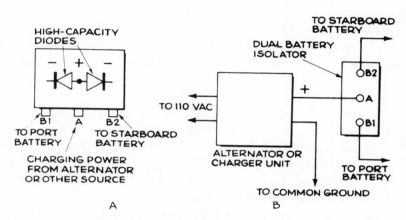

Fig. 24-4 A battery isolator consists of two diodes connected as shown in (a). It is used to divide the charge between two batteries (b) and prevent one battery from discharging into the other.

more. The positive side of the diodes will be connected together so this should be the case of the diode that will come in contact with the heat sink. This item will, therefore, be "hot" electrically and must be mounted on an insulated base.

If isolating diodes are used, it will be necessary to increase the charging voltage to offset the 0.7-volt drop across each diode. This can be done by a mechanical adjustment of the regulator, or by feeding the input to the regulator through a diode that has a similar voltage drop; this causes the alternator's regulator to raise the alternator's output voltage automatically. This diode need not be as large as the others; a rating of a few amperes is sufficient, and much less heat will have to be dissipated.

Many 120-volt AC battery chargers will have built-in isolators; these models will have separate positive terminals for each battery to be charged, and a common negative terminal. A separate isolator is not needed here, and it should not be used because of the added voltage drop. Such an isolator will, however, still be needed if multiple batteries are to be charged from an engine-driven alternator.

DRY CELLS

Much has been written about "dry cells"—those used in flash-lights, calculators, etc—not being really "dry" but rather containing a moist paste electrolyte. We will not repeat that story again here. But we consider the various types of dry cells and how they can be most advantageously used on a boat.

Basic Types

The two basic types are the nickel-cadmium (Ni-Cad) cells intended for recharging, and the others that are not intended for recharging but that can have a fraction of their capacity restored by a "charging" process. (These latter types are actually "primary" cells using a one-way, nonreversible chemical process, but forcing a current back through them in a reverse direction will overcome internal conditions that have been limiting the discharge of energy. Rather than recharging, you are actually "rejuvenating" them so that you get all possible energy from the chemical process in the cell.) The charging of both of these types of dry cells will be discussed below.

Zinc-carbon cells are marketed in several categories including "general purpose"—sometimes called "flashlight"; "transistor"; and "heavy duty" (actually zinc-chloride). These come in various voltages and energy capacities. Typical 1.5-volt cells, from physically larger to smaller, are D, C, and AA sizes. At higher voltages, there are 6-volt batteries for lanterns and anchor lights, and small 9-volt batteries used in radio receivers and other electronic devices. (Remember, one cell is a "cell"; several cells connected together, usually in series, form a "battery.")

There is also a related category of "alkaline" cells that cost several times as much but that can supply up to 10 times the energy; these are nearly always the most economical in the long run. All of these types of cells give a nominal 1.5 volts, with batteries some multiple of that value. Their chemical composition and internal designs, however, differ, and some are better than others for light or heavy loads and for continuous or intermittent service.

Service Life

The selection of the type of dry cell to purchase should be governed by the use to which it will be put. The life of various types of dry cells in different usages is shown in Table 24-1; the data are taken from the engineering handbook of Union Carbide, manufacturers of Eveready-brand cells and batteries. The figures shown are for D cells but would be proportionate for the smaller C and AA sizes. Load currents used in developing these data were appropriate to the cell and type of use.

	Type of service					
	Light intermittent	Heavy intermittent	Continuous	Cassette recorder	Portable radio	Shelf life
Standard carbon-zinc	650 min.	340 min.	105 min.	22 hrs.	107 hrs.	3 yrs.
Transistor-grade carbon-zinc	325 min.	—	150 min.	—	200 hrs.	3 yrs.
Heavy-duty carbon-zinc	502 min.	960 min.	319 min.	37 hrs.	128 hrs.	3 yrs.
Alkaline	835 min.	815 min.	780 min.	57 hrs.	219 hrs.	5 yrs.
Rechargeable nickel-cadium	175 min.**	175 min.**	144 min.	6 hrs.**	25 hrs.**	3 mos.

** *Motor Boating & Sailing* estimates

Table 24-1

The life figures shown should not cause you to believe that the voltage will remain constant to the end. Except for the nickel-cadmium cells, all batteries (especially zinc-carbon) grow weaker with use. Ni-Cads maintain essentially full voltage (1.2 or 1.25 volts rather than 1.5 volts) until they are nearly exhausted; this is nice to have, but it results in little or no warning before the flashlight goes out or the radio goes dead.

The most important conclusion to be drawn is that the life of most types of batteries depends on how they are used. General-purpose zinc-carbon and heavy-duty cells last longer if use is not continuous and they are allowed to "rest" for intervals, during which they recover a bit of their capacity.

Alkaline batteries are designed for truly continuous use and are recommended for emergency or distress lights. They would be a waste of money for any other lighting application unless you want the longest possible service regardless of cost. They are a good buy, however, for cassette recorders and calculators.

Similarly, the transistor-type battery is great for the light drain of portable radios or direction finders but quite unsatisfactory for the heavier drain of flashlights.

Rechargeable nickel-cadmium cells are something of a mixed blessing for a boatman. They will save a great deal of money over an extended period of time, but their energy capacity is less, and frequent recharging will be required. If you opt for Ni-Cads, you will need to keep one or more fully charged sets on board as spares; but be aware that they self-discharge and have a quite limited shelf life before recharging is necessary. (This is why the instructions for electronic devices with internal Ni-Cad batteries always say "Charge before using.")

Recharging Dry Cells

Chargers for Ni-Cads are readily available at stores such as Radio Shack, but most of these operate from 120-volt AC sources. Even if you have an on-board light plant, or an inverter, you have a problem, as full recharging may take 14 to 16 hours. However, you can make your own very simple charger operate from your boat's 12-volt DC system. The circuit shown in Figure 24-5 will allow 16-hour charging of either 2 or 4 size D or C Ni-Cad cells. Resistance values are given for charging 2 or 4 cells, which must be connected in series. A few commercial models of Ni-Cad chargers using a 12-volt DC source are now available (Radio Shack item #23-139). The Ni-Cad batteries of some small hand-held VHF radios can be recharged from the boat's battery, 12 to 14 volts DC, using a special charger cord that plugs into a cigarette-lighter type of socket.

"Chargers" for zinc-carbon cells are available (Radio Shack item #23-120), but do not expect the capacity for repeated cycling that you get with nickel-cadmium cells. These operate from 120-volt AC sources. You will get a better "rejuvenation" effect on zinc-carbon cells if it is done when they are about half discharged; completely dead cells cannot be brought back to life.

If you are using dry cells other than Ni-Cads, be sure you have enough spares on board; but don't overstock, as a fresher battery is always a better battery.

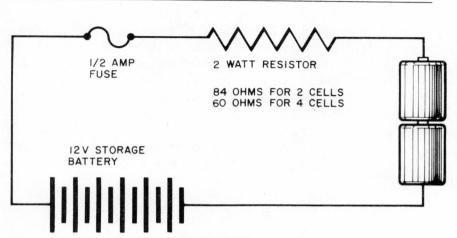

Fig. 24-5 Simple circuit for charging two NiCad cells. Select proper size resistor for type of cells to be charged; the cells *must be in series.*

Effect of Temperature

If you use Ni-Cads, it is important that you let them discharge fully, or almost so, before recharging fully. Repeated light discharge and recharge may create a "memory" effect that reduces capacity. If this occurs, the cells must be very deeply discharged and then recharged to restore their capacity; this may have to be repeated several times. Ni-Cads also do not like to be discharged and then left in that condition.

Whatever type of dry cells you use, they will provide less energy in cold weather. A zinc-carbon battery, for example, will in freezing temperatures have only half the capacity it would have in moderate 70-degree F to 80-degree F surroundings. In an emergency, some additional life can be obtained from a "dead" carbon-zinc cell by warming it thoroughly, but do not overheat it.

Heat is an enemy of battery shelf life. If practicable, general-purpose and heavy-dry cells should be stored in a refrigerator; alkaline cells can be satisfactorily stored at room temperature. Don't store any cells or batteries where they will be warmed or get hot.

Battery-Powered Lanterns

A hand-held electric lantern will have many uses on your boat; these usually use a square 6-volt battery with spring terminals on top. (A similar battery, with binding-post terminals, is used in many anchor lights.) A heavy-duty zinc-carbon battery will give the longest service, but there is now available a rechargeable battery of the same size and voltage with interchangeable terminals of either type. Chargers are available to work from either 120-volt AC or 12-volt DC sources. The initial cost is, of course, much higher, but in the long run this is a more economical source of energy for a battery lantern.

CHAPTER 25

VHF/FM Radios

RADIO COMMUNICATIONS for small craft are now almost entirely based on the use of very-high-frequency, frequency-modulated (VHF/FM) equipment. Use of medium- and high-frequency, single-sideband (SSB) radios is limited to offshore cruising yachts, and few of them are so equipped; see Chapter 27. Citizens Band (CB) radios are installed on quite a number of boats, but in most cases as additional equipment rather than the basic means of communications; see Chapter 26.

The development of VHF sets has progressed to a point in terms of compactness and reasonable cost where a boat has to be very small indeed not to be suitable for such an installation. And the VHF marine communications system has grown to such a stage that safety communications are available to at least 20 miles offshore along all our coastline and over much of our inland waters. Continuous weather broadcasts are now being made from more than 300 locations around the country, each reaching out to at least 40 miles and some to 150 miles or more. Marine operator connections into the land telephone system are not as completely available, but the service is widespread and still growing. Communications to marinas, boat and yacht clubs, and bridge and lock tenders all increase convenience; and, of course, boat-to-boat contacts are always useful. So really, a VHF transceiver should be part of your boating equipment—for safety, convenience, and enjoyment, too.

SELECTION

VHF radios are available to you in such a wide range of models that selection of a specific set for your boat requires careful consideration. The range of features and of prices is great—you must decide what you need, what you would like to have, and how much you are able to pay.

Several characteristics of VHF marine radios are so universal that they form no part of a selection process; they are noted and quickly passed over. All sets (except hand-helds) will have a 25-watt output power rating, with the capability of reducing that power to 1 watt or less, as required by the regulations of the Federal Communications Commission (FCC). All will include a microphone, usually firmly attached to the set by a cable but sometimes connected with a plug and socket combination (desirable). All will have a squelch control for eliminating background noise when no signal is being received. All will operate on 12-volt DC power with a current draw of 0.5 to 1.2 amperes while receiving (even less when squelched), and 4 to 6 amperes when transmitting on full power.

Channels

VHF/FM communications are conducted over a number of fixed frequencies designated by channel numbers. VHF channels are grouped in accordance with the type of communications that are legally permissible on them—distress and safety, including communications with the Coast Guard; calling; ship-to-ship (in the FCC rules and regulations, boats are "ships"); ship-to-shore to marinas, yacht clubs, etc.; communications to bridges and locks; and communications to marine operators for connection into a land telephone system. Table 25-1 lists the various channel assignments. Forget about frequencies in megahertz (MHz); you only need to know and use channel numbers.

The days of VHF sets with a limited number of channels is long gone. Except for a very few hand-helds, all new transceivers will have every channel you can legally use, whether you are in commercial or noncommercial operation. Regrettably, *they will also have many channels on which you cannot legally transmit* (although you can listen). This requires some study and

Priority List of VHF-FM Channels for Recreational Boats

Channel Number	Frequency (MHz) Transmit	Receive	Communications Purpose
16	156.800	156.800	DISTRESS SAFETY and CALLING (mandatory)
06	156.300	156.300	Intership safety communications (mandatory)
22	157.100	157.100	Primary Liaison with USCG vessels and USCG shore stations, and for Coast Guard marine information broadcasts
68	156.425	156.425	Non-commercial intership and ship to coast (marinas, yacht-clubs, etc.)
09	156.450	156.450	Commercial and non-commercial intership and ship to coast (commercial docks, marinas, & some clubs)
26	157.300	161.900	Public telephone, first priority
28	157.400	162.000	Public telephone, first priority
25	157.250	161.850	Public telephone (Also 24, 27, 84, 85, 86, 87, 88)
13	156.650	156.650	Navigational—Bridge to Bridge (1 watt only). Mandatory for ocean vessels, dredges in channels, and large tugs while towing. Army installing for communications with drawtenders on many highway and railroad bridges.
14	156.700	156.700	Port Operations channel for communications with bridge and lock tenders. Some Coast Guard shore stations have this channel for working.
70	156.525	156.525	Distress and Safety Calling, and general purpose calling, *using Digital Selective Calling ONLY*
12	156.600	156.600	Port Operations—traffic advisory—still being used as channel to work USCG shore stations
72	156.625	156.625	Non-commercial intership (2nd priority)
WX-1		162.550	Weather broadcasts
WX-2		162.400	Weather broadcasts
WX-3		162.475	Weather broadcasts
69	156.475	156.475	Non-commercial intership and ship to coast
71	156.575	156.575	Non-commercial intership and ship to coast
78	156.925	156.925	Non-commercial intership and ship to coast

knowledge to avoid use of channels prohibited to your type of boat and operation. Advertisements of VHF sets will feature the number of channels covered—generally between 40 and 109; often the number of receiving channels is greater than the number of transmitting channels. These figures are rather meaningless when it is realized that the legal maximum for a noncommercial boat to transmit on is only 30, and for a commercial craft it is no greater than 38. To summarize: Any set you might buy will have every authorized channel, whether your operation is recreational or commercial.

Some VHF/FM transceivers are advertised as having "expansion" or "private" channels. These can be activated by an internal switch, and they do work, *but* their use is *illegal* at this time—stay on the authorized channels *only*. This feature should not be a factor in the selection of a set.

Channel selection is generally by use of a keypad similar to that of a telephone, although a few sets use one or two rotary knobs, or push buttons for up-down channel changes. If you are using a keypad, remember that you must always enter 2 digits—add 0 before the channel number for a single-digit channel (for example, Channel 6 becomes "06").

Channel numbers, and some other information—such as "high power" or "low power"—are shown by either liquid crystal displays (LCD) or light-emitting diodes (LED).

Mandatory Channels

FCC regulations require that all marine VHF radios sold must have the capacity to transmit and receive on Channels 16 and 6 plus a "working" channel. This ensures that a boat can make a distress call and hear the distress calls of others. Channel 6 is also required to ensure that all vessels have a common frequency to which they can move, freeing the distress channel for other craft. The three-channel minimum is not really meaningful, as all transceivers will have many, many others.

Coast Guard Channels

For communicating with Coast Guard shore stations and vessels, you will need a working channel to shift to after making initial contact on Channel 16. The recommended channel is 22A, although Channel 12 is sometimes used when 22A is overloaded with traffic. (And here we come to our first complication—for technical reasons that need not be considered here. Although 22A—spoken on the radio as "22 Alpha"—is the correct terminology, it is often referred to simply as "22"; these are exactly the same, and either is acceptable in everyday use. Similar situations exist for Channels 1A, 5A, 7A, and certain others up to 88A).

Boat-to-Boat Channels

For communications with noncommercial craft, Channel 68 is most widely used, although it has no legal preference over 69, 71, 72, or 78A. Because 68 is so heavily used, plan to use one of the others whenever possible, especially on weekends.

Vessels of all sizes in commercial operation have their own group of VHF channels; these are 1A, 7A, 8, 10, 11, 18A, 19A, 67, 79A, 80A, and 88A. Recreational boats are *not* authorized to use these channels, just as commercial craft are not authorized to use the channels listed in the preceding paragraph.

One channel is special: Channel 9 is authorized for both commercial and noncommercial vessels; it is the only channel that can properly be used for routine intership communications between these different categories of vessels. (Both categories will also have Channel 6, but this is limited by the FCC to "safety" communications.)

Channel 70 is now in a special category: It is reserved for distress, safety, and general-purpose calling *using digital selective calling only*. This is a new "high tech" service that has been internationally authorized but has not yet been implemented with equipment. For all practical purposes it is unusable at this time.

Boat-to-Shore Channels

Certain of the ship-to-ship channels for noncommercial craft can also be used for ship-to-shore communications to "limited coast stations" such as marinas and yacht clubs. These are channels 9, 68, 69, 71, and 78.

For commercial craft, the authorized channels are 1A, 7A, 9, 10, 11, 18A, 19A, 79A, and 80A.

Marine Operator Channels

Next in consideration will be channels to marine operators. The FCC has designated Channels 26 and 28 as jointly being the first choice for assignment. This means that the other "public correspondence" channels—24, 25, 27, 84, 85, 86, 87, and 88— will not be used except where the shore stations are so close together that additional use of either 26 or 28 would result in interference. As a result, roughly 70% of all marine operators are on one or the other of these two channels. You must check listings for your local area, and areas into which you may cruise, to determine just which ones you will be using.

Other Channels

Miscellaneous channels include "port operations," principally Channels 12 and 14, and the navigational "bridge to bridge" Channel 13. The "bridges" were originally those of ships, but now many highway and railroad spans are radio-equipped, and 13 is often used as the working channel with the bridgetender.

And finally we have the receive-only weather channels with their continuous broadcasts. Channels WX-1 and WX-2 are used for most locations, with WX-3 used where interference might result from too-close spacing. Other channels—WX-4 through WX-7—are occasionally used in limited special situations.

Miscellaneous Features

All VHF marine transceivers will operate on the appropriate channels and will have the basic characteristics previously described in this chapter. Most will also have one or more of the following "special features" in various combinations—and more such special features seem to come along every year.

Nearly all sets will have a separate push button—often of a distinctive color, such as red—that will instantly switch transmission and reception to the distress and calling channel, 16. Some units will have a holding bracket for the microphone that includes a switch that will automatically shift the set to Channel 16 whenever the mike is hung up after use; this is very useful, as it eliminates the frequent error of failing to remember to switch back to 16 after talking with another station on a working channel. (Of course, if the set is already on 16, no switching occurs.)

Some sets have a reversible slanting front panel that adds convenience to an overhead mounting if such is desired. Some have provisions for a telephone-type handset in lieu of, or in addition to, the regular microphone; this provides privacy and better hearing in noisy surroundings.

A necessary feature on some boats is the capability of having a remote unit so that the same radio can be operated from a fly bridge as well as from a lower helm station. (An alternative solution that should be considered is having two separate sets; this adds redundancy for greater reliability and safety, as both sets are not likely to have trouble at the same time. The secondary set could be a less-expensive model with fewer special features.)

Many current models now have a "memory" feature that allows ten to twenty channels to be set up for easier and quicker access. Some sets feature scanning in various modes—all channels, all memory channels, all weather channels, etc.; these may include a "lockout" capability to eliminate temporarily one or more selected channels from the scanning process. In any scanning mode, Channel 16 is usually given "priority" status—the set will go to there, and stay there, as long as signals are being received. "Dual watch" is another very useful feature, which allows simultaneous continuous monitoring on two channels, normally 16 and one working channel.

An intercom capability is built into some VHF sets, useful for interior communications on larger boats. Some models advertise a loud hailer capability, but the low level of audio power, usually 4 to 6 watts, is really not enough unless an external amplifier of 25 or so watts is added.

A digital clock can be displayed on the dial of one model, and essentially all sets can be connected to an external unit for automatic direction-finding (ADF) if that capability is not a built-in feature.

The selection of an antenna will be considered below as part of the installation project.

Hand-Held Transceivers

Small, internal-battery-powered hand-held sets are usually considered portable units to be used in conjunction with full-size sets installed on various craft. They can, however, provide a "quick and easy" capability for smaller boats. No wiring need be run, and the units are easily taken off the boat for added security when the craft is not in use.

Essentially all hand-held transceivers provide a full range of channels, selected by either a keypad or two thumbwheels. Maximum power will range from 3 to 6 watts. The higher power levels, however, do not provide much increase in range, and they do run down the internal Ni-Cad battery that much faster. Battery life is variable, depending upon the ratio of transmit time to receive time. Sets are usually sold with a flexible "rubber ducky" antenna; these are convenient, but they result in a more limited range of operation. Greater range can be obtained through use of a pullout extensible antenna roughly 46 inches in length; when collapsed, such antennas are no longer than a rubber ducky and do not detract from the handiness of the set. When connected to a regular-size installed antenna, these small radios can provide a much greater working range.

FCC regulations allow the use of portable sets *only* between the "mother" craft and a dinghy or other related small craft when such sets are used in conjunction with a regularly licensed radio. If they are separately licensed, they can be used in any normal way. Use of portable transceivers onshore, or from shore to any boat is *not* permitted, nor is on-board use from one part to another of a yacht.

INSTALLATION

Installation of a marine VHF-FM radiotelephone is a relatively simple and easy project. This is, however, an electronic device that radiates a signal over considerable distances and thus is capable of causing interference to the communications of others. As the licensee of the station, you are held responsible by the FCC for its proper operation. You may make the physical installation yourself, and normally all will go well. But if there is any doubt as to the proper functioning of the transmitter, you should stop any use of the set until it has been checked out by a technician holding a general class FCC commercial operator license.

Location

The transceiver unit—and a remote unit if one is used—should be located so as to be convenient for use yet reasonably protected from the adverse effects of rain and spray. The hang-up bracket for the microphone or handset should also be located where it will be convenient for use and so the cord will not be in the way.

Wiring

At their maximum current drain, when transmitting on full power, VHF radios draw only a moderate amount of current. To ensure, however, that there is not an excessive voltage drop, consult Figure 3-9 on page 58 to determine the proper wire size. In an emergency you might be using your radio under conditions of fading battery power, and you want to be sure of having a minimum voltage drop in the power leads to the set.

Ventilation

As no electronic device is 100% efficient, there will always be some heat to be dissipated to the surrounding air. On VHF radios this usually comes mostly from a finned "heat sink" on the rear panel. Most sets are mounted in the clear, and heat radiation will be no problem. If, however, you are mounting your VHF radio recessed into a bulkhead or panel, make sure there is provision for air circulation so the set will not overheat and be damaged.

Antennas for Powerboats

The installation of the antenna will depend on the type selected, and several choices are normally available. The larger (longer) the antenna is, the greater range you will get, and hence the more desirable that antenna is. Smaller, open boats can carry a 4½-foot "sailboat" antenna (commonly described as a "3 db gain" antenna, although this is not fully correct by exact technical standards). Slightly larger craft can mount a "6 db" antenna, which may vary in length from 8 to 10 feet. Such an antenna should be on a ratchet-type or "lift and lay"-style base so it can be swung down to horizontal when necessary. Even longer antennas may be mounted on larger powerboats by using an upper support bracket. The greater length may be an 18- to 19-foot "8" or "9-db" antenna or in the form of a 6-db antenna mounted atop a 10-foot tubular extension to give it added height. Height is the key to greater VHF range, and the 6-db antenna on an extender is preferred by many technicians to the

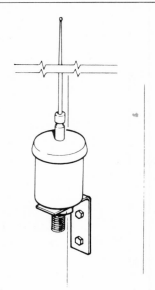

Fig. 25-1 An excellent antenna for sailboats, or trawler-types with masts, is the metal whip above a base-loading coil. The entire assembly is at ground potential for DC and can serve for lightning protection, as a fiberglass whip cannot.

9-db antenna's possibly excessively sharp directivity in the vertical plane—this could cause fading if the boat rolled or pitched heavily in rough waters.

Sailboat Antennas

The installation of a VHF antenna on a sailboat offers two basic choices. A masthead antenna has the considerable advantage of increased height, but at a risk of losing the ability to call for help after a dismasting. The other possible location, at the transom, is quite low but should survive any loss of the mast. Two possible compromises are possible: (1) nominal use of a masthead antenna, but with a base mounted and wired at the transom, with a spare antenna available to be screwed on if and when needed; or (2) on a ketch or yawl, an antenna at the top of the mizzenmast, which is less likely than the mainmast to suffer damage.

A sailboat masthead antenna can be a simple 4½-foot fiberglass whip; greater gain and vertical directivity at this height are not desirable. Alternatively, you can use one of the newer 36-inch stainless steel base-loaded whips for which 6-db gain is claimed. An advantage of this is that the whip, the base coil case, and the outer braid of the coax cable can all be at DC ground potential, providing some lightning protection; this is not possible with a fiberglass whip; see Figure 25-1.

Cables and Connectors

Marine VHF antennas for powerboats normally come with an attached length, typically 20 feet, of coax cable; unless the instructions specifically forbid, this can be cut to shorten it if the full length is not needed and would just get in the way. It may also be desirable, or necessary, to cut off the connector at the end of the cable so it may be passed through a smaller hole in the side of the cabin or other surface. A new PL-259 connector (Radio Shack #278-205) must then be added; see Chapter 43. This cable will usually be type RG-58/U, about the diameter of a lead pencil. Such cable is satisfactory for short runs, but all cables have losses that vary directly with length, and for a 50-foot length of RG-58 only about half of the power that you put in one end will come out the other! For runs to mastheads and other longer-than-usual distances, it is wiser to use RG-8/U or RG-8A/U, which have less than half the line loss of the smaller cable. Newer coax cable types include RG-213/U, which might be described as a better-quality RG-8, and RG-8X, which is smaller than regular RG-8 but still a lower-loss type. Most cables can be obtained with white outer covering if you don't like the normal black.

If the cable that came with your set is not long enough, you can add a section to cover the additional distance, but you can't splice and solder, as you would with two wires. You must use PL-259 connectors on each end of the added cable, and join the two sections with a PL-258 "barrel" coupler (R/S #278-1369).

Coax cable should never be bent sharply, especially near a connector. If the space behind your VHF radio is limited, or if you want to run the cable off in a side direction for some other reason, use a UG-646 right-angle adapter (R/S #278-199) between the socket on the set and the plug on the end of the cable.

The antenna connection on a hand-held VHF transceiver is normally a "female BNC" connector. If you want to use such a set with an installed antenna whose cable ends in a PL-259 plug, you must use a UG-255 adapter (R/S #278-120).

MAINTENANCE

As with other relatively complex electronic equipment, maintenance by the owner is quite limited, even more so for VHF radios because of FCC requirements for a technician with a commercial operator general class license to do any work or make any adjustments on the transmitter. You can, however, keep on board several spare fuses of the proper type, and you can in case of a complete "dead" set check the input power connections for tightness and proper voltage. Never press the microphone button with the set turned on unless the antenna cable is connected to the set, and to an antenna at the other end. Should you be concerned about antenna failure only, there are available small emergency antennas in the form of a flat, narrow spring-steel tape that can be plugged directly into the set—it stores rolled up like a measuring tape and straightens to the correct length when released. This will have limited range because of its lack of length and height, but it will transmit and receive over limited distances when you have nothing better.

If you are unable to hear anything on your set, or to make contact with other stations, a logical first step is to try to isolate the trouble to either your transceiver or your antenna; it is not likely to be both at the same time. Take your set on board another boat and connect it to that craft's antenna. If it works there, the problem is most likely in your antenna; if it still will not operate normally, then it is probable that your antenna is OK but the set itself has problems. If practicable, try another transceiver on your boat's antenna.

VHF sets may, over a period of time, drift slightly off frequency. As licensee of the station, you are held responsible by the FCC that your transmissions are on frequency to close tolerances. It is not a bad idea to take your set in to a well-equipped service shop every year or two for a frequency check. Should you receive repeated reports that your signal is "fuzzy," or if you notice that other signals are not as clear as they have been, take your set in for a frequency check without delay. Otherwise, modern, solid-state VHF/FM marine radios are very reliable and should require little maintenance of any kind.

CHAPTER 26

CB Radios

FIRST: CITIZENS Band (CB) radios are *not* a substitute for the safety communications of VHF/FM marine radios.

Second: There are valid applications for CB sets on board boats.

These two statements are not as contradictory as they might seem on first reading. In areas where there is shore-station coverage of VHF marine channels by the Coast Guard, yacht clubs, and marinas, and marine telephone operators, plus many other boats with VHF sets, you should not put *only* a CB set on your boat even though many other craft are so equipped. CB radios do not have as much range capability, and there is less assurance of someone maintaining a listening watch for calls for help; more interference is also likely. Most CB transceivers are built to lower standards than marine VHF/FM sets and therefore may be less reliable. If VHF channels are active in your area, equip your boat to use them, and do use them in emergencies. Coast Guard shore stations attempt to monitor CB Channel 9, but this is on a secondary basis to VHF channels; local police and sheriff monitoring stations are often too far inland to be of much help to a coastal boater, considering the relatively short range of CB sets.

If you are in an inland boating area, there may not be activity on marine VHF channels. Here a CB set will quite properly be your primary means of radio communications. In such concentrations of boating activity there will probably be some monitoring of channels by local law-enforcement officials, boat clubs, or CB operator groups.

CB As Well As VHF/FM

Even where VHF/FM is the primary means of communication for your boat, you may want to install a CB transceiver also—the cost is small, and you will find many uses for it. With CB you can talk from boat to boat regarding fishing results, social plans, sports news, and other topics that are *not* authorized for marine VHF channels. A CB channel is excellent for use among a group of boats cruising together. CB communications are legally allowed to a home station or car to keep family members in touch with one another; marine channels cannot be so used directly. Small boat clubs not willing to undertake the expense and licensing formalities for a VHF limited coast station can simply and easily install a CB base station with a good antenna high enough to provide excellent coverage out over the water. Hand-held CB sets provide excellent coverage among a marina office, attendants out on piers, and approaching boats—slip assignment and docking assistance go much more smoothly with communications between or among all parties concerned. Handie-talkies also provide a means of communication from persons out in a dinghy or on the beach back to your boat in an anchorage. (Remember that a marine VHF hand-held *cannot* be used for communications from a person onshore to a boat, or between persons onshore.)

SELECTION

The selection of a CB set for your boat presents less of a problem than that of a VHF/FM radio, as covered in Chapter 25—fewer points have to be considered before a decision can be made.

Features

Channels: All CB sets will have the full forty available channels; sets with only the original twenty-three channels may no longer be marketed. (An exception is some of the portable hand-held units.) Remember: CB "channels" are *not* the same as the channels on a VHF/FM marine radio. As with VHF, there is no need to learn or use frequencies in megahertz; channels numbers are sufficient.

Power: As the power is limited by the FCC to only 4 watts of output (some may be advertised as "5 watts," but this is input power and no different), all sets—again, except most handhelds—have this maximum level.

Modulation: FCC rules allow both double- and single-sideband operation on CB channels. For normal boat-to-boat and boat-to-house, or boat-to-car communication, the less complex, and much less expensive, double-sideband CB sets are adequate and preferable because of their greater simplicity of operation.

Marine Quality

An important consideration in the selection of a CB set for your boat is the purchase of a "marine" unit. While it is true that most boat owners will have installed a less-expensive unit intended for automobile use, the harsher environment in which a CB set exists on a boat should be taken into consideration. This is especially true for equipment on small, open boats, where there is little protection from spray and rain. The two types of sets are similar in their channels, power rating, and operation; the difference is internally, where parts have been specially selected and circuit boards and connections have been coated. A true marine set may have gaskets at joints in the case and O-ring seals where shafts come through the front panel; toggle switches will be weatherproofed. The set might not survive total immersion, but it could take a lot of spray and rain, plus just plain salt air. Marine CB sets are relatively few on the market in comparison with the "ordinary" kind. But marine CB sets can be found by careful shopping, and often the difference is worth the added effort (and some additional cost). However, don't be sold the wrong type by a dealer or salesperson who doesn't know one from the other!

Noise Rejection

Noise suppression is most important for your marine CB receiver, but unfortunately it is difficult to judge the effectiveness of one set over another until one is purchased and installed. All sets will have an "automatic noise limiter" (ANL) circuit, and most will have a front-panel switch to turn it off when not needed; this is desirable but not mandatory, as the set is slightly less sensitive to incoming signals when the ANL is on. A few sets may have a "noise blanker" circuit that is even more effective in eliminating pulse-type noise, such as comes from ignition systems.

Specifications for CB equipment will include figures for "sensitivity" and "adjacent channel rejection." Without going into technical details, it is sufficient for you to know that the smaller the figure for sensitivity, the better; and the larger the figure for adjacent channel rejection, the more desirable the set.

Miscellaneous Features

There are several special features, found on automotive or marine CB sets, that you might consider. Your set definitely should have a type of channel indicator that can be easily read in bright light; many sets with LED (light-emitting diode) displays fail this requirement. Some sets have a separate switch that puts you immediately on Channel 9, the CB emergency frequency, regardless of where your main dial is set; this is especially useful if your dial is difficult to read in bright light. At least one model has two added buttons on the microphone that allows up-down changing of channels without reaching for the set's front panel controls. The most advanced sets can scan all or selected channels, but this feature is not really needed by a boatman.

A squelch control—to silence background noise when no signals are being received—is so universally included now that it is no longer a factor in selection. Many, if not most, CB sets have a "PA" capability, an ability to use the microphone and audio section to drive an external speaker as a public address system. This capability, however, is rather limited, as typically the audio power of CB sets is only 4 to 6 watts. This may serve an on-board function but falls short of the power needed for a satisfactory "loud hailer"; see Chapter 30. A "monitor" switch—usually marked "MON"—allows the continued monitoring of a CB channel even while the set is used in the PA mode. There may also be provisions for an external speaker that can be so placed that incoming signals are much better heard than through the built-in speaker all sets have.

A meter that reads received signal strength and relative transmitted power is nice to have, but hardly a necessity. Some meters will also measure "SWR," an indication of antenna matching; this is a "plus" in selecting a set. A separate "RF Gain" control, found on some more expensive models, is useful when receiving signals from a transmitter that is quite close by; otherwise it is left turned up full and might as well not be there!

A single-sideband (SSB) CB set can use the same forty channels in the DSB mode, and in addition, forty upper-sideband and forty lower-sideband channels, but only with another SSB transceiver. The SSB transmissions are more efficient and may give greater range, but the equipment is significantly more expensive.

INSTALLATION

The installation of a CB radio on your boat is a quite straightforward project. The transceiver should be located where it is protected from spray and rain but where the dial can be easily read and the controls comfortably reached. On smaller, open boats, these requirements may conflict, and compromise may be necessary.

Wiring

The connection to your boat's 12-volt DC system should be made in accordance with Chapter 23 and in such a way as to minimize noise pickup. With an in-line fuse, as used by most sets, you can run your power wires directly to the battery or master disconnect switch (see Chapter 24). Keep this line well away from any engine with its ignition wires and reasonably separated from other circuits, such as those for pumps and lights. Keep it clear also from wiring associated with electrical gauges and the alternator and regulator. If you have a noise problem, try to isolate the source by turning off or disconnecting one possible source at a time. Ignition makes a popping noise and alternators make a singing or whining sound; both of these vary with

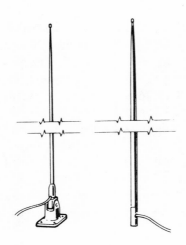

Fig. 26-1 Antennas for CB sets on boats are different from those used on automobiles because of the absence of the metal surface of the car's body. Do not cut a cable that is attached to a marine CB antenna; however an additional extension length can be connected if needed.

engine speed. Instruments and gauges can make many types of sounds, including clicks and crackles. See Chapters 20 and 41.

Antenna

The place to be careful, and perhaps spend a few extra dollars, is in the selection and installation of your antenna. As all transmitters put out the same 4 watts of power, the difference in signal strengths will come from the antennas. On a boat, you *must* use a marine-type CB antenna. The styles of antennas sold

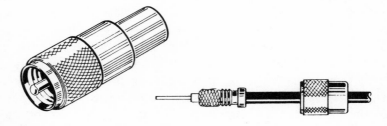

Fig. 26-2 Antennas for a VHF/FM set (and CB sets also) are connected by a coaxial cable terminated in a PL-259 plug. This is used with an adapter for the smaller RG-58/U cable, and without the adapter for the larger RG-58/U coax.

for use on cars are designed to "work against" the metal of the car's body; this metal under the antenna functions as a "ground plane" or "counterpoise" and is part of the antenna circuit. On a wooden or fiberglass boat, you do not have such a broad metal surface at the base of the antenna. Hence a different design is required, and only this marine-type CB antenna will operate efficiently on boats; with only 4 watts of power, you can't afford to waste any! A marine CB antenna will also be better constructed to resist the ravages of a harsh atmosphere. These antennas come with an attached length of coax cable—*do not shorten this lead-in*. It can, however, be lengthened by adding an extension cable of the same type of coax having a male plug (PL-259) at each end and using a double female "barrel" coupler (PL-258); see Chapter 43 for installing connectors on coax cable.

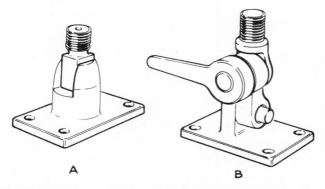

A   B

Fig. 26-3 CB radio antennas, as well as those for VHF/FM sets, often have to be turned down to a horizontal position to reduce the vertical clearance required. Shown here are a "lift and lay" mount (a) and a "ratchet" laydown mount (b).

Antennas come in various lengths; use the longest that can reasonably be fitted on your boat. Some have an integral mounting base; others screw into a separate base. Use a type of base that permits the antenna to be rotated to a horizontal position when not in use; this is especially necessary for trailered craft.

Locate the antenna base so it will be as high as practical—height means greater range. But be sure to consider how the antenna will lie when it is in the horizontal position—don't risk an easily broken antenna; a slim fiberglass whip is not overly strong. Give consideration also to the route you will have to take with the coax cable to get to the transceiver. If the cable must come in through a cabin side, use a proper fitting to avoid having a leak at this point.

MAINTENANCE

Owner-maintenance on a CB set will generally be limited to carrying several spare fuses of the proper size and keeping connections clean and tight. If the set fails to operate, it will usually have to be taken into a service shop. If this becomes necessary, it is always helpful to take along the instruction book that came with the set; this will contain a schematic circuit diagram that will speed repairs—and should reduce your repair bill, too! As with marine VHF/FM transceivers, you may be able to save money by isolating the trouble to either the set or the antenna; it is not likely to be both at the same time. See Chapter 25.

CHAPTER 27

Single-Sideband Radiotelephones

THE MARINE VHF/FM radio system has many desirable features—clear reception with no static, multiple channels, good voice quality, etc. *But* it has one major disadvantage: limited range. VHF is the mainstay of communications for small craft, and it will meet the everyday needs of nearly all boaters. Some, however, will need a longer-range communications system—this requires the installation of a marine single-sideband (SSB) radiotelephone set.

SSB radios will provide the offshore skipper with the capability to communicate over long distances with the Coast Guard, with other boats, with onshore activities, and with marine operators to connect into the worldwide telephone network for business and personal contacts; see Fig. 27-1. Amateur ("ham")

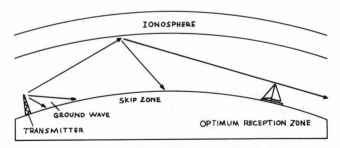

Fig. 27-1 Single-sideband transmissions reach out to hundreds and thousands of miles because the signals are reflected back to earth by layers of the ionosphere. The height of the ionosphere varies with the time of day, and frequencies must be selected for that and the distance to the other station.

radio will cover the same distances, and it is great for some purposes (it will be considered in Chapter 42), but it can*not* be used for business purposes and should not be relied on for emergency communications; it also requires separate operator and station licenses.

Marine SSB radios are relatively expensive to purchase and install when compared to the usual VHF/FM set, but if you require communications over more than 30 or so miles, an SSB radio can be essential.

SELECTION

Marine radios using single-sideband modulation operate on a number of specific frequencies in several medium-frequency (MF) and high-frequency (HF) bands between roughly 2 and 23 megahertz (MHz). Various channels are assigned for distress and calling, ship-to-ship, ship-to-shore, and marine operator traffic. (Remember that the FCC considers all vessels to be "ships" regardless of their size or type.) By selection of a suitable frequency for the time of day and the distance to the other station, reliable communications can be established over hundreds and thousands of miles.

There are two basic components of a marine SSB installation: the transmitter-receiver unit (commonly called a "transceiver") and the antenna-ground system. Both are vital to successful communications, and both must be carefully selected.

Transceivers

Marine SSB radios are complex internally but simple to operate, and some have features that make them even simpler to use than others; see Fig. 27-2. Modern SSB transceivers technically can operate on literally thousands of frequencies—*but not legally!* You must use *only* the authorized channels in each band. To aid in this, sets can be pretuned to desired channels, and these selected by a simple knob or keypad. The number of bands covered, and the number of channels that can be set up in advance will vary with the general price range of the equipment.

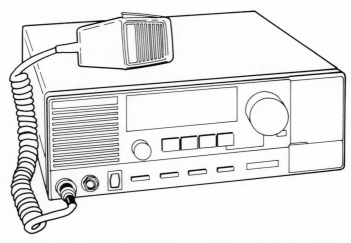

Fig. 27-2 A single-sideband transceiver may be complex internally, but it is simple to operate. Multiple channels are preprogrammed, stored in memory, and selected by a single knob. Squelch and frequency scanning are features of this modern set. A radio telephone alarm signal generator can be added.

Frequency Bands

Specific frequencies are allocated within seven bands near 2, 4, 6, 8, 12, 16, and 22 MHz. Within each band there are a number of channels for separate designated purposes, such as distress and calling, ship-to-ship, ship-to-shore, etc. All SSB sets will have the lower and middle bands; not all will go up as high in frequency as the 16 and 22 MHz bands, but you may not need these anyway.

The propagation characteristics of the various bands can be roughly summarized as follows:

2 MHz—up to 100 to 150 miles during daytime (but you must use VHF if it will reach); 100 to perhaps 300 miles at night

4 MHz—up to 250 miles during daytime; 150 to 1000 miles at night

6 MHz—50 to 100 miles during daytime; 250 to 1,800

miles at night (used mostly on the Mississippi River and other Western Rivers)

8 MHz—250 to 500 miles during the daytime; 300 to 3,000 miles at night

12 MHz—400 to 4,000 miles or more in late afternoon and at night

16 MHz—1,000 to 6,000 miles or more in daytime

22 MHz—1,200 to 8,000 miles or more in daytime, but may be seasonal and less predictable than lower frequencies

In most instances, the operator manual that came with your SSB transceiver will contain excellent information as to the use of specific channels and the best frequencies for a given set of conditions.

Channel Selection

Nearly any SSB transceiver you select will have an adequate overall number of channels available to you. The number of memories that can be set up will range from about 24 to hundreds. Some will require that you "program" the set for the various frequencies; others will have channels preprogrammed by the manufacturer; and still others will have a combination of both of these. Transceivers should be designed so you cannot accidentally *transmit* on an unauthorized channel; listening is OK.

Other related desirable features to consider in selecting your SSB set include scanning of a number of channels in memory, and one-button access to 2,182 kHz, the distress and calling frequency.

Power

The maximum authorized power for SSB transmitters on boats is 150 watts. Most sets operate at this level, but if a less expensive radio has all the other desirable features, a power of 75 or 100 watts should be adequate for your normal needs.

Other Features

Distress calls are most effective if they are preceded by the transmission of the *radiotelephone alarm signal*—an alternating two-tone sound to very specific specifications that is used in some instances to activate special receivers, but in any case is so distinctive as to receive the immediate attention of anyone listening on that channel. Some SSB sets have internal circuitry that will generate the alarm signal when a switch is turned or a button is pressed; this is a very desirable feature to be considered when selecting your equipment.

Sets with "general coverage" receiver sections—the ability to receive on all frequencies, not just those of the marine service—are desirable. With these, you can listen to news and entertainment broadcasts, receive time signals, eavesdrop on the ham radio bands, etc.

Some more expensive models of marine SSB transceivers will have terminals that can be connected to a telex machine for sending and receiving "hard copy" message traffic. Modems are available that will permit interfacing personal microcomputers to SSB sets and use over radio circuits.

Several models of SSB sets are available with remote control units. With these sets, the main unit, the transceiver, can be located where it will be less in the way, can have protection from the weather, have shorter power and antenna leads, etc. A much smaller control unit, often weatherproof, can be conveniently located at the helm; or several remote control units can be installed around a larger craft, wherever they are needed.

An audio-activated squelch circuit will keep your SSB receiver totally silent between calls, similar to the operation of your VHF/FM set. A fine-tune (or "clarifier") control will permit you to adjust your receiver precisely for more natural-sounding speech.

Antennas and Couplers

An effective antenna and ground system are absolutely essential for the proper operation of a marine SSB transceiver. Some signals may be received using almost any length of wire, but effective transmission requires a correctly installed and tuned antenna.

You will immediately notice that any antenna you select for your SSB installation is *large!* A "quarter-wavelength" antenna, the simplest type, for VHF/FM radios is only about 19 inches in length; but for the MF/HF channels of SSB radios, they would be many *feet*—for 2,182 kHz, for example, a quarter-wavelength antenna would have to be more than 107 feet tall! This is obviously impractical for any boat, or even on many ships. To have the antenna shorter physically, but still the same length "electrically," it must be "loaded" by the addition of inductance and capacitance; this is normally done in a coupler (also called a "tuner"), a separate unit near the base of the antenna.

The typical marine SSB antenna is 23 feet in actual length, with the balance made up electronically by the coupler. A two-section white fiberglass whip is usually used. The coupler can be integral with the transceiver but typically is an external unit; see Fig. 27-3. These can be purchased independently of the trans-

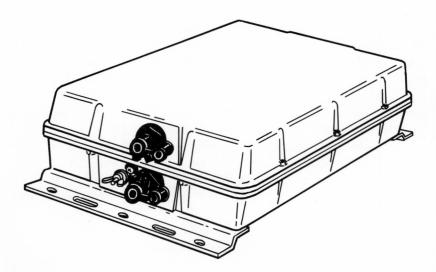

Fig. 27-3 For single-sideband radio installations, the antenna must be "matched" to the transceiver for the most effective transmission and reception. This is most easily done using an automatic coupler, normally a separate unit.

ceiver, but generally there will be less problems if both units come from the same manufacturer. Automatic antenna couplers are now almost universally used; these are microprocessor-controlled to sense the electronic characteristics of the antenna, and then use relays to switch in varying quantities of inductance and capacitance so the antennas will correctly "match" the output circuit of the transmitter.

For some installations you might select a "trap" antenna rather than a fiberglass whip and coupler combination. This consists of tubular aluminum sections with a number of electronic trap circuits between each section. Typically this antenna is about 20 feet in length and has five traps, one for each frequency band to be used. All loading inductance and capacitance is in the traps on the antenna, which may be connected directly to the transceiver without a coupler. In contrast to the fiberglass antenna and automatic coupler, which will load up on any frequency, a trap antenna will work only within several limited portions of the radio spectrum. Its advantage, however, is that no

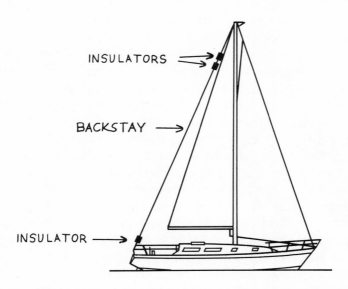

Fig. 27-4 Sailboats can have a very effective antenna for high-frequency SSB transmission and reception. Insulators are inserted in the backstay near its top and bottom, and the wire between them is used as the antenna.

375

coupler is required, and you are relieved of the possibility that a complex electronic device might fail just when it is most needed. Trap antennas are less expensive than whip antennas with automatic couplers; you can select just which bands/traps you wish when ordering such an antenna.

Sailboats present an excellent situation for a MF/HF antenna—put insulators at the top and bottom of the backstay and you have a fine "long wire" antenna; a coupler will be required; see Fig. 27-4. To be doubly safe in case of a dismasting, you can mount a fiberglass antenna at the stern (or mount just the base and have the antenna stowed); this can be a spare to be connected to the coupler when and if needed.

INSTALLATION

The installation of a SSB radiotelephone consists of the physical installation of the transceiver, antenna, and ground system, and the tuning up of the equipment.

A boat owner who is reasonably proficient with hand tools and has a basic set of them should have no problem with mounting the transceiver and the antenna (he or she may need some expert advice in locating the latter). Connection to a source of 12-volt DC power is also relatively simple—but remember that while transmitting, the set may draw 20 amperes or more (check the owner's manual). The newer microprocessor-based automatic antenna tuners will (in theory, at least) match any antenna to the set at any frequency.

The establishment of a *fully adequate* radio-frequency (RF) ground system (more properly called a "counterpoise") is absolutely necessary for effective operation—and this is often not an easy task; this is quite different from the negative 12-volt DC (ground) wire from the set. A vertical quarter-wavelength antenna is only half of the radiating system; the other half is a mirror image of the antenna that is formed by a "ground plane" beneath it. Ideally, it should be large—100 square feet is an absolute minimum, and several times that will do a better job—and it should be centered under the antenna and coupler. If the craft has a metal hull and superstructure, your problem is solved. But if, as is usually the case, construction is of fiberglass, then a ground plane must be specifically prepared. The best solution is for the builder of the boat to include a large area of metal foil or tight-mesh screen within the fiberglass layers of the deck or cabintop, with a lead of wide copper foil coming out at a location that will minimize the length of this connection—6 inches or less to the coupler is desirable. If a built-in ground plane does not exist, you or the installer must provide one in the most practicable manner. It also helps to bond together large metal objects, such as the engines, tuna tower, etc., and connect these to the ground plane by a wide copper strap as short as possible (see also Chapter 10).

When the installation is completed, the effectiveness of the ground system can be roughly evaluated by touching a neon lamp or small fluorescent lamp tube to various metal objects in the general vicinity of the transceiver. If this lights up on modulation peaks (when you speak into the microphone), then you have stray radio-frequency energy, and further work is desirable on your RF ground system. Rethink your work, and if you can't get a solution, call in a service technician who is experienced in such installations—the results will be worth the cost.

MAINTENANCE

As with most modern high-tech electronic equipment, there is little that you as the owner can do in the way of maintenance. Keep all connections—power, antenna, and ground—clean and tight. Be alert for decreased performance of your set when in contact with stations that you communicate with regularly. At intervals of six months or so, check the voltage at the input power terminals of the transceiver when it is transmitting at full power (when someone is talking into the microphone); you need full voltage for the equipment to operate properly. If your set goes dead, check the power lead, and fuses or circuit breaker. If nothing that you do gets the set working, take it to a qualified service shop, and be sure to take the manuals.

CHAPTER 28

Electronic Depth Sounders

MANY PERSONS approach the operation of a boat on the water, especially smaller craft, with the idea that it is much like driving a car down a highway—they soon find out differently! Probably the biggest difference—after the lack of brakes—is that when piloting a boat, you can't see many of the obstacles ahead of you. With a car, you can see the box or other objects in the road that you must drive around; you can see and avoid the potholes. With a boat, you cannot see submerged hazards—the underwater rocks, sandbars, coral reefs, and the just plain too-shallow areas. While charts will advise you in general terms of such hazards, often you do not know your position so precisely that you can be sure of avoiding specific dangers. Thus a depth sounder is normally one of the very first items of electronic equipment added to a boat; there is almost no lower limit to the size of a craft that can benefit from the installation of such a device.

A second reason for having a depth sounder on your boat is that information on the depth of the water directly beneath you is often useful in navigation. Added to other information, such as visual bearings, your position can be more clearly determined. Depth data can be very valuable in disproving a fix obtained from other means—if your measured depth is quite different from that shown on the chart for your "fix," it is highly likely that there is some error in your previous work. While a depth reading closely matching the charted depths as adjusted for the tidal level at that time does not absolutely confirm the accuracy of your positioning—any specific depth occurs in a vast number of places on a chart—it can lend a degree of credibility to your plot.

A third application for depth sounders is "fish finding." Many models of simple direct-reading sounders will indicate schools of fish or a single large fish with some degree of reliability. All sounders can be used as a navigation aid to find the proper depth of a particularly good fishing "hole" or artificial reef. More complex models of depth recorders are usually installed primarily for their application to fishing.

SELECTION

In "days of old," skippers and navigators had to depend on mechanical means of determining depth—sounding poles and lead (pronounced "led") lines where such means would reach. Later, sounding machines, which substituted fine wire for the rope of lead lines, enabled greater depths to be measured. To-day, the small-craft operator has generally substituted an electronic depth sounder for mechanical means, although a boat hook marked for use as a sounding pole and/or a simple lead line are still useful items to be carried on board. (The correct term is "depth sounder," or sometimes "echo sounder"; don't broadly use the term "Fathometer"—this is the trademarked name for the sounders of only one manufacturer, Raytheon.)

Indicator or Recorder?

In selecting a depth sounder for your boat, the first decision is of the basic type—indicator or recorder—that will best fit your needs. Recording depth sounders provide a permanent record on paper of the depth of the water, and in many instances, the presence of fish. This permits you to look backward in time and note depths and bottom conditions you have passed over during the past few minutes. The paper tape can be also annotated with the position, date, time, etc., to provide a rather complete record for future use. A more recent development is a sounder with a TV picture type of display that can provide graphic information over a short, variable time span, but no permanent record.

Depth Indicators

Recording, and video, depth sounders are quite a bit more expensive than units of the simple indicating style. For most skippers, an indicator-type depth sounder is all that is needed. Now the selection must be made of the type of indication—rotating flashing light or digital; there are a few other specialized types of indicators, but these are rarely used.

The rotating flashing light was the original model and is still very popular. A neon bulb or light-emitting diode (LED) flashes when a pulse is sent out from the transducer (more on this later) to mark the "0" on the scale, and it flashes again after the rotating arm of the indicator has made a partial revolution to indicate the depth of the water on a scale that runs clockwise around the face of the display. With a good sounder and a little experience, you can tell not only the depth, but also something of the nature of the bottom—hard or soft, rocky, etc.—with a flashing-light sounder. This capability, plus somewhat lower prices, and the popularity of digital displays, are what have kept the indicator type popular.

A more recent "high tech" development is a display that resembles the rotating arm flasher but is actually composed of many LEDs or a large segmented LCD, with no mechanical rotation; the LEDs may even be in various colors.

Digital Displays

Digital depth sounders offer a quickly and easily read, unambiguous display. They permit indications of shallower depths in tenths of feet, although this level of precision is not necessarily evidence of higher accuracy. (See Chapter 36 for a discussion of the terms "precision" and "accuracy," and the difference between them.) The actual type of display will vary with different models. Digits of LEDs are easily read at night, but sometimes are difficult to see in bright light unless well shaded by a hood. A very popular type of readout uses a liquid crystal display (LCD) for each number. These are very easily read in bright light, but require a source of illumination to be seen at night. Other types of displays have digital segments whose brightness can be varied over a wide range to suit your eyes, whether running in full sunlight or with a darkened helm at night. The electrical meter type of depth sounder preceded digital displays but has largely been superseded by them; it was easy to read in daylight, and its scale could be illuminated at night.

On some models of depth sounders, the transducer housing also contains a temperature sensor, and the display can be switched from depth readings to show water temperature in degrees, or degrees and tenths, on either the Fahrenheit or Celsius scale, or both.

Maximum and Minimum Range

For some skippers, a point to be considered in the selection of a depth sounder is the maximum depth that can be measured. This is primarily desirable where offshore navigation or deep-sea fishing is planned. In the majority of instances, however, you should be more concerned with the ability of the sounder to indicate clearly shallow depths, measurements of a few feet more than your craft's draft, for this is important in avoiding running aground. For flashing-light sounders this typically means a maximum range of 60 feet on the linear scale around the face of the indicator. Some models have a minimum range of 20 or 30 feet; this is even better for shallow-water navigation. If the range is greater—100 or 120 feet, for example—the first 10 feet of scale will be crowed and less easy to read to a precise depth. (Some 0–60 feet sounders will have a second, smaller set of numbers to 120 feet for "second time around" readings; this does not change the basic 0–60 feet scale.) With digital displays, the extent of maximum depth readings will not affect the lower end of the scale, but be sure that your selection will read in tenths of a foot for the shallowest waters, typically under 10 feet.

A digital display should show depth in units and tenths up to 10 units (feet, fathoms, or meters), and in whole units for greater depths.

Multiple Ranges

Modern electronic circuitry makes it easy to design depth sounders with multiple ranges, or ones that will read in different units, such as fathoms as well as feet. For use in foreign waters, some models also read in meters and decimeters. A multirange capability most often exists in sounders of the digital display type but is also available in some flashing-light models.

Depth Recorders

Selection of a depth recorder will involve such factors as maximum depth; ability to expand a portion of the overall range; variable paper speeds (slower for better economy or faster for better definition); straight-line versus curved-line recording; the "white line" feature to sharpen indications near the bottom; variable sensitivity; and width, cost, and availability of recording paper. A few models of depth recorders also include a flashing-light indicator so the unit can be used without chart paper consumption when that feature is not desired.

Video Sounders

The term "video depth recorder" is often used to describe a more recent development. But it is really a misnomer, as depths are displayed over a short interval of time and distance but are *not permanently recorded,* except for a few expensive models that can output to a video cassette recorder (VCR), as used with TV sets.

A video sounder has a display that is much like a section of a paper chart recorder. Some models provide their information in colors, others in shades of gray, on a TV-like screen. Black-and-white displays usually use a LCD type of presentation. A "zoom" capability allows many models to focus attention on a portion of the depth range and expand this for greater clarity of detail. Often a screen of information can be temporarily "frozen" for closer examination. More expensive models can scroll back to the previous screen if something was missed as it went by. Many models can show other information on the screen, such as water temperature, and speed and distance from a starting point; deluxe models can even display the craft's position in latitude and longitude derived from a Loran-C receiver.

Operating Frequency and Power

Depth sounders, regardless of their type of display, operate by projecting downward brief pulses of ultrasonic energy and receiving back the echoes from the bottom (and sometimes from fish). The frequency of these ultrasonic pulses determines the depth to which they can penetrate the water and the sharpness of the beam (which in turn determines the level of detail on the display). Although there are a few odd frequencies, 50 kHz and 200 kHz predominate. Use of the lower frequency makes possible a greater maximum range, but use of the higher frequency provides a sharper beam. (Dual 200 kHz transducers are now available that permit switching from a sharp beam to a broader one, but depth penetration remains limited by the higher frequency.) Consider how your depth sounder will be most used when you make your selection.

Depth sounders may be rated in average (also called "RMS") power of their output, or in peak-to-peak pulse power; the ratio is 1:8 between the two forms of measurement. Small differences are not significant in selecting between typical indicator models; many advertisements do not even list a figure for power. Recording and video models are more likely to be rated, with peak-to-peak powers from about 400 to more than 1,000 watts; the higher powers are more significant in reaching greater depths.

Depth Alarms

An audible alarm is a desirable feature on any type of depth sounder, and many models have them. This should be adjustable either in fixed steps or smoothly to any value selected by the operator. While most obviously used to warn of shoaling water to avoid running aground, an alarm set at greater depths can also be a useful part of your navigation plan; it can advise you, for example, of when you should make a change of course.

An interesting feature recently added to some models of depth sounder is the dual alarm; it should receive particular consideration in your selection process. It is used after anchoring by setting one alarm depth slightly less than the water you are in and the other somewhat greater. Now if your anchor should drag, and you not notice it, an alarm will sound whether you are moving inshore or farther from land—a definite safety feature, but you must remember to allow for tidal changes. Another type of anchor alarm can be set for any one of several values of depth *change* plus or minus; these will sound if the actual depth varies more than the preset value from what it was when the alarm was turned on.

There are also available external accessory alarm units that can be installed as an add-on to an existing depth sounder in many instances.

At least one model of depth sounder has the desirable feature of a "forward-looking" depth alarm. In this unit, the *trend* of depth measurements is considered. together with the craft's speed, and the alarm is sounded in advance if it appears that the preset depth will soon be reached.

Fish Alarms

Depth sounders intended primarily as "fish finders" often have a special alarm that will sound when definite echoes are received from levels above the bottom of the water.

Other Features

Many depth sounders of all types also provide data on water temperature—a sensor is easily built into the transducer mount. A paddle-wheel sensor for speed and distance measurement is also built into some transducers, with the information being shown on the same digital display as depth.

A highly desirable feature is a depth reading offset adjustment that can be set to allow the display to show either clearance depth under the keel, or water depth from the surface, highly useful in navigation. (Transducers are located somewhere between the surface and the keel and thus show neither of the above depths without an offset.)

If you don't want to have to watch your electronic sounder to get continuous depth information, there is an accessory that can be connected to many models. It will sound off in synthesized speech, either when depths change, or at regular selectable intervals, your choice. It can operate in an alarm mode, remaining silent until the depth decreases to a value you have preset; in this mode it can also serve as an anchor alarm.

Other special features vary from one manufacturer to another; several models should be considered before making your final selection.

INSTALLATION

A modern electronic depth sounder consists of two units: a display unit that includes all electronic circuits, and a transducer that acts as both a "loudspeaker" and a "microphone" to send out pulses of sound energy and receive back the weak echoes. There is an interconnecting cable between these units, and DC input electrical power leads will be required.

Installing the Display Unit

The display unit should be located where it can easily be read in your normal sitting or standing position at the helm. Most models have brackets that allow tilting, and perhaps rotation as well, for the best viewing angle. The unit should not be so near the compass as to affect that most important navigation instrument. With your boat absolutely motionless—preferably made fast to a pier—bring the display unit, power turned off, from a point 10 feet or more away from the compass to its intended mounting position, and observe for even the slightest movement of the compass card. Now turn the unit on (with cable connected to transducer), watching the compass card closely. Do this several times with your boat on a north–south heading, then repeat on an east–west heading. If there is any effect on your compass, try to find another location. If this is not practicable, recompensate your compass after installing the depth sounder. If turning the sounder off and on causes the compass card to move, and you can't relocate the display unit, you will have to have two deviation tables for your compass, one for use when the sounder is in use and the other for when it is off.

Wiring

The display unit will need a source of power and must be connected to the boat's electrical system. Requirements are not great: .33 ampere or less for indicator-type units; roughly 2 amperes for video sounders; and 5 amperes, more or less, for paper chart recorders. Make all connections in accordance with the guidelines in Chapter 23.

Installing the Transducer

Some smaller boats have the transducer installed on a bracket at the transom, and on a few craft the transducer is mounted internally, but in the vast majority of installations the transducer is external to the hull and has its stem extending through, into the inside bilge. As with the installation of any electronic gear, read the manufacturer's instructions carefully before starting any work, then read them once again—and be sure to follow them.

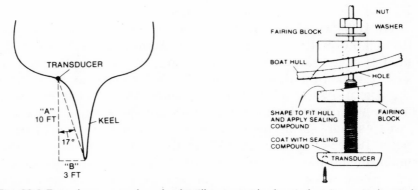

Fig. 28-1 Transducer on a deep-keel sailboat must be located so its conical sound beam does not intersect the keel. Right: Use a pair of fairing blocks when a transducer is mounted on a surface that is not horizontal.

The location for the transducer should be carefully selected. It must, of course, be a spot on the hull that does not come out of the water as the craft rolls and pitches. The location must avoid areas of turbulent flow in normal operation. On displacement or moderate-speed planing hulls almost any spot aft of midships will be smooth, bubble-free water; the slower the boat, the farther forward the transducer may be placed. Ultra high-speed craft may have to be slowed to take depth readings, as the transducer may be out of the water at the characteristically steep bow angles. On sailboats, turbulence is not normally a problem, but if there is a deep keel or centerboard, the transducer must be outboard from the centerline enough that the keel does not appear in the conical beam of sound energy projected downward. For boats of radical design, the best advice is to consult the manufacturer or owners of similar craft. The transducer must not be in an area of disturbed water flow, such as near the struts; cooling water intakes; or other projections, such as speed sensing units. For its own protection, it should not be mounted on the bottom of the keel. Since this last requirement means that the transducer will be mounted on the hull to one side of the keel, you will need fairing blocks so that it points directly downward. If the transducer points downward at an angle, echoes may not be received back, and any depth readings will be inaccurate because of the longer path traveled by the signals. A pair of blocks is used, one outside the hull and one inside. It is also desirable that the outside block be streamlined on a fore-and-aft axis to minimize disturbances in the water flow past the transducer. An important consideration in locating the transducer is access on the inside of the boat so you can tighten up the stem nut and run the connecting cable properly—check this carefully before drilling the hole in the bottom of your boat.

Transom Mounting

A transom-mounted transducer may well be necessary for a trailered boat to prevent damage to it when launching or reloading. This position, however, is somewhat less than desirable from the viewpoint of water turbulence; locate the transducer to one side, outside the wake of propellers and rudders. The mounting angle can be critical, and an adjustable bracket is usually necessary. Depth sounders with transducers so mounted may operate properly at relatively slow speeds only.

Antifouling Protection

An external transducer, whether mounted through the hull or on a transom bracket, should be protected from fouling. Do not use your regular antifouling paint; special thinned-out transducer paints are available, but you can do just as well with a good grade of oil-based bottom paint. Don't use vinyl or epoxy paints, as they may react with the rubber or plastic of the trans-

387

ducer housing. And don't apply more than one light coat of thinned-out bottom paint; any heavier coating may seriously reduce the sounder's sensitivity and limit the depths to which it can reach.

An "Inside Job"

An inside-the-hull mounting for a transducer eliminates the need for having your boat hauled out for installation, but otherwise it is generally a more complex job. There will always be

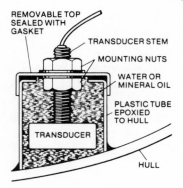

REMOVABLE TOP
SEALED WITH
GASKET

TRANSDUCER STEM

MOUNTING NUTS

WATER OR
MINERAL OIL

PLASTIC TUBE
EPOXIED
TO HULL

TRANSDUCER

HULL

Fig. 28-2 A transducer can be mounted inside the hull as shown, with no loss of accuracy, but probably with some loss of maximum range.

some loss of power as the signal, and the echo, must travel through the hull; this will affect the maximum depth at which measurements can be taken but will not adversely affect the accuracy of any reading. The hull must be of solid, not cored, construction; there must be no bubbles or buoyancy voids in the fiberglass at the chosen location. You must be careful to avoid areas where there will be turbulence on the outside of the hull. One way to find a good location is to complete the installation of the display unit and then make tests with the transducer temporarily mounted inside the hull; this unit can be placed in a plastic bag filled with water, or it may simply be stuck to the hull with chewing gum! Take your boat out to where the water is approximately 50 feet deep and try various locations inside the hull until you get a good, consistent reading while the boat is drifting. If you don't at first find a suitable location, try in somewhat shallower water; if you are interested in deeper readings, start your tests in 100 feet of water. When you think you have found a good mounting location, bring your boat up to cruising speed and check that the operation of the sounder is still satisfactory. (This procedure is also useful for finding a turbulence-free location for an externally mounted transducer.)

Once you have a satisfactory location, proceed with the permanent installation. The transducer should be mounted in a fluid-filled "bubble"—these are available commercially, or you can make your own. The fluid can be seawater or freshwater, but the best is mineral oil. The transducer head must be fully submerged, and the face can butt against the hull. An alternative mounting method is to bond the transducer directly to the inside of your boat's hull, using a good-quality clear silicone-type marine sealant (but it must point directly downward). Make sure there are no bubbles in the sealant or on the face of the transducer.

Connecting the Transducer

The transducer will come with a length of cable connected permanently to it, with a fitting at the other end to match the display unit. If this cable is longer than is required for your installation, *do not cut it;* coil up any excess at some point along its length and tuck it out of the way. If the cable is too short, consult the manufacturer's manual that came with the sounder. The best solution is to use a factory-made extension cable; if one is not available, visit a service shop for advice—a cable can be spliced, but this is a job for a technician. An increase in cable length should not affect the accuracy of depth measurements, but it may require retuning the unit to avoid a slight decrease in the maximum depth that can be read.

The connecting cable should be routed between the transducer and display unit so it is well clear of all other electrical wiring, especially such "noisy" wires as those of the ignition system. Modern depth sounders have antinoise circuits built in, but avoidance is the best policy.

CHECKOUT AND FAMILIARIZATION

Once your installation is complete, test it under different conditions—at various speeds, over different types of bottoms, during the day, and at night. Use your sounder, and become familiar with its operation well before the day when its use may be critical to your craft's safety. Some models have internal circuits for automatic sensitivity control, but others have a knob on the front panel for a "sensitivity" or "gain" control, and you should know the proper settings for various operating conditions; again, see the manufacturer's instructions.

Electronic depth sounders measure distance from the face of the transducer. If your unit does not have a depth offset, you should know how far this is below your boat's waterline so you can add this amount to the indicated depth to get actual water depth for navigation. You should also know the distance that the transducer is up from the lowest point on your boat so that you can subtract this amount to get the clearance depth for safety.

Check your depth sounder readings in shallow water with a marked lead line—make one up temporarily if you don't carry one regularly. Don't depend on charted depths for checking accuracy, and don't expect absolute accuracy—typical depth sounders for small craft are rated at ± 5% (plus one digit for digital displays), and this is more than good enough for safety and navigation.

MAINTENANCE

Depth sounders required little or no maintenance, but do carefully check the manufacturer's instruction, if any, on such actions. Flasher models using a neon bulb may grow dim and require replacement of this lamp after several hundred hours of use, but LEDs will not require this service. Depth recorders will need periodic resupplying with fresh rolls of paper, and perhaps a cleaning of the stylus. There is nothing that an owner need, or can, do with a digital display.

If the depth sounder fails completely or operates erratically, about all that you can do is check that there is voltage at the input, the fuse is not blown, and that the transducer cable connection is clean and tight. If all these check out, remove the display unit only and take it to a shop; there they will have a test transducer to use on your set. If the display unit checks out at the shop, it may be necessary for the technician to come to your boat to check the transducer as the probable cause of the trouble. If a neighboring skipper has an identical model, you might first try exchanging display units; this will let you know whether the trouble is in the display unit (likely), or in the transducer and cable (unlikely). Do not, however, switch units on different models of depth sounders—you could change a small problem into a larger one.

If your boat is to be out of service for several months or more, it is generally advisable to remove the display unit and store it in a safe place not subject to extremes of temperature or humidity.

CHAPTER 29

Speedometers and Logs

A SKIPPER-NAVIGATOR can, after accumulating some experience with his or her boat, make a reasonably accurate *guess* as to the speed of the craft and how far he or she has come since a specific starting time. This level of precision and accuracy will suffice for ordinary daytime cruising under favorable conditions, but it falls far short of what is required for good navigation, especially at night or in fog and other conditions of reduced visibility. It is also not adequate for sail racing or powerboat predicted log contests. For these latter situations, electronic instrumentation—sensors and displays—are necessary.

The first step in using speed and distance traveled information is the recognition that there are two kinds of each. These quantities can be measured "through the water" and "over the bottom," to use generally accepted terms. Nearly all instruments installed on a boat for measuring speed and distance produce "through the water" data; this is the most easily obtained measurement. For inland boating on a lake, this is essentially the same as "over the bottom"; but let the water itself have motion with respect to the earth—horizontal motion, that is—and this equality is lost. If the water flows, as it does everywhere there is a current—river, tidal, or ocean—then the speed and distance traveled over the bottom are a combination of the boat's motion within the body of water and the motion of that water with respect to the earth.

Actually, speed over the bottom can be measured by an electronic instrument aboard your boat, but it is a sort of secondary output. True speed can be measured as a change in geographic position—you could even do it in a trailered boat going down a highway! But seriously, most Loran-C receivers have an output of speed as an averaged change in position; this is normally read from the main display by pushing a button, if it is not continuously shown on an additional line. In some installations, such speed information can be interfaced to another navigation device, such as a radar display, and also shown there.

It is essential that the two different types of speed information be recognized and always kept in mind when such data are used for navigation or other purposes.

At one time the terms "speedometer" and "log" had somewhat different meanings, but now time has blurred them into essentially interchangeable usage. For the sake of simplicity, "speedometer" will be used in this chapter to refer to all instruments that measure speed and/or distance.

Selection

There are a number of factors to be considered in selecting a speedometer for your boat. As noted below, essentially all sensors are now of one general type, but a recent trend seems to be the combination of a speed sensor into a single unit with a sensor for water temperature, and sometimes also a depth sounder's transducer. Displays come in a variety of types and sizes; there should be no problem in selecting one to meet your needs and physical limitations.

Distance traveled is often shown in two different ways in the same instrument. First is an accumulated measurement of total distance since the instrument was installed; there is no external means for resetting the reading to zero. Many speedometers will also measure "trip distance"—this is a separate display that can be reset to zero whenever you wish merely by pressing a button or a switch. Both readings have their uses—the first as a means of recording the total travels of the boat, and the second in ordinary navigation, such as dead reckoning or piloting. It may be satisfactory to reset the trip reading to zero for each day's travel, or it may be more useful to reset to zero for each leg of a pas-

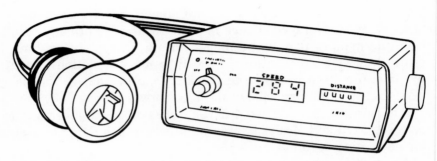

Fig. 29-1 Speedometers for boats usually use a paddle-wheel type of sensor. The small wheel turns in the flow of water past the hull, generating an electrical signal that is proportional to the craft's speed. Distance can be measured by an integration of speed with time.

sage, as an aid to anticipating when the next change of course will be occurring.

Sensors

Nearly all speedometers for boats use a sensor that resembles a very small paddle wheel; see Fig. 29-1. This is turned by the flow of water past it as the boat moves ahead. One older model used a propeller-type spinner, and there have been a few high-tech models that electronically detected the flow of water past a flush sensor with no moving parts. A simple speed-only paddle wheel sensor can often be retracted into the boat and the through-hull fitting capped off. This is a desirable feature for boats that sit for long periods without use; it will help to keep the sensor from fouling with marine growth. Only a cupful or so of water will enter the boat if the cap is held ready to apply as soon as the sensor is pulled up and out of its housing.

A separate sensor for distance is not required, as this information is derived electronically from speed by a mathematical integration process.

Displays

The display of speed information can be either analog with a rotating pointer on a clocklike dial, or digital with a liquid crystal display (LCD).

Distance is usually shown by a mechanical counter if the display is of the pointer-and-dial type. With LCD digital displays of speed, distance can be shown by a separate set of numbers, or by switching the same digits as used for indicating speed.

The speedometer display is also used on some models to show water temperature, or even depth.

Select a display that has internal provisions for illuminating the display at night.

Other Features

In some instances you will have to select a speedometer for use with either statute miles and miles per hour or with nautical miles and knots, depending upon the waters on which you do your boating. Other models allow for positioning a switch for whichever set of units you are concerned with, and an easy change back and forth between them.

The level of precision in the measurement of speed and distance will also vary among different models. For digital displays, a satisfactory style of readout for speed would show whole units above 10 mph or knots, with units and tenths at slower speeds. Some models read to .01 mph/knot, but internal averaging is required to "smooth" the data and keep the display from fluc-

Fig. 29-2 Some speedometer/logs for sailboats can be switched to a "delta speed" function that emphasizes small increases and decreases in speed through the water. The unit shown above displays a "+" or a "−" to indicate acceleration or deceleration.

tuating rapidly and constantly; the accuracy of speedometers is not really great enough to validate readings in hundredths of a speed unit. (See comments on accuracy under "Installation" below.)

Distance will be shown in nautical or statute miles, normally to tenths, and sometimes to hundredths.

Speedometers for sailboats will often have an incremental speed feature, a "delta speed" display. This is of considerable value in racing but can also be useful in cruising. When this "delta" speed indication is switched in, a more sensitive, more precise readout is used to show slight variations in speed resulting from small adjustments of heading and sail trim. Absolute speed is not shown at this time, only small changes faster or slower; see Fig. 29-2.

Some models with digital readouts also include a timer that can be set to show elapsed time from when it was started, or to show a countdown of time to an expected event, such as arrival at a turning point.

Alarms are included in some speedometer models that will sound when the timer is used, or when a preset distance has been reached, or when speed varies from a preset value.

If you are planning on use of satellite navigation, you should select a speedometer that will interface with your SatNav receiver and provide a speed input to that device.

INSTALLATION

Installation of a speedometer will require some advance planning. The sensor is external to the hull and below the waterline—this is obviously a job to be done when the boat is out of the water for storage or other work. The location for the sensor must be chosen carefully, considering both the flow of water around the hull (to get accurate readings) and accessibility from inside the boat (it must not be under some major item where it can't be reached, especially if you plan to retract the sensor when the boat is not in use).

Mounting the Display

The display unit is small enough that there usually is no problem deciding where it is to be placed, although often there are many items that "must" be easily seen by the helmsman. If the display is to be flush-mounted, plan carefully before cutting any holes in a panel or bulkhead. An LCD display probably will have no effect on a compass, but make a test to be sure. A meter-type analog display is more likely to have a magnetic field—keep it well away from the compass and test carefully. Both of these tests should be made with some value of speed being shown on the display.

Wiring

For larger craft, consider the distance between the sensor and the display unit as compared to the length of the cable supplied with the instrument; it can be lengthened, but don't get caught short in midjob.

The wiring between the sensor and display unit is a small, light cable that can be routed wherever convenient. Wires must also be run to a source of 12-volt DC power, but very little amperage is used, and these wires, too, can be small and light. (A few models are self-powered, or have internal batteries, but these may need an electrical power connection for display illumination.) If wires come anywhere near a compass, they should be twisted together in accordance with standard practice.

Accuracy

The accuracy of a marine speedometer is far from guaranteed; the speed indicated will be highly dependent on the location of the sensor on the hull and the flow of water past it. Most models will provide for an adjustment of the reading within reasonable limits; any given setting of this control, however, may not make readings accurate over the entire range of the instrument. You must expect to have to run calibration trials over known distances; when you do this, record the data in your boat's log and be sure to note the prevailing conditions: state of fuel and water tanks; number of persons on board (if significant); cleanliness, or lack thereof, of the bottom and propeller, etc. If there is no means of adjustment provided, you still should run calibration trials; tabulate the error at various speeds, and refer to these values when speed or distance data are later needed for precise navigation.

MAINTENANCE

Except for a few meter-type analog speedometer indicators, speedometers are all of solid-state electronics requiring no maintenance. Keep electrical connections clean and tight, and replace a fuse if one should ever blow. (The fuses are of very small size; make sure you carry the proper spares.)

The moving parts of the sensor must be kept clean of marine fouling growth if they are to retain their accuracy. If yours is not of the retractable type, take advantage of every opportunity to clean it off; if you boat in warm and clear waters, don't forget it when you go for a swim. Follow the manufacturer's instructions regarding the use, or nonuse, of antifouling paint.

CHAPTER 30

Loud-hailers and Intercoms

THERE WILL be many occasions in your boating activities when you desire to, or absolutely must, speak to another person who is out of range of your normal voice. On board, you may need to call a crew member up from belowdecks to assist you in some essential action; or you may merely want to go below and take a rest, knowing that the person at the helm can instantly and surely communicate with you if he or she needs advice or help. Externally, you may merely need to converse with a person on a pier as you approach; or it may be vital communications when you are assisting another vessel, or receiving help from one. In all these cases, your unreinforced speaking voice is likely to be inadequate.

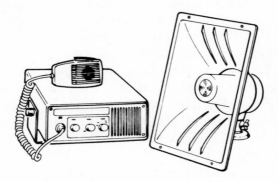

Fig. 30-1 In addition to the external speaker, a boat's loud hailer includes a control unit mounted near the helm. This has an attached microphone for calling out and an internal speaker for listening.

To a limited extent, you can overcome your limitations by shouting or by changing your position, such as leaving the helm to call down the companionway. But it may not be adequate in the first case, or safe in the second. The better solution is the use of appropriate electronic equipment—a loud-hailer for communications external to your boat, or an intercom system to exchange information within or about your craft. You may want to install one or the other—or both.

LOUD-HAILERS

For a boat, a loud-hailer is a moderate-power audio system consisting of a microphone (almost always referred to as a "mike"), an amplifier, and one or more speakers. This system may be assembled from individual components, but more often it is purchased as a unit.

Types of Hailers

Loud-hailers on boats may be either hand-held portable units or installed fixed systems; each has its advantages and disadvantages. Once again, plan ahead carefully: Consider what your needs and intended uses are, and buy to meet them. Portable units—frequently called "power megaphones"—have less audio strength, 10–25 watts, as they are powered by internal batteries. This can be offset, however, with greater directivity, enabling the available audio output to be directed specifically toward the intended hearer. Hand-held hailers can be compact and stowed out of the way when not needed for use.

Installed hailer systems, on the other hand, can have as much power as desired, as they draw from your boat's 12-volt DC electrical system. A louder output is often needed as the speaker is normally fixed in direction and the intended recipient of your communications may be off the axis of maximum sound. As will be seen later in this chapter, however, there are ways of overcoming this fixed-direction limitation.

It is quite possible that your various applications for amplified voice communications will make it desirable to have *both* an installed loud-hailer and a hand-held electronic megaphone; this is not as redundant as one might first think.

Selection

First of all, the equipment must be truly "marine quality"—capable of withstanding the harsh environment found in most boating situations. The microphone should be a standard hand-held unit for voice frequencies with a "push to talk" button switch. It will be similar to those used on VHF and CB radios. A "noise-canceling" mike is one of special design that responds only to sounds spoken directly into it at close distances, with no sensitivity to general background sounds. This is a desirable feature, particularly on noisy powerboats, but not a mandatory one if your budget is a bit tight. The amplifier must have enough power to be useful, but excessive levels are of no particular advantage. It is monaural, of course, not stereo! Power ratings are typically 15 to 40 watts, which are fully ample, but one available unit is rated at 80 watts. Quite often you will find CB radios and some VHF/FM marine transceivers with a "P.A." switch on the front panel and an output jack or pair of terminals similarly marked on the back of the set. The audio power available is typically only 4 to 6 watts, considerably less than needed to be effective. This limited audio power is really useful only for on-board communications.

Speaker Selection

The speaker is the critical element of a loud-hailer installation; select with care, and pay enough to get a good one. The speaker must be waterproof, as it is almost always placed where it will receive the full force of rain and at least some spray. It should have been designed for voice frequencies rather than music, and it must have a power rating to match the amplifier that will drive it. Finally, get information on the speaker's directivity pattern; consider what your requirements are, and match a speaker to them.

Special Features

Most loud-hailers offer one or more special features in addition to their normal function of amplifying your voice; these can add considerably to the usability and desirability of this electronic accessory.

Many hailers additionally have a listening capability in which the external speaker doubles as a microphone to pick up distant sounds that are too faint for you to hear directly with your ears. These sounds are amplified and heard either through a speaker in the amplifier/control unit or through the normal microphone, then doubling as a small speaker you can hold to your ear. This capability makes possible two-way voice communications out to the farthest range of the hailer. Using this feature, you may also be able to hear fog signals or aids to navigation at greater distances than otherwise would be possible. A separate volume control is often provided for this mode of operation.

Another useful feature is the ability of some loud-hailers to serve as an automatic (or manual) fog signal for your craft. A suitable tone is generated within the amplifier at accurately spaced intervals of two minutes, as specified by the Navigation Rules. Caution: It is possible that your fog signals could get "in step" with those of another vessel being sounded automatically at precisely the same intervals—you would not hear the other vessel's signals if they were drowned out by your own. It is advisable to break your sequence at odd intervals to listen for the signals of others. Some units that automatically repeat fog signals at regular intervals have a control that allows adjustment of this interval; the Navigation Rules merely require the sounding at intervals of "not more than two minutes." Some but not all hand-held hailers have an internal fog signal capability but do not sound automatically at fixed intervals.

Another electronically generated signal can be described as a siren or "yelp." This is useful for attracting attention, but don't use it in any way that might lead to your being accused of impersonating a law-enforcement vessel.

Some loud-hailer systems have an auxiliary input for connection to the receiver of your VHF/FM radiotelephone so that you can monitor a channel while out on deck, or nearby in the dinghy. Or you can connect to a low-level output from a music system and serenade all those around you—hoping that they like your selections!

A few loud-hailer systems have audio output at reduced power for internal speakers in order to operate as an intercom system. This function can be switched to separately so that messages to those belowdecks are not broadcast at full power over the hailer's external horn.

In many cases, a foghorn or other signal can also be connected to various sensors to sound the alarm for fire, high bilge water, unauthorized entry, etc.

One hand-held hailer has a built-in light that can be flashed in Morse code for emergency signaling—*if* you and the other individual know the code! But most boaters would recognize three dots—three dashes—three dots as an "SOS."

Installation

The "installation" of a hand-held power megaphone consists simply of arranging secure and protected, as well as convenient, storage for the unit when it is not in use. If the batteries of your hailer can be recharged from the boat's 12-volt DC electrical system, you must have an outlet for this that will mate with the connector on the charger's power cord; this can be either a cigarette-lighter connection or a polarized plug and socket combination.

For a fixed hailer, the audio amplifier unit will contain the controls for the system—the on-off switch, gain or volume control, etc.—and must be located where these are convenient for use. The microphone is plugged into this unit, and it, too, must be located convenient for use; it should have a coiled cord that will extend to where you will normally use it, but retract to a shorter length for keeping out of the way. If the amplifier/control unit has an internal speaker for listening, this will have a powerful permanent magnet that will affect your boat's compass. Try bringing this unit slowly to its intended mounting place from a distance of 6 to 10 feet away while another person carefully observes the compass card; do this on both N–S and E–W headings of your boat. If an effect is seen on your compass on either heading, you have two options: (1) Select another location for the amplifier/control unit, or (2) make a complete new deviation table for the compass. Do not attempt navigation without taking one or the other of these actions!

Speaker Location

One of the most important elements in an effective loud-hailer installation is the speaker location on the boat. Be sure it is high enough to be clear of any major obstructions that would block or deflect its sound waves. It is also necessary that the speaker be mounted where maximum acoustical separation from the microphone can be achieved; this will reduce the chance of feedback howls and squeals when the output is turned up high. The greater the acoustical isolation of mike and speakers, by distance or by the imposition of a sound barrier between them, or a combination of both, the higher the amplifier gain can be set without getting feedback.

Both glass and plywood or fiberglass make poor sound barriers, so don't count on the cabin itself to be of much help in preventing feedback. One of the worst cases is a microphone on a flying bridge with the speaker mounted on the forward side and just below—feedback is guaranteed here! On a powerboat with a mast or tuna tower, locate the speaker as high as possible. If there is no way to get the speaker up, then get as much horizontal distance as possible between the microphone and the speaker; keep the mike location behind the speaker. On a sailboat, the speaker can be mounted quite high up the mast, usually at the level of the spreaders. Here, with the mike back in the cockpit, there usually is no feedback problem.

In some boat installations you may want to mount a second speaker, perhaps a smaller one, facing aft; consult the manufacturer's manual to determine if such a second speaker can be used, and if so, how it should be connected. Your amplifier controls may allow you to switch between the two speakers, selecting the one pointed nearer to the direction in which you wish to communicate; or use both at the same time if that is desired.

Speaker Orientation

The speaker will normally be installed facing directly forward. One with a circular opening to the horn will be properly oriented in any position, but one with a rectangular opening must be properly turned—there is a correct orientation for the most desirable distribution of sound. With this type of speaker the

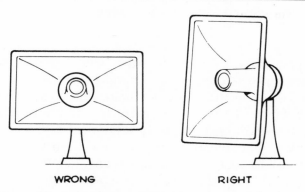

WRONG   RIGHT

Fig. 30-2 A rectangular speaker of a boat's loud hailer is often mounted incorrectly. For the best distribution of sound in the horizontal plane, the long axis of the speaker's opening should be *vertical*.

distribution in the horizontal plane will not be the same as in a vertical plane. It is usually desired to have the wider angle horizontally and the narrower angle vertically—potential hearers are more likely to be off to one side rather than high overhead. Many rectangular speakers are seen mounted incorrectly, as such might seem more "logical" if the technical features are not studied carefully. The correct orientation is with the longer axis *vertical*.

Alternative Speaker Locations

An interesting possibility is that of placing the speaker on a mount above a pilothouse top similar to that used for a searchlight. This permits the speaker, preferably one with a round horn opening, not only to be rotated but also to be tilted upward to converse with bridge tenders or dock personnel. Sometimes the speaker will be mounted on a bracket alongside the boat's searchlight, but a separate mount usually works better.

This combination of a speaker so mounted and a hailer that can also listen will result in an "audio direction finder," very useful in reduced visibility for determining the direction of, or homing in on, fog signals from aids to navigation or other vessels. Bearings can be taken to a quite remarkable degree of precision by swinging the speaker back and forth across the sound to detect the direction from which it is the loudest.

Wiring

The installation of speaker wires will generally follow the guidelines for low-voltage DC electrical systems as described in Chapter 23; the manufacturer's manual will contain information as to the gauge of wires to be used. It is almost inevitable that speaker wires will have to go through a cabin top or side; take special care that a leak is not created. Wiring for electrical power from the boat's system should also follow the practices in Chapter 23. After installation, it is a good idea to measure the DC voltage at the power input terminals of the amplifier when it is operating at full power; low voltage will do more than anything else to rob a hailer of its audio output.

Maintenance

As with other modern, solid-state electronic equipment, there is little that you should or can do. Blown fuses can be replaced (be sure you carry spares of the correct size, and don't put in one that is too large because you don't have the right one!), and connections kept clean and tight; but otherwise service in an electronics shop will be required.

INTERCOM SYSTEMS

If your boat has a control station abovedeck with a cabin below, you are a candidate for a simple intercom system. If your yacht has several cabins below—particularly an aft cabin down and behind the companionway—you should consider a multistation intercom system. On medium- and larger-size craft, communications from the cockpit or pilothouse to the foredeck is a decided advantage in anchoring, picking up a mooring, or docking. This can be done by using the loud-hailer with the output volume turned down, but it also can be accomplished by installing well forward a weatherproof "outdoor type" unit in your boat's intercom system. If you don't have an intercom system but your VHF or CB set has a "PA" output, this should be adequate for foredeck communication.

Selection

Often an installed loud-hailer will have connections for a three- or four-station intercom system; but if not, you will need a separate unit. While a marine-type intercom system is, of course, preferable, you may not be able to find one to fit your needs. A simple "house"-type system can be used, but it must be adequately protected from the weather.

If a simple *one-way* "system" will meet your needs, you can use the PA output from your CB set or VHF/FM radiotelephone. Install a small speaker of suitable impedance and power rating in a box just large enough to hold it. Mount this box at a suitable location in the cabin and you will be able to call to a person below, although he or she cannot talk back to you.

If *two-way* communications are needed or desired, an inexpensive battery-powered system of two or more units can be installed. These will require wiring from the master to the remote units, and between masters if more than one is used. Unfortunately, the "wireless" intercom units that offer the greatest flexibility and ease of installation can be used only in limited cases, as they require a continuous source of 120-volt AC electric power.

Some larger intercom systems will have an input connection for background music or will include an integral FM radio tuner.

Installation and Maintenance

Master and remote units can be installed into bulkheads and side panels if desired; or they can be simply set on shelves and brackets, being securely fastened down to prevent falling when you run into rough weather. If the amplifier/control unit is mounted into a bulkhead or panel, provide enough ventilation to ensure that heat generated by the equipment can be dissipated by an adequate circulation of air. Interconnecting wires/cables are small and light, and they can be run where convenient and inconspicuous; they should be secured in place and protected from physical damage, as for low-voltage DC wiring.

Maintenance will be limited to replacement of any blown fuses and checking to see that all connections are clean and tight.

CHAPTER 31

Loran-C Receivers

FOR THE American boatman who has no globe-circling plans, the Loran-C electronic navigation system offers all-weather positioning to a good degree of accuracy. Compared to satellite navigation, Loran provides continuous position information from somewhat less expensive equipment. Its coverage is limited, however, to the U.S. and Canadian coasts, the upper North Atlantic Ocean, the Mediterranean Sea, and a portion of the far western Pacific Ocean in the area of Japan and the Philippines. There is some adequate coverage in the vicinity of Hawaii, but signal strengths are weak between there and the U.S. Pacific Coast. Loran signals in the lower North Atlantic Ocean and the Caribbean Sea are marginal at best. The South Atlantic, South Pacific, and Indian oceans lack any Loran coverage.

SELECTION

The "state of the art" in receivers for the Loran-C radionavigation system has advanced dramatically in recent years. Many features have been added, and use of a set has become much simpler and easier. The physical size of Loran receivers has shrunk, as has the price. For a skipper whose boating activities make Loran navigation applicable, there is little reason not to be so equipped.

System Operation

The basic output of a Loran-C receiver is one or more "time differences" from pairs of stations, numbers that correspond to

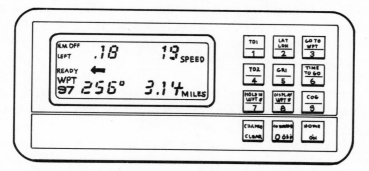

Fig. 31-1 On this model, two full time differences are shown simultaneously, facilitating plotting. Tuning to the desired station is done with knobs.

lines of position (LOP) on a chart. To obtain a fix, it is necessary to have two LOPs; three are desirable. These are normally obtained from the different station pairs of the same Loran-C chain, so the receiver need not be retuned. Receivers have at least two lines in their displays so that a pair of position data can be simultaneously shown. Many models have one or more additional data lines to show such information as speed, distance (and perhaps time) to go, course made good, etc. On some sets, the position and other data will be shown in alternately selectable displays on the same screen.

Once set to a Loran-C chain, the receiver automatically selects the strongest two station pairs; several minutes may be required for the set to "settle down" and output stable information. If a third Loran pair is being tracked, it is normally necessary to operate controls on the front of the set to have its output information displayed in lieu of one of the stations pairs originally selected.

Position Plotting

To find your position most accurately, you will need to use a chart that has been overprinted with Loran-C lines of position. Using the time difference information from your set, take one of the readings and locate your LOP of the moment between the printed lines for values on either side of your readout. Do this for a second time difference, and you have a Loran fix. If a third time difference can be obtained, the third LOP will give greater confidence in your position. Don't expect the three LOPs to intersect at a single point, but the triangle that they form should be small; a large triangle indicates an error in either reading the display or in plotting.

Essentially all Loran-C receivers now have an internal microprocessor that converts time-difference data into a simultaneous display of latitude and longitude. With such sets, charts with overprinted Loran lines are not necessary. A word of caution, however: Many charts that do not have Loran lines may have omitted them for good reason, such as unreliable Loran reception in the area. Positions from latitude-longitude readouts may not be as accurate as those manually plotted from time differences—compromises may have been made within the receiver in the conversion process.

Loran-C receivers typically display latitude and longitude in degrees and minutes with two decimal places, and one model even carries this to three decimal places. For latitude, 0.01' equals only 60 feet, and 0.001' is just 6 feet; both are less for longitude. Such a high level of precision is not warranted by the overall accuracy of the Loran-C radionavigation system. Plotting to 0.01' of latitude or longitude is not realistic in absolute position, but it may be valid for return to a location using Loran's excellent "repeatability" characteristic. (See Chapter 36 for a general discussion of the terms "accuracy" and "precision" and the difference between them.)

Notch Filters

A consideration in making your selection of a Loran-C receiver is the number and type of "notch filters." Loran-C pulses are subject to interference from other signals on nearby frequencies. Such unwanted signals are eliminated—"notched out"—by filters sharply tuned to those frequencies. Loran-C receivers will have from four to eight such notch filters, and these may be factory-tuned, operator-tunable, or a combination of both; on more expensive models, some or all of the filters may automatically seek the interfering signals and tune them out. The number of filters needed will depend on the interference conditions in your operating area or areas; consult with both shop technicians and other local Loran-C users. If your vessel stays in one general area, you may not need tunable filters or as many preset filters; if you cruise widely, you may need the capability of adjusting to different interference situations. In general terms, a combination of preset notch filters (internally adjustable) and externally adjustable or automatic filters will provide excellent interference protection and adequate flexibility.

Displays

The size and type of display used by a Loran-C receiver are significant considerations in making a selection. The display must be large enough to be read clearly and of a type adequately visible in bright daylight, or in the almost total darkness of a helm station when under way at night.

The most common type of display is liquid crystal (LCD), which is easily read in daylight and can be backlit for nighttime use (a variable control on the intensity of the backlighting is most desirable). The newer "super twist" types of LCD screens have sharper characters with greater contrast against the background; they are also more easily read when standing off to one side of the set.

One model shows the Loran-derived position on a chartlike display. The display, which can be in a wide range of scales, can be manually drawn in, or automatically taken from plug-in modules.

A desirable safety feature is the ability to "freeze" a Loran display—to temporarily stop the readings from being updated as the craft moves. This makes it possible for the readings to be written down before the set is allowed to resume reading current position. In person-overboard situations, freezing the Loran reading is an important immediate action.

Course Determination: Way Points and Routes

Nearly all Loran receivers can also compute a great circle (shortest distance) or rhumb line (constant course) track from your present position to any destination whose latitude and longitude (or pair of time differences, or direction and distance) you enter by means of a calculatorlike keypad. Intermediate "waypoints"—from nine to more than a hundred—can be similarly entered if you are not to go directly to the destination. Large numbers of waypoints can be predetermined, and then entered and retained in the set's memory even when the set is turned off; this uses an internal battery that is recharged when the set is turned back on. On deluxe sets, each waypoint can be given a brief alphanumeric name, as well as a sequential number, for easier recall and identification. Some sets can string a number of selected waypoints into "routes," with automatic transfer to the next one as each is reached; it is desirable that each route can be run in either direction. There may also be provision for entering any present position as a waypoint by pressing a single button. For long great-circle tracks, many sets will compute rhumb line courses for waypoints along that track.

The courses computed are derived from differences in geographic coordinates and thus are true courses. Some sets automatically apply the variation for that area from data stored in internal memory; others allow the entry of variations manually, using the keypad. Deviation, which varies from vessel to vessel, cannot be stored and must be entered manually. Entry of variation and deviation results in magnetic courses that can be compared to the craft's steering compass and/or used by an autopilot.

A Loran receiver, by continuously tracking your position, can indicate to you whether you are on course, or off to the right or left. It can compute course and speed made good and tell you the distance and time to go to your destination or next waypoint. It can be set to alert when you are a specified distance away as you approach a waypoint or your destination, and it will tell you when you have arrived!

Alarms

Various alarms are available on Loran receivers. Most essential is one that indicates a unsatisfactory quality of the received signals. There are times when Loran information must not be relied upon, and special signals are transmitted at these times;

the receiver automatically detects this situation and warns the navigator. Receivers that indicate off-course distances may also have an alarm that sounds when the crosstrack error exceeds a specified amount. An "anchor alarm" may be set to sound when the measured position varies more than a set amount from that established when the craft was first anchored. This is an excellent alert for a dragging anchor, but do allow for the size of the normal swinging circle.

Interfacing to Other Electronic Devices

A very practical and useful feature of some Loran receivers is an electronic output that can be "interfaced" with an autopilot. This allows the crosstrack errors to provide an input to the autopilot that will steer the craft so as to bring it back on course. Properly connected and adjusted to eliminate overshooting, your boat will be kept very close to the direct optimum track, saving time and fuel; this is particularly advantageous when crossing a major current such as the Gulf Stream, but it is useful in any current that is not directly ahead or astern. As the Loran track is in terms of true directions, and the automatic pilot is guided by sensing magnetic directions, inputs of variation and deviation must be made either automatically or manually.

Another interface that is possible with a few Loran-C receivers is one to a SatNav receiver. In areas of duplicate coverage by both systems, the highly accurate, but intermittent, SatNav fixes are complemented by the continuous Loran position data. This provides better plots of the vessel's location than depending on DR alone between satellite passes.

Special Features

Loran-C signals are affected by their passage over large landmasses. This must be compensated for by the entry of "Additional Secondary Factor (ASF)" corrections. The entry of such corrections may be manual or automatic from information stored internally in the set. Entry of exact latitude and longitude at a known position can be used to refine the output of some Loran receivers further and ensure more correct readouts for further cruising in that general area.

All Loran receivers come with instruction manuals, of course, but at least one manufacturer supplements this with a videocassette tape showing the proper installation and operation of the unit.

INSTALLATION

A Loran-C receiver is not a large package: Some models will be about the same shape and size as a VHF/FM receiver, others may be somewhat larger; some sets have the longer axis horizontal, others have it vertical. If the set does not have a steering indicator (display of how far the craft is off to the left or the right of the direct track to the destination or waypoint, called "cross-track error"), there is no need to mount it within the direct vision of the helmsman, and it can be located anywhere convenient for general navigational use. At least one model, however, has an optional steering-only indicator, a much smaller package, that can be placed forward of the helm, with the main unit at the navigator's station. Other sets have optional display units with full readout capability.

Ventilation

Do not flush-mount a Loran-C receiver in a bulkhead unless adequate provision is made for ventilation of the heat produced in the operation of the set.

Antenna

Receivers for Loran-C will require their own antenna. As this is a very-low-frequency (VLF) system, an external coupler (loading coil) is needed. A whip antenna about 8 or 9 feet in length is usually used—a CB fiberglass whip (full-length, not loaded, and not "marine-type") works well; if an antenna is part of the receiver package when purchased, be sure to use that one. Cables to connect the antenna coupler to the receiver will be supplied by the set manufacturer and must be used. The antenna must be mounted high and well clear of other antennas.

The physical installation of a Loran-C receiver and its antenna is not difficult and should easily be within the capabilities of the average boatman. But getting it to work properly may be another matter—electrical noise on your boat can be a serious problem. Every spark, even the tiniest ones from brushes of a motor such as a bilge pump, is a radio frequency signal, and the power leads to that pump or other accessory act as an antenna to radiate that signal. Electrical noise often comes from generators or alternators, and from their regulators. There may be a number of noise sources that must be suppressed for reliable Loran-C reception.

You can call in an experienced service technician, but there is no reason why you should not first try your own hand at noise suppression (it will help on radio and TV reception, too!); see Chapters 20 and 41.

In many instances a standard television set, color or black-and-white, will cause interference to Loran-C reception. The simple solution is to turn off the TV set; but if this is not practicable, try a standard high-pass filter installed between the TV set and its antenna. Fluorescent lights are often a particularly troublesome source of electrical noise.

Wiring

The input power requirements of Loran-C receivers are quite small, from less than 0.01 to about 1.2 amperes from your boat's 12-volt DC system. Thus these sets do not require a separate circuit breaker on the distribution panel and can be connected to the same circuit that powers the radio or radios. Some sets may be temporarily powered from a small 9-volt "transistor" battery; this provides for use if the boat's power system fails, and for taking the receiver off the boat for preloading waypoints while preparing at home for a cruise.

Electrical wiring should be installed in accordance with Chapter 23. A good ground connection directly to the engine block or keel bolts is absolutely essential.

MAINTENANCE

The maintenance that you can perform on your Loran-C receiver is quite limited. Keep the set clean and dry, and keep it securely mounted. Keep electrical connections clean and tight—this includes connections for the antenna, power leads, and all noise-suppression capacitors and chokes. Your set may have a small cartridge fuse in a holder on the chassis—typically a 1- or 2-ampere, type 3AG fuse; keep on hand several spares, but if a newly replaced fuse blows immediately upon turning the set on, cease trying to use the Loran-C receiver and take it to a service shop or call a technician to come to your boat.

If your boat is to be out of service for several months or more, it is generally advisable to remove the Loran receiver and store it in a safe place where it will not be subjected to extremes of heat or humidity.

CHAPTER 32

Autopilots

THE TERM "autopilot" is not a strictly true description, but this does not diminish the usefulness of this unit. A more precise name would be "automatic steering device," for it does not "pilot" your boat in the usual sense of that term. You (perhaps assisted by another electronic unit) must still do the piloting—the determination of course to be steered—by the usual navigation procedures. The electromechanical autopilot will only hold your boat on the heading that is set into it; and it will have no control over the throttle—it's not smart enough to know to stop when there's danger ahead.

Advantages and Disadvantages

While you must continued to do the navigation for your craft, the autopilot has several significant "good points" that well justify its installation and use. Although you may be able to steer a better course initially—and this is by no means certain—it is highly likely that after a while you will get tired or bored and your attention may wander, resulting in less precise steering. On the other hand, your autopilot never tires and does just as good a job hour after hour. Both time and fuel will be saved by the straighter course made good.

An autopilot on your boat will also permit you to divert your attention for short periods of time—this is especially important and necessary when cruising single-handed or with only a mate—*but this must be done sparingly and only with the utmost caution*! While on watch, you can set the autopilot on course,

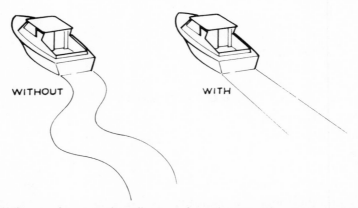

Fig. 32-1 The use of an autopilot will get you from "here" to "there" in a straight line with less human effort.

engage it, and do other piloting chores such as taking bearings, plotting on the chart, and making navigational calculations. All this time, however, you *must* frequently glance around the horizon for other vessels, hazards, etc. If absolutely necessary, you can even leave the helm position for brief periods to check the engine, prepare a snack, or take care of other necessary functions. If your craft is radar-equipped, a monitor with audible alarm can give you an added assurance of safety while you're absent from the helm. Even if you don't have your own radar set, a directional radar detector with audible alarm will give you additional confidence that all is well while you are below-decks or when your attention is focused on other tasks; see Chapter 33.

Autopilot Systems

Autopilots are manufactured to work with mechanical or hydraulic steering systems on boats, and for wheel or tiller helms. The principal components are the direction-sensing unit, which may be incorporated within the control box; the power unit for actually steering the craft; and a follow-up sensor, which monitors the position of the rudder and provides feedback information to the control system.

On boats and small motor vessels the sensing element is usually a magnetic compass; this can be a conventional card-in-a bowl type with optical sensing, or the more modern flux-gate compass with electronic sensing that will give steadier output data. Signals are generated to indicate that the boat is off the established heading, and to which side. One model uses a "directional gyroscope" that cannot measure direction but that will maintain a preset orientation for several hours. Larger vessels will have a "gyroscopic compass" that determines true north and that can be linked into an autopilot. Models of this type have been developed for small craft, but they were too expensive to become widely used.

Some more expensive autopilots will have a visual display of the boat's heading at any instant in addition to the course that has been set in; this provides a quick indication of the degree to which the craft might be off-heading at any time. This display may also show the current rudder angle.

Many autopilots now include a capability for being "interfaced" with other electronic systems. Most Loran and SatNav receivers can internally compute the course (corrected for variation and deviation) to a destination, or the next waypoint, that has been keyed in by the navigator. A continuous monitoring of the craft's position relative to the computed track yields off-course data that are automatically converted to steering correc-

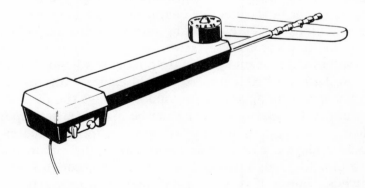

Fig. 32-2 Special models of autopilots are available for sailboats that use tiller steering.

tions. These heading changes are communicated to the auto-pilot, and the vessel is directed smoothly back onto the correct track. If the Loran set is automatically sequencing a series of waypoints, it is advisable to disconnect the interface function temporarily at the time of each change of course and reconnect after the craft settles down on the new heading.

Autopilots for sailboats may have the capability of being interfaced to the output from a wind vane, and so steer the craft for a constant relative wind angle. Even with this capability, steering referenced to a compass is normally more satisfactory.

System Operation

Signals from the sensing unit (and commands from a radionavigation set, if connected) are amplified electronically through the control box and used to actuate a reversible motor that moves the rudder. A small follow-up unit senses the rudder position and supplies that information to the control unit. Data on the amount of off-heading angle and the rudder position— sometimes with information as to the rate at which these values are changing—are combined to yield smooth, on-course steering without the zigzags of oversteering. (Older autopilots may lack this refinement; "hunting" types steered continously to stay on course, and "deadband" models only apply steering corrections when the off-course error exceeds a preset amount.) There are usually one or more controls to vary the response of the auto-pilot to better fit the steering characteristics of the boat and the sea conditions currently affecting her; some units automatically sense and adjust for these factors.

Another component of most autopilots is a hand-held remote unit at the end of 20 feet or so of light cable. With this unit you can engage or disengage the autopilot; change the direction setting either for a normal change in course or just temporarily, called "dodging"; or use the system for "power steering," in which mode the compass sensor is out of the circuit and you have direct left–right control of the rudder through a switch or switches. This is a very desirable feature where a boat has a flying bridge or you must partially climb a mast to see any rocks or coral heads in your projected track; it also permits directional control from a fishing cockput, but remember that a hand-held remote unit of an autopilot gives you no control over throttle settings or the gearshift in any of these applications.

Specialized models of autopilots are available for sailboats that use a tiller rather than a wheel for steering. The electrical principles are the same; only the mechanical drive is different.

Off-heading alarms can be set for any desired number of degrees of steering error, as determined by sea conditions and the craft's ability to cope with them.

Any autopilot that you consider for selection should have a provision for quick and easy manual takeover of steering in the event of an emergency.

Accessories

Optional accessories for some small-craft autopilots include a hand-held remote control unit (if it is not part of the basic system), a second-station control unit if your vessel has two helm positions, a rudder-angle indicator, and one or more digital readouts of the system's direction-sensing compass. These can be combined or used individually to fit your particular needs.

There is also now available a "portable helm" that provides the capability to shift gears and adjust throttle settings from a small box at the end of a cable, as well as to make course changes. This is an expensive addition to an autopilot installation, but it does result in full remote control.

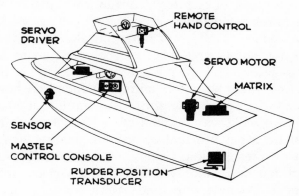

Fig. 32-3 The complete autopilot system.

INSTALLATION

The installation of an autopilot on a boat will require moderate capabilities for carpentry, mechanical, and electrical work, and sometimes hydraulic work, too. The degree of skill in each area, however, is not beyond that of a boat owner who has a good set of tools and is handy with them. Study the problems carefully and don't hesitate to tackle the project *if* it seems to be within your abilities. As with any major project, careful advance planning will pay off—look before you leap, so to speak; in this case, look and plan before picking up a single tool.

The control unit must be mounted within easy reach of the helmsman, although it need not be near his normal line of vision. If the compass component of the autopilot is within the control unit, as it is on some models, this complicates the siting problem. It cannot be closer than three feet from the boat's steering compass, and a greater separation is desirable. The control unit must not be located near items of iron or steel, nor near a radio speaker with its magnets. If the direction-sensing unit can be remotely located, more possibilities are opened up. The sensing unit should be located as low and as near amidships as practicable to reduce the effects of the craft's inevitable motions. It is frequently put in the back of a clothes locker—but then don't use coat hangers made of iron wire. Keep the sensing unit clear of large metal masses such as the engine, and also clear of DC wires unless they are twisted together. Tests should be made for any effects from currents flowing in any nearby wires in the same manner as you would do when installing a steering compass. Make your initial installation of the autopilot binnacle unit solid but temporary; be prepared to have to try several locations.

The location of the power unit will depend on how that unit drives the boat's steering system. Instructions that come with the autopilot will cover a wide variety of situations. From these, with perhaps a bit of ingenuity and imagination, you will work out your own installation. Finally, mount the follow-up or feedback unit and mechanically link it to the arm at the top of the rudder post. Connect wires and cables between the units (and hydraulic lines, if applicable), and you are ready to go. Follow the guidance of Chapter 23 in installing power leads in particular, and all wires and cables in general. The autopilot should be on its own separate electrical circuit having a fuse or breaker with an ampere rating suited to the maximum load of the device (this occurs intermittently with the operation of the motor).

CHECKOUT AND MAINTENANCE

You will probably need to make some mechanical and/or electrical adjustments to get your autopilot working as smoothly as you would like. Changes may have to be made in gears or sprocket drives to obtain the correct ratio of autopilot action to rudder angle.

While under way in open, smooth waters under autopilot control, tests should be made of the effect of operating various items of electrical and electronic equipment. On one craft, each time the 120-volt AC light plant started up, there would be a 90° turn to port or starboard! On another boat, transmission on the VHF radio caused a gradual turn to port. Such reactions cannot be predicted—each device and load must be turned on and then off while observing the steering compass for any effect. The entire series of trials should be done on two headings, one north or south, and the other east or west.

If your model of autopilot has one or more controls to adjust for the steering characteristics of the vessel and/or sea conditions, try different settings and make notes as to which give the most satisfactory results. Instruction manuals will explain how these are used, but experience while under way in varying conditions will be needed before you can use them most effectively.

Routine preventive maintenance may be required for the motors and chain drives of some autopilots. If the unit uses internal fuses, several spares should be on board of each size used. Other maintenance and repairs will normally require the services of a trained technician (no FCC license is required).

CHAPTER 33

Radars and Related Equipment

RADARS ARE not items for every boat, but continued developments in solid-state electronics in recent years have made them suitable for more craft than one might think, and less expensive, too! They offer safety and operational benefits obtainable with no other equipment. But even if you decide against a radar for your boat, there are reflectors and detectors that can be used at much less cost for the improved safety of your craft and all those on board.

SELECTION

A marine radar is a complex piece of electronic equipment with many technical specifications. Most of these will be of little interest to a small-craft skipper, and here, as an aid in the selection of a specific radar set, we will try to sort them out as to their relative importance to you.

Operational Specifications

The operating characteristics of a radar that will be of the greatest interest are: (1) *minimum* range, (2) range resolution, and (3) bearing resolution. These determine how well you can detect *and sort out* radar-reflecting objects—commonly called "targets"—that are close to you or close to each other. A close-in ability is important, for example, when in zero visibility you are running down a channel marked by buoys and in use by other vessels. Better discrimination ability will facilitate distinguishing land shapes for comparison with charts and make more clear any collision possibilities in heavy traffic.

Maximum range is of lesser importance on most boats, as the height at which the antenna can be mounted will be a greater limitation to the range than the design of the equipment. Radar waves bend only slightly, and nominal radar range is the distance to the visible horizon plus roughly 7%. An exception to this small-craft limitation is a sailboat with a ketch rig; here the mizzenmast provides an opportunity to get an antenna height of 20 to 30 feet on moderate-size craft.

There should be an adequate number of range scales, usually six to eight, so that various areas of interest, close in or distant, can be expanded for clarity. The shortest range setting should be no greater than ¼ nautical mile so that nearby objects will stand out and be identifiable. If the set uses range rings, there should be from two to six of them at suitable intervals on each range for the estimation of distance from the face of the radarscope.

Better than range rings are "variable range markers" (VRM); this high-tech development makes possible the precise and accurate measurement of distance to a target much better than an estimate of the distance between range rings on either side. A VRM is essentially a continuously variable range ring that can be moved in or out from the center of the display by means of a front-panel control until it is on top of the echo representing a target. Distance to the current setting of the VRM is then shown digitally in a corner of the screen.

Displays

Modern solid-state electronics have brought many improvements to small-craft radars, but none more apparent and significant than the change in the way in which information is displayed. Older sets, and a few current models, use a rotating line sweeping around the face of the radarscope in synchronization with the antenna. A detected object will show up as a "blip," a patch of brighter light on the screen. Most sets now use microprocessor chips to digitize the returning signals and show them on a screen much like that of a TV set. These "raster-scan" displays have more uniform brightness—no fading of a blip before the sweep line completes a revolution and comes back to "repaint" it.

The actual display could be square or rectangular, but usually it is round, and may even include a rotating line (essentially meaningless except to indicate the rotation of the antenna); the corners of the display tube are used to show a variety of information from the radar set and other electronic navigation devices in alphanumeric format. Internal circuitry retains the brightness of each picture element (pixel) until new information is generated on the next sweep of the antenna. Digitally processed display data can also be processed to remove noise, sea return from nearby waves, and other undesired signals. On some sets, a raster-scan display can be temporarily "frozen" for more detailed examination.

Raster-scan displays are brighter than those of traditional radarscopes and can easily be read in the daytime without a viewing hood; they also can be read by several persons at the same time. Displays are often in green on a black background, but increasingly colors are being used to distinguish among different types or varying strengths of echoes—these processes are known as "single-level quantization" and "multilevel quantization," respectively. Raster-scan displays often show operating parameters, such as the range scale in use, settings of controls, etc., on the screen, where they will not interfere with the display of targets.

In addition to variable range markers described above, many radars will have an "electronic bearing marker" (EBM), a radial line on the screen that can be positioned over a blip by using a front-panel control, with the direction (relative bearing) shown digitally in a corner of the display.

A unique type of display uses a raster of LCD elements. The resolution of the screen is coarser, but the display unit can be made much smaller, with a front-to-back dimension of only a few inches, as compared with other raster-scan models that require 12 or more inches of depth for the picture tube.

Some radar sets can establish "guard zones" and will activate a visual and audible alarm if any targets are detected therein. The angular limits of such a sector are established using one or two EBM settings, and its depth by one or two VRM settings; the "guard zone" can be shown on the radar's screen.

Technical Specifications

Peak power output is often stressed in advertisements for radar but is of not too great importance because of the height limitation on range discussed above. Of greater importance is antenna size, which will determine horizontal beam width and hence bearing discrimination. An antenna should be as large as can be handled on your boat. A larger antenna means a narrower beam horizontally and a sharper discrimination in bearing. Your selection must also include a choice between an antenna that is enclosed in a radome and one that rotates in the open. For sailboats, a radome is almost a necessity; for powerboats, an open antenna can often be used, and consideration should be given to this type, as they are usually larger.

Better resolution in range and improved close-in performance are achieved with shorter pulses of outgoing RF energy; shorter pulses, however, have less energy and are less desirable for longer-range detection. Normally a radar will use several different pulse lengths, switched automatically with changes in range scale. Pulse repetition rate will also vary with range, being greater at the shorter ranges with shorter pulses.

Modern solid-state electronics have greatly reduced the consideration that must be given to the amount of power required from your boat's electrical system to operate the radar. Don't be confused by the "kilowatts" of the peak power; the input DC power will be far less—from 25 to 100 watts—no more than 2 to 8 amperes from a 12-volt system. This can easily be tolerated by the electrical system of most boats, especially when the engine is operating and the load is carried by the alternator rather than the batteries.

Physical Characteristics

Radars for small craft are comprised of two basic units. The antenna and part of the electronic circuits should be mounted as high and as clear as possible. One word of caution here: Antenna units have a not-inconsiderable weight, from 35 to 100 pounds, and if mounted high on a mast it is advisable to consult with a professional naval architect regarding any possible adverse effect on your craft's stability.

The other portion of the radar is the display unit. This will be mounted near the helm position, where weight is not a problem but where space may be. Very roughly, this unit might be 1 foot by 1 foot by 1½ feet. Consideration must also be given to the routing of the several interconnecting cables between the antenna unit and the display unit.

INSTALLATION

The installation of a radar set on a boat is a major project requiring careful and detailed advance planning. Each job is sufficiently different so that only broad, general guidance can be offered here. Much of the work is carpentry and electrical rather than electronic. If you are experienced in working on boats and have a good general toolbox, you need not hesitate to tackle the physical installation and electrical power portions of the project. Follow the guidelines of Chapter 23 with respect to electrical power connections; be sure to use a separate circuit breaker of proper rating and wire heavy enough to carry the required current with no more than a 3% voltage drop; see Chapters 2 and 23.

Consider carefully how the radar will most likely be used on your boat. In most instances the same person will not read the radar display and steer the boat; this is too much to do justice to either important task. A good location is adjacent to the helm position with enough separation so that the radar observer does not interfere with the helmsman, but close enough that information and steering orders can be passed in a normal voice.

Since a radar transmitter sends out energy, it must have an FCC license. This will be a part of the license for your radio equipment; if radar frequencies were not included in your original application, you must get the license modified.

If the radar set you have selected was designed and approved for owner installation, this task may be done by you or someone under your supervision without having to have a FCC operator license (no license is required for the use of a radar). Otherwise, the installation and checkout must be done by an individual holding a general-class commercial radio operator license with a ship-radar endorsement. Even if you do the work yourself, you may get better results from your radar if you have it checked and tuned by a qualified technician and have him or her show you how to operate it for best results.

MAINTENANCE

The maintenance that you as a nontechnician can perform on your radar will be quite limited. Fuses in the set can be replaced if they blow, but if a specific fuse opens more than twice, you should cease any attempts to use the radar and contact a properly manned and equipped service shop.

Some radars will require periodic routine maintenance, such as lubrication of moving parts. Check your owner's manual and don't neglect this minor but important chore.

ACCESSORY EQUIPMENT

Most radars are complete units, but in some cases it is possible to enhance the capabilities or convenience of a set by the addition of one or more accessories.

Radar Monitors

If not an integral part of your radar, a valuable accessory is a monitor unit that can be connected to your equipment to give an audible and/or visual alarm when a target appears in a preset guard zone around your craft. The extent of this zone can be limited to a specified angular sector if an all-around guard is not desired. More advanced models feature both an outer "early-warning zone" and a closer-in "alarm zone." A radar monitor is a highly desirable accessory for a radar-equipped boat that also has, and uses, an autopilot.

With the advent of microprocessor-controlled electronic equipment comes the ability to interface various units with the radar—loran, depth sounder, satellite navigation receiver, digital fluxgate compass, speed and distance logs, etc. This capability may be built into some deluxe radars, or it may be added by an external accessory unit. Interfaces have become highly standardized, but there is still some equipment that doesn't work well with others—select the components of your "integrated system" with some caution.

RELATED EQUIPMENT

Even if your boat does not have its own radar, there are items of safety equipment that you should very definitely consider: passive reflectors and active detectors.

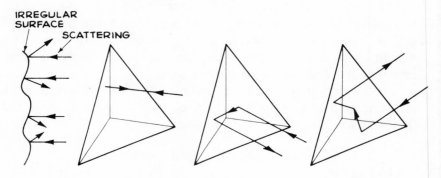

Fig. 33-1 A radar reflector will return an echo *directly* back to the set rather than scatter it as an irregular surface would. The radar pulse may be reflected from one or more surfaces of the reflector as determined by the angle at which it arrives.

Radar Reflectors

Every boat that operates in water traveled by radar-equipped vessels should carry a *radar reflector* and be prepared to use it— to repeat, that is *every boat*. Boats of fiberglass or wooden construction do *not* show up well on radarscopes. Even craft with aluminum or steel hulls show up poorly, especially when the waters are rough and there is significant "sea return." A small-craft's radar echo can be greatly increased by a simple, inexpensive radar corner reflector of three metal sheets meeting one another at right angles. It is essential that the planes be quite rigid with respect to each other and that the angle of intersection be very close to 90 degrees. If these angles are correct to within ± 1 degree, the incoming radar pulses will be strongly reflected back in the direction from which they came rather than being scattered randomly; see Figure 33-1.

Mounting a Reflector

Radar reflectors should be mounted or hoisted as high as possible, as this adds to the range at which you will be detected. Use a downhaul from the bottom of the reflector to minimize swinging in the wind. Many skippers leave their radar reflectors up in good weather as well as in conditions of reduced visibility; this is desirable if you venture into or across shipping lanes, as the visual lookout on big ships usually leaves much to be de-

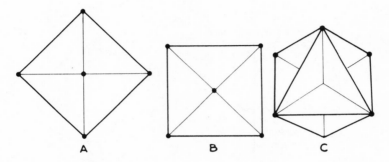

Fig. 33-2 Radar reflectors are most often suspended by one corner (a), but this is the least effective mounting. Hanging with one plate vertical but top edge horizontal (b) is better, but not the best. The "raincatcher" position (c) is best, at least in theory, with nearly all the horizon covered by a reflecting corner.

sired. It has been said that the "rain catcher" position for a radar reflector (see Figure 33-2) adds to its effectiveness, but be sure that there are drain holes! Two radar reflectors are better than one, though not fully twice as good.

Make Your Own

Radar reflectors are not expensive items, but if you are a do-it-yourselfer it's not a difficult project, and a dollar saved is a dollar earned! Within limits, the larger your radar reflector the more effective it is, but larger ones are more affected by the wind. Smooth metal is more effective than rough surfaces or wire mesh, although the latter is sometimes used because of its lightness and lesser wind resistance. The individual plates can be square or round; for our project let us use round plates and a diameter of 10 inches.

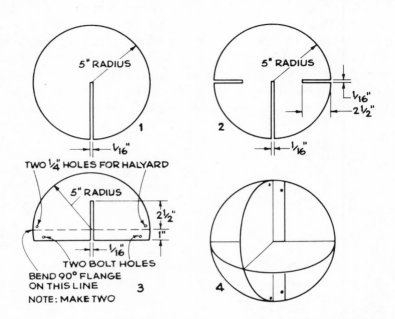

Fig. 33-3 If carefully made from the instructions in the text and the above sketches, a home-made radar reflector will do the job as well as one purchased at a greater cost.

A piece of ¹⁄₁₆-inch aluminum, 20 by 24 inches, is large enough for the four required pieces. Don't use thicker metal, as the additional weight is undesirable, and cutting the slots will be more difficult.

Lay out the patterns as shown in Figure 33-3; you will need two of the half-circle pieces shown at c. Be sure to mark the center of the circle on each piece, as it will serve as a handy reference point for your layout. Use a square to ensure that the slots shown in b are precisely at right angles to each other.

Cut out the four pieces—a band saw is best, but a hand saber saw can be used (a bit of unevenness around the outer edge makes no difference except in appearance). For the slots, use a blade with offset alternate teeth that will make a cut just a tiny bit wider than ¹⁄₁₆ inch.

Next, bend the flanges on the two half-circle pieces as shown in c. Bend the flanges on each side of the slot separately, using a vise and an angle iron to extend the jaws wide enough. Index both flanges of each piece to the same place on the vise so they will line up after being bent; a pencil line on the aluminum plate is a help. Turn the flanges on both sides of the slot in the same direction.

Assemble the pieces as shown in d, holding them together with C-clamps, while you drill holes for the assembly bolts. Two #10 bolts with nuts and washers (stainless steel) are fine. Add two more holes, one at the top and one at the bottom, to attach the halyard and downhaul. Check the squareness of your corner angles, and you now have a radar reflector!

Radar Detectors

Another device for a boat not equipped with radar is a *radar detector*. Models used on highways to evade law-enforcement speed monitors are not useful on the water, but there are units designed specifically for marine use. This is a small receiver for radar frequencies, powered by internal rechargeable batteries or connected to the craft's 12-volt system with a very small drain. This unit detects the pulses of another vessel's radar at ranges of up to about 5 miles; the alarm can be audible, visual, or both. An omnidirectional antenna provides for full-horizon coverage, but a separate unidirectional antenna can then be switched in to obtain a rough bearing on the source of the radar signals. If signals from more than one radar are being picked up, the unit can distinguish between or among the different sets of pulses.

Radar Transponders

A radar reflector is a passive device, merely enhancing the return of a very minute portion of the radar pulse's energy. A *transponder,* on the other hand, is an active device that sends out a pulse of its own when triggered by receipt of the radar's pulse; this obviously presents a larger and brighter spot on the radarscope. Transponders have been in use for aircraft for many

433

years and now are required equipment on many planes. They are just now being developed for marine use. A transponder can be a simple echo-enhancing device, or it can, as aircraft models do, transmit a considerable amount of information concerning the vehicle carrying it.

CHAPTER 34

Satellite Navigation Receivers

NAVIGATION OF vessels by means of radio signals received from satellites in space is becoming increasingly popular. It is supplementing, and in some cases even replacing, Loran-C. The present system—commonly called "Transit" or "SatNav"—became operational for Navy missile-firing submarines in 1964, and for civilian ships and boats in 1967; acceptance and use have gradually expanded as the initial high cost of receivers has steadily come down. A replacement, the Global Positioning System— "GPS" or "NavStar"—is now in limited use, with full operational status somewhat uncertain because of delays in the launching of satellites resulting from the Space Shuttle *Challenger* disaster.

Compared to Loran-C system, satellite navigation—usually contracted to just "SatNav"—has advantages and disadvantages. On the plus side, coverage is worldwide, and accuracy is somewhat better now, with the expectation of being even better when GPS becomes fully operational. On the negative side, the Transit system does not provide continuous positioning information, but only when a satellite is passing by, and for full accuracy on a moving vessel there must be an accurate input of course and speed; both of these limitations, however, will disappear with GPS.

SELECTION

SatNav receivers for the Transit system are available from a number of different manufacturers, with varying levels of prices

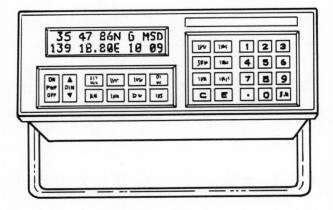

Fig. 34-1 Receivers for the Transit satellite navigation system display a boat's position directly in latitude and longitude. Courses and distances to destinations or waypoints, and other data, can be calculated and displayed in lieu of position information.

and features—a range wide enough to warrant careful study before you make your selection; see Fig. 34-1. The cost is greater than for Loran-C, but not so much so as to eliminate SatNav receivers from competitive consideration.

Way Points and Computed Courses

Similar to Loran-C receivers, a destination, or multiple waypoints, can be entered in terms of latitude and longitude by use of a keypad. The number of waypoints will generally vary with the price of the SatNav receiver, but even the fewest offered should be more than enough for practical navigation. Courses and distances to such points are internally computed in terms of either great circle tracks or rhumb lines; automatic or manual corrections for magnetic variation, and manual corrections for deviation, allow for conversion to compass courses. Waypoints can be programmed into routes, and then the set will automatically sequence to the next one as each is reached; arrival (or closest point of approach) alarms can be set.

Displays and Alarms

The typical display is two lines, either liquid crystal display (LCD) or vacuum-fluorescent. Position is shown directly in latitude and longitude, in degrees and minutes to two decimal places. After pressing one or two buttons, much other information may be shown in the same display: distance traveled since reset; course and distance to next waypoint; time to go; crosstrack error; speed and heading being made good; set and drift; calendar date and time (local or UTC) with alarm clock; and other items, varying with the particular receiver.

In addition to the destination/waypoint alarm described above, many Transit receivers also have visible and/or audible alarms for such situations as off-course, dragging anchor, and satellite acquisition.

Initialization

SatNav receivers require a bit of initial input data to get started. On some models an approximate location must be entered manually using the keypad, but on more expensive sets the initial location is automatically generated within the set. These sets may also prompt the user with plain English displays at to what other information must be entered, and will check such information rejecting it if it is not reasonable.

Need for Course and Speed Input

Postion information from Transit satellite signals is generated during a two-minute period of reception of signals (and for a number of repeated periods during a normal satellite pass). If the receiver is moving during each period, as would normally be the case on a vessel at sea, then the internal microcomputer needs an input of course and speed for its calculation of position. On all receivers this can be done manually, but the deluxe models have interfaces that can take the needed data from a compass and a speed sensor. Such sets often also have outputs for interfacing position data to other displays, such as on radarscopes or video plotters. When operating in an area covered by Loran-C, some sets can interface that radionavigation system to the SatNav receiver to supply course, speed, and position data between satellite passes. For some models, interfaces may be an option to be added later.

From the course and speed information supplied to the receiver, its internal computer can continuously calculate and display dead reckoning (DR) positions between the times of inputs of satellite fixes, and use such fixes to start a new DR track.

Storage of Data in Memories

SatNav receivers can compute the predicted time of future satellite passes and store such information in nonvolatile internal memory. This memory will also store data from a number of recent passes if it is necessary to go back to check past plots. Data in this memory are retained for several months or more, even if power to the receiver is turned off.

Antennas

The Transit satellite signals that are used by civilian vessels are in the UHF band near 400 MHz. For this reason, antennas are small and light. Most are "passive," but for some receivers an "active" antenna containing a preamplifier may be selected as an option. Antennas are furnished complete with connecting cable.

Power Requirements

SatNav receivers do not consume much power from the craft's 12-volt DC electrical system—typically 1 ampere or less—but to save on battery power some units can be put in a extremely low drain standby, "sleep," mode and then turn themselves back on just before the time of the next satellite pass. This could be a consideration in the selection of a SatNav receiver for a sailboat.

INSTALLATION

Satellite navigation receivers are neither large nor heavy, and they can be located nearly anywhere on your boat. Although crosstrack error can be shown on many sets, it is not normally necessary that a SatNav receiver be located in the direct vision of the helmsman; it is often installed at a "navigator's station" belowdecks, especially on sailing craft. Physical mounting of the set and wiring to a source of 12-volt DC power should be within the capabilities of any skipper who is handy with tools.

A SatNav antenna should be mounted high and clear of other antennas; its small size and light weight make many locations possible. The small size coax cable from the antenna to the receiver should also present no problems of installation, but be sure to seal adequately the opening in the cabintop or other surface where it comes inside the boat.

MAINTENANCE

A satellite navigation receiver is about as "high tech" as you will get on a boat, and owner maintenance is out of the question. In fact, it is entirely possible that local electronic shops may not have the knowledge or components to repair a defective receiver, so the unit may have to go back to the manufacturer. When you do take your set in for servicing, be sure to take along all manuals that came with it.

THE GLOBAL POSITIONING SYSTEM

Full operation of the Global Positioning System has been postponed by the delays in the launching of Space Shuttles— they carry the satellites into low orbit, from where they power themselves the rest of the way to 10,000 miles up. The full GPS system will have eighteen satellites in orbit (plus spares); these will provide continuous coverage and positioning in three di-

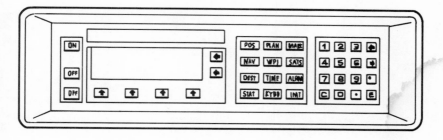

Fig. 34-2 A receiver for the Global Positioning System (GPS) appears much like one for the older Transit SatNav system. Operation is also much the same, but a different set of satellites is used, and position information is continuous.

mensions (the third dimension is altitude, not of too much interest to boaters!). GPS is, however, now in partial operation, and part-time, two-dimensional (latitude and longitude) use of the system is possible.

GPS receivers are now being made and installed on vessels of all sizes; the price at this time is several times that of a set for SatNav navigation; see Fig. 34-2. Some manufacturers are selling Transit receivers that can be later upgraded for GPS. Other features, installation, and maintenance characteristics are generally the same as discussed above for present-day satellite navigation equipment.

CHAPTER 35

Electronic Charts and Plotters

THE COMPUTER AGE has come to boating in many ways, not the least of which is the availability of "electronic charts." This has occurred in two ways, one of which will eventually come to affect all boaters; the other will involve a smaller group of boaters, who elect to equip their craft with a video plotter.

Computerized Paper Charts

The National Ocean Survey (NOS) has had a program under way for several years to computerize their charts. All information on a chart is "digitized." This includes every point, every letter and figure, all lines and shapes, all colors—*everything* is reduced to the "1's" and "0's" of computer binary language. These are then stored on magnetic disks and tapes and can be used to guide laser printers for the actual production of charts. The advantage of this high-tech method is that the stored data can be easily changed whenever necessary, and the production of new editions is facilitated. If the same area appears on more than one chart, as often happens with overlapping charts and charts of the same area at different scales, then each item of data need be created and stored only once, and a single update serves for multiple charts.

Years will be required to build up a complete data base, but more and more NOS charts are now being produced by this computer-assisted process. Such a chart is totally indistinguishable from a chart prepared by the older, manual processes; only a brief note in the margin reveals the method by which it was prepared.

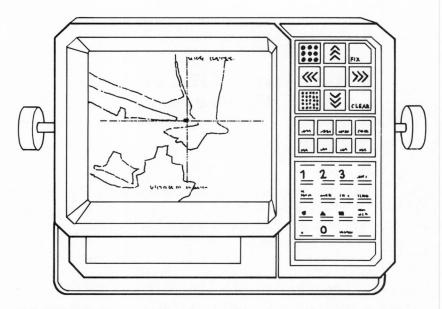

Fig. 35-1 Video plotters can show a reasonably complete chart on a television-like screen; some units display in monochrome, others in full color. Many different charts can be stored in a single magnetic-chip module, on a "floppy" disk, or on a laser disk.

Electronic Charts for Vessels

Boaters now can have electronic charts directly on their craft. This is not really a "chart" in the conventional sense of a large sheet of paper, but rather a display on a cathode-ray tube (CRT) like that of a TV set or computer, or one of the new raster-scan radarscopes. It does serve, however, as a nearly complete replacement for a paper chart. Stored digital information can be shown on the screen to produce a "chart" adequate for most navigational purposes. Multiple electronic charts can be stored in a single memory module, and the chart you need can be called up at a suitable scale of your selection; different methods of magnetic or optical storage are used, as will be described below; see Fig. 35-1.

As with most things, there are advantages and disadvantages with electronic charts. On the plus side, storage requirments are drastically reduced—a very small cartridge or disk can hold up to several dozen charts. The display can be presented "north-up," as are most paper charts, or it can be shown "heading-up," which is easier to use, especially when traveling along a river or other waterway. Lighted aids to navigation can be shown as chart symbols, or actually made to flash in the same pattern as the light itself. You can "zoom" in to expand a selected area for greater ease of reading. The digitized data often combine information from the NOS data base and digitizing done by the manufacturer of the electronic chart equipment. Chart updating consists of merely replacing a memory module with a new one.

On the negative side, because memory is expensive and has finite limits, there will always be some loss of detail as compared with a NOS paper chart. This is not all bad, as there is much on a chart that is of little immediate interest; but it can present problems—for example, few electronic charts include soundings, although some may show depth contours.

Using Electronic Charts

A significant feature of electronic charts is the ability to overlay position and track information directly on the screen—no requirement for plotting! Courses can be "drawn" directly on the screen using a "joystick" or "trackball"; the microprocessor will compute the magnetic or compass direction and distance—all this faster and easier than you could do it on paper.

Direction and speed sensors can feed movement information to the screen; a Loran-C or satellite navigation receiver can provide position data; and a radar display can be added—everything together on a single display for both navigation and collision avoidance. Other alphanumeric data, such as readings from a depth sounder or a digital compass, or the current date and time, can be shown in a corner of the screen, or wherever they will not interfere with information of greater importance. With some models you can plot additional information on the screen, such as a favorite fishing spot, or some detail from a paper chart that has not been included and is of particular interest to you; you may then be able to store it for use again at a later time.

SELECTION

There are a number of different manufacturers and models from which you can make your selection of an electronic chart unit, often called a "video plotter." These offer a wide range of features and prices.

Displays

For lower cost, the display may be on a monochrome screen in green, or in black and white with shades of gray, but full color is available and makes information stand out more clearly. For some monochrome green units, the land areas are merely outlined by the shoreline; on others the land is shown in solid green, with the water left blank (black) except for plotted lines and symbols.

If available, different colors can be used to show different types of information. For example, the lines of latitude and longitude could be in one color and the track line of your vessel in another color; land areas and aids to navigation could be in different colors, etc. As many as eight colors are used by some models.

Data Input and Storage

You will be giving the plotter directions and inputting information to the chart with a keypad. This will have the usual numeric keys plus others for special functions—select a plotter on which these are clearly labeled for ease of use. Note also how simple or complicated it is to change memory modules, and to select the specific chart from among the many stored in each module. Some modules have an overall outline chart, much like an NOS chart catalog, that shows the area coverage of each chart in that module; this is a desirable feature.

The type of memory storage used is a factor in making the selection of a video plotter. The digitized chart data can be stored in read-only memory (ROM) "chips" that are mounted in a plug-in module for ease of insertion and removal. A number of charts can be stored in a single module, and different modules will be available for different general areas. Another form of chart data storage is the magnetic disk as used in personal computers. Recent advances in technology have greatly increased the storage capacity of disks, which no longer can be called "floppies," as the latest come in hard plastic cases; more charts can be stored on a disk than in a single set of ROM chips. One model uses magnetic storage, but in the form of tape in a small cassette.

The latest type of data storage is the CD-ROM or laser disk, very similar to the compact disks now used for high-quality audio recording. These have an almost unbelievable capacity for data, equal to that of many disks, and hence can store more charts, or greater detail for the same number of charts, or a combination of both.

Interfacing to Other Devices

If you plan to use your electronic chart with an input from a Loran-C or SatNav receiver—and you should—then you must be sure that both units have compatible interfaces. There are industry standards, but these have changed over the years and grown more sophisticated; some manufacturers use their own interface designs that cannot be mixed with others. Two-way data exchange is desirable—the ability to establish way points on your electronic chart, and then have this information sent back to the Loran or SatNav unit.

The ability to interface a fluxgate compass and a speed sensor is desirable so a dead reckoning plot can be carried forward during the absence of position data from a radionavigation system. You may even be able to enter your planned speed and get predicted times at a destination or way points.

Chart Availability

Electronic charts are not available for all areas, and what is available varies with the manufacturer. Consider what is available for your local area and any to which you might expect to cruise. Most manufacturers are planning to expand their coverage, but be cautious about predictions of new module availability that could be overly optimistic.

Other Features

A desirable feature found on all video plotters is the ability to "zoom" in and out, showing more or less detail as called for by your navigation situation. Some models will have more flexibility in this process than others; consider this in making your selection.

It is useful if you can easily plot on your electronic chart such items as lines of position derived from compass or relative bearings, or other means. You will not often want to record these permanently, but some other types of infomation you may want to add to your chart data in memory. This may be possible on units using magnetic storage, but not on laser disks.

It is desirable that the video plotter can show the date and time on some portion of the electronic chart display.

One model is unique in that it *combines* a video plotter with a Loran receiver—no interface required! Chart modules are available, or the user can draw in his or her own coastlines and other details. The screen is a liquid crystal display (LCD) that does not have as good resolution as a CRT, but the combination of two units, and in one quite small package, does have its advantages, especially in space-limited installations.

Personal Computers

The electronic chart units discussed above have all been "dedicated" devices—they are not usable for other purposes. Another possibility for video plotting is the use of a personal computer with special software. Programs and digitized chart data are available for several different types of microcomputers; these are stored on the same type of media as other programs for that particular computer. The obvious advantage of going this route for electronic charts is a lesser cost if you already have the computer, plus its availability for other uses, including, but not limited to, celestial navigation, tide predictions and calculations, vessel management, and any nonboating applications you might use at home or in the office. Some computers and programs allow the storage on disk of position data so a passage or cruise can be replayed at a later date.

Apple Macintosh

A computer that is particularly suitable for electronic chart use is the *Apple Macintosh;* it features a very-high-definition screen and a user-friendly operating system. Several software

Fig. 35-2 Programs available for many personal computers that will turn them into video plotters. Position data from radionavigation systems can be added to the electronic chart. The computer is also available for many other applications besides navigation.

publishers are marketing video plotter programs for this computer; see Fig. 35-2. The "Mac's" limitation is that its display is monochrome (except for the Macintosh II, a very-high-priced model); this is partially overcome by the use of multiple shades of gray. The Mac uses no keyboard in this application, only a "mouse" to control the movement of a cursor on the screen.

Place the cursor on an item of the display, such as an aid to navigation; then click the button on the mouse, and a "window" will appear in a corner of the screen with detailed information on position, type, color, light characteristics, etc. Latitude and longitude lines can be displayed or not, as the user desires. Depth information can be shown on demand.

Other Computers

A number of other computer programs are available for various models of *IBM* and *IBM-compatible* computers, and one for an *Atari 130XE*.

Electrical Power Requirements

A possible limitation on the use of a personal computer on a boat for electronic charts and other purposes is the input power required. (Video plotters will operate from a boat's 12-volt DC system.) Except for portables, computers will need 120-volt AC electricity at power levels of 75 to 200 watts; even portables will require such power for recharging their internal batteries after only a few hours' use. If this is not available from an onboard auxiliary generating plant, it may be possible to use an inverter, but check that the output from such a unit is compatible with the computer's power needs.

Installation and Maintenance

Video plotters are made for use on vessels, and should have been designed and constructed for operation in a marine environment. Protection from rain and spray is essential, but otherwise only a secure mounting should be necessary. Personal computers put to such use may require more careful installation; see Chapter 36.

CHAPTER 36

Calculators and Computers

A CALCULATOR can be used on most boats, and a computer can be used on more boats than you would think possible. Various applications for either device relate to navigation, the management of the craft, and business and personal matters. The availability and use of calculators has become so widespread that it would be a most unusual boater who did not have at least one at home or in the office—and the use of personal computers follows close behind.

Precision and Accuracy

In any consideration of calculators and computers, and radionavigation systems as well, one must be aware of the proper meanings of "precision" and "accuracy"—what each term means and how they differ. Accuracy and precision are not the same; they should be used correctly and not interchangeably.

"Precision" relates to how finely a measurement is stated—how many significant figures, how many decimal places. To say "4.00" is not the same as to state a measurement as "4.0" or "4"; to say "563," the "3" must be a significant value; otherwise, say just "560." Calculators and computers, and other electronic devices that do internal calculations, often present results to many digits and decimal places, far more than is warranted by the input data. You must be aware of this and not assume a level of precision in calculated results that is not justified.

"Accuracy" is a gauge of how close a measurement, whatever its precision, is to the "true" or "correct" value of a quantity.

CALCULATORS

Personal calculators came into existence in the late 1960s as realtively expensive "gadgets" of limited capabilities. In the years since then, advances in microelectronics have vastly increased what can be done with calculators and greatly reduced them in size and price. Scientific, navigational, and financial calculators now can perform functions that were not even thought possible when calculators first appeared on the market. Originally about a handful in size, they now can be so small that they are often incorporated into a wristwatch. Although some advanced models still cost hundreds of dollars, many calculators that can do considerably more than the early models are now priced under $10.

Selection

The simplest and least expensive calculators will perform the four basic mathematical functions—addition, subtraction, multiplication, and division—with perhaps a few more advanced operations, such as square roots and percentages; many will have a single memory that is useful for more complex computations. From here on up, specialized functions are added until one has

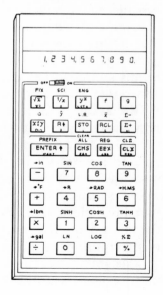

Fig. 36-1 General-purpose calculators of varying degrees of complexity and capabilities can find many uses on board boats; see text for details of various applications.

almost the equivalent of a computer. Stored mathematical constants, such as "pi" (π), trigonometric functions, metric conversion factors, statistical functions, and multiple memories are only the beginning; see Fig. 36-1. Upper-level calculators are programmable, some directly by the user, some "hard-wired" by the manufacturer with internally stored programs, and others are capable of loading in magnetically stored programs either written by the user or purchased. Calculators may be preprogrammed by the manufacturer for such applications as celestial navigation, specialized piloting techniques, and business and financial problem solving. In some instances, celestial navigation is one; tabular data as well as programs will already have been internally stored when the calculator is purchased.

Displays

The displays of early calculators nearly always used light-emitting diodes (LEDs), but these have been largely replaced by liquid-crystal displays (LCDs) because of the much lesser power drain of the latter type; some calculators for operation on 120-volt AC lines use a vacuum fluorescent display that is very readable.

A few models of calculators have an integral printer, or the capability of being connected to an external printer; it is often desirable to have the results, or even the full flow of calculations, recorded on paper for analysis or filing.

Power Sources

Calculators for use on boats most often will have small dry cells that will have to be replaced after a period of time, depending upon the amount of use of the unit. To reduce the battery supply problem for long voyages, many calculators have "gone solar" with a small area of solar cells that will keep a tiny internal rechargeable battery up to working voltage. Some larger or older models are powered by Ni-Cads that can be recharged from either a 120-volt AC outlet or a 12-volt DC source (the power taken from a boat's battery is insignificant). Calculators that have a printout capability are generally powered by dry cells or from an AC source.

Applications

Even the simplest of calculators can find many uses on a boat—distance-speed-time calculations, fuel consumption, cruise and boatyard expenses, and others. Calculators are much handier than paper and pencil for making conversions between units in different measurement systems—conventional to metric units, nautical to statute miles, etc.

Add trigonometric functions to the calculator and you can do your current sailing problems mathematically rather than graphically, and to a better degree of accuracy and precision. Closely related are true and relative wind calculations and relative motion problems. Calculators with trig functions can also be used to solve problems of tide height and tidal current strength, and also for positioning solutions using techniques such as two bearings on an object and the run between.

Equations for all of the above applications will be found in Chapter 21 of *Chapman's Piloting, Seamanship, and Small Boat Handling.*

Traverse Sailing

Sailboats, and other craft running a series of legs in different directions and perhaps at different speeds, can use *traverse sailing* to compute the net change of position. The trig functions are used to break down each tack or course leg into its north–south and east–west components. The components are then added algebraically, and the net N–S and E–W values are used to determine the course and distance made good. A calculator having a polar-to-rectangular, and vice versa, conversion capabilities will speed this type of computation.

Celestial Navigation

Computations for celestial navigation can be done on any calculator that includes trig functions plus squares and square roots, but they can get complicated! These processes can be done relatively simply and quickly using calculators that either have appropriate programs stored internally or that can be programmed by inserting magnetic strips or small plug-in modules. With such units, all that need be done is to insert the input data.

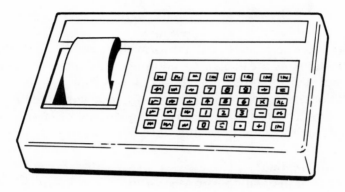

Fig. 36-2 Special calculators dedicated to the solution of celestial navigation problems are available, including models that can print out the results. Operation is simple compared to use of data tables and manual calculations.

Some navigation calculators will have, in addition to the programs, internally stored data such as a partial *Nautical Almanac*. Top-of-the-line models will not only calculate lines of position, but even the geographic coordinates of a fix from multiple LOPs—and print them out on a paper tape for record purposes!; see Fig. 36-2. The reduction of celestial observations is made easier on many calculators by plain English "prompts" appearing in the display to guide you in the entry of the next item of input data.

Typically, calculators that can solve celestial navigation problems can also compute great circle and rhumb line courses to distant destinations or way points.

Computers

It is becoming increasingly difficult to identify the boundary between calculators and computers. Calculators have become ever more capable, and computers are steadily becoming smaller and lighter without sacrificing any of their performance. Some computers may be too bulky and require too much input power for any craft other than the larger yachts, but many models could be used on almost the smallest of boats. These are the transportable and "laptop" computers that are becoming very popular.

Applications

Computers can, of course, perform the same basic mathematical functions as a calculator—addition, subtraction, multiplication, and division—but not always as conveniently! For simple calculations, use your calculator. Save your computer for complex computations and those involving storage of large amounts of data (such as video plotting—see pp. 446–48).

Navigation Programs

Trig functions and conversion constants can be stored as part of a computer program that requires their use. Programs for celestial navigation that include full almanac data for the sun, and the fifty-seven navigational stars for many years to come can be purchased on magnetic disks; information for the moon and planets may or may not be included, as this requires storage of considerable amounts of data.

With inputs of location and sextant data, a computer program can compute a line of position in terms of intercept and azimuth. This LOP need not be plotted, as the process can be carried farther, to the point of yielding a fix after you have determined a second line of position. Give the computer your DR position, and the intercept and azimuth for each of two bodies, and it will give you your latitude and longitude at the time of observation.

The U.S. Naval Observatory publishes a comprehensive *Almanac for Computers* in annual editions. This is available either in printed form or on disks usable on IBM and IBM-compatible computers. Items of daily almanac information are computed using complex equations and stored data tables.

Star Identification

Star identification can be accomplished from inputs of date and time, latitude and longitude, and observed altitude and azimuth. Inversely, the computer can be used as a star-finder— input the date and time, plus your latitude and longitude, and get out a screen display or printed list of the altitude and azimuth of all fifty-seven stars (a negative altitude indicates that the star is below the horizon and therefore not visible at the specified location and time).

Other programs are available that take advantage of the computer's screen to show the heavens graphically. The sun, moon, planets, and stars are shown on views every 45 degrees around the horizon, plus directly overhead. In addition to the representation of the sky, the screen can show alphanumeric information on the azimuth and altitude of the body, and its time of rising and setting with the azimuth at those times.

Dead Reckoning

Celestial navigation software usually includes the ability to carry forth dead reckoning positions from inputs of starting latitude and longitude, plus course and distance traveled. Such programs can compute rhumb line and great circle courses from inputs of the latitude and longitude of the starting and ending points.

The computer software described above is available on disks (3.5-inch or 5.25-inch) or on tape cassettes for many computers, including the Apple II and Macintosh families, IBM PC and compatibles, Commodore, and certain TRS models.

Other Navigational Applications

Programs are available for some computers that will calculate tidal information—time of highs and lows, and height at any given time—for a large number of locations. Data disks are prepared for various regions; these also include the times of sunrise and sunset. Tidal cycles can be shown graphically on the computer's screen.

Computers are often used with special software to produce electronic charts or video plots; for more information on such use, see Chapter 35.

Input Power Requirements

Transportable computers normally require a source of 120-volt AC power, but only a small amount—75 to 200 watts—is needed; see Fig. 36-3. Be cautious in the use of an inverter to

Fig. 36-3 Small personal computers can be used on boats if they are adequately protected from spray and rain. Some models require 120-volt A.C. power, but others run on internal rechargeable batteries.

get your AC power from the boat's DC system; many such units provide "square wave" AC that some computers or peripheral equipment may find indigestible. Power from onboard auxiliary generating plants will be satisfactory provided the frequency does not stray too far from the standard 60 Hz. At a somewhat higher price, inverters are available that will output sine-wave electricity.

Laptop models are generally capable of being run for several hours from internal rechargeable batteries, but a source of electrical power for recharging will soon become necessary on any long passage or cruise. Square-wave AC electricity from a standard inverter should be satisfactory for battery recharging, but make sure before setting out on a cruise depending on that inverter.

Installation and Maintenance
Personal computers are made for on-shore use; they lack any design or manufacturing features for the more harsh marine environment. A computer must be installed or placed so that it is

adequately protected from spray and rain, and it must also be protected from falling due to violent motions of the boat in rough weather at sea. Normal air circulation or air-conditioning of the craft will probably prevent damage from humidity extremes, but a computer should be removed from the boat if neither boat nor computer is to be used for an extended period of time.

IMPORTANCE OF A BACKUP METHOD

To use a calculator or computer safely for navigation on your boat, you must, of course, know how to use it, *but* you must *also* know how to make the necessary calculations yourself with the necessary reference books and tables, paper and pencil. Enjoy the convenience and speed of electronic computations, *but you must have a backup method*! Calculators and microcomputers are normally quite reliable, *but you must not be totally dependent on them;* you must have a thorough understanding of the procedures and equations that your computer is "automating" for you.

CHAPTER 37

Safety and Security Systems

BELLS, HORNS, whistles, and sirens—they're not just for the signals of the navigation rules. They can also be a part of one or more systems on your boat for increased safety at dock or under way, or for greater security when not under way. A wide variety of *sensors* and *alarms* can be combined into simple yet highly effective *systems*. The presence of such "systems" must never lessen a skipper's responsibility to be on guard for dangers, but they can provide a constantly alert "companion" in the interests of safety and security.

Other systems, also to be considered in this chapter, might be termed "convenience" systems; these do not directly relate to safety or security, but they aid in preventing various misfortunes or embarrassments.

Any of the systems in this chapter can be installed by a boat owner who is even moderately skilled with tools. Components will come mostly from marine supply stores, with a few items from electronics parts sources, such as Radio Shack stores, or from hardware or automotive parts stores.

SYSTEMS FUNDAMENTALS

Boating is *not* an inherently dangerous activity, but the wise skipper takes every precaution he or she can to ensure that no accident happens. Almost every boat has one or more *safety systems*—electrical and/or electronic components that will give warning of a hazardous condition. You probably will not want to have every possible safety system, but you owe it to yourself and your boat to be knowledgeable as to what is available and to make a reasoned decision as to what to select for installation. The purpose of this chapter is just that—to acquaint you with various available systems and how each should be installed if you decide it is for you.

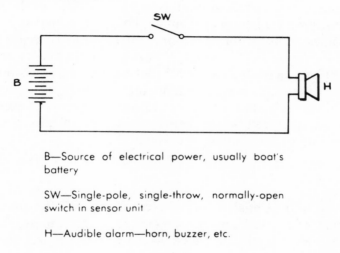

B—Source of electrical power, usually boat's battery

SW—Single-pole, single-throw, normally-open switch in sensor unit

H—Audible alarm—horn, buzzer, etc.

Fig. 37-1 Circuit of basic alarm system; visual as well as audible signals can be used.

Circuits

Alarm systems are basically very simple electrical circuits. Some detectors are electronic devices, but the system consists primarily of various switches, plus audible and/or visual signals connected with wires to each other and to a source of electrical power. Alarm activation is based either on a start-up of current flow through the wires, or an interruption to a steady flow of current—that's all there is to it!

Switches

Switches are usually "single-pole, single-throw" (SPST), which merely means that they have a single set of contacts and two terminals. They may be "normally open" (N-O) or "normally closed" (N-C)—a statement of their status when not operated by some external action. These switches may be activated mechanically, thermally, or by a change in an electronic sensing device. A system with normally closed switches is generally considered more reliable, as any accidental break in the circuit will sound an alarm, just as would the operation of one of the hazard or security sensors. A disadvantage, however, is that such a system, unless it incorporates additional electronic circuitry, will draw at least a small amount of current continuously, and this may not be practicable for a boat that has long intervals between periods of use. A system employing normally open switches draws no current, but a break in wiring will go undetected, and protection may well be lost between the time of failure and the next testing of the system; see Figure 37-1.

Alarms

Visual alarm signals, usually red lights, are often used, but they have the disadvantage of possibly going unnoticed. Such warning lights should always be placed where they will be within your field of vision when you are operating the boat. Even so, a visual alarm for a hazardous condition that might occur when not under way could easily be overlooked. Hence an audible signal is highly desirable, one loud enough to wake you if a malfunction should occur while you are asleep. The alarm signal can be a separately installed horn or bell, or it could be your craft's regular signaling horn. In almost all installations an "override" switch to disconnect the audible alarm is desirable, as the hazardous condition may take longer to correct than you are willing to listen to the continuous sounding of a horn or bell! This may be a simple manual switch, or it may be an automatic time-delay switch that will open after 30, 60, or more seconds of alarm signal. The automatic type is highly desirable for an unattended boat at a marina, where continued sounding of the alarm would be objectionable to other persons, and it could add greatly to battery drain just when all available power was needed, such as to operate bilge pumps.

SAFETY ALARMS

There is usually a small control box or panel—perhaps several of these—for a safety alarm system. Typically these contain switches to turn the system off and on, to test the alarms, and an overriding cutout switch. This box or panel will have the visual alarm and either an audible alarm or terminals to which such a device can be connected. Additional circuitry may be included for some more sophisticated alarm systems.

Bilge Water Alarms

Although fuel vapor alarms are perhaps the basic safety system, and they will be considered below, let us start off with very simple things: a switch, a bell or horn, and a few feet of wire. Typical of such a system is an alarm for an excessively high level of water in the bilge. A float of some sort is mechanically linked to a normally open switch that is connected in a circuit with the alarm bell or horn and electrical power from the boat's DC system; a combined float and switch, like the units used to control automatic bilge pumps, can be used. Power should be taken from a circuit that has a switch or circuit breaker that can be turned off when working on the system, but make sure that this circuit will be "hot" both under way *and in port.*

Automatic Bilge Pumps

Most boats have electric bilge pumps, and many of these are connected to an automatic switch in the lower part of the bilge. Typically there is a small control panel with a fuse, a three-position toggle switch (off-manual-automatic), and a red indicator lamp; see Figure 37-2a. This red light, however, may not be located where it is readily seen, and in any case it gives no warning when the helm position is unoccupied, as at night with the crew asleep; an additional, audible alarm is quite desirable. It may be possible to hook a horn or bell in parallel with the light, but caution must be exercised that the total current for the pump's motor and the horn is not excessive for the contacts of the automatic switch. If that should be the case, a simple horn relay, available at any automotive parts store, can be used. To silence the audible alarm, an SPST toggle switch is included, but

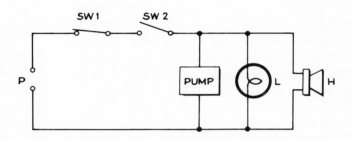

P—Source of power from a fused circuit at
  distribution panel.
SW₁—Normally-closed control switch
SW₂—Normally-open switch operated by float
  sensor
L—Visual alarm; usually a red lamp
H—Audible alarm; buzzer, bell, etc.

Fig. 37-2a Circuit for alarm for operation of automatic bilge pump. Sensor switch SW₂ must be capable of handling additional current of alarm device; this can be considerable for a horn or bell.

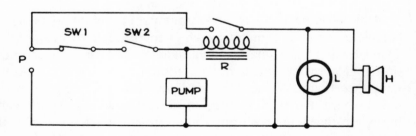

R—12-volt DC relay with normally-open contacts
rated at least 10 amperes.

Fig. 37-2b

care must be taken that it is not accidentally left in the off position so that you would be without its protection; see Figure 37-2b. This circuit can serve as a high-bilge-water alarm as well as an automatic control for bilge pumping. For the greatest safety, however, a separate high-water alarm, as described above, is recommended, with the sensor located somewhat *above* the level at which automatic pumping begins. This will warn you if either the automatic pump switch fails to operate, or if the rate of incoming water is greater than the capacity of the electric bilge pump or pumps.

Both of these systems can be easily tested, and they should be checked on a regular schedule, such as monthly, by deliberately running water into the bilge until the automatic pump switch and/or high water level alarm sensor operates, or until it is obvious that they have failed to function.

Counters

For boats that are left unattached for days at a time, it is possible to connect a device to automatic-bilge-pump circuits that will count the number of times the pump has operated since it was last reset. It would even be possible to connect a running-time meter that would tell you the total time in hours and tenths of hours that the pump had run since the meter was last read. Such accessory devices have a safety role in that they will bring to your attention slow leaks and drips that might go undetected under normal operating conditions, but that should be corrected before they develop into major hazards.

Vapor Detectors

Systems to sense the presence of gasoline vapors and sound an alarm are probably the oldest and most widely used safety systems for boats. Steady progress has been made in the development of the sensing element, and several quite different types are now marketed. The technical details of how each type of sensor works is beyond the scope of this book. It is sufficient to know that there are "hot" and "cold" sensors. It is important that you understand something of the explosive nature of gasoline fumes—it is possible to have such a *high* concentration of

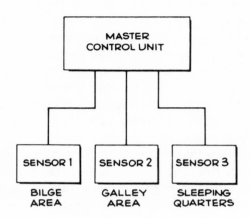

Fig. 37-3 A fuel vapor detector consists of a control and monitoring panel plus one or more sensors placed in appropriate locations (see text).

fumes in the air that the mix is *not* explosive. There is a lower explosive limit (LEL) of 1.4%, below which the mixture is too lean to explode; there is also an upper explosive limit (UEL) of 7.6%, beyond which no explosion will take place. But beware: As air is added into a too-rich mixture (by running a blower or merely by operating the engine), it will thin down into the explosive range.

Fuel vapor detectors are primarily intended to warn of gasoline fumes. Some types of sensors for that purpose can additionally warn of gases from other sources, such as one or more of the following: liquified petroleum gas (LPG—propane or butane), alcohol, or hydrogen (from battery charging), plus such nonexplosive but still hazardous conditions as carbon monoxide or simple smoke. When selecting your fuel vapor detector, consider carefully what additional protection you can achieve from it, or the possible need to have more than one system; some systems allow the use of multiple sensors for different types of vapors, such as propane or compressed natural gas (CNG).

Although not explosive, carbon monoxide fumes can be deadly! A separate detector and alarm is required for such protection, but this is a small, relatively inexpensive unit, easily installed and well worth the cost and effort.

Installation

The installation of a hazardous-vapor alarm requires merely the mounting of a control unit (near the helm station) and the sensor (in the engine compartment well above the normal level of bilge water and near likely sources of fuel spill such as carburetor and fuel pump). An interconnecting cable is run between these units plus wires from a source of DC electrical power. Installation should, of course, be done carefully, in accordance with the manufacturer's instructions—don't take shortcuts with safety! Wiring should be installed in accordance with the guidelines of Chapter 23; electrical power should *not* be taken from the ignition switch, but rather from a point on the distribution panel that is continuously on.

If your craft is a larger one, with gasoline tanks in a compartment separate from that containing the engines, or if a 120-volt AC generating plant is located in an isolated compartment, *each* such area should have its own sensor. When selecting a fuel vapor alarm system, check to see how many sensors the control unit can accommodate; see Figure 37-3. If you cook on your boat with LPG fuel, and if your system is sensitive to such vapors, you might want to consider installing a sensor below the stove, as such vapors are heavier than air and will sink down to the lowest level they can reach.

The control box of a fuel vapor detector will have a warning light or a meter that indicates the percentage of LEL vapor present. If an *audible* alarm is not a standard feature of your detector, it can *and should* be added.

Testing

Most fueling vapor detectors will have a "test" button, but this only simulates sensor action to test the alarm circuit and warning signals; *it does not test the sensor.* At regular intervals you should fully test the system by exposing the sensor to actual fumes. You can—very carefully—pour invisible *fumes* (not liquid) over the sensor from a small can partially filled with gasoline or carbon tet. Absolutely and positively, hatches must be open, electrical devices turned off, and the no-smoking rule strictly enforced! Even better, you can make the test by pouring a small amount of gasoline or other suitable liquid on a rag and then bringing that rag near to the sensor—this avoids any possibility of spill of liquid fuel.

The extremely low-current cold-sensor models may be left turned on all the time—this is a particularly desirable feature. Some such models do not even have an off-on switch and continuously guard the safety of your craft. Cold-sensor models are adaptable to use two sensors; these can be purchased as a dual-sensor model, or an additional sensor can be installed at a later date.

Fire Sensors

Sensors to detect a fire—or even better, an overly hot engine compartment before a fire can start—can be installed overhead or high on a bulkhead. These remain "silent" until the temperature exceeds a normal, safe condition, typically 135 degrees F, at which time a switch closes to activate an alarm. As these are simple N–O switches, any number can be installed and wired in parallel to the same control unit and signal. Other areas that might be so protected include the galley and sleeping areas if smokers are normally aboard.

Engine Alarms

An engine alarm system may not be considered as much of a "safety" device as a fuel vapor detector, for example, but there are many boating situations in which a loss of engine power could definitely hazard your boat and crew. These alarms can be quite simple—a switch or two, a horn or bell, and a few feet of wire. The most widely used system is for low oil pressure and/or high cooling-water temperature; quite often one or more of each of these types of sensors is hooked to a single audible alarm. The low-oil-pressure switch is of the "normally closed" type, and it is held open in the "safe" condition by oil pressure slightly less than the minimum required for proper operation of the engine. It is installed by screwing into a threaded hole in the cylinder block that connects with an oil gallery. (If there is not a "spare" hole closed with a plug, you can use the same one as for the oil pressure gauge sender by employing a "T" fitting.)

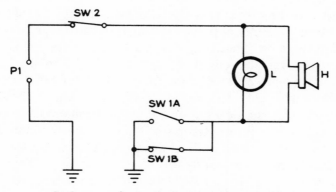

P—Source of electrical power from ignition switch

SW.ₐ—Overheat sensor; normally open, but closes if engine coolant temperature rises over safe limit

SW.ₑ—Low oil pressure sensor; normally closed but held open by safe oil pressure; closes to sound alarm if oil pressure drops while engine is operating

SW₂—Over-ride switch; normally closed but can be held open to silence alarm while starting and until oil pressure builds up. Must be a push button momentary (non-locking) switch

L—Visual alarm; usually a red lamp

H—Audible alarm; horn, buzzer, bell, etc.

Fig. 37-4 Engine alarm system for overheating or low oil pressure.

The sensor for water temperature is a normally open switch that is closed by thermal action above a predetermined level. It can be screwed into the water jacket of the block or connected by use of a "T" fitting where cooling water comes *out* of the block to go to a circulatory pump; it will offer better protection there than if it is installed where water *enters* the block. From the diagram in Figure 37-4 you can see that the operation of either switch completes the circuit from the alarm, shown here as a horn, to ground. This is one of few instances in boat electrical systems where a single-wire circuit is used with an engine block forming the "return" side—this is done as the sensors are screwed into the block or connecting pipe fittings and have only one terminal. Electrical power is drawn from the ignition switch (or equivalent on diesel engines) so that the system is always active whenever the engine is running. To eliminate a brief "false alarm" after the ignition is switched on but before the engine builds up oil pressure, an N–C switch can be installed in the circuit. This should be a push-button, momentary (nonlocking) switch that will only temporarily inactivate the system; it is held down for a few seconds at each time of starting the engine (until the oil pressure builds up).

This system can be *partially* tested at each starting by *not* holding down the push-button switch. This tests the low-oil-pressure sensor, but there is no test for the high-water-temperature sensor short of removing it and placing it in a pan of water on a stove with an ohmmeter across its terminals. Place a cooking thermometer in the water but not in contact with the container; light the stove; and watch both ohmmeter and thermometer to see at what temperature the switch closes.

Additional Alarms

Another type of simple engine alarm is one that gives warning of any interruption in the flow of cooling water coming in from outside. A sensor unit replaces a short length of hose between the seacock (or strainer) and the raw water pump. This will give an immediate alarm before the engine reaches a dangerously high temperature that would activate the sensor at or near the engine block. It is *not* a duplication to have a raw-water-flow alarm *and* a high-temperature alarm. You need both, as the latter will also warn of other troubles, such as a broken belt to the internal water pump or a loss of coolant in a closed freshwater system.

Similar alarms can and should be installed for the gasoline or diesel engine of a 120-volt AC generating plant.

Often overlooked, but nearly as important, are alarms for low oil pressure and/or high oil temperature in a hydraulic reduction/reverse gearbox. Some marine transmissions operate at quite high hydraulic pressures, and a sensor must be selected accordingly.

Dual Alarms

The various sensors for an engine can be wired to a single alarm bell or horn for economy; there should, however, be separate alarm systems for each engine if there are two or more. And don't forget the engine of the auxiliary 120-volt AC generating plant—it, too, needs protection.

An alarm sounding will not tell you the nature of the problem, only that something is abnormal. This should be satisfactory, as your initial action in any event should be to shut down the engine; then you can investigate the cause by reading gauges, looking, smelling, etc.

Gauges

Although not strictly "alarm systems," gauges can often provide timely warnings of impending troubles. You should know, and have recorded in your engine log, the normal values, or ranges of value, for each instrument. In addition to the normal oil pressure and water temperature gauges, other desirable measurements include battery/alternator voltage and charge or dis-

Fig. 37-5 Single meters with dual opposing needles are excellent for twin-engine boats—differences between engines are immediately apparent and may signal trouble. The gauge shown above measures transmission (drive) oil pressure, but any function could be displayed in a similar manner.

charge current, fuel pressure on each side of the filters, and exhaust temperature using a pyrometer (some models also have an alarm capability).

For twin-engine craft there are available gauges with two opposite, facing needles that conserve instrument panel space and also greatly facilitate comparison of the condition of one engine with that of the other; see Figure 37-5.

CONVENIENCE ALARMS

In this category are alarms that may save you much trouble or embarrassment. Devices and systems are available to warn you of such diverse conditions as reversed polarity on the shore-power cord, a holding tank approaching a full state, a fuel or water tank nearing empty, too high a temperature in a refrigerator or freezer box, or the fact that you have neglected to disconnect your shore-power cable and/or water hose as you prepare to leave the pier. Such alarm systems will vary in applicability with different boats and skippers; you should know what is available and make your own decisions. Installation will vary with the device, and the only guidance that can be given here is to follow, step by step, the instructions that came with the unit.

Use your imagination to design other systems not mentioned above that would particularly fit your craft and your boating style.

SECURITY ALARMS

Many skippers moor or berth their craft where measures must be taken to prevent theft or vandalism. In addition to good mechanical security—locks and latches—an electronic security system is often advisable. Not all sensors that are usable ashore in a home or shop can be used afloat because of the normal motion of a boat, but a more than adequate variety remains.

Security alarms can be wired to flash a light, sound a horn, or both; some can interface into the telephone system to give the alarm at a distant location such as the dockmaster's office or even your home. (Such interfaces will normally also accept signals from in-port safety alarms for such as fire or high bilge water.)

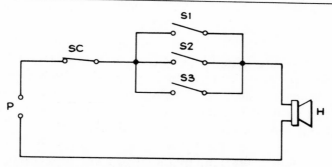

S₁, S₂, S₃, etc.—Normally-open sensor switches—
as many as desired
Sc—Control switch, may be hidden toggle or
visible key-operated switch

Fig. 37-6 The closing of any one of the normally-open sensor switches will cause the alarm to sound.

Probably the best security systems are of the "fail-safe" variety, whereby any opening of the circuit activates circuitry that sounds the alarm, but a system using normally open switches (see Figure 37-6) is simpler electrically and easier to install; some systems may include both N–C and N–O switches. Individual sensors can be homemade or purchased, either separately or as part of an overall system; they need not be complex.

System Design

Sensors can be placed so they will be activated by a person merely stepping on board, or only if a forcible entry is attempted. The possibilities will be limited only by the extent of your imagination: Trip wires can be placed in strategic locations; pressure-sensitive switches can be placed under deck mats or carpets, or where a deck flexes slightly under a person's weight; foil conductors can be put around a window or door glass; contact switches can be placed at a door or hatch, etc. More sophisticated sensors can be used, such as beams of light or ultrasonic sound waves, but they are more expensive and are not really needed. Study your boat to determine the possible points of unauthorized access—they will vary widely with the type and size of the craft.

Sensors

Trip "wires" are actually lengths of very light monofilament fishing line connected to a sensitive switch, often a "microswitch." Switches called "pull traps" can be fashioned from two small metal strips attached to a wooden or plastic clothespin. A thin piece of insulating material normally holds the metal strips apart, but when pulled out by action of a trip line, the opening of a door or hatch, etc., the metal strips come into contact with each other, completing the circuit; see Figure 37-7. Foil around a window glass can act as a sensor in a circuit that uses normally closed switches; breaking the glass will break the foil, open the circuit, and so activate the alarm.

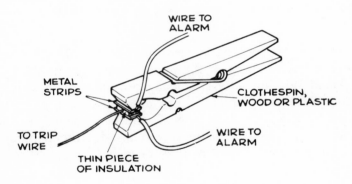

Fig. 37-7 When the trip wire pulls the insulator from between the jaws of the clothes pin, the two wires come into contact and complete the alarm circuit.

Magnetic switches are widely used in security systems ashore, and these can readily be adapted for use on boats. Such switches can be either N–O or N–C types and be operated by either bringing a small magnet near the switch or by removing a magnet that is normally adjacent to the switch; see Figure 37-8. Especially designed for boats is a system of wired snaps for a canvas cover that can be connected into a security alarm system.

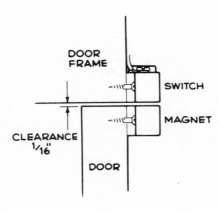

Fig. 37-8 Magnetic switches for security alarm systems consist of two units, one containing a switch that is operated by the presence of a permanent magnet in the other unit. Contacts may be either normally-open or normally-closed.

Alarms

Your boat's air or electric horn can serve as the alarm signal, but a separate horn and/or light can be used if you so desire. Several added features will be desirable; first you will need to use a "hold-in" relay to keep the signal sounding even if, for example, an unauthorized foot is removed from a pressure switch. You can buy a latching relay for 12 volts, or you can make your own by modifying a standard automotive horn relay as shown in Figure 37-9a and connecting it in the circuit of Figure 37-9b as shown. But you will not want the alarm to sound endlessly because of battery drain—and possible objections from neighbors. This requires adding a timer that will shut off the alarm signal after several minutes; a unit sold by automotive parts stores for use on cars, trucks, campers, etc., works fine on the boat's 12-volt system—it stays on for 2 minutes, then goes off and automatically resets itself.

An intermittent sound or a flashing light will normally attract greater and faster attention than a steady signal. This can be achieved by use of an automotive turn-signal flasher; because of

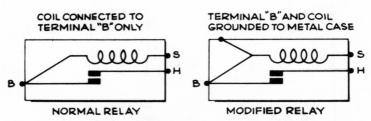

Fig. 37-9a An inexpensive automobile horn relay can be easily modified to serve as a "latching relay" that will keep an alarm system on even though the sensor switch is restored to normal.

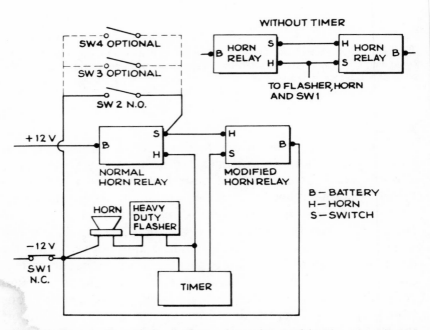

Fig. 37-9b Alarm system including latching relay and timer. If the timer is not desired, merely connect from "H" on normal relay to "S" on modified relay.

the current load of a horn, be sure to use a "heavy duty" unit, such as one intended for use when towing a trailer having additional lamps besides those on the car.

474

Control Switch

The final element of your security alarm system is an on-off, or activate-deactivate, switch. This may be a simple toggle switch, well hidden, whose location is known only to a trusted few. Alternately, it can be a highly visible key switch with a warning notice that the boat has a theft-protection system. In either case, you and other "in" people must always remember to deactivate before entering the system to avoid embarrassment to yourself and annoyance to others.

CHAPTER 38

Bilge Ventilation Systems

FOR MANY years, the legal requirements of Coast Guard regulations were merely for natural ventilation of engine and fuel tank compartments using one or more pair of ducts leading from each compartment to the outside atmosphere. For safety reasons, however, a considerable percentage of boats also were equipped with exhaust blowers, especially on gasoline-fueled boats but also on diesel-engine craft. These air movers are powered by an electric motor operated from the boat's electrical system. If the powered blower were operated for 4 or 5 minutes before any action was taken to start a gasoline engine, and you made a "sniff test," you could be assured that no explosion would occur when the starter switch was activated, or a minute or so later.

How Explosions Occur

Let us pause here for a brief bit of theory. Gasoline vapors and air form an explosive mixture *only* within a certain range of proportions. A *too-lean* mixture, not enough gasoline vapor, is not explosive. But a *too-rich* mixture is also nonexplosive! The concentration of gasoline fumes can be too high to "go boom." Three situations are possible. First, if a starter switch is pressed, or if some other spark jumps, such as from a leaky spark-plug wire, when the concentration is below the lower explosive limit (LEL), all is well—there will be no explosion. If the fumes resulted from spillage, the concentration will be further weakened as the engine runs and more air is sucked in; if the fumes resulted from a gasoline leak, then anything can happen. Second, if the concentration is between the LEL and the upper explosive limit (UEL), an explosion will occur just as soon as the necessary spark occurs. The third case is when the vapor concentration is greater than the UEL when the engine is started. No explosion will occur when the starter is operated, but one can very well occur a minute or so later, when the inflow of fresh air to replace that used by the engine gradually reduces the fume concentration into the explosive range. Here the spark will come from faulty wiring or some electric motor or device that is not "ignitionproof." Why a boat will explode, not on starting the engine, but when it has moved a few hundred yards off the ramp or pier has sometimes puzzled people; this is the explanation. A test of the engine space with a "fuel vapor detector" (more on this is in Chapter 37)—or better yet, a sniff with your nose— would have revealed any of the above situations. Powered bilge ventilation is excellent, but it is wise to be doubly safe.

Coast Guard Regulations

The legal situation on powered ventilation systems changed on August 1, 1980, for all craft equipped with gasoline engines for propulsion, electrical generation, or mechanical power. From that date for all *new* boats, each compartment that has a permanently installed gasoline engine must be ventilated by a powered exhaust blower unless the space is "open to the atmosphere" as defined in Coast Guard regulations. Each exhaust blower, or combination of blowers, must be rated for an airflow of not less than a value computed on the net volume of the engine compartment plus other compartments that are open to it. After installation, the effectiveness of the blower or blowers must have been tested to ensure that air was actually moved at at least a minimum rate determined by other equations. The engine compartment, and other compartments open to the engine compartment where the aggregate area of openings exceeds 2% of the area between the compartments, must also have a natural system intake and exhaust ducts. Additionally, each compartment with a permanently installed gasoline tank must have its own natural ventilation if it contains any electrical device that is not "ignition protected" in accordance with Coast Guard electrical standards for boats. These regulations specify the required cross-sectional area of ducts for natural ventilation systems based on compartment volume, and how the ducts must be installed. They further specify that the bottom end of the intake duct for an exhaust blower must be in the lower third of the compartment but above the normal level of accumulated bilge water.

These requirements are placed on the manufacturer of the boat when it is built, but the purchaser, and any subsequent owner, is responsible for maintaining the powered ventilation system in good and effective operating condition.

Improving Your Boat

While the above ventilations requirements are not applicable in a legal sense to boats built on or before July 31, 1980, they do provide excellent guidance for the safety-minded skipper. They are based on engineering knowledge and experience acquired over the many years since the development of the natural-ventilation requirements in 1966. You can check the existing ventilation system on your boat against the Coast Guard standards, and either be assured that you are in voluntary compliance, or take the necessary actions to upgrade your craft.

Checking Your Boat

The first step in checking the adequacy of your present bilge ventilation system is to determine the "net compartment volume of engine compartment and compartments that open thereto, in cubic feet." To do this, start by measuring or estimating the gross volume, the volume of the compartment empty of the engine and other solid objects; it may be necessary to subdivide mentally an irregular volume into several subspaces and add the volumes of each of them. Next, make similar measurements or estimations for the space occupied by the solid objects within the compartment, and subtract their total volume from the gross figure to get the net volume.

The value for net volume in cubic feet is used in Table 38-1 (column A) to determine the minimum acceptable "rated blower capacity" (column B) in cubic feet per minute. It will not

Col. A [1]	Col B [2]	Col. C [3]
Below		
34	Fr = 50	Fo = 20
34 to		
100	Fr = 1.5V	Fo = 0.6v
Over		
100	Fr = V/2 + 100	Fo = 0.2V + 40

[1] Net compartment volume of engine compartment and compartments open thereto (V) cubic feet

[2] Rated blower capacity (Fr) cubic feet per minute

[3] Blower system output (Fo) cubic feet per minute

Table 38-1 Exhaust blower rated capacity and actual output is determined by net compartment volume.

be practicable for you as an individual to measure actual "blower system output" (column C). Note that these values are uniformly 40% of the rated capacity values; you can reasonably assume that if you have enough rated capacity, you will be obtaining enough actual output. You may be able to find a rated capacity on the nameplate of your blower, but if it is not there, take down the manufacturer's name and model number and consult a catalog or write to the manufacturer for capacity data. If the nameplate is illegible—quite likely on older craft—you may have to write to the boat manufacturer for this information. Larger craft may have more than one bilge blower operated from a single switch; if so, the capacities of each unit may be added together toward meeting the requirement.

Installing a Blower

If you find that your blower is below standards, or if you do not have one at all, the installation of an acceptable unit should present no great problem if you are reasonably handy with tools; it will be even easier to install natural ventilation openings and ducts. Coast Guard regulations specify the standards to be used in determining the required rated capacity of a blower. You will probably have to accept the manufacturer's rating based on their good reputation, but don't buy a blower on a salesman's say-so;

insist on a nameplate rating or the equivalent information on a manufacturer's data sheet. The blower motor must definitely be UL-listed as "ignition protected" so it can handle explosive vapors.

Plan your installation carefully before buying any materials or cutting any holes in the boat. The blower should be mounted high in or adjacent to the compartment. A length of duct will be required on the intake side and may be needed on the exhaust side (mounting the blower right at the opening in the hull or superstructure increases the exposure of the device to the corrosive effects of spray). The duct should be of plastic material suited to the environment in which it will be used—resistant to the effects of water, gasoline, oil, detergents, etc. It must also be flexible and wire-reinforced so that bends can be made without the duct collapsing. Keep all turns as gentle as possible, as sharp bends restrict the flow of air.

A powered exhaust blower does not require a cowl for its proper functioning, but one is normally installed, with the opening facing aft, to aid in preventing spray and rain from entering the duct and running down onto the blower motor.

The electrical wiring for the exhaust blower should be installed in accordance with the general procedures given in Chap-

Fig. 38-1 With this type of switch power is automatically applied to the exhaust blower *before* the engine's ignition system. The blower should be run for at least four minutes before attempting to start a gasoline engine.

ter 23. A separate switch may be used for this circuit, or for even greater safety, a combination ignition-blower switch can be used that requires you to turn on the blower before you can start your engine. Even so, there should be a warning sign near the ignition switch that the blower should be run for at least four minutes, and a "sniff test" made, before the ignition switch is turned on.

When planning overload protection for the blower circuit, remember that this is a motor load and hence there will be much greater load when starting than a few seconds later, when the motor is up to speed. Use a "slo-blow" motor-type fuse or a circuit breaker that is intended for use on circuits having briefly heavier starting currents.

Natural Ventilation

A boat built before the effective date of the current Coast Guard regulations for powered ventilation must have an acceptable natural ventilation system for its bilge—and don't forget that boats required to have a powered ventilation system must also have natural ventilation. Openings into the engine compartment for the entry of air for the carburetor are in addition to requirements for the ventilation system.

Although natural ventilation is not an electrical project, it must be done properly to complement the powered exhaust system. Natural ventilation is supplied by a pair of vents, one to bring in a supply of fresh air and the other to exhaust old air possibly contaminated by fuel vapors. The regulations no longer require that the intake and exhaust vents have cowls facing in specific directions, but it is a good practice to use the following guidelines. The supply vent opening should be on the exterior surface of the boat and have a cowl that faces forward so there will be a flow of air into and out of the vents when the boat is moving forward, or from the wind when the boat is at anchor or at a mooring. The cowl on the exhaust vent should face aft to take advantage of any suction effect from the passing wind. The intake vent must be farther forward on the boat than the exhaust vent to lessen the chance of any recirculation of fuel vapors out of the exhaust vent and back into the intake vent. The intake vent should also be located so it will not pick up vapors from fueling operations.

One distinct weakness of natural ventilation systems is the fact that for a great majority of boats docked in slips or at a pier, the wind does not consistently blow from bow to stern; it may even be exactly the reverse!

DIESEL CRAFT

The legal requirements for both powered and natural ventilation are placed only on boats using gasoline as a fuel. The commonsense safety aspects are likewise focused on such craft. But powered exhaust blowers will commonly be found on diesel-powered vessels also. This probably stems, at least in part, from production line economies of making all boats alike regardless of the engine fuel to be used. Diesel fumes are not explosive, but it is still desirable to get them out of a boat, and there are other secondary applications for a powered ventilation system. When working in an engine space on a larger boat that has been entered from one end rather than by raising hatches in the cabin deck, running the blower to exhaust some air will result in bringing in replacement fresh air, which will certainly help your personal comfort—the standards are based on more than one complete air change every minute. In hot weather I make it a practice on my diesel-powered trawler to run the blower for ten minutes or more *after* shutting off the engine from a run. This removes from the interior of the boat hot air that would otherwise raise the temperature of the cabin. Remember that a diesel engine is a large mass of iron that has been run at high temperatures and will no longer have cooling water passing through it after it is stopped. The engine will take some time to cool down; run the blower until the air coming out its exhaust vent no longer is significantly warmer than the outside air.

MAINTENANCE

An exhaust blower should be run at least once a month to keep the motor shaft from freezing up. On a gasoline-powered boat that is in regular use, this will be no problem if the blower is faithfully used each time before starting the engine. On a boat that is used infrequently, or on a diesel-powered craft in cooler climates, an exhaust blower tends to be neglected. In such circumstances, add an item reading "Run exhaust blower" to your list of "monthly safety checks and routine maintenance items." (You do have such a checklist, don't you?)

Exhaust blower motors may or may not require periodic lubrication. Check your blower, and the instruction sheet that came with it, to determine whether this is an action that should be taken at regular intervals.

If your fuse or circuit breaker is of the proper type and rating, it should never open up. If you are troubled with blown fuses or tripped breakers, check your blower for a mechanical obstruction or binding as the impeller rotates—it must turn very freely, as it operates at high speeds. It is also a good idea to check the voltage at the motor while it is operating, to be sure it is adequate. If it is too low—under 11 volts—check for poor connections and/or replace wire with heavier-gauge conductors.

CHAPTER 39

Stereo Systems and TV

BOATING IN itself is fun (and safe boating is more fun, as the experts say), but sometimes the enjoyment can be enhanced with the addition of one or two "luxuries" afloat, such as a good stereo system or a TV receiver. By keeping the size of these units consistent with the size of the boat, both fine-quality music and television entertainment can be enjoyed on a wide range of craft.

Back in the days of double-sideband marine communications, most such sets also could receive AM broadcast stations for news, music, and other radio entertainment. Today's VHF sets do not have that capability, although many radio direction finders (RDFs) do. The ready availability of small transistorized receivers has made the reception of both AM and FM stations a simple matter anywhere, including on boats. But these can best be described as "low-fi" and fall far short of meeting the music quality standards of many people, whether their interest is in popular music, country and western, or classical.

Selection of Audio Equipment

For some years, the demand for better-fidelity sound on boats had to be met by the installation of stereo systems designed and manufactured for use in automobiles. These had the advantage of working on 12-volt DC power, thus making unnecessary any shore power connection or the running of an on-board 120-volt AC generating plant. (Inverters—see Chapter 42—produce 120-volt AC power from a 12-volt DC system, but in most cases the output is not a sine wave, frequency can wander, and voltage regulation is poor. This can be tolerated for some applications, but not "hi-fi" equipment.) Automotive stereo systems are still widely used, but now increasing numbers of music systems designed and manufactured especially for marine installation are becoming available.

In planning a stereo system, factors that must be considered include the source of program material—FM radio, records, or tape cassettes; where you will want output; amplifier power needed; and input power to be used—AC or DC, or both. Answers to these questions must be thought out before you consider the selection of specific equipment.

Stereo Systems

Automotive stereo systems may be considered, especially the higher-quality units. They offer advantages of compact size, easy adaptability to the boat's electrical system, and a wide variety of models from which to choose. All types of input, except records, are available, as well as combinations. Except in the smallest of boats, however, you will probably do better with speakers other than those designed to fit into the limited spaces of cars. The principal disadvantage of automobile systems is their lack of protection from the harshness of a marine environment; this is where the newer units, designed especially for on-the-water use, are superior. Still, at a proper location on board, with protection from spray and rain, automotive stereo units can give years of service.

True marine stereo still should be protected from direct rain and spray, but they are manufactured specifically for use in a boating environment. The cases of many units are sealed, with gaskets placed around the shafts of controls; doors for cassette insertion are specially designed; and all printed-circuit boards have been sprayed with a protective coating. Vibration protection is provided for some models. All the usual features of a home stereo system are included. A few marine units can also receive the continuous-weather-broadcast frequencies, WX-1 and WX-2; this, however, is not a significant feature, as these

channels will always be available on the VHF-FM communications transceiver.

One model has a microphone input and can be used for internal communications.

Record Players

Record playing presents two particular problems on boats.
Unless turntable speed is adjustable, musical pitch may be off
when the frequency of AC power is not exactly 60 Hz. This is
not a problem when connected to shore power, but it can be a
matter of concern when under way or at anchor. Even with the
larger on-board generating plants, the AC system frequency may
be off by a Hertz or two, and the error will vary with changing
loads on the system. Frequency meters can be easily installed,
but the result will more likely be knowledge of the frequency
error rather than correction to exactly 60 Hz, as this is not a
simple, easy adjustment. An adjustable-speed turntable can
compensate for off-frequency power, but adjustments may be
needed at frequent intervals if you are a purist as to pitch. The
second problem is that of keeping the pickup head in the proper
groove on the record. Stylus pressures are feather-light, and
even the slightest movement of the boat will have a tendency to
make the arm go skittering across the record. At least one
model of turntable now available, however, is designed to overcome this problem. A radial guide rail carries the phono cartridge and permits no sliding from its proper place, regardless of
motion of the unit as a whole. The cartridge is stabilized in its
position by a servomechanism that instantly corrects any tendency to jump out of the groove. This record player will work
well at anchor or under way—but it's not inexpensive!

The new compact disk (CD) players may be the solution for
the playing of music records on boats. In these units, the disk is
scanned by a low-power laser beam, and there is no "needle" to
be kept in a groove. The CDs also provide a smaller record, but
with a longer-playing capability—more than 300 laser tracks can
fit in the space of a single needle groove! Music quality is exceptionally good—fidelity that is nearly perfect and no background
noise. CD players can be programmed to play only selected por-

tions of a disk, and in many other special ways. There is no wear on the disk from the laser beam; with proper care, a CD player and its disks can last for many years. Models specifically designed for marine use have not yet appeared on the market, so "home" or "automobile" units must be installed and proper protection provided from the weather.

Tape Players

Cassette tape players present no problems for boat hi-fi systems, whether they are automobile, home-type, or the new marine-designed units (8-track tape players are now essentially obsolete and should not be considered for new installations). Special care should be given, however, to the storage of tape cassettes. Conditions of heat and humidity, especially when a boat is shut up tightly during periods of nonuse, far exceed those found in a home or office. You must protect tapes from direct sunlight and excessive moisture, but even so, expect reduced life and eventual playing problems.

Digital audio tape (DAT) provides music of outstanding fidelity in a most convenient package; it should be considered when players become available at acceptable prices. DAT cas-

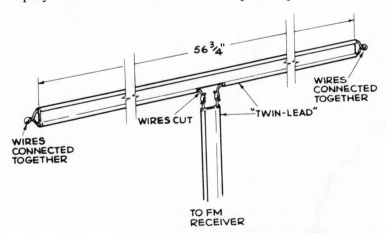

Fig. 39-1 A simple antenna for FM broadcast reception can be made from "300-Ohm twin-lead" often used for TV lead-ins. A piece 56¾" is cut, the wires are connected together at each end, and one side is opened at the midpoint, where another length of twin-lead, long enough to reach the receiver, is connected.

sette players may well be the eventual replacement for CD players on boats—the same quality of output, plus being smaller, lighter, and with the capability of recording in addition to playing back.

FM Radio Reception

An FM tuner will undoubtedly be part of your on-board stereo system, since much boating is done within the range of such stations. Recognize, however, that the normal range of an FM broadcast station rarely exceeds 50 miles, and some of your cruising may be too far out from the nearest station (here is where your tape player will come into its own). For achieving the greatest possible range of FM reception you will need a good antenna. A "folded dipole" antenna can easily be made from a length of 300-ohm "twin lead" as commonly used for TV reception; see Figure 39-1. This has maximum sensitivity at right angles to its long axis; you may want to mount a pair of such antennas oriented 90° to each other. These can be hidden behind furniture or drapes but should be as high as possible for the best results.

For even better reception, and to greater distances, an external, rotatable antenna can be used, one similar to those used for TV sets; the antenna for shipboard TV can be used if a multiset coupler with FM output is added. See comments later in this chapter regarding TV antennas.

Space, always a problem on a boat, can be saved if you select combination units—a receiver with built-in tape player, or a combined receiver-amplifier. Don't try to impress your friends with a massive display of multiple units.

Amplifiers

Since boat cabins are generally quite a bit smaller than house rooms, not as much audio power will be required. Amplifiers with 20 to 30 watts per channel are fully adequate. With modern solid-state design, amplifiers of this power rating can be both small in size and highly efficient. Higher-power amplifiers can be used, but these will rarely ever be turned up anywhere near full output. Most marine stereo systems will include an amplifier of adequate output power in a single package with the AM-FM tuner and a cassette tape player.

Speakers

Speakers from automotive stereo systems, especially surface-mounted units, will often prove a disappointment on boats because their design has been optimized for quite different surroundings. It is generally preferable to use speakers intended for use ashore in apartment-size rooms. Small size is a definite limitation to the low-frequency response of a speaker, but the best models of small speakers are not too bad. There are good small speakers, and there are bad small speakers—ask around, and, if possible, try several before buying. Speakers designed for a marine environment will have special protective features against high humidity and direct sunlight.

The cabin of a boat provides an excellent setting for four-speaker "surround sound." If you install four, however, be sure to include a fader control to adjust the sound between pairs of speakers. Left–right sound balance is handled by controls on the receiver or tape player.

If you want your music out on deck, you may have to give up some of the "hi" in "hi-fi," as nearly all fully weatherproofed speakers have been designed and manufactured for the narrower frequency range of speech rather than music. Exceptions do exist, however, and careful shopping combined with consultation with qualified technicians may yield satisfactory results.

Installation and Maintenance

There are few unique problems to installing a stereo system in a boat. The location for the combined unit, or separate tuner, tape or record player, and amplifier units should be selected so it is protected from rain and spray. Often all units are built into a bulkhead or cabinet; if so, adequate ventilation must be provided to get rid of the heat that is generated. Fortunately, this is very much reduced with solid-state components but is still not something that can be ignored. If units are not built in, then they must be secured in place so they will not fall or be thrown about in rough weather or under heeling conditions. Some units are designed to mount under a shelf as well as on it, or to be built in.

Models that mount by means of a "snap-in" bracket can do double duty, being moved from car to boat and back again, with the only added expense being an additional bracket; such units can be removed from either location and taken home for added security.

Electrical installation is straightforward, and it, too, should present no problems. Input electrical power should be wired as for any added piece of equipment. Units operated from 12-volt DC sources should be wired in accordance with the guidance of Chapter 23; 120-volt AC-operated equipment should be supplied with power as described for added circuits in Chapter 22. Audio wiring to speakers should be of the gauge recommended by the manufacturer of the speaker or amplifier used; the physical installation of these wires should be in conformance with previously described good practices on boats.

Maintenance requirements are steadily declining with the increased use of transistorized and integrated-circuit designs. No additional or unusual maintenance problem should be expected just because the equipment is afloat; perhaps the only difficulty

Fig. 39-2 Improved TV reception on boats can be obtained by using a special antenna mounted as high as possible, but *never* on the whip antenna of a VHF or other two-way radio. Some models are complete with internal rotator.

will be if you have trouble while away on a cruise and don't have your familiar repair shop to take your troubles to!

TELEVISION AFLOAT

A television set makes the transition from house to boat quite easily. Any black-and-white or color set will operate on board if there is a source of 120-volt AC power; even inverters will do, as a TV receiver is usually not as "fussy" about the frequency and wave shape as stereo systems are. Modern solid-state TVs draw about 100 watts, a bit more or quite a bit less depending on whether it is a color set and the size of the picture tube; this load is easily accommodated by on-board AC sources. Many good-quality TV sets are now available that are operable directly from 12-volt DC power sources, or even from internal batteries, rechargeable or dry cells. There are now some models specifically designed for operation in the environment found on boats.

Antennas

Built-in extensible rod or "rabbit ear" antennas will be satisfactory only for short-range reception. For full cruising use, your TV set will need an external antenna mounted as high as practicable. Simple "omnidirectional" antennas, as seen on large cars and limousines, can be used, but the best results will be obtained from a "unidirectional" antenna that can be rotated for better reception from a specific direction. Several models of these can be found in marine or recreational vehicle stores. An antenna of special design is placed in a pancake-shape housing about 2 feet in diameter and several inches thick, together with a preamplifier to boost signal strength. A small control box to direct the rotation of the antenna is placed near the TV set. Such an antenna can be used for both VHF and UHF television signals, and additionally for FM radio reception, at greater distances than would otherwise be possible.

CHAPTER 40

Air-Conditioning and Heating

IN SUMMERTIME in most areas, when under way and away from shore, the breezes will usually make living comfortable. But docked in a marina or anchored in a well-sheltered cove, it can be just plain hot! In wintertime, under way or alongside, it can be too cold for comfort. Going boating is a way of getting back in touch with nature, but there's nothing that says you have to be miserably hot or cold. Thus on medium-size and larger craft, air-conditioning and/or heating make sense.

AIR-CONDITIONING

Basically, "air-conditioning" consists of cooling the air within a confined space, such as your boat's cabin. In this process, some moisture is removed from the air; this lowers the relative humidity and further adds to comfort.

The principal function of any air conditioner is to move the heat that is within the space concerned to some place outside and dissipate it there. In a true marine-type air conditioner the removed heat is transferred to the water in which the craft floats. This requires an additional raw water inlet, with seacock and strainer, plus one or more circulating pumps. Some air conditioners used on boats are single-unit types in which the "compressor" and "evaporator" portions are located within a single cabinet set in a corner of a cabin or built into a bulkhead. Many others, however, are of multiple-unit design in which the compressor is located belowdecks, often the engine compartment, and the evaporator element in the cabin where the cooling effect is desired. Insulated copper tubing, and control wires, must be run between these units, an added complication, but it does permit considerable space savings in the cabin area where it is most needed. Some boats are designed so that a single evaporator unit can be located in a storage locker between two cabins and discharge cooled air in both directions, thus cooling each space.

Cooled air can also be ducted from a remotely located evaporator unit to an outlet grill in a space where it is needed.

In some instances, "house-type" room air conditioners may be installed on a boat. These air-cooled machines are mounted in a window, as in a house, or are built into the side of a cabin. Another style of air-cooled unit is that designed for recreational vehicles and mounted on a cabintop. In general, both of these types will function just as well as a marine water-cooled unit, but will almost surely have a shorter operating life, as they were not designed to withstand the harshness of a marine environment, especially when the boat is used on salt water.

Installation

The installation of any of the above models of air conditioners on a boat is not a simple project; it is probably the most complex project covered in this book, but it is possible to do. If you are accustomed to doing boat carpentry and electrical work and have good tools, there is no reason not to undertake the work yourself.

Planning

As with any project, success will be best ensured by detailed and complete advance planning. The first step will be the determination of the size of the unit your boat should have. Air conditioners are rated in "BTUs" of cooling power; you will probably need the outside advice of an expert in figuring out the necessary size to be installed.

Before cutting into a bulkhead or cabin side (these holes will be large), think the action through and be sure that this is what you want to do. Plan the runs for wires and refrigerant tubing— make sure you have a feasible route all the way, and measure

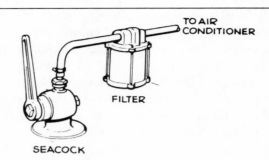

Fig. 40-1 Marine air conditioners require a flow of raw water to remove the heat collected in the compressor unit. The intake should have a seacock and strainer; the outflow can be above the waterline.

the length of material you will need. Consider where you will place the compressor unit, where you will cut a hole in your boat's bottom for raw water intake, and where topside for the cooling water discharge. Follow up your thorough planning with careful execution and you can have your air-conditioning at a considerable saving of money. Some "skipper-done" installations look even better than "yard" jobs!

Installing a water-cooled air conditioner will require a new through-hull fitting—don't "tee" off of an engine-cooling-water intake. Plan the location of this new hole carefully, considering both the inside and the outside of the hull. As this work will require the boat to be out of the water, integrate your plans for air-conditioning installation with other tasks to be done when your craft is next hauled out.

Raw-water pumps are of two types: centrifugal and positive-displacement. Displacement pumps offer more flexibility in location, but they use a neoprene impeller that is subject to wear and periodic replacement. Centrifugal pumps avoid this problem and operate with less noise. They have a disadvantage, however, in that they are not self-priming and so must be located well below the waterline. The physical characteristics of your boat may dictate the use of an impeller displacement pump, but if you have a choice, the centrifugal type should be selected.

All rubber hoses below the waterline should be of the highest-quality reinforced type similar to that used in engine cooling systems.

Wiring

Wiring for 120-volt AC power should be installed in accordance with the guidelines of Chapter 22. Air conditioners draw a considerable amount of 120-volt AC power when running, and briefly quite a bit more when starting. Most air-conditioned craft also have on-board electric plants so that the benefits of cooling can be had at anchor; be sure that this load is within the rating of your present or planned 120-volt AC plant. Air-conditioning will surely be wanted when you are in port, and on boats without an on-board generator, this is the only time when the unit can be run. It is normal to wire the air-conditioning load to a shore-power inlet separate from that used for other loads such as lights, battery charging, refrigerator, cooking, etc. This permits the use of multiple loads without overburdening the shore-power cord or its connectors at either end. You will have a higher voltage for other loads while operating the air conditioner or conditioners if such are on their own line. You will, of course, need to have a separate main breaker, and a separate transfer switch if an on-board generating plant is used.

Maintenance

Owner maintenance on a marine air conditioner will consist primarily of ensuring an uninterrupted and unrestricted flow of cooling water through the unit. The exhaust flow will normally be through the topsides, where it can be seen; it should be visually checked frequently. The raw-water strainer should be inspected for grass, weeds, mud, etc., on a regular basis and additionally whenever there is the possibility of picking up material that could clog it, such as after running aground or when anchoring in very shallow water over a grassy bottom. The seacock should be operated from full open to full closed and back on a regular schedule, usually monthly, to keep it free and available for shutting off the flow when the strainer must be disassembled for cleaning. (Do not install a brass gate-valve—this can and usually will get a barnacle or other growth in the opening such that the valve cannot be fully closed to shut off the water flow completely. Boats have sunk because of the use of gate valves that couldn't be closed when needed!)

There are electric motors on the compressor and the fan behind the evaporator coils. Normally these will not require lubrication or other attention, but be guided in this, and any other required periodic attention, by the manufacturer's instruction manual. Circulating-raw-water pumps that have neoprene impellers will require periodic inspection—perhaps semiannually—and replacement of the impellers when they show signs of wear.

Accessories

The water removed from the atmosphere—called "condensate"—must be drained away from the evaporator unit into the bilge or over the side. This can, however, be filtered and sterilized, and then added to your boat's freshwater tank. Complete equipment is commercially available for this purpose, or you can assemble your own components; up to 10 or more gallons of potable water per day can be obtained from this source—a significant quantity when cruising offshore.

Dehumidifiers

High relative humidity is a major factor in personal discomfort during hot weather and is the principal cause of mildew damage in a boat that is closed up for days at a time. An electric dehumidifier can be purchased and used on a boat at a small fraction of the cost of installing an air conditioner.

Portable Units

There are quite compact portable units, perhaps 1 to 1½ feet square by 1½ to 2 feet high. Power requirements are moderate, and such units can be plugged into any 120-volt AC duplex outlet on the boat, or run off an ordinary extension cord from the pier. If needed, an additional duplex outlet can be installed at a suitable location by following the procedures of Chapter 22. A dehumidifier can be placed anywhere, but proper provision must be made for the water that will be drawn out of the air; this can be from 3 to 10 gallons per day. It is undesirable merely to drain the water into the bilge, even with an automatic bilge pump. A simple solution is to set the unit on a countertop in the galley or head, with the drain hose running to the sink or basin. Care should be taken to fasten the unit in place securely, lest it be upset by the boat rolling from side to side by the wakes of passing craft.

Controls

An electric dehumidifier need not be operated continuously. It can be controlled automatically by a "humidistat"—an internal or external device that reacts to humidity levels much as a thermostat does to temperature changes. Alternately, and less expensively, a timer can be used to turn the dehumidifier on and then off after an hour or so of operation twice each day; the frequency of running periods, and their length, can be varied to determine what is required for various seasons.

Operation of a dehumidifier on a boat that is not air-conditioned will both prevent mildew damage and make it a much more pleasant environment to step on board to on a Friday afternoon after the craft has been closed up for nearly a week.

HEATERS

Even on boats that require air-conditioning in summer months, there may be other months, still suitable for boating, when a bit of heat in the cabin will feel very pleasant. Electric heating has the advantage of not consuming oxygen as do charcoal or LPG heaters and stoves, and there is consequently no danger of asphyxiation or carbon monoxide poisoning. Electric heat is also more controllable than other methods, and it can be operated automatically for your desired temperature level.

Reverse-Cycle Air Conditioners

Many models of marine air conditioners can be operated on "reverse cycle" to heat rather than cool the air that passes through them. In this mode, heat is extracted from the raw water that is pumped in and then out, and the warmth is circulated in the cabins. A disadvantage of this method of heating is that the air-conditioning outlets are normally located high in cabins. This is where cooled air should be inserted into an enclosed space, but it is *not* where warmed air should be dumped—quite the opposite! A limitation on the reverse-cycle method is the temperature of the water in which your boat is floating. The effectiveness and efficiency of the air conditioner decrease as the water gets colder and there is a lower limit below which the heating mode will not operate; this varies with the unit being used but is typically about 40° F.

Some models of household or recreation-vehicle air conditioners may be able to provide heat either from a reverse-cycle mode of operation or by passing the air over resistance coils. Not all such units will have this capability, so investigate before making your selection if you have the need for heating as well as cooling.

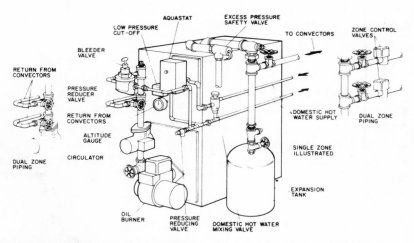

Fig. 40-2 Year-around live-aboard boats in northern waters will require some sort of heating system. Electric space heaters are seldom adequate. The furnace system shown here uses diesel fuel from the boat's tanks.

Electric Space Heaters

Household "space heaters" can also be used on a boat having access to 120-volt AC power. These units may provide heat by either radiant or convective means, or a combination of the two; they may or may not have a built-in fan. Such heaters can be either manually or automatically controlled and must have a protective "tilt" switch that shuts them off should they fall over from an upright position; units that are "long and low," rather than those that have a small base and are tall, are preferable for use on boats, where the deck may move about much more than the floor of a house. Electric space heaters draw quite a bit of power—a "high heat" rating of 1,500 watts is common—but can be operated from an ordinary duplex outlet if only a few, and light, other loads are on the same circuit. If you are going to use a heater regularly at a specific location on your boat, consider installing a new outlet on its own separate circuit; see Chapter 22.

Quite separate from heating for "creature comfort" is the installation of small, very-low-wattage heaters permanently placed in lockers to provide just enough warmth to reduce relative humidity and prevent mildew.

Furnaces

Larger boats and yachts can have a heating system that uses a small furnace burning diesel oil (which is actually #2 heating oil with lowered impurities) from the vessel's fuel tanks. Such a furnace requires a source of air for combustion and a vent for smoke and fumes. Heated air is circulated about the craft by a means of ducts with louvered outlets at locations where heat is desired.

An alternative—less dry and dusty, but more complex and expensive—is a heating system that circulates hot water from a boiler in the engine room to convectors located where heat is needed. These units can have built-in blowers to aid in air circulation. Automatic control by thermostat and timer is possible; heat can be fed to where it is needed, and shut off where it is not desired. Packaged units are available, and installation, while a major project, is not particularly complex. Conventional baseboard radiators can be used instead of the fan-powered convectors, but these must be considerably larger to yield the same heating effect. As for the hot-air furnace, fuel can be diesel from the boat's regular tanks.

CHAPTER 41

Electrical Noise Suppression

WHILE A VHF/FM radio on your boat may be relatively immune from problems caused by electrical noise, not so your
depth sounder, radio direction finder, AM broadcast radio receiver, CB set, loran receiver, or single-sideband radio—all of
these can be rendered less efficient or even totally inoperative.
Information in Chapter 20 and in this chapter will help you in
suppressing the electrical noise problem on your boat.

Electrical noise primarily comes from sparks—electricity
jumping across tiny gaps. The "hotter" the spark, the worse the
noise. Each spark acts as a tiny radio transmitter with a broad
frequency output, radiating its signal through the air and along
the wires on either side of the gap. Noise suppression is
achieved by "short-circuiting" these radio waves, by giving them
a short, easy path directly to ground. Some sparks may be in-
tentional, such as in the spark plugs of a gasoline engine; some
may be unavoidable, such as the sparks in a distributor or at the
brushes of an alternator; and some are entirely avoidable, such
as leakage on high-voltage ignition wires, or loose and dirty
electrical connections of any kind.

Finding the Source

The first action in suppressing electrical noise is to find the
source, and the first step in this is to listen. Each noise source
has its own distinctive sound. Ignition noise is a popping sound
that increases in tempo with engine speed and stops instantly
when the keyswitch is turned off while at a fast idle. Alternator

501

noise is a high-pitched musical whine that increases in pitch with higher engine speed. It does not stop instantly when the key-switch is turned off (unless the field coil of the alternator is fed from that switch). Voltage regulator noise is a ragged, rasping, "frying" sound and usually accompanies alternator or generator noise. Instrument noise consists of random crackling or hissing sounds; verify by jarring the instrument suspected. Electronic tachometers can also create noise; verify by turning off and on. Electrical noise from motors can be identified by switching each pump, fan, windshield wiper, etc., off and on while listening; noise from fluorescent lights can likewise be identified by switching individual circuits and fixtures on and off.

Noise Layers

Electrical noise can be said to come in "layers" according to the intensity of the spark producing it, and as you "peel off" one layer by suppressing it, you then hear the next—one that was there all the time, only covered up by the louder noise. If you start by checking on minor noise sources, you may not be able to judge the effectiveness of your work. Look for the major electrical noise sources with a pocket-size transistor AM receiver or with a search coil on a shortwave receiver as described in Chapter 20. You can bring your "noise sniffer" near a suspected source and listen for an increased level of noise; or you can switch off a motor or pump, for example, and listen for a decrease in noise. You can also install suppression measures and then listen for a change in noise level.

Ignition Systems

If you have one or more gasoline engines on your boat, start with them, as ignition noise is usually the overriding layer. Spark plugs must, of course, have a spark, but the radiated electrical noise can be reduced. First check your entire ignition system and bring it up to good operating condition. Check spark plugs, breaker points, and distributor rotor; if in doubt about any item, replace it. Also inspect all ignition wiring and terminals, especially high-voltage ones, for loose connections. Jiggling

502

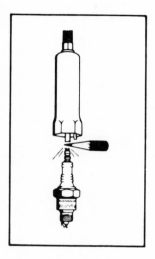

Fig. 41-1 Incorrect polarity of an ignition coil can cause an increase in radio noise. It is easily checked, see text for procedure. Always use a wooden pencil and stay clear of the metal ferrule on the eraser end.

all wiring while listening to the noise level on the AM radio can flush out bad circuits and connections.

First try the suppression measures on pages 296–298; if these do not give enough noise direction, continue as described below. In bad cases, you can combine resistor spark plugs and resistance wire from the distributor to the plugs; make sure that you are using the type of plug recommended by the engine manufacturer and are setting the gap as specified. If your ignition system is in good shape, engine performance will not suffer from this double-barreled action. Always check coil polarity; wires to the primary side could have gotten reversed when the coil was removed. Insert a pencil (wooden shaft only) into the high-voltage circuit as shown in Figure 41-1. The spark should flare orange on the plug side of the pencil; if it doesn't, reverse the primary wires to the ignition coil. Reversed polarity requires more voltage to fire the plugs and hence produces stronger electrical noise.

Sometimes you will find nonignition wires bundled with or routed alongside ignition wiring—this obviously increases the potential for noise to be radiated. All power and signal wiring to

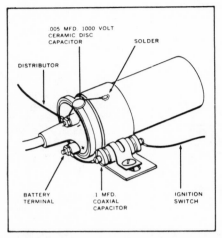

Fig. 41-2 Capacitors can be added to an ignition coil to reduce radio noise. Use the proper type and size; install *only* as shown above.

electronic equipment should be kept well away from the engine.

Noisy ignition coils can be improved by adding capacitors as shown in Figure 41-2. Noisy ignition switch wiring or electric tachometer cables may require the use of shielded wire, with the braid grounded *at each end*. (The operation of some tachometers may be adversely affected by such shielding.)

Shielding

If the above measures fail and you must have less radio interference from your engine, you will have to consider a fully shielded ignition system. This involves special spark plug shields, metallic-braid-covered wires, and shields for distributor and coil. These systems are bulky, expensive, and should be installed by an expert.

A possible alternative is to shield the entire engine box or compartment. This is done with well-grounded copper screening material. The job must be absolutely complete, no gaps where noise can "leak out." The screen must allow access for maintenance, yet be complete when the hatches are closed. Every wire

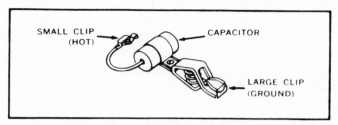

Fig. 41-3 A by-pass capacitor of 0.5 mfd can be fitted with clips and used to test for noise suppression at various motors, instruments, alternator, etc. Observe cautions given in text.

leading into or out of the compartment must have a capacitor to "clean" it of any noise pulses. Such shields can be effective, but installing one can be a major project.

Charging Circuits

Alternator and regulator noise are easier to diagnose. Assemble a capacitor probe as in Figure 41-3. With the engine running, and using your portable radio as a listening device, ground the large clip and touch the small clip briefly to each hot terminal on

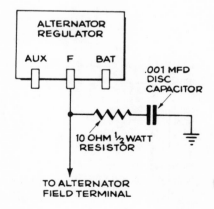

Fig. 41-4 Never connect a capacitor to the field terminal of a regulator or alternator without using a series resistor as shown above.

the alternator and the regulator but *not* to the field terminal on an alternator. If the noise stops or lessons, you have "a," but not necessarily "the," source. The noise of alternators can be suppressed effectively with 0.5 microfarad *coaxial* capacitors or combination filters made specifically for this purpose. These units must have a current-carrying rating equal to the maximum current of the circuit on which they are to be used. They are available at electronic parts stores such as Radio Shack (R/S #272-1085). Do *not* connect a capacitor to the field terminal of an alternator.

Make sure that the metal case of a coaxial capacitor is well grounded. If additional noise suppression is required for a voltage regulator, connect a .001 microfarad capacitor (R/S #272-126) in series with a 10-ohm, ½-watt resistor (R/S #271-001) from the field terminal to ground; see Figure 41-4. In extreme cases of noise it may be necessary to use shielded wires between the regulator and the alternator, with the braid grounded *at both ends*. You might consider replacing an older-design electromechanical regulator with a newer-design solid-state electronic regulator that will have no sparking contacts; consult your engine mechanic for information on the availability of such a unit for your engine's alternator.

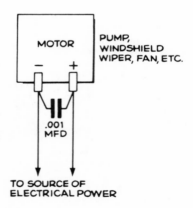

Fig. 41-5 To suppress normal electrical noise from a motor, a small disc capacitor can be connected directly across the terminals. If the unit has wire leads, connect the capacitor as close (electrically) as possible to the motor.

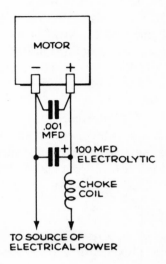

Fig. 41-6 If the electrical noise problem is exceptionally severe, try adding an electrolytic capacitor in parallel with the disc capacitor (observe polarity). A small choke coil can also be used in series in the positive lead.

Noise Filters

Multielement noise filters are manufactured for a number of applications. Units are made in various ampere ratings for use at an alternator or other noise source. Different units are designed for use at affected electronic devices, such as depth sounders and Loran-C receivers.

Electric Motors

Small motors—bilge pumps, freshwater-system pumps, fans, windshield wipers, etc.—can often be silenced with small .01 microfarad disc ceramic capacitors costing only a few cents each at a Radio Shack store (R/S #272-131). These are connected directly across the power terminals of the motor as close to it as possible; see Figure 41-5. Usually this is all that is required, but if the noise is not adequately suppressed, you might try adding an electrolytic capacitor of 100 microfarads at 50-volt working rating (R/S #272-1044) in parallel with the disc ceramic capacitor already installed and/or a small choke coil in series with the positive lead (make sure this coil is rated for the current drawn by the motor, and check afterward for voltage drop). See Figure 41-6 for how these components are added to the circuit; be sure to match polarity markings when connecting an electrolytic capacitor.

Gauges

Some electrically operated gauges and instruments may also cause noise. Try using a .01 microfarad disc capacitor across the terminals or a 0.5 microfarad coaxial capacitor (case-grounded) in series with the "hot" lead. Do *not* do this on an electronic tachometer.

Diesel Engines

If your engine is diesel-rather than gasoline-fueled, you are spared all the electrical noise that comes from the ignition system. You will, of course, still have possible noise sources in alternators, voltage regulators, gauges, etc., of the engine, plus the motors of your boat's electrical system.

If your craft is large enough to have an auxiliary generating plant for 120-volt AC power, don't forget to check its components for radio noise and take suppression action where needed. This is especially necessary if the engine uses gasoline as its fuel.

Outboard Motors

Outboard motors, particularly those with high-voltage capacitive-discharge ignition, can make quite a bit of noise. Adapt, as well as you can with the limited available space, any of the methods discussed above. Some outboard motor manufacturers offer ignition shielding kits that may help reduce noise. Household aluminum foil can be fastened to the inside of the fiberglass engine-cover with contact cement; separate pieces of foil must be well connected together, and the shield as a whole must be grounded to the engine. This will cut off much but not all of the radiated noise. Any electrical wires back to the battery, which also supplies power for the radio and depth sounder, should have bypass capacitors installed.

Inboard-outboard propulsion systems should have electrical noise problems attacked in the same manner as for inboard engines.

CHAPTER 42

Miscellaneous Equipment

THERE ARE a number of items of electrical or electronic equipment that have a more limited applicability or appeal to boat owners but that should not be overlooked entirely. These will be presented briefly in this chapter so you can make an informed decision as to whether one or more of them should be selected for your craft.

Radio Direction Finders

Radio direction finding is a radionavigation technique that has been around almost as long as radio itself—but it is still a very valid method of finding your position. The equipment is much less complex than more modern systems, but it is not simpler to use in finding your position on the water. Its principle advantage is that a radio direction finder (RDF) is less expensive.

The radio direction finding system consists of transmitters at charted locations and modified receivers on vessels. The primary application of an RDF is to take bearings on two or more sources of radio signals, then plot them in order to fix your boat's position, much as visual bearings are used. The advantage of radio bearings is that they can be received at greater distances and in conditions of reduced visibility. (The disadvantage is that radio bearings are less precise than visual ones.) The taking of bearings can be either manual or automatic, in which case the set is called an automatic direction finder (ADF).

A second use of RDFs and ADFs is for homing on the source of a signal, but great caution must be used in doing this.

The transmitters used for direction finding are usually in the low- and medium-frequency bands—radio beacons and AM broadcast stations plotted on regular navigation charts. Increasingly, however, DFing is being done on the VHF band—homing on other vessels and taking bearings on VHF transmitters onshore whose location can be clearly identified, such as continuous weather broadcasts.

Equipment for Low- and Medium-Frequency Bands

Radio direction finders for reception of radio beacons and AM broadcast-band stations consist of conventional solid-state receivers with a rotatable antenna and a "null" indicator. In some situations, there may be doubt as to which of two reciprocal directions is the correct bearing; for such times, a separate sense antenna is desirable. With manual RDFs, the antenna is rotated by hand, and the direction is read from a scale around its base. For the more expensive ADFs, the antenna is rotated electronically, and the direction is read from a dial or small display.

There is essentially no "installation" required for an RDF or ADF, as they are normally powered by internal dry-cell batteries, although some models can be connected to the boat's 12-volt DC system (very light drain). One caution, however: The set *must* be calibrated for "radio deviation" at a specific location on the boat, and it must always be used from that location, or a new deviation table will be needed.

Hand-held RDFs are available that include a built-in compass for direct reading of the direction to the source of the radio signals.

Equipment for VHF Direction Finding

Automatic radio direction finding on VHF radio signals can be done with either a special model of communications transceiver or with an accessory unit that can be connected to any regular VHF/FM radiotelephone. In either case, a special antenna must be installed in addition to the normal VHF whip for sending and receiving.

Radio bearings on VHF are often less precise than on the

lower frequencies. The most often used application is in homing on signals from other vessels.

EPIRBs

The full name is so long—Emergency Position-Indicating Radio Beacon—that the acronym is universally used. This is a small device, powered by an internal battery, that when activated sends out a signal indicating distress. Present models do not identify the vessel in distress or the nature of the problem, nor is there any communications capability. Its sole functions are first to alert authorities that there is a ship or a boat in distress, and second to assist search and rescue units in locating that vessel. Incidentally, the signals that are transmitted are identical to those from a downed airplane—the EPIRB is a marine version of an aircraft's Emergency Locator Transmitter (ELT).

Class A and Class B EPIRBs

There are two general categories of EPIRBs, with two types in one of them. Class A and Class B units operate on two *aircraft* VHF frequencies, 121.5 and 243 MHz. These are the "guard" or emergency frequencies that are listened to by many planes, both civilian and military. An aircraft pilot hearing an EPIRB signal informs air traffic control authorities, who in turn notify the Coast Guard. In some instances, the pilot can roughly determine the location of the distress situation by observing changes in the signal strength as the plane passes by, or the location can be approximated from two or more reports. The signals from these types of EPIRBs are also received on certain U.S. and Soviet satellites and retransmitted to any ground stations that may be within "sight." This method of signal relay is not continuously available, but it has been effective in many emergency situations.

The difference between Class A and Class B units is that the former are capable of floating free from a sinking vessel and activating automatically; these are required on small, passenger-carrying vessels. The Class B EPIRBs are simpler in design and less costly; they are carried voluntarily on many recreational and fishing craft. If your boating takes you out of range for VHF/FM communications and if the cost of an SSB transceiver is not justified, you surely should consider carrying an EPIRB on your boat; these small units have brought prompt help to many a boater in trouble far offshore.

Class C EPIRBs

The Class C EPIRB is a newer type and quite different in operation from the older ones, although generally similar in size and appearance. It, too, provides an alerting and locating signal without communications capacity, but this type operates in the VHF/FM marine communications band. A very brief signal is sent out on Channel 16, the distress and calling frequency, followed by longer but not continuous transmissions on Channel 15. The transmitted sound is the standard radiotelephone alarm signal of two different tones alternated rapidly, an easily recognized signal of distress.

These units were primarily developed to be carried by small craft that were not fitted with a VHF/FM radiotelephone; the concept was to give these boats an inexpensive means of calling for help when in distress. In actuality, their cost is greater than for the least expensive VHF transceivers with much more power plus full communications capabilities, and thus they have never become popular. The range of a Class C EPIRB is not greater than that of a VHF/FM radio and normally will be considerably less. Their carriage on boats with communication radios is unnecessary, except as a backup in case of failure of the main radio, or to be taken off in a life raft if one has to "abandon ship."

Licenses

EPIRBs of any type are self-contained units and require no installation other than perhaps a bracket to hold the set securely in rough weather. An FCC license is required, as this device transmits a radio signal. A Class C EPIRB is already covered by your license for a VHF/FM radio station if you have one, but a Class A or Class B unit will require modification of that license to add the new frequencies if you did not check the box for its frequencies when you filled out the application form. If you have no station license, you will have to get one.

"Second generation" EPIRBs

Because of the limitations of the EPIRB system at 121.5 and 243.0 MHz, development is well under way on a new system to operate at 406.25 MHz. A satellite in this new system will receive the EPIRB signal and be able to store it until its next pass over a ground station, at which time it will retransmit the signal—this will provide worldwide coverage. The 406.25 MHz signals will also carry much more information than at present, such as an identification number, and perhaps the nature of the emergency plus location data if the EPIRB is interfaced with a Loran-C or other radionavigation receiver.

The new EPIRBs will be much more valuable to boatmen and mariners, but they will also be much more expensive, at least initially, with a price several times that of current models.

Inverters

An electric power inverter for your boat is just the opposite of a battery charger. With an inverter, the input is low-voltage DC power and the output is 120-volt, 60 Hz AC electricity. If your boat does not have an auxiliary engine-driven AC generating plant (see Chapter 8), you will find an inverter useful for TV sets, stereo systems, tape recorders, electric typewriters, and similar electrical or electronic loads. Inverters are *not* suitable for heavy-load devices such as stoves, coffee makers, etc. Under some conditions, however, inverters can be used to power an "apartment size" 120-volt AC refrigerator to avoid running an auxiliary generating plant while under way or at anchor.

Inverters are available in a wide range of power ratings, but as the ratings go up, the input current requirements get very high! (For 12-volt boats, divide the load wattage by 12, then multiply by 1.2 for solid-state inverters or 1.5 for mechanical units—this gives the amperes to be drawn from the DC system.) A practical limit for 12-volt DC inverters is about 500 watts, although units are available up to 1,250 watts—figure that out for yourself in terms of amperes from your battery! On 32-volt DC systems, inverters for loads from 1,000 up to 2,500 watts are feasible. These ratings are for continuous loads; all models can take momentary surges—such as for the starting of motors—up to three to five times as great as the steady-state rating.

Solid-State or Mechanical?

Inverters operate by either rotating machinery or solid-state electronics. Each method has its advantages and its disadvantages. A solid-state inverter will operate at higher efficiency (up to 90%), but the output will typically be a square wave rather than the normal sine wave of shore AC power, and the frequency may be off from 60 Hz by a few Hertz; this can be a problem with some electronic equipment. At least one manufacturer offers a solid-state inverter with a "modified sine wave" output—this may solve the difficulty with devices that are "fussy" about the type of AC power supplied to them. A DC motor turning an AC alternator—sometimes called a "motor-generator set"—will produce pure sine-wave AC power with better voltage regulation for varying load conditions. The efficiency of operation will be less, on the order of 65% for 12-volt models, and thus more input power will be taken from your boat's battery for the same AC output. In some models there will be a single armature with two separate windings, for the DC input and the AC output.

Installation

Inverters must be located where the heat generated by their less-than-100% efficiency can be adequately dissipated. The DC input current will be great; therefore, leads should run directly to the battery and be as short as possible. Be sure to use heavy enough wire (see Chapter 3); check the input voltage at the inverter with the heaviest normal load applied.

Control Circuits

Some solid-state inverters draw a small but continuous "idling" current even if there is no AC load. This can be eliminated by use of a load-sensing device that will turn the unit completely off in the absence of any demands for output, but will turn it on automatically whenever AC power is required. Also available as accessories are voltmeters and ammeters to monitor the output, and automatic switchover devices to transfer the load immediately to shore-power circuits when such electricity becomes available.

A great convenience is to have a double-pole, double-throw (DPDT) switch of adequate capacity to switch the circuits of AC duplex outlets throughout your boat from the shore-power line to the inverter output. This will provide you with 120-volt AC electricity wherever you might need it, but be sure when you shift to inverter power that some heavy load is not plugged in and turned on!

Refrigeration

Refrigeration for food and drink on a boat is a system much like air-conditioning—the removal of heat from where it is undesirable, and its disposal where it can do no harm. These are fundamentally mechanical processes, but electrical energy is used for pumps and compressors and for control functions.

Mechanical or Electrical?

A wide variety of designs is available and various combinations should be considered in selecting the best system for your boat. The compressor can be mechanically operated by a belt drive from the main engine, or it can be operated by an electrical motor. The heat removed from the box can be dissipated into the air of the interior of the boat; or it can be absorbed by a flow of water drawn from the body in which the craft is floating and discharged back into that body. There can be a combined refrigerator-freezer, or one or both units separately.

A mechanically driven compressor eliminates one electric motor and a major battery drain, but it requires that space be available near the engine. Insulated tubing must be run to and from the evaporator unit in the refrigerator or freezer. Refrigerating action is available only when running the engine. In general, use of this type will require closer attention to insulation of the box because of the more intermittent nature of heat removal.

Direct radiation of removed heat into the boat eliminates the need for one electric motor-driven pump, plus a through-hull fitting, seacock, and raw-water strainer. This heat, however, may not be desirable in the interior of your boat in hot weather. (If you are running your air conditioner, this heat will have to be moved again, this time to outside the boat!)

Planning

Study the options carefully—their advantages and disadvantages—including the electrical power required for each. Consider the physical mounting problems as well as the wiring requirements. A refrigeration project will require carpentry and mechanical as well as electrical skills, but these should not be beyond the abilities of a skipper who has suitable tools and who works carefully. Install any necessary switches and power wires in accordance with Chapter 23.

NavText Receivers

Weather information is transmitted continuously from many locations on special VHF channels; these, however, have a rather limited range. To extend the reception range for such data, and also other forms of safety information of interest to mariners, the NavText service has been established. In U.S. waters, Coast Guard-operated transmitters on 518 kHz have regular schedules, coordinated among stations to avoid interference; the service is also operated in many foreign countries. These broadcasts are received on special receivers on vessels. For large ships that are required to have NavText receivers, the plain-text English-language information is printed out on paper. Such sets can be used on boats, but less expensive models are available that have an LCD display of several lines of text that can be scrolled up or down.

The high-tech design of NavText receivers permits storing messages, so the receiver need not be continuously attended. As messages are later viewed or printed out, they are removed from memory to make room for new incoming information. A receiver can be programmed to ignore certain types of messages if these are of no interest to that craft but will always record dis-

YOUR BOAT'S ELECTRICAL SYSTEM

tress and urgent safety broadcasts. Alarms can be set to sound when any message is received, or only when a distress or an urgent message is received; on printing models, a paper-out alarm can be set.

Cellular Telephones

Cellular mobile telephones have become almost a necessity for business and professional men and women whose activities keep them in their automobiles a good part of each working day. They have even become something of a status symbol for individuals who may not find them a necessity! While not part of the marine radio service, cellular telephones can be used on boats, and frequently to very good advantage.

The cellular telephone service offers several advantages over connections through a marine operator on the channels that are part of every marine VHF transceiver. Many more channels are available, with no delays; direct dialing out (no operator needed) and direct dialing in to you; clearer, more readable transmissions; and complete privacy for your conversations. Full telephone services, such as call waiting, call forwarding, speed dialing, connection to a computer modem, etc., are possible. On the negative side, cellular telephones are relatively expensive, and their range will normally be less than that of the VHF ship-to-shore service. Cellular service is also more expensive, and prior arrangements may be necessary to use your set beyond the limits of your local company.

Cellular telephones are available in models that are for permanent installation, transportable units, and hand-helds. All of these can be used on boats; a model intended for installation in a car can also be used on a boat if a duplicate mounting bracket is purchased.

There is no installation required for a transportable or hand-held unit, as this has a built-in battery power supply and an antenna. A cellular phone of the automobile type will require mounting of its bracket, and connection to an antenna and a source of 12-volt DC power. On your boat, a proper marine-type antenna should be used if the greatest range is to be obtained; it should be mounted as high as practicable, but the length of coax cable should be kept as short as possible.

"Ham" Radio

Amateur radio operation is a "natural" for boating. Equipment is more complex in operation, but less expensive and more flexible in use than marine single-sideband sets. A wide range of frequencies is available, and there are a number of "nets" operated by seagoing hams for safety and fellowship purposes. The FCC requires that both equipment and operator be licensed in the amateur service. The operator license requires a knowledge of both radio theory and Morse code. There is, however, a graduated series of licenses—you can start as a "novice" and work your way up to technician, general, advanced, and extra class. There are increasing operating privileges at each level, and you can move up as fast as you are able. Information on amateur radio licenses, and on the hobby as a whole, can be obtained from local stores that specialize in ham equipment, or by mail from the American Radio Relay League, Newington, CT 06111.

Installation will be much like that for a marine SSB transceiver. Electrical noise can be a problem for single-sideband radio reception, either marine service or amateur service; see Chapters 20 and 41 for suppression measures.

Weather Facsimile Receivers

Many types of weather maps are constantly being transmitted by radio; some of these can be of great value to an offshore skipper. Facsimile ("fax") units receive the signals and print them out as a weather map—current surface conditions, forecasts, and specialized maps such as conditions at various altitudes. Models of facsimile equipment are available that include the radio receiver or that can be connected to an existing receiver. Either type is an expensive item, but one that could save your life on an ocean passage.

Installation consists only of securely mounting the unit, and connecting to an antenna and source of 12-volt DC power.

Rudder Angle Indicators

A small, inexpensive electrical device, but one that can be very useful, is a rudder angle indicator. A sender unit is connected to the arm or quadrant at the top of the rudder post, and a meter-type indicator is mounted near the helm position, where it can be easily read. A small cable between these units and a pair of power leads complete the job. (The sender is much like the rudder position sensor used in some autopilots, but the same unit cannot be used for both purposes, unless the autopilot system is so designed.) The current drain is quite slight, but a small SPST switch should be included in the positive power lead so the device can be turned off when its use is not needed.

With careful attention to the installation instructions for the mechanical linkage from sensor to rudder arm, the indicator will read the actual rudder angle in degrees on its calibrated scale. Information on rudder position is desirable when initially getting under way and in performing maneuvers in tight spaces. It's hardly a necessary instrument, but it can be very useful.

Omega Navigation Receivers

The Loran-C electronic navigation system described in Chapter 31 provides excellent positioning information where it has coverage—U.S. coastal waters, plus portions of the North Atlantic Ocean and the Mediterranean Sea. It is not a global system, however, and the cruising yachtsman deep in the Caribbean, the South Atlantic, the South Pacific, or other distant waters must use another system. The Omega Navigation System uses very-low-frequency (VLF) signals from eight transmitters to cover essentially the whole earth. A complex receiver is required, but through the marvels of integrated circuits and microprocessors, operation by you is simplicity itself, with output in terms of latitude and longitude. Omega receivers will also provide navigational computations such as great circle tracks. Omega is a competitor to satellite navigation—it does not provide as accurate locations, but it does provide a continuous flow of position data.

The installation of an Omega receiver consists of little more than mounting the set and a simple whip antenna, plus making a power connection to your boat's electrical system. (Incidentally, an Omega receiver must be left on continuously to track the signals; if tracking is interrupted, it must be reset at a position of known coordinates.) If you follow the manufacturer's instructions carefully, you probably will not need the services of a technician; an FCC license is not required.

CHAPTER 43

Miscellaneous Projects

THIS CHAPTER will include a number of smaller projects that do not fit into one of the major subdivisions of this book. Also included will be several items of "shop practice," hints and kinks about the use of tools in boat electrical and electronic projects.

Battery Paralleling

In Chapter 24 it was recommended that your boat have two batteries, one for engine starting and the other for general service loads such as lights, pump, radios, etc. This (in theory, at least) ensures that you will always have an adequately charged

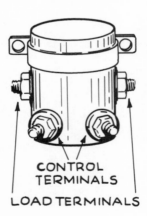

CONTROL
TERMINALS

LOAD TERMINALS

Fig. 43-1 A "starting solenoid," or relay, can be used for any type of heavy-duty switching. Some models have only one control terminal with the other end of the coil connected internally to one of the load terminals, or grounded to the case.

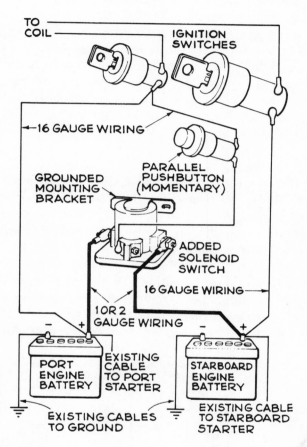

Fig. 43-2 By adding a new solenoid and a push-button momentary switch, you can parallel the two batteries any time you wish by merely pressing the push-button switch.

battery for starting your engine after a period at anchor or at a pier without shore power. Alas, this is not always so, due to charging failures, circuit leakage, or other causes. The need then is for a means of paralleling both batteries to get the engine started, after which, it is hoped, the alternator can recharge the low battery.

Paralleling can be accomplished by the use of "jumper ca-bles," as used between two automobiles. This is, however, awk-ward and can be a safety hazard. Since in this case the two batteries are quite near to each other and solidly secured, the paralleling wires can be permanently installed, to be activated when needed by a remote switch mounted conveniently near the starting switch. As the currents in engine starting are very great, it is necessary to use a heavy-duty relay, generally called a start-ing solenoid; see Figure 43-1 and Chapter 9. A simple circuit for this shown in Figure 43-2.

Automatic Paralleling

A variation of emergency paralleling procedures is shown in Figure 43-3. Here a twin-engine boat has a separate starting bat-tery for each engine. Turning either ignition switch parallels the two batteries to start that engine. The batteries are paralleled only for as long as the key switch is turned against spring pres-sure to the "start" position; the paralleling is disconnected in the "run" or "ignition on" position. Two small diodes—whose cur-rent rating need only be large enough to handle the solenoid coil current, an ampere or two—are used to isolate the two key switches so that each starts its own engine only. Be certain to

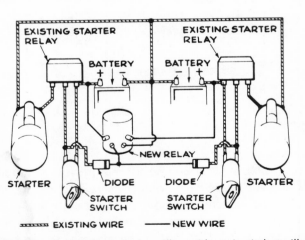

Fig 43-3 Adding one relay and two diodes will provide a circuit that will start either engine using both batteries in parallel.

install the diodes in the correct orientation so that current can flow in the desired direction, but the opposite flow will be blocked. Use of this circuit will routinely use both batteries for every start, thus reducing to half the maximum load that is ever placed on either battery.

Alternate Energy Sources

Yes, there are alternate electrical energy sources for boats—perhaps not nuclear or coal, but definitely solar, wind, and hydro. These are (for now, anyway) quite limited in their power output and relatively expensive, but they do exist, and technological advances are surely ahead.

Solar Power

Photovoltaic cells produce DC electricity directly from sunlight. A number of cells are mounted together to form a solar panel, which typically is square or rectangular, with a surface area of one to five square feet; multiple panels can be installed. The panels are light in weight and not more than one inch thick; they can be mounted on almost any surface, and can even be walked on if a protective clear glass or Plexiglas cover is installed. The individual cells are connected in series to produce the desired voltage, usually about 14 to 16 volts for batteries. Such strings of cells in series can then be connected in parallel to provide a greater current output. The positive line from the solar panel to the battery should have an in-line fuse of appropriate rating. A regulator is desirable for all but the smallest installations; but if one is not used, be sure to put a small diode in the line to prevent reverse current from discharging the battery at night and on cloudy, rainy days.

Only a relatively small amount of electricity can be produced by present-day cells; but for any boat on a mooring away from shore power, or for a sailboat on a long cruise under sail, every little bit helps. A storage battery loses charge at the rate of about 8 to 10% per week even if no loads are applied; any intermittent operation of a bilge pump adds to this loss of charge. A lead-acid storage battery will have a longer life if kept up to full charge, and a solar panel is excellent for this; a small one will do, but a larger one will be needed if other loads are to be placed on your boat's battery. The greatest amount would be generated if the cells were on an angled mount so as to be at a right angle to the rays of sunlight, and rotated to track the sun. This is not feasible on a boat, and solar panels usually are mounted horizontally—it has been said that a panel so mounted will produce in 8 hours the same amount of electrical energy as a sun-tracking panel would in 6 hours. This would most likely be valid in lower latitudes, where the sun is more nearly overhead at all times of the year, but effectiveness would be even less in high latitudes, especially in winter. In many situations, the output of a solar panel on a boat actually may not be more than a third of its manufacturer's rating. Presently available solar panels, costing several hundred dollars, produce ½ to 2½ amperes of current. Multiply this by the hours of full sunlight or only very light haze that you can expect per day or per week and you get the number of ampere-hours (AH) of battery charging you can expect from a day of sailing or a week of nonuse while sitting at a mooring. It is not much, but it can keep a well-charged, good-condition storage battery "topped off." This is "trickle charging" at its best; any possibility of overcharging probably will be offset by the occasional consumption of power by a bilge pump or other intermittent light load. Heavy loads, such as refrigerators, are out, and foggy or cloudy days don't count! Solar panels have one feature that is often overlooked: They are totally quiet—no noise to disturb you on a quiet sail or that afternoon at anchor!

In some applications, solar energy is put directly to work. Ventilators are available that can be installed in a cabintop and that contain both a small fan and an integral solar panel. One model includes its own Ni-Cad battery to keep the fan running when the sun goes under a cloud, or sets for the night. Other models consist of two separate units—a small fan for interior air circulation that is wired directly to its own solar panel on the exterior of the boat.

Solar cell panels are almost, but not quite, maintenance-free. To maintain their efficiency in conversion of light to electricity, they must be kept clean. Wash regularly with soap and water, and more often if they accumulate a coating of salt.

Wind power

A wind generator—the seagoing counterpart of a farmer's windmill—is a possibility under way, at anchor, or at a mooring. If you are under way there will, of course, be some relative wind (except when going downwind at wind speed); on a mooring or at anchor, the wind will be less uniform and less dependable. Because, however, this device is electromechanical, a greater amount of energy than solar cells can be produced, with some units up to 4 amperes or more, at a voltage high enough to charge a 12-volt battery.

Size, and available space to mount it so it can swivel into the wind from any direction, are the principal limitations to a wind-driven generator on a boat. (It also is not any too "nautical" and may attract some comments from your fellow boaters.) Approximately 10 knots of wind are required to start generation of electricity, and the output increases with stronger winds; voltage regulators are required with all but the smallest units. All available units have a maximum wind rating, and some provision must be made for the removal, disassembly, and safe storage of a wind generator when a storm threatens. The cost of a wind generator varies with the size; generally it is more than for a solar panel, but remember that the output is several times greater.

Water Power

Electrical energy can also be derived from turning a rotor by its movement through the water resulting from the forward speed of your boat. The generator concerned is quite like that turned by the wind's action—in fact, one model uses the same generating unit for either application, with windmill-like vanes for air-driven action and with a towed rotor, much like an old-fashioned taffrail log, for water-driven action. Another version of a hydrogenerator looks quite like a small outboard motor of 2 horsepower or so. It clamps onto the rail or a bracket and extends down into the water at the stern of your boat. In general, water-driven generators are intended for sailboats with speeds in the 3- to 8-knot range. They are, of course, not suited for use on boats at moorings for extended periods—here wind-driven generators or solar panels should be used.

A hydrogenerator does add a bit of drag to your boat's forward motion, but not enough to be of any concern in nonracing situations. Costs of water-driven units are comparable with those of wind generators; the combination air- and water-driven model is the most expensive. Power ratings are at least as good as for wind-driven designs, and some are better.

On-board Telephone Service

If you live aboard, or if you spend much time on board while moored in a marina slip, it can be a great convenience to have telephone service on your boat. Special inlet fittings can be installed on the side of your boat or where convenient in the cockpit. A matching plug and cord provide the connection to the telephone lines on the pier.

Within your boat you can install modular telephone jacks (available from stores such as Radio Shack) at one or more suitable places and move a compact phone (also available at Radio Shack or the telephone company) from location to location to fit your activities.

Lighting with 12-Volt AC Power

Many boats that are based at a marina or yacht club spend most of their time moored in their slip. When owners work or relax inside their boats at such times, it is often convenient to use the regular 12-volt cabin lights powered by the craft's storage battery.

Unless the boat is equipped with an automatic charging system, there is the continual problem of maintaining the batteries in a fully charged condition. This is especially true of smaller craft that use an outboard motor for power. It is a total problem when the boat is laid up for the winter and the battery has been removed. The only way to get light inside while working on board, especially under a cover, is to bring a portable droplight aboard or to use flashlights.

A simple solution to these problems will cost less than $20 or so plus an hour or so of your time. This will permit lights to be used as much as you wish without harm to your battery—or even if there is no battery aboard. The solution involves powering your boat's regular 12-volt lights with 12 volts AC rather than with DC power from the battery. Unlike most of the low-voltage electronic and electrical devices on your boat, lights will not be harmed by alternating current; they will work equally well on AC or DC.

Installation

All that is needed is a single-pole, double-throw (SPDT) switch, an SPST switch, and a small transformer with a secondary winding rated for 12.6 volts at 5 or 6 amperes (more or less, depending on the number of lights that may be turned on). A small bulb will draw 1 to 1.5 amperes, while a house-size 25-watt bulb will draw 2 amperes. The hookup is simple: Disconnect the feed wire for "cabin lights" at the distribution panel and run it

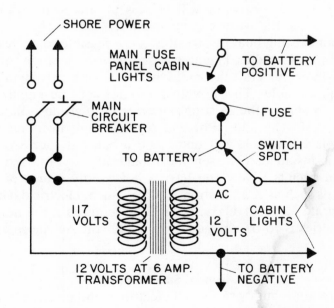

Fig. 43-4 Often overlooked is the possibility of using AC to power a boat's lights when dockside and connected to shorepower.

to the center terminal of the newly installed SPDT switch. Mount the transformer in a convenient, protected location and wire in its primary through a new SPST off-on switch. Connect one side of the transformer secondary to ground and the other to one side of the SPDT switch; connect the other side of that switch to the battery's positive terminal. The completed circuit will look like Figure 43-4. If you do not have an onboard connection for shore power, you can connect the transformer to a long cord with a male plug at the end; this can be plugged into an outlet on the pier when needed.

A 32-Volt Electrical System

Nearly all recreational boats have 12-volt DC electric systems. If one or more very heavy loads are installed, or planned, the merits of a 32-volt DC system should be considered. Machinery and other devices will operate at greater efficiency. Some equipment not practical at 12 volts will become feasible at 32 volts. Inverters for heavier AC loads become practical at the higher voltage. Current in wires will be less for the same amount of power; hence the wires can be smaller.

On an existing boat, it probably is not feasible to make a total conversion, including engine starting motors, ignition, etc. But on a twin-engine craft the addition of a 32-volt subsystem can be quite practicable. The 12-volt alternator on one engine is retained to charge the existing batteries through an isolator; see Chapter 24. The alternator and regulator on the other engine are replaced with 32-volt units, and a bank of four 8-volt batteries is installed. (This engine retains its 12-volt starting and ignition circuits.) Now you have a heavy-duty source of power for loads such as refrigeration, anchor winch, electric davits, etc. A separate 32-volt DC charger will be required if the new bank of batteries is to be charged from a 120-volt AC shore connection.

Assorted Small Projects

There are a number of small electronic and electrical projects that can profitably occupy your time during the off-season, or even on a day when the weather makes it inadvisable to leave your slip or mooring but when it is still a pleasure just to be on board your craft. These will be mentioned here as "food for thought" without detailed instructions—just the general guidance to plan thoroughly before buying material, to follow the manufacturer's instructions, and to check all your work carefully before turning on the power switch for the first time.

You can install an automatic fuel shutoff valve controlled by the ignition key switch. This valve goes as close to the fuel tank as possible and is a definite "plus" for safety. Additionally, it can provide a degree of theft protection if located as inconspicuously as possible.

Closely related to the above project is an electrically controlled shutoff valve for LPG fuel if you have that type of stove. A small panel can be located adjacent to the stove, with the actual valve at the propane tank—another "plus" for safety.

Replace an old electrical distribution panel that uses fuses with a modern one having circuit breakers. If the panel has been in use for a number of years, it is likely that both the switches and the fuseholders have deteriorated from the malign effects of a marine environment. Anticipate problems; head them off before they develop.

Inspect all wiring, especially in the engine compartment, where temperatures are higher than elsewhere. Check insulation for cracks and frayed places. Terminals and connectors deserve special attention; clean or replace as needed.

Treat your engine to an electronic ignition system. With the dampness normal in a boat, it's a wonder that most engines start as easily as they do. If yours is a hard starter, a capacitor-discharge system can help. Installation is easy, and a bypass switch is included if the electronic components give trouble later.

If there are more than 20 feet of coax cable between your VHF radio and its antenna, and if you are using the small RG-58 type, get some new, low-loss RG-8X (or, better yet, RG-213) cable, and get more signal into the air.

HINTS AND KINKS

Making Coax Cable Connections

Coaxial cable—commonly called just "coax"—is used between VHF and CB radios and their antennas. Often when you buy an antenna, the cable will be connected (molded in) at the antenna end, and there will be a connector on the other end ready to be plugged into the set. There will be times, however, when you want to shorten a lead-in, cut the cable to pass it through a cabin side, make up an extension, or for some other reason need to install a connector on coax cable. Although this may appear complicated, with the right tools it's no problem.

For the smaller cable RG-58 (never use the similar-appearing RG-59!), you will need a PL-259 plug with a UG-175 adapter—these are military designations but have been commonly adopted; the Radio Shack part numbers are 278-705 and 278-206, respectively. For the larger coax cable, type RG-8 or RG-213, which should be used for any lengths over 20 feet, use the PL-259 without the adapter. These cables, both sizes, have a vinyl outer jacket, a braided shield, inner insulation, and a center conductor. The PL-259 plug must be used to match the coax cable properly at each end, both mechanically and electronically.

The series of illustrations in Figure 43-5 show you step by step

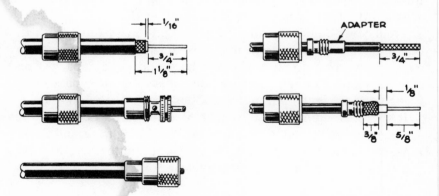

Fig. 43-5 Instructions for installing connectors on larger (RG-8/U) and smaller (RG-58/U) coaxial cable.

how to put a PL-259 connector on RG-58 cable, using the adapter. Use of the "solderless" type of PL-259 is not recommended.

A connector is placed on RG-8 cable by stripping back the outer vinyl covering and inner braid to the dimensions also shown in Figure 43-5. Slide the connecting ring on, threads facing the exposed braid. Then screw the body of the plug onto the cable; it will make its own threads in the vinyl outer jacket. Solder the braid through the holes as you did for the smaller cable,

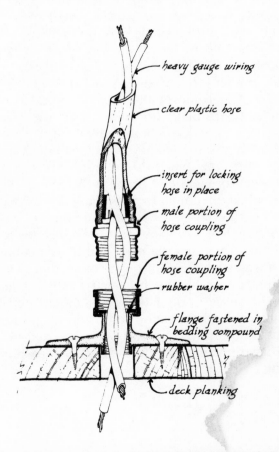

heavy gauge wiring

clear plastic hose

insert for locking hose in place

male portion of hose coupling

female portion of hose coupling

rubber washer

flange fastened in bedding compound

deck planking

Fig. 43-6 A water-tight method of bringing heavy-gauge electrical wires through a weather deck or other exposed surface.

then solder the central conductor as before. Screw the coupling ring down on the plug, and you're finished—simpler even than when the adapter is used.

Through-Deck Fittings for Heavy Wires

You may have situations in which you must feed a pair of heavy-gauge wires through the deck of your boat in a manner that will not result in leaks—for example, to power an anchor winch or an electric davit.

Marine stores sell waterproof fittings that generally are designed for passing an antenna wire or small coax cable; these, however, are limited to a single wire up to about ¼-inch diameter. Fittings suitable for large wires or pairs of large wire are more difficult to find. You can make your own as follows:

Use a water-inlet fitting designed for hooking up to a dockside water supply. This comes with a female-threaded collar for accepting the standard male-threaded end of a garden hose. Run the heavy-gauge electric wires through a short length of ¾-inch clear vinyl tubing; to the end of this tubing attach a male garden hose fitting—the type that is sold at hardware stores for making repairs when an original end fitting wears out or is damaged.

Drill a hole large enough to pass the wires through the deck. Mount the inlet fitting on the deck, bedding it in well with compound to avoid any leaks. Now pass the wires down through the fitting and hole, then join the male and female connections, and you have a watertight feed-through connection. The clear vinyl tubing should extend up to the electric motor being powered, and there the space around the wires should be plugged with silicone rubber or other sealing compound to prevent the entry of water at the point; an up-and-over, inverted-U bend in the tubing will also prevent any downward passage of water in the clear tubing.

CHAPTER 44

Preventive Maintenance

THE "TROUBLESHOOTING" aspects of electrical and electronic equipment maintenance have been discussed in the various chapters on different types of equipment. Here we will cover "preventive maintenance"—efforts you should make on a regular basis to, insofar as possible, eliminate in advance any need for troubleshooting. Preventive maintenance is often referred to as "PM"; this is fine, as the same initials also stand for "planned maintenance."

Basic Actions

Preventive maintenance consists of careful inspections, plus various actions such as lubricating, tightening, cleaning, etc. *The most important thing about preventive maintenance is that it must be done on a regular, scheduled basis.* This does not mean that an entire checklist will be executed every time—some items will require monthly attention, others weekly, or only semiannual or annual attention—but it does mean that you should stick to your schedule, whatever it is.

Inspection is a vital part of preventive maintenance and is often overlooked. Some checklist items may be of a dual nature—always inspect, but act only if required by what you see. You may not have to take any action at all at some points in your electrical system, but you must look to assure yourself that all is well. A checklist is a very personalized matter—it is specific to you and your boat. You cannot just go out and buy one that will fit, although such may serve as a starter for your own

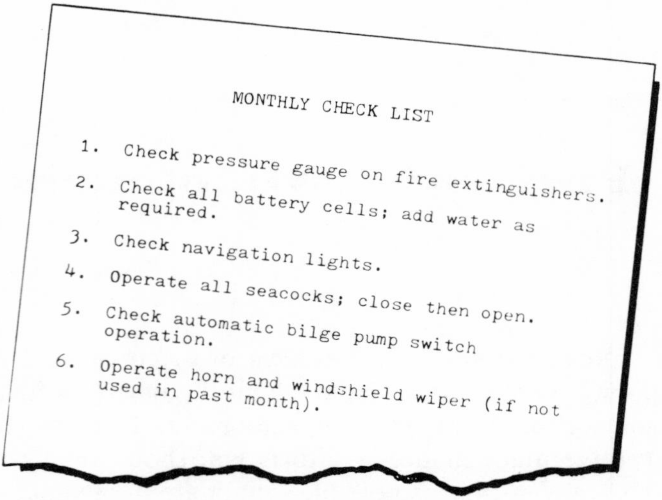

```
                    MONTHLY CHECK LIST

   1.  Check pressure gauge on fire extinguishers.
   2.  Check all battery cells; add water as
       required.
   3.  Check navigation lights.
   4.  Operate all seacocks; close then open.
   5.  Check automatic bilge pump switch
       operation.
   6.  Operate horn and windshield wiper (if not
       used in past month).
```

Fig. 44-1 Typical monthly check list (extract).

personalized list. Think out your checklist very carefully, and expect to add to it from time to time.

BATTERIES

The most obvious item of storage battery preventive maintenance is regular checks of fluid level in each cell, but there are other items that should be done on a set schedule. The top surfaces of a battery should be cleaned semiannually (more often if needed) with a cloth moistened in a solution of baking soda and water. Make sure that all caps are on tightly, and do not get any of the cleaning solution down into the cells. After cleaning, wipe off with a rag moistened with clean water and then dry the battery top completely. Careful attention to this routine maintenance will aid in preventing formation of corrosion and leakage of charge across the battery's top between terminals.

Terminals

Corrosion and looseness at battery terminals affect the entire electrical system, but more so for heavy loads, and worst of all the engine starting circuit, with its hundreds of amperes. Conditions at a battery terminal may be such that electrical power is available for lights, radios, etc., but the starting motor will be unable to crank the engine. Thorough cleaning of terminals of the "post" type can be accomplished with a special wire brush tool obtainable at automotive supply stores. Terminals of the "lug" (bus) type can be cleaned with a knife and an ordinary wire brush. Special chemically treated pads shaped like doughnuts that will eliminate or greatly reduce corrosion are available to fit over post terminals. There are terminal protective coatings now sold in spray cans that may also be used; these can reach into smaller spaces and crevices than the more traditional smeared-on coat of petroleum jelly, but the latter can be used if no better method is available.

Voltage Regulator

The voltage regulator is a vital part of your boat's electrical system. An electromechanical regulator is more likely to need attention than the alternator; a solid-state regulator is less likely to have troubles. Watch your ammeter—and voltmeter, if you have one—to be sure all is well. Adjustment of a voltage regulator is covered in Chapter 6, but this requires a rather delicate touch, and you may want to refer this task to an experienced service technician. Replacement of an external voltage regulator is a simple do-it-yourself project.

Fig. 44-2 Frayed insulation indicates mechanical damage; look for cause and correct it. It can cause electrical leakage and eventual deterioration of the current-carrying conductor.

WIRING

If current is the "life-giving blood" of the many electrical and electronic devices on your boat, the wires are the "arteries and veins." Wiring is too often forgotten as a possible, even probable, source of system troubles; careful inspection is the key item of preventive maintenance.

Wires must carry the needed current with a voltage drop that is not excessive—use 3% for critical loads such as electronic devices and 10% for noncritical loads such as cabin lights, pumps, etc. Even if the initial installation job was done correctly, excessive voltage drops can develop later from broken strands in the wire, corrosion in terminal lugs, dirty contacts at terminals, and mechanical connections that have loosened up. Wires that have been reduced in size by broken strands, and corroded terminals, must be replaced, but bad connections can be cleaned with a knife or sandpaper and then retightened.

Fuses

If you use fuses—either in clips at a distribution panel or in in-line holders—check each end of each fuse for dirty or corroded contacts. If the fuses are in clips or other friction holders, check the tension of the holder. Make sure the spring of an in-line holder still supplies enough pressure against the ends of the fuse for good, low-resistance contact and that corrosion has not developed.

Leakage

Leakage can occur from electrical wires, just as it can from hoses and tubing. Damaged insulation is the usual cause, but this will also require moisture and dirt. Wires that have had their insulation chafed may be salvaged with tape, or they may have to be replaced; be sure to make physical changes as required to prevent the chafing action from continuing. Keep wires up, well clear of bilge water; install more support clips if needed (see Chapter 23). "Hot" wires should not pass over sharp metal edges, especially those of grounded metal objects such as engines. Insulation in high-temperature areas such as engine compartments may become brittle and cracked; this is less likely to occur if the proper type has been used (see Chapter 2). Leakage is a particular source of trouble with the high-voltage wiring of an ignition system.

Leakage in your boat's 12-volt DC electrical system can be checked by removing the cable from the battery's positive terminal when all loads are turned off. First, bridge the gap with a test light as shown in Chapter 19. If the bulb glows, you probably have left something turned on. If it does not glow, you can make a more sensitive test for leakage current by substituting a milliammeter for the test light—start with higher current scales and work down to lower ranges to make a measurement. Ideally, the reading should be 0, but a few milliamperes probably will show on the meter.

ELECTRICAL EQUIPMENT

The principal preventive maintenance action for electrical equipment is ensuring adequate voltage as discussed above. Pumps, motors of all types, and lights need adequate voltage. Lubrication may be required of some motors, but not for many used on boats. Larger motors may need to have their brushes checked for excessive wear. Submersible bilge pumps are particular candidates for leakage tests; with the motor off, a milliammeter in the positive lead should show no current flow.

Bonding circuits should be carefully checked for good contacts to ensure the system's effectiveness.

Electrical gauges and instruments will not read correctly if contacts have become dirty or corroded and resistance has built up. Annually, all contacts on the instrument panel should be cleaned—take off only one wire at a time, or carefully label each wire to get it back on the correct terminal. For continued adequate instrument illumination, remove panel lights and clean their contacts; also at this time, clean any dust and dirt off the bulbs. If any pair of DC wires is not twisted together, take this opportunity to do so to lessen their effect on your boat's compass (if you do this, however, you should recheck your deviation table). After completion of this work, spray the entire back side of the panel with a moisture-and-corrosion-inhibiting aerosol spray.

ELECTRONIC EQUIPMENT

Cleanliness and dryness are essential to the proper operation of electronic equipment. Much of newer, solid-state electronic equipment will be in sealed cases that restrict the entrance of dirt and moisture. Some units, however, will have vents for dissipating internal heat. Here you will have to remove covers, clean dust and dirt out with a soft brush, and use a moisture-inhibiting spray. When such gear is not in use, it can be partially protected with fitted covers of canvas or other heavy fabrics; do not use plastic, as moisture may be trapped and conditions made worse rather than better.

Radiotelephones

Modern VHF/FM radios require little preventive maintenance, but this is no reason to omit what is desirable. Measure voltage at the terminals with the set turned off, while receiving, and while transmitting on full power. The change in voltage should be very slight, well under ½ volt; if it is more, check the power wiring.

If you have not used your radio for a month or more, make an on-the-air "radio check"—but use a working channel rather than Channel 16. *Radio checks at more frequent intervals are not needed.* You can also buy a quite inexpensive field-strength monitor that will tell you your signal strength immediately without calling another station; it will give indications of any gradual decline in output if it is mounted and kept in the same place. Make notations of the meter readings.

Also, make sure that the flexible lead on the microphone is in good condition.

You are legally responsible that your radio transmitter is on frequency. If you have any doubts, or receive reports of a weak or distorted signal, take your set to a licensed technician in a properly equipped shop. A check every two years is desirable even if there is no known or suspected trouble.

Antennas

Antenna connections must be clean and tight. Make sure there are no sharp bends in the coax antenna lead and that the outer vinyl insulation has not cracked or been cut. A cracked fiberglass whip antenna can sometimes be repaired with a sealant material, but a broken whip must be replaced. For coax cable that is exposed to direct sunlight, replacement every two or three years is worth the cost and effort.

Depth Sounders

A flashing-light type of depth sounder that uses a neon bulb will show dimmer readings after prolonged use. This bulb can be replaced, but this is usually a shop job, as the rotating arm must be kept in good balance. LED flashers do not have this problem, and digital displays normally require no service. Depth recorders will require regular periodic maintenance; consult the manufacturer's instruction manual for details of what should be done, and when, for your particular equipment.

Transducer

The transducer of all depth sounders is a component that requires regular maintenance. The face of a unit mounted externally on a hull will collect marine growth that reduces the sounder's sensitivity, although it will not affect its accuracy. It should be cleaned each time your boat is hauled for bottom painting or other work. You can do this yourself, but take care not to cut or gouge the active surface. If you have the yard workers paint the bottom of your boat while it is hauled out, tell them *not* to paint the face of the transducer with regular bottom paint; then, before launching, check that you instructions have been followed. The active face of a transducer must be left unpainted, or painted only with paint specially prepared for that purpose.

If your waters are clear and warm enough for you to dive with a face mask, the transducer face should be checked monthly—this will pay off well in continued good performance.

Radio Direction Finders

The principal items of attention for portable RDFs are the batteries and their holders. Dry cells should have been removed if the unit has been out of service for any period of time. If not, corrosion is very possible. Annual replacement of batteries is highly desirable so they will have adequate power when direction finding is needed. If you make much regular use of your RDF, a change of batteries may be needed semiannually—do not let the cells go completely dead in the set and start to leak! If any corrosion has built up, clean all contacts thoroughly with a knife and/or wire brush; check all springs for adequate tension.

Other Major Equipment

Items of electronic navigation equipment, such as Loran-C and satellite navigation receivers, and single-sideband transceivers and other high-tech devices, are so complex that owner-operator maintenance is not possible. Clean, tight connections for power and antenna leads are about all the preventive maintenance you can do, other than keeping the set clean and dry, but do make checks regularly.

Radars and autopilots may require periodic lubrication of moving mechanical components but little or no preventive maintenance of electronic components. Check the manufacturer's manual for what you should do regularly, and add these items to the preventive maintenance checklist for your boat.

A Few Useful Formulas

Ohms Law

The most frequently used equations in electricity are those of Ohm's Law. These useful expressions are: $I = \dfrac{E}{R}$, $R = \dfrac{E}{I}$, $E = I\,R$. Where I is the current in amps; E is the potential in volts; and R is the resistance in ohms. Entering the equation with any two knowns, you may extract the unknown. Thus if the voltage is 12 and the resistance is six, the current is two. The serious electrical boatkeeper might want to memorize Ohm's Law.

Power

1. Watts equal volts times amperes in direct current circuits.
2. Watts equal volts times amperes times power factor in AC circuits.
3. The heating of a conductor, or resistance element, is I^2R, the result expressed in watts. Thus five amps flowing through 10 ohms equals 250 watts.
4. 746 watts equal one horsepower at 100% conversion efficiency.

Resistors in Series

The total resistance of several resistive components in series is equal to the sum of the resistances. Thus if resistors of four, 10, and 15 ohms are wired in series, the total resistance will be 29 ohms: $R_1 + R_2 + R_3 + R_{etc} = R_{tot}$.

Two Resistors in Parallel

The equivalent resistance of two resistors in parallel is found as follows:

$$R_e = \frac{R_1 \times R_2}{R_1 + R_2}$$

Where: R_e is the equivalent resistance; R_1 and R_2 are the resistances in parallel. Thus resistances of four and 10 ohms in parallel equal 2.86 ohms equivalent resistance.

Three or More Resistances in Parallel

The equivalent resistance of several resistances in parallel is found as follows:

$$R_e = \frac{1}{\dfrac{1}{R_1} + \dfrac{1}{R_2} + \dfrac{1}{R_3} + etc.}$$

Thus if resistors of four, 10, and 15 ohms are wired in parallel, the equivalent resistance will be 2.4 ohms approximately. The equivalent resistance is always smaller than that of any resistor in the network.

Capacitors in Parallel

Several capacitors wired across the line, as for power factor correction or noise suppression, have total capacitance $C_1 + C_2 + C_3 + C_{etc}$. Thus capacitors of four, 10, and 15 microfarads in parallel equal 29 μF.

Capacitors in Series

The same formula applies to capacitors in series as to resistors in parallel. Thus capacitors of four, 10, and 15 μF in series have an equivalent capacitance of 2.4 μF approximately. Note: Series and parallel capacitors are just the *reverse* relationships of series and parallel resistors.

APPENDIX B

Thoughts on Shop Practice

• Whenever at all possible, take electrical parts and accessories home or to a shore-based shop for trouble-shooting and repair. It's much easier to work where you have elbow room, tools, and equipment.

• Use a muffin pan or a series of short jars to hold nuts, bolts, washers, and other small parts as they are disassembled from an accessory under repair. The receptacles can be grouped according to the section from which the parts were removed, preventing mixups when things go back together.

• When taking apart an intricate device, shoot "Instant" pictures of the assembly as it comes apart. These photographs will be a blessing as you reassemble things, reminding you of the order in which things go together.

• Try small spring clips, paper clips, and clothes pins to hold parts together when you are soldering or arranging delicate assemblies.

• Keep one hand in your pocket when working on conductors carrying a dangerous bite. Stand on a dry rubber mat.

• Solder electric joints using rosin core radio solder, never using acid fluxes, even those said to be non-corroding. Sandpaper the metal shiny bright; apply heat with a clean, tinned iron; then feed on a sparing length of small diameter solder. Heat the work, letting the work heat the solder. Don't apply the heat directly to the solder.

• After fastening cable clamps to the storage battery posts, apply a healthy coat of battery terminal compound. Viscous stuff, it is sold in auto supply stores, and does a better job of discouraging "acid toadstool" than does grease or petroleum jelly.

• When using a multi-meter, always set the selector switch on a scale higher than the voltage (or current) you think you're measuring. Then, after hooking up, click down to the correct scale. The practice may save you many a blown meter.

• Always, but always, look at the meter selector switch before touching the test prods to the work.

• Use your engine-timing strobe light only as required for a good job. Unnecessary flash time shortens the length of tube life, which is rated in X number of flashes, expressed in hundreds of thousands.

• Slip lockwashers under nuts when attaching terminal lugs to studs. Boat vibrations have an uncanny way of backing off seemingly tight nuts.

• Be awfully careful when working around storage batteries with metal tools. A short circuit across the battery posts or all connecting straps can trigger a frightful arc, welding the tool, and burning you painfully.

• Take frequent short breaks when doing tedious jobs. After a sip of tea, or a short chat with a fellow boatman, thorny things seem to go together much easier.

• Try to arrange for a helper on big jobs. Often, two boatkeepers can finish a job in a third of the time required by one. Having a mate read a meter on the far side of a bulkhead can save hours of improvising and cussing when you're alone.

• Don't depend upon solder for strength in a connection. First, make a secure mechanical connection, then flow in solder to assure a perfect, noise-free electrical junction.

On-Board Spare Parts And Supplies

THE FARTHER the cruising man ventures from the pier, the more complete should be his stock of spare parts and electrical supplies. There are no electrical shops "out yonder" where gear is most likely to break down. Below is a reminder list of spares and supplies; and the reader is urged to modify it to suit his individual needs:

- Set of spark plugs
- Set of ignition points
- Ignition condenser
- Distributor cap and rotor
- Ignition-system ballast resistor
- Ignition coil
- Alternator V-belt
- Several of each size fuse on the boat
- One or more of each size light bulb, especially for navigation lights
- Brushes for much-used motors
- Roll of rosin-core electrical solder
- Roll of electrical tape
- Spray can of moisture inhibitor
- Junk box of choice terminals, lugs, lengths of wire, screws, nuts, bolts, washers, cotters, and all the other stuff so dear to the heart of the electrical tinkerer.

Useful Tools
For Electrical Work

IN ADDITION to the usual boatkeeping tools such as ordinary pliers, wrenches, vice-grips, and an assortment of screwdrivers, the Boatman-electrician will find the following tools and instruments of help in his electrical maintenance and trouble shooting:

- Electrician's combination cutter-plier
- Combination wire stripper and lug crimper
- Thin, long-nosed pliers
- Pair diagonal cutters
- Scout knife
- Ignition tool set with feeler gauges
- Flashlight
- Trouble-light
- Volt-ohm meter
- Snap-on alternating current ammeter
- Battery hydrometer
- Half dozen test leads with alligator clip each end
- Set of battery jumper cables
- Electric soldering iron or gun
- Plug-in polarity tester for AC receptacles
- Ignition timing light
- Dwell meter

Handy Addresses

American Boat and Yacht Council, Inc.
P.O. Box 806
Amityville, N.Y. 11701
(Safety information and standards)

Allied Radio & Electronics
2400 W. Washington Blvd.
Chicago, Ill. 60612
(Electrical parts, switches, capacitors, wire, tools)

Cole-Hersee Co.
20 Old Colony Avenue
Boston, Mass. 02127
(Heavy duty marine switches)

Heath Company
Benton Harbor, Mich. 49022
(Electronic kits, instruments, tools)

Hubbell Division
Harvey Hubbell, Inc.
Bridgeport, Conn. 06602
(Marine wiring devices and fixtures, ground fault interrupters)

James Bliss & Co., Inc.
Route 128
Dedham, Mass. 02026

(Marine electrical hardware and fixtures)

Kohler Company
Kohler, Wis. 54044
(Electric generating plants)

LaMarche Mfg. Co.
Route 2, Box 82C
Annapolis, Md. 21401
(Battery chargers)

Marine Development Corp.
P.O. Box 8675
Richmond, Va. 23226
(Battery chargers)

Marinetics Corp.
P.O. Box 2676
Newport Beach, CA 92663
(Marine electrical panels, switchboards, and instruments)

Mercantile Mfg. Co., Inc.
P.O. Box 895
Minden, Louisiana 71055
(Engine driven AC power plants)

National Fire Protection Assn.
60 Batterymarch St.

Boston, Mass. 02110
(Safety information and standards)

National Marine Manufacturers
    Association
666 Third Ave.
New York, N.Y. 10017
(General boating information)

Onan
1400 73rd Ave. N.E.
Minneapolis, Minn. 55432
(Electric generating plants)

Pass & Seymour, Inc.
Syracuse, N.Y. 13209
(Ground fault interrupters)

Raritan Engineering Co.
1025 N. High St.
Millville, N.J. 08332
(Battery chargers)

Ratelco Inc.
610 Pontius Ave.
Seattle, Wash. 98109
(Battery chargers)

Research Enterprises, Inc.
P.O. Box 232
Nutley, N.J. 07110
(Approved type electric fuel shut-
    off)

A. L. Rogers Development Corp.
107 Vanderbilt Ave.
W. Hartford, Conn. 06110
(Heavy battery switches)

Ray Jefferson
Main & Cotton Streets
Philadelphia, Pa. 19127
(Battery chargers)

Scott & Fetzer Co.
Adalet Div., 4801 W. 150th St.
Cleveland, Ohio 44135
(Power centers)

Sprague Electric Co.
North Adams, Mass. 01247
(Capacitors)

Starrett Corp.
4522 W. Ohio Ave.
P.O. Box 15497
Tampa, Fla. 33614

Westerbeke Corp.
35 Tenean Street
Boston, Mass. 02122
(Electric generating plants)

Good Reading

Electronic Corrosion Control for Boats, John D. Lenk, Howard Sams & Co., Inc., Indianapolis, Ind.

Fractional HP Motor & Control Handbook, Bodine Electric Co., 2500 W. Bradley Place, Chicago, Ill. 60618.

National Electric Code, National Fire Protection Assn., 60 Batterymarch St., Boston, Mass. 02110.

Motor Craft, M.F.P.A. No. 302, National Fire Protection Assn.

Marinas and Boatyards, N.F.P.A. No. 303, National Fire Protection Assn.

Lightning Protection Code, N.F.P.A. No. 78, National Fire Protection Assn.

Safety Standards for Small Craft, American Boat and Yacht Council, Inc., 15 East 26th St., New York, N.Y. 10010.

Small Boat Engines, Conrad Miller, Sheridan House, New York

Basic Electricity Kit Course, Heath Co., Benton Harbor, Mich. 49022.

(This is a manual and kit to demonstrate electric theory, and the kit builds a d.c. volt-ohm-milliameter.) Kit EK-1.

INDEX

553

556

558

559